M.deb. Hachlas, Ph.D.

MINORITIES

M. dk C. Nachlas, Ph. D.

MINORITIES
A Text with Readings
in Intergroup Relations

B. EUGENE GRIESSMAN

Auburn University

THE DRYDEN PRESS

Hinsdale, Illinois

Library of Congress Cataloging in Publication Data

Griessman, B. Eugene, comp.
　　Minorities.

　　　Bibliography: p. 367
　　　Includes index.
　　　1.　Race problems—Addresses, essays, lectures.
2.　Minorities—Addresses, essays, lectures.　3.　Social
groups—Addresses, essays, lectures.　I.　Title.
HT1521.G74　　　301.45'1'042　　　74-28207
ISBN 0-03-077675-9

ACKNOWLEDGMENTS

For permission to reprint materials copyrighted by authors, publishers, and agents, the author
　　is indebted to the following:
"What Mothers Worry About," excerpt from *Hawaii*, by James A. Michener. Copyright ©
　　1959 by James A. Michener. Reprinted by permission of Random House, Inc.
The Painted Bird, by Jerzy N. Kosinski. Copyright © 1965 by Jerzy N. Kosinski. Reprinted
　　by permission of Houghton Mifflin Company.
Return to Laughter, by Elenore Smith Bowen (Laura Bohannan). Copyright © 1955 by
　　Elenore Smith Bowen. Reprinted by permission of Curtis Brown, Ltd.
"Me," from the NEA Tucson Survey on the Teaching of Spanish to the Spanish Speaking.
　　Department of Rural Education, NEA, 1966.
"Men and Jobs," excerpted from *Tally's Corner* by Elliot Liebow. Copyright © 1967 by Little
　　Brown and Co. (Inc.) and reprinted by permission.
"Polarity in the Approach to Comparative Research in Ethnic Relations," by Richard A.
　　Schermerhorn. Reprinted by permission of the author, University of Southern California,
　　from *Sociology and Social Research*, LI (January 1967), 235–240.
"Preface," from *The Mind of Primitive Man*, by Franz Boas. Copyright © 1963 by The
　　Free Press and reprinted by permission.
The U.S. Census Definition of Race. Reprinted from the U.S. Bureau of Census, Census
　　of Population, 1970. General Social and Economic Characteristics.
"Decisive Genes," by Hans J. Eysenck and "Indecisive Genes," by Leon Kamin from "War
　　of IQ." Excerpted and reprinted from *Educational Change*, vol. 5, no. 7, by permission.
"Genetics of Race Equality," by Theodosius Dobzhansky. Reprinted from *Eugenics Quarterly*,
　　vol. 10, pp. 151–160, by permission.
"The Plantation as a Race-Making Situation," by Edgar T. Thompson. Presented at the Con-
　　ference on Race Relations in World Perspective, University of Hawaii, July 1954.
　　Abridged and adapted by permission of Edgar T. Thompson.
"The Meaning of Israel," by Harry Golden. Reprinted from *Holiday* © 1967. By permission
　　of *Holiday* and the author.
"Pig and Policy: Boundary Maintenance and the Chinese Muslims," by Barbara Kroll Pills-
　　bury, from *International Journal of Ethnic Studies*, vol. 1, no. 2, 1975. Reprinted by
　　permission.
"Introduction," from *Ethnic Minorities in the Soviet Union*, by Erich Goldhagen. Reprinted
　　by permission of Praeger Publishers, Inc., 1968.

"National Languages and Interlingual Communication," by Yuri Desheriyev. Courtesy of *Soviet Life Magazine*, vol. 8, no. 203:18, 19 (August 1973); published by permission of *Soviet Life*.

"Maori Attitudes toward Integration," by Thomas K. Fitzgerald. Reprinted by permission of the author.

"The One Hundred Percent American," by Ralph Linton. Reprinted by permission from *The American Mercury*, 40 (April 1937), pp. 427–429.

"Bigotry Money Gets Tight." Reprinted with permission of The Atlanta *Constitution* and *Journal*, August 12, 1973.

"The Shock of Black Recognition," by James Farmer and Ralph Bunche. Reprinted from *Esquire Magazine*, © 1969 by Esquire, Inc.

"The Lumbee Indian in the City," by John Gregory Peck. Reprinted by permission of the author.

Excerpt from *Manchild in the Promised Land*, by Claude Brown. Reprinted with permission of the Macmillan Company and Jonathan Cape, Ltd. Copyright © by Claude Brown, 1965.

"Prisoners of Caste Segregation," by W.E.B. DuBois. Reprinted from *Dusk of Dawn*, 1940.

"Rhodesia's Good, White Life," from *Newsweek*. Copyright *Newsweek*, Inc., 1972, and reprinted by permission.

"They Did Not Know It Was Illegal To Kill Indians," from *Wassaja*, vol. 1, no. 6 (September 1973), p. 1.

War behind Walls, by Edward Bunker. First published in *Harper's* Magazine, vol. 244, no. 1461 (Feb. 1972). Copyright © 1973 by A. Watkins, Inc. and reprinted by permission.

"Improving the Economic Status of the Negro," by James Tobin. Reprinted by permission from *Daedalus*, Journal of the American Academy of Arts and Sciences, Boston, Mass., vol. 94, no. 4 (Fall 1965).

"How Segregation Ended in the Early Thirties," by Charles F. Eyre, as abridged in the *Intellectual Digest* of February 1973 as "The Bonus That Saved the Republic." Reprinted by permission of *National Review*, Nov. 1971. Copyright © 1971 by National Review, Inc., 150 East 35 Street, New York, N.Y., 10016.

"Cairo, Illinois: A Town in Troubled Water," by James M. Hanson, Community Development Services Newsletter of Southern Illinois University (May–June, 1971).

"The Improbable Change Agent and the Ph.B.," by Mark Hanson. Reprinted by permission.

PREFACE

Minorities is a textbook designed for college students who are beginning to study intergroup relations. It is a somewhat unique approach to the topic in that it presents a general discussion of intergroup relations that is integrated with selected readings. *Minorities* attempts to present as simply as possible the basic concepts, principles, and ideas of leading scholars. A number of important theories and research findings are abstracted or summarized. The social sciences have produced a variety of theoretical positions, some of which do a good job of explaining and predicting selected aspects of intergroup relations. Several of these approaches are presented in the text along with brief discussions of their strengths, weaknesses, and applications. The book brings together ideas that are sometimes taught in two separate courses: "Minorities" and "Race Relations." This objective is undertaken by presenting readings and discussions about specific groups, but within the framework of basic concepts. Moreover, the approach is cross-cultural. Illustrative mate-

rial is drawn from sociology, anthropology, social work, psychology, history, economics, art, literature, and political science. Readings from earlier times and places
are merged with materials from contemporary American society. The rationale for
this use of data is two-fold:

1. To show that continuities extend across the boundaries of time and space, and
   from one type of behavior to another
2. To interpret specific situations by comparing them with others; data, after all,
   are understood only as they are compared with other data

The selection of readings includes fresh up-to-date accounts plus a good number of the "classics." The idea is that by combining accounts of specific situations
with a discussion about general principles, the student will come away from the
course knowing more than bits of interesting, but discrete and unrelated information about Blacks, Gypsies, Chicanos, and so forth.

Several academic affiliations are represented in the readings, but a few of the
contributors bear no academic label—James Michener; Joel Chandler Harris;
Harry Golden. They all display a concern for human experience—ambitions, prejudices, kindnesses, hatreds, faiths, and loves. Some writers have dwelt on the inner
feelings, sentiments, preferences, and beliefs of individuals. Others have described
the group settings for these experiences, the stimuli which excited them, and the
social boundaries which limited them.

A word about the title: The concept that provides the title for this book
implies several additional concepts. There are no *minorities*, for instance, unless
there also are *majorities*. The existence of minorities and majorities suggests that
there are various types of *relationships* which occur between them. Groups relate to
each other in terms of differential prestige and power. Hence, a minority may be
either a dominant group or a subdominant group. Such relationships imply definitions—groups cannot relate to each other as minority and majority unless the
members of those groups establish ways of recognizing one another.

Sometimes a field of inquiry can be summed up with a basic question. In the
case of minorities and majorities, the basic question is: *What happens when unlike
peoples meet?* The usefulness of this question derives from the fact that it leads to
further inquiry about how groups become "unlike" in the first place, and what
signs are used to set them apart. What conditions make for hostile relations or
friendly ones? Even a superficial reading of history jolts us with the almost endless
chronicles of angry, bloody fighting between unlike peoples. We read about vanished
civilizations and lost tribes, and we perceive that some of them vanished because
only one group survived an ancient battleground. But some unlike peoples amicably associate with each other, intermarry, and eventually merge into a single people.
Others manage to maintain distinctive features and a separate identity in pluralistic
arrangements.

Is it possible to draw valid generalizations from a study of relationships that have such varied outcomes? Earlier writers thought so, and wrote about "race relations cycles" that were irreversible and practically inevitable. Few scholars would make that kind of claim today, but it is recognized that there are general patterns which characterize relationships between peoples. That is what this book is all about.

Many groups and social categories can be legitimately studied as minorities—homosexuals, the deaf, the blind, women, juveniles, hippies, etc. Indeed, many of the ideas discussed in this book apply to these social entities. However, this book deals *specifically* with groups that are considered to be a minority on the basis of ethnicity (classifications based on language, nationality, religion) or race (classifications based on physical features presumed to be socially significant).

I agree with those who believe that we should try to understand society in order to change it. It is my hope that this book will contribute to the understanding, and to the change.

A number of friends have helped with critical comments and suggestions. They include: J. Ken Dane, Charles Glasgow, Hardy T. Frye, Marjorie Kelley, Mary King, Gerhard Lenski, Ray Marshall, Elyce Misher, Richard C. Owen, David Riesman, M. M. Sawhney, Kathleen Sharp, Robin Williams, Jr., and, especially, my colleagues at Auburn.

B. Eugene Griessman

Auburn, Alabama
November 1974

CONTENTS

MINORITIES

1

The Human Condition: The Setting for Intergroup Relations

> My nature is rational and social; and my city and country, so far as I am Antoninus, is Rome; but so far as I am a man, it is the world.
> —Marcus Aurelius Antoninus,
>
> *Meditations*, VI, 44

It is widely recognized that intergroup relations should be considered an explosive world problem, and with good reason. In academic sources alone, as many as a thousand books, monographs, and journal articles appear on the topic in a single year. This plethora of documents does not include feature stories and news releases in the mass media, novels, or motion pictures. It is not generally understood, however, that intergroup relations can be studied rigorously and systematically.

The starting point of this book is the belief that intergroup relations can be approached in ways similar to those used to study other types of social behavior. Such study is greatly needed, but it is not easy. Few substantive areas in the social sciences are more sensitive than this one, partly because a great deal of our information has been drawn from situations that are charged with emotion. The topic thus tends to generate more heat than light, more fervor than knowledge. Frantz Fanon, for one, has warned of its dangers: "I do not trust fervor. . . . Every time it has burst out somewhere, it has brought fire, famine, misery. . . . And contempt for man" (1967, p. 9).

Social scientists may sometimes delude themselves that they have no biases because they avoid emotional excesses or because they use only scholarly sources of information. But these feelings too are biases. The truth is that we are all biased, and we all lean toward certain points of view. "We cannot be impartial," the historin Gaetano Salvemini has written: "we can only be intellectually honest; that is, aware of our own passions, on our guard against them and prepared to warn our readers of the dangers into which our partial views may lead them" (1954).

Even though there is no ultimate solution to this basic epistemological question, there are partial solutions that can help to correct for biases. One approach is to use cross-cultural and historical data. By learning what has happened in other places and at other times, we can counter the tendency to perceive selectively those things that we are close to, as well as those things that we have a stake in.

Another way to correct for individual and collective distortions is to seek information from individuals who have different perspectives. Scholars, house-wives, merchants, and laborers all have their stories. Because intergroup situations can be viewed as particular instances of more general social facts, sociologists, psy-chologists, anthropologists, economists, and historians can all make real contribu-tions to systematic study of intergroup relations.

The well-known propensity of scholars to criticize one another's work provides still another corrective for biases and is more basic to the growth of knowledge than is generally recognized. Knowledge grows through *conjectures* (tentative regularities that we try actively to impose upon the world) and *refutations* (criti-cisms, experiments, tests). Those explanations, or conjectures, that appear to be better approximations of truth than competitive explanations come to be accepted as the "science" of a particular period. The attempt to refute conjectures, either by scholars themselves or by others, gives to science a critical and progressive quality (Popper, 1962, p. vii).

Karl R. Popper has argued that this attempt to reject conjectures by means of "risky" tests is the touchstone that distinguishes science from pseudo-science, myths from scientific theories. Any interpretation of reality so vague that it cannot be rejected by test is a myth, not a scientific theory. Truth is arrived at scientifically, wrote Popper, when the researcher poses the conjecture in such a way that it can be tested and refuted. Scientific knowledge grows, according to this view, not by the mere accumulation of observations but by the "repeated overthrow of scientific theories and their replacement by better or more satisfactory ones" (Popper, 1962, pp. 36, 37, 215). Knowledge is thus tentative and progressive. Knowledge, to use the word precisely, is *warranted* belief. Information drawn from many sources provides evidence that can be used to test the warrants.

Intergroup relations is not a unique subject, different in kind from other aspects of human behavior. At one level of analysis all the relations found among ethnic groups are also found among groups that are not ethnically based. The study of intergroup relations is the study of human behavior; to be more specific, it focuses on the ways in which human relations are influenced by ethnic or racial considerations.

In order to cast the present discussion within a broad framework, we shall consider several key elements in human existence. As a point of departure three broad generalizations can be made: Every person, in certain respects, is like every other person, like some other persons, and like no other person (Kluckhohn and Murray, 1953, p. 53). These generalizations have been derived by means of approaching the subject matter from three different levels of abstraction. (The same kind of statement can be made about trees or horses, for example: "Every tree is like every other tree, like some other trees, and like no other tree.")

Like All Others . . .

The statement that every person is in some respects like every other, self-evident as it may appear, has not always been universally believed—not even in the scientific world. Only quite recently in human history has it come to be fairly widely accepted that all people belong to one species, *Homo sapiens.*

As late as the 1840s one of the early anthropologists, James Cowles Prichard, found it necessary to deal with a "problem" of his times: whether or not the "primitive" peoples that had come under the colonial authority of European powers were truly human. Presumably, the answer to that question would have a bearing upon the responsibilities of the colonial administrators toward those peoples.

In *The Natural History of Man* (1843) Prichard examined the available evidence on the physical and moral characteristics of different peoples, his aim being to see whether or not an empirical study would confirm the biblical teaching that "it pleased the Almighty Creator to make of one blood all the nations of the Earth" (*Acts*, 17:26). He wrote:

> If the Negro and Australian are not our fellow creatures and of one family with ourselves but beings of an inferior order, and if our duties toward them were not contemplated, as we may in that case presume them not to have been, in any of the positive commands on which the morality of the Christian world is founded, our relations to these tribes will appear to be not very different from those which might be imagined to subsist between us and a race of orangutans. (Quoted in Lienhardt, 1966, p. 4)

He concluded that scientific inquiry did support belief in the basic unity of the species, in similarities that outweigh all conspicuous differences.

Prichard's conclusion has been rather dramatically confirmed by the common medical practice of making blood transfusions between persons of the same blood type, regardless of their racial identifications. Not only blood transfusions, but even heart transplants too have been performed between people of different groups. In one of the first of the latter, the heart of a South African Coloured person, Olive Haupt, was transplanted to the body of a White, Philip Blaiberg.

A number of illustrious names have been associated with the study of human differences: Herodotus described the customs of the Scythians, Egyptians, and other "barbarians." Tacitus, the Roman historian, produced a famous study of Germanic peoples. Marco Polo amazed Venetians with tales of travel and adventure in the Orient. To this day, explorers and travelers can find a market for interestingly written, though often inaccurate, descriptions of strange and bizarre customs.

Human differences, though fascinating to study, should not be allowed to obscure the broad similarities that exist among all peoples. It is essential that the student of intergroup relations understand the basic underlying sameness that extends to all humanity.

Biological Similarities

A *species* is generally defined as a category of morphologically similar organisms possessing the ability to interbreed naturally and to produce fertile offspring. The boundaries between species, however, are not always clear-cut. Some species are made up of many local populations, each of which can be interbred with its nearer neighbors though not with its distant ones. And, in some instances, two different species from quite different environments have proved interfertile. All modern peoples and some prehistoric types, however, are generally placed in the single species *sapiens*.

Considered from the physiological point of view, certain needs, drives, and capacities—sleeping, eating, breathing, and the like—are common to the species. Human beings, unlike other mammals, are in permanent sexual readiness throughout their mature years. Human beings come into life helpless and must be nurtured over relatively long periods of time. They have relatively large brains, and the capacity for speaking and hearing is common to the species, as is the physiological capacity for such emotional responses as laughing, smiling, and weeping. Humans have the unique ability to use symbols. Such behavior is the basis of the human *ethogram*, the behavioral inventory of the animal. It determines the broad conditions under which culture and society operate: the "biological constant."

Social Similarities

Not only do human beings resemble one another along the lines suggested, but also they live in societies that are similar to one another in a number of important ways. Cross-cultural studies have underscored the fact that all human societies, despite their obvious differences, have common features.

These common features arise from the biological constant and the requirements for survival. The interplay between the biological and the social can be clearly seen at a number of points. Take, for example, the long period of time required for the human infant to mature. The child's helpless condition requires that every society provide some mechanism for feeding, clothing, instructing, and protecting him for many years. The family is one solution to this "problem." A set of relations to the family or to some substitute provided by society is thus a part of the life history of every human being.

There are other unavoidable dilemmas, or "problems," that all human societies face. An examination of various groups the world over indicates that they engage in activities that can be grouped in several broadly inclusive categories. Social scientists call them *functional prerequisites*. Functional prerequisites are "the things that must get done in any society if it is to continue as a going concern, i.e., the generalized conditions necessary for the maintenance of the system concerned" (Aberle *et al.*, 1950, p. 100). They include producing and distributing goods and services, reproducing new members, socializing new members into functioning adults, maintaining order, and maintaining motivation and a sense of meaning.

The idea of functional prerequisites does not imply that all societies are identical. Obviously they are not. It only suggests *what* must be done, not *how*. For example all societies somehow allocate goods and services, but a particular society may change from one method to another without destroying itself.

The functional prerequisites of a society have consequences for individual society members. For example, the fact that all human societies must maintain order means that all human beings will have had some experience with normative order, even though specific normative patterns vary from society to society.

The activities classified as functional prerequisites are characteristic of all social life. Along with biologically inherited factors, they provide the setting and define the range within which human variation occurs. "Not any single area, but all of them taken together and viewed as a network of social activities constitute the framework of human society—the condition of man" (Aberle *et al.*, 1950, p. 111).

Like Some Others . . .

The generalization that every person is like some other persons suggests that the level of abstraction has shifted from all humanity viewed as one entity, or species, to the various aggregates and groups that characterize humanity. These groups constitute an important dimension of human life because, in the strict sense of the word, there is no such thing as a "solitary" person. Human life is to some extent always group-related.

Theories of Interpersonal Attraction and Association

Various theories have been proposed to account for the principles that hold groups together in varying types of human association. In one form or another society as a concept has never ceased to be the object of philosophical concern. Yet much remains to be discovered. Thomas M. Newcomb, in his presidential address to the American Psychological Association, commented, "I think it not much of an exaggeration to say that there exists no very adequate theory of interpersonal attraction" (1966, p. 1969).

The fact that human propensity for *group* life is a universal feature has led some to suggest that human beings possess something akin to a social instinct or "need for positive affect" (Goldschmidt, 1959, p. 26). Others trace the origin of human social nature to the physiological relationship between parent and offspring. Still others see human groupings as the result of force and coercion: People are believed to do what they do, not because they really want to, but because their real alternatives are not many. These interpretations, however, do not attempt to account for the kaleidoscopic forms that various human aggregates take.

Proponents of one explanation view individuals—who presumably are by nature free—as rationally and deliberately forming various types of association. Hence, society. Volition, assent, and contract are the key concepts. Franklin Giddings (1855–1921) used the phrase "consciousness of kind," which grew out of this approach. He explicitly acknowledged his indebtedness for the idea to Adam Smith, who in the *Theory of Moral Sentiments* (1759), had commented on the importance of "reflective sympathy" in social life. Giddings conceived consciousness of kind as a pleasurable state of mind that involves the perception of resemblance, reflective sympathy, affection, and desire for recognition. He claimed that individuals united through consciousness of kind simultaneously feel the same emotions, arrive at the same judgments, and sometimes act in concert.

The concept "consciousness of kind," once very much in vogue, is not often used by social scientists today. It has been recognized that perceived likenesses only partially explain human associations and that dissimilarities and unlike needs are also significant factors in bringing people together in functioning aggregates. The integration of societies with highly developed divisions of labor derives from the fact that society members are specialists, rather than generalists, and therefore need one another for various services. Nonetheless it is true, as Giddings showed, that perceptions of likeness play an important role in many human associations.

Writers in the Marxian tradition have stressed interests and economic determinants as overriding concerns in human associations. They maintain that every historical period is characterized by a predominant mode of production and, based upon it, a class structure consisting of a ruling and an oppressed class. Relation to the economic order in turn determine the values, institutions, social aggregations, and life chances of individuals within a respective class (see Bendix and Lipset, 1966).

A number of social scientists stress *values*, rather than *interests*, in accounting for social action and human association. Preferred ways of solving human problems become part of the social legacy that is transmitted to members of the respective groups. Various mechanisms of social control operate so that the individuals will conform, within tolerable limits, to the norms of the group. This "social binding" continues throughout an individual's life. One consequence is that similarities within a group are produced and maintained (see Benedict, 1959).

So far, our discussion has focused on groups rather than on categories, that is, on aggregates whose members have a sense of common identity, or a "we" feeling. But human beings can be classified according to *arbitrarily* defined categories. Physiological features, among other things, may be selected as the basis for classification. Indeed, such efforts have had a very long history. Scientific classification in biology, however, is generally thought to have begun with Carolus von Linnaeus about 200 years ago (1707–1778). It was Linnaeus who bestowed upon human beings the Latin name *Homo sapiens*.

Linnaeus' method of classifying plants and animals is still used. The classification includes the categories *species, genus, family, order*. The species are grouped into genera, the genera into families, and so on, according to their various degrees of resemblance.

In the early days of taxonomy an investigator would shoot a bird or animal, keep its skin and skull, compare it with others in existing collections to determine whether or not it was new, and write up a detailed description. If it was new, it became a type specimen, or *holotype*, of its species, and future collectors would compare their discoveries with it. Johann Blumenbach, who classified mankind in a five-part skin-color system, selected a handsome skull from a collection as the type or specimen of the Europeans. As it had belonged in life to a native of the Caucasus mountains, Whites came to be called Caucasians or Caucasoids and still are (Vallois, 1953, p. 150).

In Chapter 3 some of these classifications will be discussed. At this point it is sufficient to observe that human beings have been classified in biological terms and that various taxonomies that use biological characters as criteria have been proposed. But the variety of these schemes reveals their arbitrary and provisional nature.

The terms most frequently used to subdivide the category *Homo sapiens* are *race, ethnic group, minority, nationality, ethclass, group,* and *people*. Of these terms "race" has been the most controversial. Many social scientists, perhaps most of them, feel uncomfortable about using it, and some argue vigorously that it ought to be abandoned altogether. So far, however, no consensus has been reached on an acceptable substitute. Some writers try to indicate the imprecision and unacceptable connotations that the term implies by enclosing it in quotation marks whenever they use it.

Caution, as well as the unsettled nature of the debate surrounding use of the word, is reflected in the flexibility of the Royal Anthropological Institute's definition of race: "A biological group or stock possessing in common an *undetermined* number of associated genetical characteristics by which it can be distinguished from other group" (Vallois, 1953, p. 150; italics added).

In terms of biological considerations, a race corresponds to a *variety* or to a *breed* of a species.[1] For purposes of this textbook, "race" refers to groups defined socially on the basis of biologically inherited features, like skin color, that are presumed to be salient for group membership and behavior.

In this sense race is what Michael Banton (1967) calls a "role sign." When physical differences are used to subdivide a population and different rights and obligations are ascribed to the divisions, outward characteristics serve to tell others what kind of treatment group members are entitled to. Such a "sign" functions much as does an insignia on a military uniform.

Use of the word "race" in the context of intergroup relations does not correspond to rigorous biological usage. Even though the logic of racial distinctions presumably is based on biological characteristics, in practice these distinctions are not based on carefully measured genetic ratios. Instead, they are *social* distinctions. An American Black is not necessarily categorized as such because of phenotype or genotype or even because he has more Black ancestors than White ones. A Black person is what customs and law define him to be.

The concept "ethnic group" refers to groups socially defined according to describes races and ethnic groups treated as subordinate peoples in a particular cultural (learned) criteria like language and religion. The term "minority" usually geographical area. However, the concept is sometimes used to refer to dominant groups that are numerical minorities. "Nationality" refers to a people (or its immediate descendents) that has lived in a particular politically defined territory for an appreciable period of time. A nationality often comprises several racial or ethnic groups. The term "ethclass" is used by some writers to designate a conjunction

---

[1] The word "race" is sometimes applied by zoologists to subdivisions of various animal species. For example, the following statement occurs in an *Encyclopaedia Britannica* article on the elephant: "The African elephants have been separated into about a dozen different races distinguished from one another chiefly by the form and size of the ears but also in some cases by differences in the shape of the skull. In the Congo there is found a dwarf race of the African elephant, perhaps only about half the normal height" (1956, vol. 8, p. 349). The 1972 edition of the same encyclopaedia, however, substitutes "variety" for "race" in the same article.

ERRATA SHEET

The last paragraph on page eight should read:

The concept "ethnic group" refers to groups socially defined according to cultural (learned) criteria like language and religion. The term "minority" usually describes races and ethnic groups treated as subordinate peoples in a particular geographical area. However, the concept is sometimes used to refer to dominant groups that are numerical minorities. "Nationality" refers to a people (or its immediate descendents) that has lived in a particular politically defined territory for an appreciable period of time. A nationality often comprises several racial or ethnic groups. The term "ethclass" is used by some writers to designate a conjunction

between ethnicity and social class. The term "group" includes so many types of human aggregates that it is usually difficult to use it with precision. Yet the term "intergroup relations" has become a convenient and acceptable way to designate relations that involve races, nationalities, and ethnic groups. It is used in this comprehensive sense in this book.

"People" is a useful alternative to "ethnic group." Its use permits avoidance of the questions about physical features that are associated with the word "race." A *people* may be either a minority or a majority; it is correct to speak of the Jewish people and the English people. The term also focuses attention upon cultural and social concerns like identity formation ("peoplehood"), territory, and group continuity.

To sum up, human groups can be categorized on the basis of age, sex, scarification, kinship, language, religion, customs, wealth or the lack of it, athletic ability, or territory. Blond hair can be as useful as yellow skin in setting a person or a group apart. The kinds of differences chosen may not be intrinsically important in themselves, but if they are perceived by the actors as real they are real in their consequences (Thomas and Thomas, 1928, p. 572).

Like No Others . . .

One obvious fact of heredity is that children resemble their mothers, sisters look somewhat like their sisters, brothers like their brothers, and so on. But, upon closer inspection, as the technique of fingerprint identification shows, no two human beings are ever absolutely identical.

Biological Sources of Variation

Genetic principles help to explain why no two human beings are exactly alike. The fusion of a male *gamete*, or *sperm*, with a female gamete, or *ovum*, produces a *zygote*, or fertilized egg. In the center of this zygote there is a nucleus, and in the nucleus are forty-six microscopically visible bodies with distinctive shapes, known as *chromosomes*. The chromosomes carry genes which are made up of deoxyribonucleic acid (D.N.A.)

D.N.A. is composed of units called *nucleotides*. In the fertilized egg approximately 5 billion nucleotides are strung together in the nucleic acid of the genes that determine the characteristics of the final human organism "How much information does this represent? Encoded in letters of the alphabet, it would be sufficient to fill about 1000 volumes, 600 pages per volume, 500 words per page" (Beadle, 1968, p. 27).

These data represent a vast increase in knowledge over that of Gregor Mendel (1822–1884) when he began to experiment with peas in a monastery garden in Austria. It was he who discovered laws for the inheritance of traits that presumably hold for all living things.

The Mendelian law of independent assortment explains how each individual, except identical twins, receives a unique total combination of inherited traits. The possible number of gene combinations for any twenty-three hypothetical traits in man located in one chromosome pair is 2^{23}, or more than 8 million. When fertilization occurs, the fusion of two gametes gives the mathematical possibility of 8 million times 8 million gene combinations. As many more than twenty-three traits are controlled by genes, the total number of possible trait combinations is astronomical (Weisz, 1963, p. 684).

Socialization as a Source of Variation

Moving to the societal level of analysis, we have already observed that mechanisms are provided in order to maintain social control, but just as surely provision is made for some deviance and variation. Several years ago Samuel Stouffer called the attention of social scientists to this fact:

> And it may be precisely the ranges of permissible behavior which most need examination, if we are to make progress in this realm which is so central in social science. For it may be the very existence of some flexibility or social slippage— but not too much—which makes behavior in groups possible. (1949, p. 717)

No two individuals are socialized in exactly the same way, not even within small, relatively homogeneous populations. Several factors contribute to such differences. In child rearing, parents emphasize some elements of culture rather than others. Individual family units are but partial representatives of generalized sets of values and normative patterns. Individual variations in the child's capacities, temperament, and responses to guidance are appreciable. Some individuals are more pliant than others. And systems of stratification perpetuate variation by providing society members with differing life chances.

In the course of socialization individuals come to learn their respective *roles*, the patterns of behavior expected of those who occupy particular status positions. But absolute role specification is virtually impossible, even in the most tightly integrated social system. Wilbert E. Moore states the idea as follows: "Thus biological individual differences interact with diverse personality and structural factors to provide a rather wide range of possible variation. On a strictly actuarial view of socialization, uniformities are somewhat more remarkable than variations" (1960, p. 814).

Cultural Dynamics as a Source of Variation

By means of the process of socialization the individual acquires a cultural repertoire. The ways in which the individual and his or her culture are related have been described by Melville J. Herskovits in the from of an analogy:

> Not every musician is a virtuoso, nor does he control the full range of orchestral instruments; and in the same manner no one individual controls his culture or is even conscious of its total resources, and no group, as a group, places the same emphases on all facets of the entire body of custom of which its members are the carriers. (1945, p. 164)

The fact that an individual's participation in a culture is never complete, not even in the most stable, conservative society is a consequence of the content of culture. Following the approach of Ralph Linton, we can divide the content of culture into three categories: *universals, specialties,* and *alternatives* (1964, pp. 272, 273). The ideas, habits, and conditioned emotional responses that are common to all sane, adult members of society are the universals. The specialties are shared only by the members of certain socially recognized categories of individuals, not by the total population. The alternatives are traits shared by certain individuals but not common to all the members of the society or even to all the members of any one of the socially recognized categories.

Scholars take account of the differences and the uniformities by statements such as: "Humanity is one; societies are many." The elements of the human condition—the interrelations among biological, social, and cultural factors—thus produce diversity, as well as similarity.

Overview

What are the social implications of the generalizations that we have considered? It appears that each lends itself to a basic humanistic approach.

If humanity is indeed one, then opportunities for cooperation extend beyond the bounds of variously defined groups, tribes, societies, and nations. "Man's inhumanity to man" grows out of failure to appreciate the broader implication of the idea that every person is, in certain respects, like every other person. Some have understood the attitude that it suggests. One such person, John Donne, stated it in the hauntingly beautiful words of his seventeenth "Devotion."

> No man is an *Island*, entire of itself; every man is a piece of the *Continent*, a part of the *Main*; if a *Clod* be washed away by the *Sea, Europe* is the less, as well as if a *Promontory* were, as well as if a *Manor* of thy friends or of thine *own* were;

any man's *death* diminishes *me*, because I am involved in *Mankind*; And therefore never send to know for whom the bell tolls; it tolls for thee.

Several years ago Jack Greenberg, who is Jewish, was asked why he continued to be active in intergroup programs. His response: "After all, civil rights is not a Negro cause; it is a human cause, a serious problem in world society. True, our organization [the NAACP] is designed primarily to aid Negroes in their push for equality, but the cause is *human, not Negro*" (quoted in Lomax, 1963, p. 202).

The second generalization highlights the reality, as well as the arbitrariness, of human groupings. Recognition of group and individual differences has had a long history. But these differences are not always recognized for what they are: variable and determined by an array of factors. Australian aborigines, Congo pygmies, or Yahgans at South America's tip are variations of one species. Humanity is one: varieties and societies are many.

Finally, the idea expressed in the third generalization—every person is like no other person—is an essential element of the humanist perspective It is alien to the racist perspective that develops when similarities within a group are so emphasized that individual differences are lost sight of. One typical form of racism is the exaggerated generalization (the stereotype): "All niggers will steal!" "You can't trust Whitey!" "Indians are naturally lazy." From a racist perspective, group differeneces are ultimate facts, and individual differences are inconsequential.

Scholars sometimes distinguish between *minimal* and *maximal* racism. Minimal racism defines other groups as different in degree but capable with training of rising to a status of equality with the dominant group. Maximal racism assumes that differences of kind, rather than of degree, distinguish the dominant group and the minority (Schermerhorn, 1970, pp. 73, 74). Both the minimal and the maximal forms of racism imply dominance and social control. "Racism," as Stokely Carmichael and Charles V. Hamilton define it, is "the predication of decisions and policies on considerations of race for the purpose of subordinating a racial group and maintaining control over that group" (1967, p. 3). It takes expression in such various forms as admitting only white doctors to a hospital staff, expelling all Asians from Uganda, confining Japanese-Americans to concentration camps, and exterminating a nation's Jews. This kind of behavior derives from a failure to perceive, or an unwillingness to tolerate, individual differences.

Some years ago Charles Drew developed a method of blood-plasma transfusion that has saved numberless lives. Later, while traveling in a southern state, he was involved in an automobile accident, and a large blood vessel was severed. Drew was refused admission to the nearest hospital because he was Black, and he died because he did not receive the help of his own medical discovery (G. B. Kennedy, 1966).

For Further Reading

Many of the items among the references cited may be considered as recommended reading as well.

Allport, Gordon W. *The Nature of Prejudice.* New York: Doubleday Anchor, 1958 (originally published by Addison-Wesley, 1954).

Banton, Michael. *Race Relations.* New York: Basic Books, 1967.

Linton, Ralph. *The Study of Man.* New York: Appleton, 1936.

Park, Robert Ezra. *Race and Culture: Essays in the Sociology of Contemporary Man.* New York: Free Press, 1964.

Schermerhorn, R. A. *Comparative Ethnic Relations: A Framework for Theory and Research.* Random House: New York, 1970.

THE MERCHANT OF VENICE

WILLIAM SHAKESPEARE

The Merchant of Venice, according to some accounts, may have been written around 1594 when popular feeling against the Jewish people was running high in England.[1] During this period, Roderigo Lopez, a Jewish physician, was hanged for allegedly plotting the death of Queen Elizabeth. In the play, Shylock is cast as a rich Jewish money-lender who enters into a contract to finance the loan of a non-Jewish merchant named Antonio. Eventually, Antonio forfeits on the debt because his ships are lost at sea, and Shylock is entitled to claim a previously agreed upon "pound of flesh" as payment. The play presents Jewish people in the most unflattering light, yet Shakespeare has given Shylock lines that are among the most eloquent expressions of human feeling ever expressed:

> . . . I am a Jew. Hath not a Jew eyes? hath not a Jew hands, organs, dimensions, senses, affections, passions? fed with the same food, hurt with the same weapons, subject to the same diseases, healed by the same means, warmed and cooled by the same winter and summer, as a Christian is? If you prick us, do we not bleed? if you tickle us, do we not laugh? if you poison us, do we not die? and if you wrong us, shall we not revenge? if we are like you in the rest, we will resemble you in that. If a Jew wrong a Christian, what is his humility? Revenge. If a Christian wrong a Jew, what should his sufferance be by Christian example? Why, revenge. The villainy you teach me, I will execute; and it shall go hard but I will better the instruction.

HAWAII

JAMES A. MICHENER

A young Japanese farmer, Kamejiro, who is about to leave for a stint as a contract laborer in Hawaii is provided with counsel for his journey by his mother. She wants Kamijero to observe the boundaries that have

---

[1] See William Addis Wright (ed.), *The Complete Works of William Shakespeare.* Garden City, N.Y.: Garden City Books, 1936, p. 446.

been set by his people. He must know how and why he is different from other people.

To exclude or admit other individuals on the basis of group identity is not uniquely human behavior. Other social animals—including those of various insect species—accept certain members of their species and reject others. They form autonomous groups, prefer members of their own communities to all others, and systematically exclude outsiders. In Kamijero's example, his mother attempts to give the proposed discriminations **meaning**: Japanese are cleaner than Chinese, girls from the north do not make good wives, Eta are subhuman.

Her advice has been given countless times. One student, who had been reared in India, commented after reading this selection: "If one changes the names and places, it is precisely the same advice my mother gave me when I left to study in the United States."

"Kamejiro, I have heard that it is a terrible thing for a man to travel overseas the way you are doing. Not that you will be robbed, because you are a strong man and able to handle such things as well as any." She was in her fifties, a small, stoop-shouldered woman with deep wrinkles from endless hours in the sun. She loved rice and could eat four bowls at any meal, but she could never afford to do that, so she remained as skinny as she had been in her youth, when Kamejiro's father had crept into her sleeping room.

"What mothers worry about, Kamejiro," she explained, "is that their sons will marry poorly. Every day that you are gone I shall be anxious, because I shall see you in the arms of some unworthy woman. Kamejiro, you must guard against this. You must not marry carelessly. When it comes time to take a wife, appoint prudent friends to study her history. Now these are the things I want you to bear in mind.

"The best thing in the world is to be a Japanese. What wonderful people the Japanese are. Hard-working, honest, clean people. Kamejiro, your father and I have heard that in Hawaii the people are careless and very dark. If you were to marry one of them . . ." She started to weep, real, mournful tears, so after a while she went to the hanging bucket at the fire and took herself a little rice in a bowl. Thus fortified, she continued. "If you were to marry such a woman, Kamejiro, we would not want you back in this village. You would have disgraced your family, your village, and all Japan."

Kamejiro listened carefully, for in these matters his mother was wise. She always collected gossip and in the last three weeks had walked fifteen miles to talk with people who had heard various bits of news about Hawaii. "Never marry a Chinese," she said firmly. "They are clever people and there are many of them in Hawaii, I am told, but don't wash themselves as often as we do and no matter

how rich they get, they remain Chinese. Under no circumstances can you return
to this village if you have a Chinese wife.

"Kamejiro, many men from Hiroshima-ken are tempted to marry girls from
the north. You've seen some of those pitiful women down here. They can't talk
decently, and say zu-zu all the time, until you feel ashamed for them. I have no
respect at all for girls from the north, and I have never seen one who made a
good wife. I will admit that they're a little better than Chinese, but not much.
If you are ever tempted to marry a northern girl, think of Masaru's wife. Zu-zu,
zu-zu! Do you want a girl like that?" she asked contemptuously.

Using chopsticks to flick the rice grains into her wrinkled but vigorous mouth
she proceeded. "A good many men try wives from the south, too, but what respectable man really wants a Yamaguchi-no-anta? Do you, in your heart, really
respect Takeshi-san's wife? Do you want a woman like that in your home? Would
you want to present such a girl to me some day and say, 'Mother, here is my wife.'?
And when I asked where she was from, would you feel satisfied if you had to
confess, 'She's a Yamaguchi-no-anta?' "

Now the wise old woman came to the most difficult part of her sermon, so
once more she fortified herself with a little rice, filling up the bowl with tea and
a garnish of dried seaweed. "I would be heartbroken," she began, "if you married
a northern girl or a southern girl, but to tell you the truth I would try to be a
very good mother to them, and you would not curse me for my actions. But there
are two marriages you may not make, Kamejiro. If you do, don't bother to come
home. You will not be welcome either in the village or in this house or in any part
of Hiroshima-ken." Solemnly she paused, looked out the door to be sure no one
was listening, and proceeded.

"If you marry when I am not at hand, Kamejiro, ask your two closest friends
to seek out the girl's history. You know the obvious problems. No disease, no in-
sanity, nobody in jail, all ancestors good, strong Japanese. But then ask your advisers
this: 'Are you sure she is not an Okinawan?' " Dramatically she stopped. Putting
down her rice bowl she pointed at her son and said, "Don't bring an Okinawa
girl to this house. If you marry such a girl, you are dead."

She waited for this ominous statement to wind its way through her son's
mind, then added, "The danger is this, Kamejiro. In Hiroshema-ken we can spot
an Okinawan instantly. I can tell when a girl comes from Okinawa if I see even
two inches of her wrist. But in Hawaii I am told people forget how to do this. There
are many Okinawans there, and their women set traps to catch decent Japanese.
I wish I could go with you to Hawaii, for I can uncover these sly Okinawans. I am
afraid you won't be able to, Kamejiro, and you will bring disgrace upon us."

She started to cry again, but rice stanched the tears, and she came to the climax
of her warning: "There is of course one problem that every devoted son looks into
before he marries, because he owes it not only to his parents but also to his brothers

and sisters. Kamejiro, I said that if you married an Okinawa girl you were dead. But if you marry an Eta, you are worse than dead."

The wave of disgust that swept over Kamejiro's face proved that he despised the Eta as much as his mother did, for they were the untouchables of Japan, the unthinkables. In past ages they had dealt in the bodies of dead animals, serving as butchers and leather tanners. Completely outside the scope of Japanese civilization, they scratched out horrible lives in misery and wherever possible fled to distant refuges like Hawaii. A single trace of Eta blood could contaminate an entire family, even to remote unattached cousins, and Kamejiro shuddered.

His mother continued dolefully: "I said I could spot an Okinawan, and I could protect you there. But with an Eta . . . I don't know. They're clever! Crawling with evil, they try to make you think they're normal people. They hide under different names. They take new occupations. I am sure that some of them must have slipped into Hawaii, and how will you know, Kamejiro? What would you do if word sneaked back to Hiroshima-ken that you had been captured by an Eta?"

Mother and son contemplated this horror for some minutes, and she concluded: "So when it comes time to marry, Kamejiro, I think it best if you marry a Hiroshima girl.

H. def. Hackler, Ph. D.

THE PAINTED BIRD
JERZY KOSINSKI

The following selection is an excerpt from Jerzy Kosinski's account of a young boy's brutal ordeal among peasant people in Eastern Europe during World War II. It is truly an "awful" story—in the most somber sense of that word—of how groups guard their boundaries, fear outsiders, and punish defenseless intruders from unlike groups.

In the first weeks of World War II, in the fall of 1939, a six-year-old boy from a large city in Eastern Europe was sent by his parents, like thousands of other children, to the shelter of a distant village.

A man traveling eastward agreed for a substantial payment to find temporary foster parents for the child. Having little choice, the parents entrusted the boy to him.

In sending their child away the parents believed that it was the best means of assuring his survival through the war. Because of the prewar anti-Nazi activities of the child's father, they themselves had to go into hiding to avoid forced labor in Germany or imprisonment in a concentration camp. They wanted to save the child from these dangers and hoped they would eventually be reunited.

Events upset their plans, however. In the confusion of war and occupation, with continuous transfers of population, the parents lost contact with the man who had placed their child in the village. They had to face the possibility of never finding their son again.

In the meantime, the boy's foster mother died within two months of his arrival, and the child was left alone to wander from one village to another, sometimes sheltered and sometimes chased away.

The villages in which he was to spend the next four years differed ethnically from the region of his birth. The local peasants, isolated and inbred, were fair-skinned with blond hair and blue or gray eyes. They boy was olive-skinned, dark-haired, and black-eyed. He spoke a language of the educated class, a language barely intelligible to the peasants of the east.

He was considered a Gypsy or Jewish stray, and harboring Gypsies or Jews, whose place was in ghettos and extermination camps, exposed individuals and communities to the harshest penalties at the hands of the Germans.

The villages in that region had been neglected for centuries. Inaccessible and distant from any urban centers, they were in the most backward parts of Eastern Europe. There were no schools or hospitals, a few paved roads or bridges, no electricity. People lived in small settlements in the manner of their great-grandfathers. Villages feuded over rights to rivers, woods, and lakes. The only law was the traditional right of the stronger and wealthier over the weaker and poorer. Divided between the Roman Catholic and the Orthodox faiths, the people were united only by their extreme superstition and the innumerable diseases plaguing men and animals alike.

They were ignorant and brutal, though not by choice. The soil was poor and the climate severe. The rivers, largely emptied of fish, frequently flooded the pastures and fields, turning them into swamps. Vast marshlands and bogs cut into the region, while dense forests traditionally sheltered bands of rebels and outlaws.

The occupation of that part of the country by the Germans only deepened its misery and backwardness. The peasants had to deliver a large part of their meager crops to the regular troops on the one hand, and to the partisans on the other. Refusal to do so could mean punitive raids on the villages, leaving them in smoldering ruins....

The mushroom season had begun. The hungry villagers welcomed it and went into the woods for their rich harvest. Every hand was needed and my master always took me along. Large parties of peasants from other villages roamed the woods in search of the small growths. My master realized that I looked like a Gypsy and, anxious not to be denounced to the Germans, he shaved my black hair. When going out I put a large old cap on my head that covered half my face and made me less conspicuous. Still, I felt uneasy under the suspicious glances of the other peasants, so I tried always to stay close to my master. I felt that I was sufficiently useful to him to be kept for a while.

On the way to the mushroom gathering we crossed the railroad running through the forest. Several times a day great puffing locomotives passed pulling long freight trains. Machine-guns thrust out of the roofs of the cars and rested on a platform in front of the steam engine. Helmeted soldiers scanned the sky and woods with binoculars.

Then a new kind of train appeared on the line. Living people were jammed in locked cattle cars. Some of the men who worked at the station brought news to the village. These trains carried Jews and Gypsies, who had been captured and sentenced to death. In each car there were two hundred of them stacked like corn-stalks, arms raised to take up less space. Old and young, men, women, and children, even babies. Some of the peasants from the neighboring village were temporarily employed on the construction of a concentration camp and brought back strange tales. They told us that after leaving the train the Jews were sorted into different groups, then stripped naked and deprived of all their possessions. Their hair was cut off, apparently for use in mattresses. The Germans also looked at their teeth, and if they were any gold ones they were immediately pulled out. The gas chambers and ovens could not cope with the great supply of people; thousands of those killed by gas were not burned but simply buried in pits around the camp.

The peasants listened to these stories thoughtfully. They said the Lord's punishment had finally reached the Jews. They had deserved it long ago, ever since they crucified Christ. God never forgot it. If He had overlooked the sins of the Jews so far, He had not forgiven them. Now the Lord was using the Germans as His instrument of justice. The Jews were to be denied the privilege of a natural death. They had to perish by fire, suffering the torments of hell here on earth. They were being justly punished for the shameful crimes of their ancestors, for refuting the only True Faith, for mercilessly killing Christian babies and drinking their blood.

The villagers now gave me even darker looks. "You Gypsy-Jew," they yelled. "You'll burn yet, bastard, you will." I pretended that this did not concern me, even when some shepherds caught me and tried to drag me to a fire and toast my heels, as was God's will. I struggled, scratching and biting them. I had no intention of being burned in such an ordinary campfire when others were incinerated in special and elaborate furnaces built by the Germans and equipped with engines more power-ful than those of the largest locomotives.

I stayed awake at night worrying whether God would punish me too. Was it possible that God's wrath was reserved only for people with black hair and eyes, who were called Gypsies? Why did my father, whom I still remem-bered well, have fair hair and blue eyes, while my mother was dark? What was the difference between a Gypsy and a Jew, since both were dusky and both were destined for the same end? Probably after the war only fair-haired, blue-eyed people would be left in the world. Then what would happen to children of blond people who might be born dark?

When the trains carrying Jews went by in the daytime or at dusk, the peasants lined up on both sides of the track and waved cheerfully to the engineer, the stoker, and the few guards. Through the small square windows at the top of the locked cars, one could sometimes glimpse a human face. These people must have climbed on the shoulders of others to see where they were going and to find out whose voices they heard outside. Seeing the friendly gestures of the peasants the people in the car must have thought that they themselves were being greeted. Then the Jewish faces would disappear and a mass of thin, pale arms would wave desperate signals.

The peasants watched the trains with curiosity, listening intently to the strange humming sound of the human throng, neither groan, cry, nor song. The train went by, and as it pulled away one could still see against the dark background of the forest disembodied human arms waving tirelessly from the windows.

Sometimes at night people traveling on the trains to the crematories would toss their small children through the windows in the hope of saving their lives. Now and then they managed to wrench up the floorboards and determined Jews might force their way through the hole, hitting the crushed stone track-bed, the rails, or the taut semaphore wire. Slashed by the wheels, their mutilated trunks rolled down the embankment into the tall grass.

Peasants wandering along the tracks in daytime would find these remains and quickly strip them of clothes and shoes. Gingerly, lest they get soiled with the diseased blood of the unbaptized, they ripped the linings off the victims' clothes in search for valuables. There were many disputes and fights over the loot. Later the stripped bodies were left on the track, between the rails, where they were found by the German motorized patrol car which passed once a day. The Germans either poured gasoline over the contaminated bodies and burned them on the spot or buried them nearby.

One day word came to the village that several trains with Jews had passed at night, one after another. The peasants finished their mushroom gathering earlier than usual and then we all went to the railroad tracks. We walked along the line on both sides, in single file, peering into the bushes, looking for signs of blood on the signal pole wires and on the edge of the embankment. There was nothing for a few miles. Then one of the women spotted some crushed branches in a thicket of wild roses. Someone spread the thorny growth and we saw a small boy of about five sprawled on the ground. His shirt and pants were in shreds. His black hair was long and his dark eyebrows arched. He seemed to be asleep or dead. One of the men stepped on his leg. The boy jerked and opened his eyes. Seeing people leaning over him he tried to say something, but pink froth came from his mouth instead and dripped slowly over his chin and neck. Afraid of his black eyes, the peasants quickly moved aside and crossed themselves.

Hearing voices behind him, the boy tried to turn over. But his bones must have been broken, because he only moaned and a large bloody bubble appeared at his mouth. He fell back and closed his eyes. The peasants watched him suspiciously from a distance. One of the women crept forward, grabbed the worn shoes on his feet, and tore them off. The boy moved, groaned, and coughed up more blood. He opened his eyes and saw the peasants, who darted out of his field of vision, crossing themselves in panic. He closed his eyes again and remained motionless. Two men grabbed him by the legs and turned him over. He was dead. They took off his jacket, shirt, and shorts and carried him to the middle of the track. He was left there and the German patrol car could not miss him.

We turned to go home. I glanced back as we went. The boy was lying on the whitish stones of the track. Only the clump of his black hair remained in view.

I tried to think what he had thought before dying. When he was tossed out of the train his parents or his friends no doubt assured him that he would find human help which would save him from a horrible death in the great furnace. He probably felt cheated, deceived. He would have preferred to cling to the warm bodies of his father and mother in the packed car, to feel the pressure and smell the hot tart odors, the presence of other people, knowing that he was not alone, told by everyone that the journey was only a misunderstanding.

Although I regretted the boy's tragedy, at the bottom of my mind lurked a feeling of relief that he was dead. Keeping him in the village would do no one any good, I thought. He would threaten the lives of all of us. If the Germans heard about a Jewish foundling, they would converge on the village. They would search every house, they would find the boy, and they would also find me in my cellar. They would probably assume that I, too, had fallen off the train and would kill both of us together on the spot, punishing the whole village later.

I pulled the cloth cap over my face, dragging my feet at the end of the line. Wouldn't it be easier to change people's eyes and hair than to build big furnaces and then catch Jews and Gypsies to burn in them?

Mushroom gathering was now a daily chore. Baskets of them were drying everywhere, basketfuls were hidden in lofts and barns. More and more grew in the woods. Every morning people dispersed into the forest with empty baskets. Heavily laden bees, carrying nectar from dying flowers, droned lazily in the autumn sun through the windless peace of the thick undergrowth, guarded by the towers of tall trees.

Bending down to pick the mushrooms, people called to each other in cheerful voices each time they found a rich cluster. They were answered by the soft cacophony of birds calling from the thickets of hazel and juniper, from the branches of oaks and hornbeams. Sometimes the sinister cry of an owl was heard, but no one could see it in its deep, hidden hole in some tree trunk. A reddish fox might scurry away into the dense bushes after a feast of partridge eggs. Vipers would crawl nervously, hissing to give themselves courage. A fat hare would bound into the bush with huge leaps.

The symphony of the forest was broken only by the puffing of a locomotive, the rattle of cars, the grinding of the brakes. People stood still, looking toward the tracks. The birds grew silent, the owl drew deeper into his hole, draping its gray cloak about itself with dignity. The hare stood up, raising its long ears high, and then, reassured, resumed its leaps.

In the weeks that followed, until the mushroom season ended, we often walked along the railroad tracks. Occasionally we passed small oblong heaps of black ashes and some charred bones, broken and trodden into the gravel. With pursed lips the men stopped and stared. Many people feared that even the burnt corpses of those jumping off the train might contaminate both men and animals, and they would hastily kick dirt over the ashes.

Once I pretended to pick up a mushroom which had dropped out of my basket and grasped a handful of this human dust. It stuck to my fingers and smelled of gasoline. I looked at it closely but could find no trace of a person. Yet this ash was not like the ash left in kitchen ovens where wood, dried peat, and moss were burned. I became frightened. It seemed to me, as I rubbed the handful of ash in my fingers, that the ghost of the burned person hovered over me, watching and remembering all of us. I knew that the ghost might never leave me, that it might follow me, haunt me at night, seep sickness into my veins and madness into my brain.

After each train had passed I saw whole battalions of ghosts with ugly, vengeful faces coming into the world. The peasants said the smoke from the crematories went straight to heaven, laying a soft carpet at God's feet, without even soiling them. I wondered whether so many Jews were necessary to compensate God for the killing of His son. Perhaps the world would soon become one vast incinerator for burning people. Had not the priest said that all were doomed to perish, to go "from ashes to ashes"?

RETURN TO LAUGHTER

ELENORE SMITH BOWEN

The capacity to laugh and cry are biological phenomena, which, at one level of analysis, are paralleled by the sounds of pleasure, terror, anger, and pain among many animal species. What is human about laughing and crying is the social arbitrariness of these responses. That which is funny in one community will be sad in another and neither in still another. In **Return to Laughter**, Laura Bohannan[1] has dramatized the ways in which Western philosophical presuppositions, even the things that make us laugh and cry, are outgrowths of the needs and values of our own society. This particular selection suggests that even the capacity to learn is affected by group membership. Here, an anthropologist in the field struggles with the basic information of a "primitive" group.

Early the next morning, I sat contentedly on my veranda drinking coffee made just to my taste. My emphatic orders—"Fruit and coffee, and then leave me alone"—had been obeyed. I don't like being rushed into a day before I am ready for it. I need to stretch my senses awake, slowly, without disturbance, just as I need to stretch my limbs into life before I get out of bed. Certainly, it's not until my third cup of coffee that I am fully awake and willing to face the consequences of that condition.

I was still drinking my second cup when Sunday suddenly materialized at my elbow. Surprised, I looked up and met at eye level a bowl of seething gray ooze. At my irritated frown, Sunday vanished as rapidly and quietly as he had come; he knew some Europeans dislike porridge. Before I could rouse my sleeping wits, he was back with a large plate of eggs and fried toast.

It was well for justice that I could expostulate only through the cook's interpretation. While he crossed the yard and Sunday stood stiffly in the doorway, I reminded myself into patience. The English like a large breakfast. Indeed, in a country like theirs, where people apply the principles of insulation and central heating to themselves rather than to their houses, a large and greasy breakfast has a certain functional value which disappears in the tropics. The Englishman abroad maintains his traditions tenaciously; he drills them into his servants. I had asked for trained servants; I had, perforce, British-trained servants. I could scarcely communicate with my boys; they had misunderstood. I must explain.

Once more I tried to tell the cook that I wanted nothing but fruit and coffee in the morning. His air of reproachful resignation showed me that he thought his skill as cook was involved. I wanted to tell him it was not so; the chef who could tempt me to breakfast does not exist. But explanation without words is impossible. "Fruit, coffee good; eggs, porridge bad." We could say no more to each other.

A stir on the path released our deadlock. Once again Kako paced slowly into the resthouse yard, followed by his bright train of notables. He had come, as he had told Sackerton he would, to teach me his language. I sent the boys out to welcome him, while I searched for a notebook and gulped my coffee like a harassed commuter.

---

[1] Elenore Smith Bowen is the *nom de plume* of Laura Bohannan.

Once again we sat outside in the shade of the tree, smiling and shaking fists in greeting. Once again Kako and his notables produced pipes; the same little boy ran into the kitchen for coals; the same two women stood behind Kako. Today, however, each action was a lesson. By the time their pipes were going, I had written and repeated pipe, pipes, coals, flint and steel. At Kako's prompting they showed me bags and spears, pointed to chairs, sheepskins and articles of dress, drilling me on each word by the simple technique of saying it a bit louder with each repetition. They opened bags: out came snuff stands, kola nuts, odd bits of cloth wrapped around shillings and pennies. With them, we came to an end.

Kako sent the younger woman and the little boy running. Through the cook he told me that now we were to start on the real pith of the lesson. I turned to a fresh page in my notebook.

Kako pointed to himself and pronounced his name. I beamed encouragingly upon him, for above all I wanted to learn people by name—as many and as quickly as possible. When Kako named, I repeated and wrote. When he pointed, I looked intently for identifying signs: that man was very thin; that one was lame; that one was reddish; that one almost purple-black. All of them were elaborately scarred, and the more distinctive patterns of sacrification proved the most reliable means of identification. Beards can be removed. What's worse, when these people shave, beard, mustache, hair and eyebrows all go, transforming a white-haired elder into a youthful billiard ball. However, this time—with all of them sitting together and in the same place—I was able to close my notebook and repeat all their names correctly. Kako informed me that I had done well.

The woman and the little boy returned, each with armfuls of leaves. Kako spread about a dozen out on the ground before me, and named them one by one; then the next dozen, and on and on. Some, he told me, were edible. By pointing at the farms to the north of the resthouse and the bush to the south, he informed me which were cultivated. Kako broke off; he needed all his attention for lighting his pipe with the matches I had given him. My instruction was taken over by Ikpoom, whose name and face I could easily remember because his eyes were so sad and he was so very ugly. Ikpoom, also pointing, taught me the words for path and bush, farm and fallow, earth and heavens, correcting my constant mistakes far more patiently than Kako had done. And I made many. Theirs is one of the simpler African languages, yet it was months before it seemed the only natural way to speak: a flow of fat, firm consonants and comfortable vowels, quite unlike the breathy hisses of English.

By nine o'clock that morning, I had several pages of words, and my tongue was limp from unaccustomed twisting. Unable to take in any more, I instituted a review by again naming the notables. I again got most of them right: the right man and almost the right sound. Kako looked on me with favor. Encouraged, I demanded the names of the women. They smiled, but Kako ignored my question and turned firmly back to the leaves. Rather reluctantly I began to name them.

With every word Kako became more dour. I spoke more loudly; my pronunciation couldn't be that bad. Ikpoom's eyes grew sadder; the women seemed incredulous. The little boy could bear it no longer. He snatched from me the leaf I was naming and handed me another. The order had been mixed, and not once had I put the right name to the right plant.

These people are farmers: to them plants are as important and familiar as people. I'd never been on a farm and am not even sure which are begonias, dahlias or petunias. Plants, like algebra, have a habit of looking alike and being different, or looking different and being alike; consequently mathematics and botany confused me. For the first time in my life I found myself in a community where ten-year-old children weren't my mathematical superiors. I also found myself in a place where every plant, wild or cultivated, had a name and a use, and where every man, woman and child knew literally hundreds of plants. None of them could ever believe that I could not if I only would.

Kako gave me that long and incredulous glare with which a brilliant father regards his backward child. Then he insisted that we start all over again. I stared at the leaves. I fingered the leaves, and drew the leaves. But the only leaf I could identify almost every time was the very distinctively pronged cassava leaf. I confused corn with guinea corn and at least three, very similar wild grasses. I couldn't and still can't tell one kind of yam leaf from the next. The little boy, no more than eight years old, stood beside me and prompted me; he knew them all. I was discouraged. Kako lost heart. He became politely bored, and promised we should try again some other, unspecified time. Then he drew his toga more closely about him and withdrew.

ME

A thirteen-year-old girl turned in the following essay for her eighth-grade English class. Her essay is an elaboration of the idea that every person, in certain respects, is like no other person.

To begin with, I am a Mexican. That sentence has a scent of bitterness as it was written. I feel that if it weren't for my nationality I would accomplish more. My being a Mexican has brought about my lack of initiative. No matter what I attempt to do, my dark skin always makes me feel that I will fail.

Another thing that "gripes" me is that I am such a coward. I absolutely will not fight for something even if I know I'm right. I do not have the vocabulary that it would take to express myself strongly enough.

Many people, including most of my teachers, have tried to tell me I'm a leader. Well, I know better! Just because I may get better grades than most of my fellow Mexicans doesn't mean a thing. I could no more get an original idea in my head than be President of the United States. I don't know how to think for myself.

I want to go to college, sure, but what do I want to be? Even worse, where do I want to go? These questions are only a few that trouble me. I'd like to prove to my parents that I can do something. Just because I don't have the gumption to go out and get a job doesn't mean that I can't become something they'll be proud of. But if I find that I can't bring myself to go to college, I'll get married and they'll still get rid of me.

After reading this, you'll probably be surprised. This is the way I feel about myself, and nobody can change me. Believe me, many have tried and failed. If God wants me to reach all my goals, I will. No parents, teachers, or priest will change the course that my life is to follow. Don't try.

2

Notes and Queries: An Annotated Checklist of Basic Questions

Those who wish to succeed must ask the
right preliminary questions.

—Aristotle

Asking a question—identifying a problem worthy of investigation—is the first step in scientific study. At first the question may be based on no more than a hunch, dimly understood, and articulated only with hesitancy. Gradually, and usually only after considerable research, it is possible to ask more precise questions. An invesigator's questions sometimes are off the mark, but one good question can lead to the acquisition of information that in turn makes possible more precisely framed questions.

An individual might observe an event that conceivably could contribute to a clear understanding of intergroup relations, but his interpretation would be faulty if his attention happened to be diverted to irrelevant details. For example, persons living in countries foreign to them are often completely oblivious to vast areas of the lives of the people of those countries unless they are directed to look for particular customs and practices. The reason is clear: One must learn what to look for.

The classic illustration of this idea comes from anthropology. In the year 1839 a paper entitled "The Extinction of Native Races" was read before a group of scholars in Birmingham, England. It aroused so much attention that a committee was appointed to prepare a questionnaire to serve as a guide to those who would come in contact with "native races." Because trained researchers were in short supply, the questionnaire was written in such a way that government administrators, merchants, missionaries, and other travelers would be able to collect uniform information that could then be analyzed by experts back home. The questionnaire that was eventually developed came to be known as *Notes and Queries on Anthropology*, now in its sixth edition.

For decades every anthropologist going to the field has packed a copy along with his other essential belongings. The reason for the checklist's enduring popularity is that it serves as a guide to researchers who want to ask important questions. Asking the right question obviously is not a problem for anthropologists alone. It is a basic consideration for every scientific undertaking (see Popper, 1962).

Questions Worth Asking

There are hazards in limiting the number of kinds of questions too strictly at the beginning of a study. One of these hazards is premature closure. It can be avoided by first surveying a topic and then listing the factors that could conceivably be relevant. Several factors, or even one factor, can then be studied intensively in the specific situation. By proceeding with general questions and narrowing the focus, the student of intergroup relations can work deliberately and systematically. In this respect, researchers are much like airline pilots who use checklists before takeoff, even though they have practically memorized the instrument panel during flight training.

The following list of questions and the brief discussions that accompany them may be considered a research checklist. The list also serves as a preview of topics that will be discussed in much greater detail later in this book. It is by no means exhaustive, nor is every item appropriate for every situation. It is hoped, however, that these questions, with their broad focus, will generate more specific questions.

What Historical Factors Seem Relevant?

Sometimes researchers ignore history and concentrate only on social arrangements prevailing at the time of the study. Anthropologists have often been forced to do so when the groups they have studied have lacked dependable written or oral history. But, when documents or other sources of historical evidence are available, these records of the past may be crucial to understanding social interactions in their present form.

Every event in the present has some connection with events in the immediate past and eventually with a larger series of events farther back. How far back should the researcher go? In some instances, not very far. The force of some events is quickly spent. To use an analogy from statistics, some events of history do not "explain" much of the variation in contemporary society. On the other hand, to understand why two Hopi communities, for example, absorbed different amounts of European-Anglo culture, we need to discover the historical fact that in the early seventeenth century a Franciscan mission was established in one village and not in the other (Doob, 1960, p. 9). A researcher who ignored that historic development and sought instead to explain the difference between the two communities in terms of personality dynamics, for instance, would be misled from the beginning.

Illustrative questions of a historical nature that might be raised include: "Does the situation involve groups that were once slaves? conquerors?" "Has a political or religious leader ever risen whose ideas about race are still believed by the people being studied?" "In the situation under study, which of the groups has been in the area the longest amount of time?" Such questions of a historical nature lead to further considerations that involve politics, economics, religion, education, and so on.

How Do Economic Factors Affect the Situation?

All human societies have systems of production and distribution. The very nature of cultural adaptation implies a division of labor that in turn brings about the need for exchange. When producer meets distributor or when buyer meets seller, there is a sense in which one person's interest is opposed to that of another. This inherent opposition results in competition and often conflict. Some order and some mutual tolerance must be maintained, however, if social life is to continue.

In many instances the economic order shapes and is shaped by racial and ethnic arrangements. One way to find out if that is so is to look at the division of labor, at occupational structures and related processes like career patterns and recruitment procedures. If jobs are ethnically typed, further investigation may show that legal barriers, customs, or inadequate educational resources help to perpetuate this condition.

Another way to explore the question is to examine wealth and income distributions. Such scrutiny can reveal not only the extent of the impact of racial and ethnic factors but also where the impact is greatest. Table 1 documents the well-known disparity among incomes that exists in the United States as well as the regions where the disparity is greatest.

We may wish to study economic phenomena in terms of the "life chances" (the probability of individual and class differentials, as measured by goods, living conditions, and personal life experiences) of members of various groups. The use

TABLE 1   FAMILIES, BY MEDIAN INCOME IN 1971, AND BLACK
           FAMILY INCOME AS A PERCENT OF WHITE, BY REGION:
           1959, 1966, 1970, AND 1971

Area	Number of Families, 1972 (millions)		Median Family Income, 1971		Negro Income as a Percentage of White Income			
	Negro	White	Negro	White	1959	1966	1970	1971
United States	5,157	47,641	$6,440	$10,672	51	58	61	60
North and West	2,581	33,544	7,596	11,057	71	71	74	69
Northeast	1,068	11,447	7,601	11,291	69	67	71	67
North Central	1,057	13,582	7,603	11,019	74	74	73	69
West	456	8,515	7,623	10,803	67	72	77	71
South	2,576	14,097	5,414	9,706	46	51	57	56

SOURCE: U.S. Department of Commerce, Social and Economic Statistics Administration, Bureau of the Census, *Current Population Reports*, 1971, Series P-23, No. 42.

of socioeconomic indicators to answer these questions involves comparison, because the data have meaning only when they are compared. In making comparisons between the economic status of Whites and Blacks, we might compare the world in which they lived in the past or with the world (both past and present) of White Americans. Comparisons might also be made between the actuality and the American ideal or between the actuality and some potential.

In industrialized nations, the question of job discrimination is crucial in understanding the distribution of wealth. A scale developed by R. M. MacIver illustrates one way in which the question of job discrimination might be studied:

> Would an individual of a given race or ethnic group typically have access to:
> (1) unskilled jobs? (2) semi-skilled jobs? (3) equal pay for equal work?
> (4) training or education necessary for skilled and professional positions?
> (5) promotions or upgrading to positions that involve responsibility? (6) positions that involve control or authority over individuals of the majority or more privileged groups? (7) positions with professional or administrative opportunities that are not limited to service within the disprivileged group itself.

In this scale, affirmative answers to 5, 6, and 7 would indicate a comparative absence of discrimination in the situation being studied.

What Political Factors are Relevant?

"Who gets what, when, how?" is the classic way that Harold Lasswell has posed the basic issues of politics (1958). Put less starkly, politics involves the distribution and the exercise of power in society. Power, by definition, is the capacity to control the actions of others.

A study of the political process inevitably leads to consideration of the state. Isolated individuals may escape to uninhabited areas where no jurisdiction reaches, but the moment that a group of such people comes together in social interaction political relations arise. The power relations that emerge may be coercive, or they may be legitimated and thus transformed into authority.

The political process involves conflict, as well as consensus and mechanisms for the easing of group tensions. So much intergroup conflict has occurred within the past three decades that it is tempting to try to analyze all intergroup relations in terms of conflict. Not surprisingly, a number of researchers have used such a perspective to good advantage. Yet a multitude of harmonious intergroup contacts occur every day in stores, on assembly lines, in schools, and at ball parks. Clearly, there can be both harmony and conflict within the same political system, and one may give rise to the other. Ralf Dahrendorf has written on this point as follows: "There are sociological problems for the explanation of which the integration theory of society provides adequate assumptions; there are other problems which can be explained only in terms of the coercion theory of society; there are finally, problems for which both theories appear adequate" (Dahrendorf, 1959, p. 159).

A researcher might focus upon the political institutions that serve the interests of certain groups. Studies of various political organizations or movements can be similarly useful. One has only to mention the Irish Republican Army (I.R.A.), the National Association for the Advancement of Colored People (N.A.A.C.P.), the Ku Klux Klan (K.K.K.), the Mau Mau of Kenya, or the Muslim League of India to realize how voluminous is the literature.

How the Situation Is Defined and Perceived by Participants

Whenever we interact in a situation, we define it. That is, we interpret and assess the situation in order to decide what behavior is appropriate. By means of certain definitions, we resolve basic relational problems that are part of group existence. Talcott Parsons has suggested that five such problems are inherent in group situations. As he presents them, they take the form of five dichotomies, or "pattern variables" (Parsons, 1951, pp. 58–67).

Qualities versus performance The first definitional problem involves the question "How are individuals to be defined, on the basis of their *abilities* or on the basis of certain *qualities?*" These opposing kinds of definition are at the root of the American problem in the treatment of minorities. One tradition says that the *performance* of any person—minority or otherwise—should be the sole criterion for judgment. Another says that the sheer *quality* of being a minority person should be the deciding factor.

Universalism versus particularism *Universalism* denotes the expectation that everyone will be treated according to abstract general principles, rather than according to personal or particular characteristics. A professor who grades students impartially according to their responses on test questions is behaving *universalistically*. A professor who favors a student who happens to be his relative or a member of a particular ethnic group is behaving *particularistically*.

Affectivity versus neutrality Individuals are permitted to be *affective* in some situations, forbidden it in others. Some cultures emphasize affectivity, and others do not. For example, the British traditionally have deemphasized affectivity, so much so that we stereotype the British as restrained and stoical. People from a society characterized by this kind of behavior probably would experience dissonance in a society characterized by "soul." Variation in these definitions among societies may influence the types of intergroup relations that develop. Individuals who have been socialized in a society that emphasizes neutrality may thus shun "soul people" or may agree to associate with them only in carefully structured settings.

Diffuseness versus specificity Definitions of situations differ in whether or not relations are specific or diffuse. In *diffuse* relations, individuals perform not one but many types of tasks for one another. In a rural society, a neighbor or a relative will be called on to help with a wide variety of tasks, but relations in modern complex societies tend to be more *specific*. A sales clerk in a large department store is expected to sell merchandise to customers, but few would expect him to visit the customers when they are sick, to lend them money, or to cook their meals.

Intergroup relations vary in diffuseness. In some countries, members of dominant groups require minority people to respond to their slightest whims. In other societies, intergroup relations are quite specific.

Self-orientation versus collectivity orientation A situation may be defined in terms of the kind of motivation that is valued. Individuals may be expected to further their own interests, thus displaying *self-orientation*, or they may be expected to subordinate their interests to the well-being of the *collectivity*.

From the point of view of intergroup relations social scientists have learned that conflicts are likely to be more intense and more violent when the contenders are oriented to the collectivity, rather than self-oriented. The reason is that the participants can then in good conscience strive for super-individual ends. As Lewis A. Coser has written, "Individuals who see themselves acting as representatives of a cause, fighting not for self but only for the ideals of a collectivity they represent, tend to be more radical and merciless than those who fight for personal advantage" (1968, pp. 232–236). Coser has also shown that intellectuals who transform conflicts of interests into conflicts of ideas, thus stripping them of merely personal aspects, help to make the conflicts more intense.

The pattern variables have been used in some research on intergroup relations. In one study of the Deep South (a region where there has been relatively little structural differentiation) it was shown that the region's prominent definitions were ascriptive, diffuse, particularistic, and affective. This finding meant that resistance to desegregation was predictable, for desegregation is most likely to occur in situations characterized by the complementary definitions: performance oriented, functionally specific, universalistic, and affectively neutral (Rubin, 1954, pp. 28–35).

Attitudes Associated with the Intergroup Situation and Their Referents

An *attitude*, according to Gordon Allport's definition, is a "mental and neural state of readiness, organized through experience, exerting a directive or dynamic influence upon the individual's response to all objects and situations with which it is related" (1935, p. 10). As generally used by social scientists, "attitude" denotes what happens between a stimulus and a response to produce an observed effect. Two persons, one from rural Mississippi and the other from Sweden, would probably respond differently to the same stimulus, perhaps an American Black. This difference is accounted for conceptually by saying that each has a different *attitude* towards Blacks.

A word of caution is in order. Even though a great many investigations presumably deal with attitudes, in some, unfortunately, the phenomena appear to be little more than verbalizations. Robin Williams, Jr., has urged,

> One of the most pressing needs is for studies which will grasp and reveal relations between verbalizations and other social actions, and will specify in considerable detail the agreement or lack of agreement between responses obtained through questionnaires or interviews and responses evoked by various types of "real situations." (1947, p. 114)

A considerable number of attitudes are related to or are grounded in groups to which the individual belongs (membership groups). Various studies indicate, however, that actions and attitudes can often be explained in terms of groups to which the individual does *not* belong. In order to account for these orientations, the term *reference group,* or *reference other,* has been used in social science to designate groups, individuals, or even abstract ideas toward which individuals orient their behavior. If there is inconsistency in behavior as a person moves from one social situation to another, it may be interpreted in terms of a change in referents. Henry David Thoreau once observed, "If a man does not keep pace with his companions, perhaps it is because he hears a different drummer."

Status problems, like the aspirations of minority groups; conflicts in group loyalty; and the dilemmas of "marginal" individuals, have been analyzed in terms of reference groups. Similar social processes may be involved in each of these ostensibly diverse situations.

Aspects of the Normative Structure Relevant to the Intergroup Situation

A *norm* is a standard of behavior regarded as socially required or acceptable in given situations. Adherence to norms makes possible an ordered society, in that individual behavior becomes fairly predictable. Many sociologists thus consider the norm to be the basic element in social organization. Norms may be classified as folkways, mores, laws, customs, conventions, and etiquette. To understand a particular intergroup situation it may be essential to learn about the norms that are observed, those that have been abandoned (for example, archaic laws or rules of etiquette), and the amount of deviation that is permitted.

Acquiring this information is no small assignment. The student of inter-group relations in industrialized nations will find that a great many norms have become formalized in legal codes, whereas others exist as etiquette or mores that vary during different time periods and in different subcultures.

Are Relations between the Sexes Associated with the Situation?

Not since Sigmund Freud have social scientists been able to ignore the influence of sex in human relations, and it has become a major focus in many important studies. "To the average, normal person in whatever type of society we find him," the anthropologist Bronislaw Malinowski once wrote, "attraction by the other sex and the passionate and sentimental episodes which follow are the most significant events in his existence, those most deeply associated with his intimate happiness and with the zest and meaning of life" (1962, p. 1).

Perhaps Malinowski overstated the point. But it is clear that customs, ideas, and institutions centered around the erotic are highly significant. In many instances, they greatly influence intergroup relations.

Parents of children in desegregated school systems are likely to be concerned about this dimension of intergroup relations, especially from the junior-high-school years on. They recognize that their children's values may be different from their own and that sexual experimentation may be beginning. Sex is also an important reason for the resistance of many private clubs (country clubs and the like) to desegregation. Clubs and schools often serve as "territory" where members of the opposite sexes meet, date, dance, and play together; guardians of these territories thus tend to be relieved when members of stigmatized groups can be excluded.

Opposition to desegregation has repeatedly been expressed in the form of the question "Would you want your daughter to marry one?" Asking this question is presumably equivalent to answering it. Historically, sexual experiences involving people of different groups have triggered harsh penalties on countless occasions. It is a matter of record that rape (alleged or actual), flirtations, and "insults" involving Black males and White females have provided occasion for many of the lynchings that have occurred in the United States.

Generally, the character of sexual relations between members of different groups is a good indicator of other aspects of intergroup situations. When intermarriage begins, a minority is on its way to complete acceptance in the larger society.

How Are Educational Processes Relevant to the Intergroup Situation?

Education may be thought of as including all learning, formal and informal, that results in the acquisition of culture by an individual (Beals and Hoijer, 1965, p. 674). It is an experience that begins at birth and continues throughout a lifetime. By means of education individuals acquire their attitudes and opinions, as well as their value systems. Actually, with such a broad definition of education, the research possibilities are practically endless. Games, work skills, songs, languages, creeds, and hundreds of other items in the human behavioral inventory are learned. Any social instrumentalities—schools, books, songs—that teach tolerance or prejudice toward members of other groups or provide information about other groups are of potential interest to students of intergroup relations.

In addition to the less structured educational activities, the researcher may wish to give particular attention to formal educational activities. Here a number of questions may be relevant: Are schools segregated? If segregated, what factors perpetuate this situation? Do textbooks and other teaching aids convey a racist approach? Is there evidence that some groups excel in intellectual pursuits? If so, what are the causes?

Is Language or Dialect Important to the Study?

Frantz Fanon considered language such a fundamental part of modern intergroup relations that he began *Black Skin, White Masks* with an essay on its importance. Fanon wrote against the background of French culture, in which a person is not fully accepted as truly French unless he or she has mastered the language. This view of things has not been limited to the French, though they have emphasized language more than have some societies. Our own word "shibboleth" attests to the fact that words are widely used to protect boundaries. "Shibboleth" is associated with an event in biblical times in which the pronunciation of the word was used to tell friends from foes. (The enemy pronounced it "sibboleth"; see *Judges*, 12:1–7).

Minorities, as well as majorities, use language for purposes of maintaining boundaries. In ethnic communities, residents will commonly resort to their own language when they wish to tell secrets or jokes, or to transact business.

Languages are conservative parts of culture, and they maintain themselves despite conquests, legal prohibitions, new religions, and economic change. Great ancient empires, like the Inca and Roman empires, bound together diverse peoples by means of common languages. Some modern nations (like India) have had serious problems because they have not been able to do so. Switzerland, by contrast, has been able to work out an amicable solution. In that country 70 percent of the population speaks Swiss-German dialects, 19 percent French, 10 percent Italian, and 1 percent Romansch. The official language in each canton (state) is the predominant language of that canton. Latin is used for stamps, certain coins, legal documents and the like, to avoid having to print them in all four national languages.

In modern society, an individual frequently interacts in several social worlds and finds that language has status functions in each of them. Certain styles of speech will be demanded in one but scorned in another. The status function of language is manifested not only in the classroom and in the world of the corporation but at parties, at football games, in bars, and in street-corner society.

American educators are presently confronting the fact that standard English is required in the classroom but is little used on the playgrounds and in the homes of many communities. Some have urged that nonstandard English be taught as a separate language in the schools. This idea has met with considerable resistance, but a proposal involving bilingual instruction for children whose first language is not English has gained support. (Massachusetts requires that school districts provide bilingual programs. A few additional states permit them.)

All these issues indicate that language is a basic consideration in intergroup relations. In a very real sense the question "Who am I?" can be answered in terms of what a person says and the way that he or she says it.

What Demographic Factors Seem Relevant?

A study of the sizes, rates of growth, geographical distributions and compositions of study populations may be particularly appropriate for the research problem. Sometimes novices in the social sciences rush into the "field"—whatever that may be—blissfully ignorant of the vast amount of information that is readily available in the form of censuses, government-agency reports, dissertations, financial reports, school reports, and so on. The appropriate "field" for some research efforts is a good library.

Various minority groups differ in terms of relative size; mortality and natality rates; age-sex ratio; residence patterns, whether rural or urban, home owning or renting; and migration patterns. These characteristics may explain a great deal about the nature of the relations in a particular area. The fact that apporoximately 42 percent of New York City's population in 1970 was of "foreign stock" (defined by the Census Bureau as foreign-born or American-born with at least one foreign-born parent) is of considerable importance when we contrast intergroup relations in that city with, for example, Indianapolis, where less than 7 percent of the population is of foreign stock. If there is a marked change in an urban area's ethnic or class composition, the ramifications of the change may affect shopping patterns, taxes, real-estate projects, schools, and voting patterns.

Is Territory a Relevant Consideration?

Territory is an important organizing principle in human society and a prominent feature of many integroup situations. Various aspects of spacing mechanisms have been explored by a number of prominent scholars (Lewin, 1948; Blumer, 1958, pp. 3–7; Lyman and Scott, 1967, pp. 236–249; Hall, 1966) by means of concepts like *social space, territoriality, personal space,* and *proxemics.* Individuals and groups view a wide range of objects as "territory." Neighborhoods, sections of cities, schools, and clubs are obvious possibilities. But there are less obvious instances of territory as well: Parents often think of their children as territory, scholars regard their disciplines as territory, and craftsmen regard their work settings and the crafts themselves as territory. In each instance, an intrusion by outsiders tends to be regarded as an invasion and is likely to be resisted.

An individual studying intergroup relations may find it useful to consider, first, what a particular group regards as its territory—a neighborhood, a school, or certain jobs; second, how this territory was obtained; third, how the boundaries of the territory are delineated; and fourth, how the territory is defended.

Is Humor Relevant to the Study?

"Jesters do oft prove prophets," William Shakespeare wrote, expanding on the idea that truth often is spoken in jest. Because humor has several social functions, it deserves attention by social scientists. Particularly important are ethnic jokes, which run a close second to sex jokes in the standard American repertoire of humor. Ethnic jokes are frequently used as vehicles for formulating and transmitting stereotypes about various groups. They exaggerate selected characteristics of each group, thus singling them out for special attention.

Humor can be used to reinforce a sense of solidarity and intimacy within a group. From the individual's point of view, successfully telling a funny story is a way of winning social approval. The very process of seeking such approval may strengthen group bonds. Humor also can sharpen group boundaries. If you have ever seen an individual about to tell an ethnic joke who first looked around carefully to see who was listening, you were observing a little social ritual that has the effect of reinforcing a boundary between "we" and "they."

Some jests and jokes express enjoyment at the discomfiture of an out-group. Humor, like insults or verbal attacks, can be a form of aggressive behavior. If a particular people's humor continually dwells on aggression and violence, it may tell of violent things to come. Wit and humor also can be safety values for social tensions. Some resentments are so intense and so explosive that there may be only two ways to deal with them openly—through violent confrontation or through humor.

> "Do you know how to save a bigot from drowning?"
> "No."
> "Good!"

What Accounts for Relatively Low Intergroup Tensions?

No general agreement has ever been reached on the extent to which social scientists, in their role as social scientists, should be involved in action programs. But few would suggest that a study of various action programs is beyond the scope of legitimate investigation.

A number of prominent social scientists have long called for such studies. "What is needed for practical purposes," MacIver once wrote, "is not so much a new series of detached studies concerning the nature, conditions and effects of intergroup prejudice and discrimination, but far more a direct and coordinated exploration of the methods by which these phenomena may be combated and controlled" (1948, p. 241).

Carefully designed studies of action programs can contribute to an improvement of such undertakings. "This dearth of appropriate research and consequent lack of a proven base for action," Williams observed almost three decades ago, "is one of the most conspicuous features of existing intergroup programs" (1947, p. 8). The general state of affairs is only slightly improved today. Much well-intentioned activity is wasteful and superficial, and some may be harmful because previous programs of a similar nature have not been rigorously evaluated.

What Religious Factors Are Relevant?

Religion is a universal, permanent, and pervasive fact of human society. "Unless we understand it," Kingsley Davis has observed, "we shall fail to understand society" (1949, p. 509). By means of religious beliefs an adherent seeks to understand and interpret the world. Because the "world" contains outsiders, an individual may look to religion for answers in dealing with unlike peoples. A researcher investigating intergroup relations may wish to find out whether or not certain religious groups approve of various peoples. It may be beyond the scope of social science to judge the truth of particular beliefs (especially those that involve the hereafter or the unseen world) but social science is legitimately interested in the ways in which persons who hold these beliefs behave. The fact that in the 1970s it could still be said that "eleven o'clock on Sunday morning is the most segregated hour of the week" suggests that there is a basic relationship between certain religious beliefs and intergroup behavior. (In 1973, according to the *Yearbook of American and Canadian Churches*, 90 percent of Black Christians belonged to mostly Black denominations.)

Sample topics involving religion include revivalist movements among subjugated peoples, the Cargo cults, the development of intergroup churches, the role of religion in the civil rights movement, and the relation between religious beliefs and prejudice.

How Are Aesthetic Activities Relevant?

According to Oliver Wendell Holmes, Jr.:

> One of the glories of man is that he does not sow seeds and weave cloth, and produce all the other economic means simply to sustain and multiply other sowers and weavers. . . . After the production of food and cloth has gone on for a certain time he stops producing and goes to the play, or he paints a picture or asks unanswerable questions about the universe, and thus delightfully consumes a part of the world's food and clothing. . . (1952: pp. 210, 211).

Ideas about other groups frequently are expressed in art forms. It is possible to ascertain prevailing attitudes toward a particular group in a given historical era by studying the ways in which the group has been represented in paintings, literature, and song. Motifs portrayed on ancient pottery, textiles, and carvings sometimes reveal information about relations among various peoples in a particular region.

In the United States, art forms have been used to communicate various ideas about intergroup relations. These ideas include the white supremacist point of view represented in the motion picture *Birth of a Nation*, the dilemma of the Blacks represented in *To Kill a Mockingbird*, and Jewish-Russian relations in the musical *Fiddler on the Roof*.

From another point of view, it may be useful to learn if members of minorities are proportionately represented among painters, dancers, actors, and the like and to attempt to discover the causes. It should be borne in mind that art tends to crystallize ideas, to disparage them or glorify them. As a field of inquiry, it certainly deserves more than the meager attention that has been given to it by social scientists. Much of contemporary art is social commentary. This emphasis is not altogether new, but it has become more common, more self-conscious, and more deliberate within the past few decades.

Occasionally we encounter a situation in which a number of the factors discussed in this chapter are conspicuous. One such example comes from Japan. This

Newsweek[1] account of the event has been analyzed by means of headings from the research guide presented in this chapter.

CALL ME MISTER

At first glance, the case of Kim Hi Ro looked like one more routine crime in Japan's turbulent underworld. In the Minx cabaret in the town of Shimzu, 90 miles south of Tokyo, 41-year-old gangster Kim shot and killed two Japanese thugs. He then fled by car to the tiny resort town of Sumatakyo and holed up in the Fujimiya Hotel, taking as hostages the owner and his family of five as well as ten guests who were there to enjoy Sumatakyo's hot-spring baths. Once barricaded in the inn with a rifle and 160 sticks of dynamite, he telephoned police to announce where he was and why.

Within hours Kim's crime and the cause he invoked to justify it were front-page news the length and breadth of Japan. And while police pondered the problem of how to capture Kim and leave his hostages unharmed, the public was accorded a dramatic reminder of a social ill most Japanese pretend does not exist in their country: race prejudice.

Political factor

For although Kim was *born* in Japan and has lived his whole life there, he is still a Korean in Japanese eyes, and, like the rest of the nation's colony of some

Demographic factor

600,000 Koreans, he is the subject of at least as much, and possibly more, discrimination than that imposed upon Negroes in the United States.

Political factor
Demographic factor

Opportunities: Koreans account for *90 percent* of all aliens in Japan, and for most of them social and economic opportunities have changed little since they

Historical,
political factor

first began arriving after *Japan conquered Korea* in 1904. During World War II, many thousands of Koreans were brought forcibly to Japan to work in mines and war plants, virtually as *slave laborers*. Many were sent throughout the Pacific in construction battalions and subsequently captured by the U.S. Though well over a million Koreans returned to their homeland at the end of the war, scores of thousands of others had by then already cut their roots with Korea. They elected to stay in Japan, but ever since, they have faced a desperate struggle to escape the classification of *second-class*

Political factor

citizens.

[1] *Newsweek*, March 11, 1968, pp. 52, 53; Copyright Newsweek, Inc. Reprinted by permission.

Economic factor	Few if any Koreans *hold jobs* with the government or top industrial firms. The vast majority of them live
Ecological factor	*in Korean ghettos* and, like besieged killer Kim, either *gravitate to the underworld* or eke out a living as best
Norms	they can at the bottom of the economic ladder. The *crime* rate among Koreans is four times higher than for
Educational factor	the rest of Japan; *private schools and universities* are not *legally bound* to accept Koreans, and many refuse to.
Definitions	For their part, the majority of Japanese persist in their old *feeling of superiority* over their onetime subjects and regard them (as they do the people of other underdeveloped Asian nations) as naturally inferior, *shiftless* and inevitably inclined to lives of crime and immorality. Those few Koreans who have managed to
Aesthetic factor	achieve prosperity (usually in the fields of *entertainment* and sports) assume Japanese names to make life "smoother" for themselves.
	Throughout the five days, he remained under siege in Sumatakyo, Kim conducted a masterful public-relations program. He called press conferences, handed out memos and spoke on tapes for TV reporters. Japanese viewers thus were able to hear Kim in such passages as:
Definitions *Attitudes*	"The idea that I am racially discriminated against never left my mind. . . . I was often called 'you dammed Korean' in my childhood."
	Finally, the police trapped Kim. They dressed themselves up as reporters and jumped him as he let them in. He put up a tough fight, and tried to commit suicide by biting off his tongue. But in the end he was subdued and hauled off to jail.
	Some Koreans feared that Kim's attempt to publicize their problem might boomerang into further prejudice, but many Japanese seemed to sympathize with lone-wolf Kim and professed admiration for his courage. As for the culprit himself, he could at least take comfort in the fact that throughout the five days he was besieged in the
Etiquette	hotel, the Japanese press and police accorded him a *courtesy* he had seldom heard before. They called him Kim-San—Mister Kim.

Errors of Analysis

What has been presented so far in the chapter is essentially a guide to key variables in intergroup relations. Identifying the key variables is an important first step. Next comes analysis—putting the variables together in a meaningful and logical manner. It is at this point that we must guard against logical fallacies and the invalid use of data, particularly in a socially sensitive area like intergroup relations, which attracts more than its share of faulty explanations. Three of the more common forms of error are described here.

Overgeneralizations

The word "overgeneralization" defines itself. An overgeneralization has a data base that is too narrow to support its inferences. When a data base is inadequate, it is usually because the instances studied are unrepresentative or simply because there are not enough cases from which to generalize with validity.

Spurious Correlations

Spurious correlations between two variables arise not from a relationship between the variables themselves but from the fact that both variables are correlated with a third variable or variables (Theodorson and Theodorson, 1969, p. 83). For example, it could be inferred from a spurious correlation that drinking lemonade is a major cause of drowning. After all, each year the rate of deaths by drowning is highest when lemonade sales are high. The fallacy of this logic is that it fails to account for a third variable—temperature. When the weather is warm more people drink lemonade, more people swim, and more people drown. The two variables are correlated with each other because they are both related to the weather. In the same way it sometimes has been claimed that race, rather than socioeconomic status, values, or ecological factors, is the cause of certain behavior patterns like illegitimacy or crime rates.

Oversimplifications and Overcomplications

Intergroup relations like all social realities, can be interpreted in such a way that the explanations are either unduly complicated or naïvely simplified. The Principle of Parsimony, also called Occam's Razor, is a strategy of logic for avoiding explanations that are needlessly complex: When two explanations seem equally good, the simplest and least complicated one should be chosen (Theodorson and Theodorson, 1969, p. 292). When this principle is ignored, social science tends to degenerate into endless qualifications or catalogues of trivia.

By contrast, an oversimplification ignores the close interlacing of social factors and leads to conclusions that are superficial and naïve. Some writers hold that "laws" of society are unattainable because social phenomena constitute a great intermixture of many "laws." Because the number of variables to be considered is so great, J. S. Mill predicted a century ago that in sociology it would be more unlikely than in any other science for two inquirers equally competent and equally disinterested to take the same view of the evidence and reach the same conclusions (1969, p. 308).

These errors of logic and analysis—overgeneralizations, spurious correlations, oversimplifications, and overcomplications—are errors because they lead to distorted pictures of reality. A researcher seeks to discover correlations, but not spurious correlations. Certain factors may be selected for special study and others ignored, but this analytical procedure involves the risk of oversimplification. Generalizations can be very helpful, but overgeneralizations seldom are.

Overview

The task of classifying facts is a major focus of this chapter. Some of the basic considerations in intergroup relations are revealed through asking a series of questions. These considerations are then briefly discussed and illustrated.

Social experiences as varied as riots, bloc voting, boycotts, school desegregation, and immigration policies are all manifestations of intergroup relations. These phenomena are tied to historical developments, economic conditions, attitudes, art, humor, and religion in that they are all subsets of basic human relations.

There is more to understanding intergroup relations than delineating key variables, however. Recognizing connections between variables and interpreting them in a meaningful and logical manner are essential. In this substantive area, as in so much of social science, overgeneralizations, spurious correlations, oversimplifications, and overcomplications are particularly hazardous.

TALLY'S CORNER

ELLIOT LIEBOW

Elliot Liebow's study of low-income Black men in Washington, D.C., contains a succinct description of the ways in which an individual—in this instance, a truck driver—can engage in easy and satisfying over-generalizations. Information for the book **Tally's Corner** was obtained by participant-observation techniques during the early 1960s in Washington's inner city. Readers of **Tally's Corner** should be careful not to make easy overgeneralizations themselves. The book is not about Black people everywhere but is instead a sensitive profile of the lives of low-income Black men in the inner city of a northern metropolitan area.

A pickup truck drives slowly down the street. The truck stops as it comes abreast of a man sitting on a cast-iron porch and the white driver calls out, asking if the man wants a day's work. The man shakes his head and the truck moves on up the block, stopping again whenever idling men come within calling distance of the driver. At the Carry-out corner, five men debate the question briefly and shake their heads no to the truck. The truck turns the corner and repeats the same performance up the next street. In the distance, one can see one man, then another, climb into the back of the truck and sit down. It starts and stops, the truck finally disappears.

What is it we have witnessed here? A labor scavenger rebuffed by his would-be prey? Lazy, irresponsible men turning down an honest day's pay for an honest day's work? Or a more complex phenomenon marking the intersection of economic forces, social values and individual states of mind and body?

Let us look again at the driver of the truck. He has been able to recruit only two or three men from each twenty or fifty he contacts. To him, it is clear that the others simply do not choose to work. Singly or in groups, belly-empty or belly-full, sullen or gregarious, drunk or sober, they confirm what he has read, heard and knows from his own experience: these men wouldn't take a job if it were handed to them on a platter.[1]

Quite apart from the question of whether or not this is true of some of the men he sees on the street, it is clearly not true of all of them. If it were, he would not

---

[1] By different methods, perhaps, some social scientists have also located the problem in the men themselves, in their unwillingness or lack of desire to work: "To improve the under-privileged worker's performance, one must help him to learn *to want* . . . higher social goals for himself and his children. . . . The problem of changing the work habits and motivation of [lower class] people . . . is a problem of changing the goals, the ambitions, and the level of cultural and occupational aspiration of the underprivileged worker." (Emphasis in original.) Allison Davis, "The Motivation of the Underprivileged Worker," p. 90.

have come here in the first place; or having come, he would have left with an empty truck. It is not even true of most of them, for most of the men he sees on the street this weekday morning do, in fact, have jobs. But since, at the moment, they are neither working nor sleeping, and since they hate the depressing room or apartment they live in, or because there is nothing to do there,[2] or because they want to get away from their wives or anyone else living there, they are out on the street, indistinguishable from those who do not have jobs or do not want them. Some, like Boley, a member of a trash-collection crew in a suburban housing development, work Saturdays and are off on this weekday. Some, like Sweets, work nights cleaning up middle-class trash, dirt, dishes and garbage, and mopping the floors of the office buildings, hotels, restaurants, toilets and other public places dirtied during the day. Some men work for retail businesses such as liquor stores which do not begin the day until ten o'clock. Some laborers, like Tally, have already come back from the job because the ground was too wet for pick and shovel or because the weather was too cold for pouring concrete. Other employed men stayed off the job for personal reasons: Clarence to go to a funeral at eleven this morning and Sea Cat to answer a subpoena as a witness in a criminal proceeding.

Also on the street, unwitting contributors to the impression taken away by the truck driver, are the halt and the lame. The man on the cast-iron steps strokes one gnarled arthritic hand with the other and says he doesn't know whether or not he'll live long enough to be eligible for Social Security. He pauses, then adds matter-of-factly, "Most times, I don't care whether I do or don't." Stoopy's left leg was polio-withered in childhood. Raymond, who looks as if he could tear out a fire hydrant, coughs up blood if he bends or moves suddenly. The quiet man who hangs out in front of the Saratoga apartments has a steel hook strapped onto his left elbow. And had the man in the truck been able to look into the wine-clouded eyes of the man in the green cap, he would have realized that the man did not even understand he was being offered a day's work.

Others, having had jobs and been laid off, are drawing unemployment compensation (up to $44 per week) and have nothing to gain by accepting work which pays little more than this and frequently less.

Still others, like Bumdoodle the numbers man, are working hard at illegal ways of making money, hustlers who are on the street to turn a dollar any way they can: buying and selling sex, liquor, narcotics, stolen goods, or anything else that turns up.

Only a handful remains unaccounted for. There is Tonk, who cannot bring himself to take a job away from the corner, because, according to the other men, he suspects his wife will be unfaithful if given the opportunity. There is Stanton, who has not reported to work for four days now, not since Bernice disappeared. He bought a brand new knife against her return. She had done this twice before,

---

[2] The comparison of sitting at home alone with being in jail is commonplace.

he said, but not for so long and not without warning, and he had forgiven her. But this time, "I ain't got it in me to forgive her again." His rage and shame are there for all to see as he paces the Carry-out and the corner, day and night, hoping to catch a glimpse of her.

And finally, there are those like Arthur, able-bodied men who have no visible means of support, legal or illegal, who neither have jobs nor want them. The truck driver, among others, believes the Arthurs to be representative of all the men he sees idling on the street during his own working hours. . . .

POLARITY IN THE APPROACH TO COMPARATIVE RESEARCH IN ETHNIC RELATIONS

RICHARD A. SCHERMERHORN

If we view intergroup relations as a subset of human relations, then the theories and research traditions that pertain to the study of human behavior generally can be fruitfully applied to the study of intergroup relations. That is what is proposed in the selection that follows. Richard A. Schermerhorn has drawn upon Georg Simmel's general views on dialectics and polarity in order to formulate an approach to the specific study of ethnic relations. A central idea that emerges is that centrifugal and centripetal tendencies are simultaneously present in every society.

This discussion is an appeal to view intergroup relations as a special case of societal relations in their broadest and most generic sense, rather than a separate and unrelated field of inquiry. It takes its departure from Simmel's insight that all groups and structures are concretions of opposed tendencies of "polar elements whose mixtures determine all relations among men."[1] Social life has more the characteristics of an event than a substance, a process rather than a permanent order. Change has a dialectical quality, an interplay of forces advancing, retreating, converging, or diverging in patterns of greater or lesser stability. Georges Gurvitch speaks of these as "structuration and destruction of types,"[2] while Peter Blau

---

[1] Georg Simmel, *Conflict*, tr. by Kurt Wolff (New York: The Free Press, a Division of the Macmillan Co., 1955), 121.

[2] Georges Gurvitch, *Determinismes Sociaux et Liberté Humaine* (Paris: Presses Universitaires de France, 1955), 37.

refers to "alternating patterns of intermittent social reorganization"[3] as the kind of movement going on. The study of ethnic relations then becomes a special application of a more comprehensive theory of social change to an area of limited concern; as it turns out, however, it is an area of crucial importance, revealing in a most illuminating way how the processes of integration and conflict interact.

For the subordinate ethnic group, as usually defined, is not indigenous to the society encompassing it. As Ruth Glass has put it, it is "the marginal location, the not-belonging or not-quite belonging"[4] that sets it off from others in the society. Whether or not it is to become incorporated, or how incorporated becomes a problematic issue, both to the larger society and to the ethnics themselves. Here the inevitable polarity of perspectives is linked with a polarity of actions that produces a series of intermittent social structures to satisfy now divergent, now convergent, now clashing social aims.

There is also a polarity of power and authority. When societies attain the complexity of the nation-state, the state itself becomes more or less identified with the interests and values of a dominant group for fulfilling the functional requirements of the entire society. Such a dominant group is that collectively within a society which has preeminent authority to function as guardians or sustainers of the controlling value system, and as prime allocators of rewards in the society. It may be a group of greater or lesser extensity, i.e., a restricted elite, incumbents of a governmental apparatus, an ethnic group, a temporary or permanent coalition of interest groups or a majority. If the fulcrum of authority is the state, the agent of the lever is the dominant group rather than the total society, since the latter forms too diffuse an entity for decision making with the peripheral exceptions of formal voting. Thus when Robert Bierstedt declares that "It is the majority, in short, which sets the culture pattern and sustains it, which is in fact responsible for whatever pattern or configuration there is in a culture. . . . It is the majority which guarantees the stability of a society,"[5] it appears that he is speaking elliptically. In his terms the "majority" is identified with the society as a whole because it is the dominant element. But unless we think in purely American terms, or in nations with structures similar to our own, the term "dominant group" is surely preferable to "majority," since both totalitarian societies and many in the developing nations have oligarchical domination of one form or another. The point is that the dominant group identifies its interests and values with those of society as

[3] Peter M. Blau, *Exchange and Power in Social Life* (New York: Wiley and Sons, 1964), 336.

[4] Ruth Glass, "Insiders-Outsiders, the Position of Minorities," *Transactions of the Fifth World Congress of Sociology*, 1962, Inter-National Sociological Association, 1964, Vol. III, 141.

[5] Robert Bierstedt, "The Sociology of Majorities," *American Sociological Review* 13 (December, 1948), 700–10.

a whole, and regards itself as responsible for maintaining stability and integration in the whole. A minority ethnic group is an obstacle to this goal, to be obliterated, suppressed, tolerated, transformed, converted, rendered harmless, ingested, etc.

How shall we think about integration? Provisionally, let us regard it as a process whereby units or elements of a society are brought into an active and coordinated compliance with the ongoing activities and objectives of the dominant group within a society. Perfect integration, however, is an ideal limit never attained. Even Talcott Parsons, accused by Ralf Dahrendorf of Utopian tendencies, makes the frank admission that "No social system can be completely integrated; there will, for many reasons, always be some discrepancies between role expectations and performance of roles."[6] Simmel's dialectical principle would here imply that unifying forces operate in conjuction with, rather than separately from diversive forces, just as he said the opposite would occur.[7] The relationship between the process of conflict is not one of pure opposition but of reciprocal interplay in concrete situations. We are reminded here of Reinard Bendix and Bennett Berger's injunction to use paired variables in research rather than single ones. As they put it, "Such paired concepts are attempts to conceptualize what we know about the range of variability of social phenomena so that we are enabled to deal abstractly with their known extremes, regardless of whether we focus on the level of interactions of institutions, or of societies as wholes."[8] W. E. Moore,[9] Pierre van den Berghe,[10] and Alvin Gouldner[11] have recently expanded this theme in suggestive ways, though time does not permit a discussion of them here.

If this clue leads us in the right direction, it follows that the task of intergroup research is to account for the modes of integration-conflict (as dependent variables) in the relationships between dominant groups and subordinate ethnic groups in different societies. It implies a search for the significant independent and intervening variables and for invariant relations between independent and dependent variables under specified conditions. This must be an exploration in macrosociology and it may well be more revealing of the nature of societies as wholes than any comparative studies now in process.

Two independent variables appear promising. The first is the degree of enclosure in the subordinate ethnic group measured by such factors as endogamy,

[6] Talcott Parsons and E. A. Shils, *Toward a General Theory of Action* (New York: Harper Torchbooks, 1962), 204.

[7] Georg Simmel, *op. cit.*, 20

[8] Reinhard Bendix and Bennett Berger, "Images of Society and Problems of Concept Formation," in Llewellyn Gross, ed., *Symposium on Sociological Theory* (Evanston, Illinois: Row Peterson and Co., 1959), 89.

[9] W. E. Moore, *Social Change* (Englewood Cliffs, New Jersey: Prentice-Hall, 1963), 67.

[10] Pierre L. van den Berghe, "Dialectic and Functionalism Toward a Theoretical Synthesis," *American Sociological Review*, 28 (October, 1963), 695–705.

[11] Alvin Gouldner, "Reciprocity and Autonomy in Functional Theory," in Llewellyn Gross, ed., *op. cit.*, 241–70.

ecological concentration, institutional duplication, associational clustering, rigidity and clarity of group definition, segmentary relations of members with outsiders, etc.[12] The second independent variable of importance is the control of scarce values by the dominant group shown by such indicators as the comparative number of members of superordinate or subordinate groups in upper echelons of political, economic, educational, or prestige hierarchies in the society. Taking only the extremes of these two variables, the high scoring and the low, it would then be possible to set up a four-fold table of possibilities to account for various patterns of integration-conflict ascertained by independent means. If we take into account the numerous intermediate forms between the extremes, a much larger range of possibilities opens up.

However, contextual features of various societies must be taken into account as an intervening variable. This can be simplified by indicating the major directions of social processes. For instance, the principle of polarity postulates that centrifugal and centripetal tendencies are simultaneously present in every society, and that each, if unchecked by the other, will exhibit cumulative growth toward its own extreme. Centrifugal tendencies move toward autonomy, independence, or in more extreme cases, toward secession of the parts. Conversely, centripetal tendencies move toward increased participation in the whole by the parts, and, in extreme cases, domination of the whole by a single part. It may be expected that each subordinate ethnic group, as part of the total society, will modally adopt a centrifugal tendency to the exclusion of the centripetal, or vice versa. Likewise, each dominant group representing the society as a whole will show a preference for strategy sustaining centrifugal tendencies or centripetal tendencies for the subordinate group. When we combine these categories into their permutations, it gives us four directional types of societal contexts within which the independent variables operate. This is illustrated in Figure I.

Thus the independent variables in their combinations may be expected to have consequences that differ in context A, context B, context C, or context D. These consequences will appear in different configurations of integration-conflict that can be specified. The trends hypothesized on the right, toward integration for AB and toward conflict for CD, are based purely on what knowledge we have of the contexts of the intervening variable. They may well be falsified by certain combinations of the independent variables. It is worth noting parenthetically that

[12] The author acknowledges indebtedness here to Pierre van den Berghe who has notably clarified this dimension in his paper, "Towards a Sociology of Africa," in Pierre L. van den Berghe, *Africa, Social Problems of Change and Conflict* (San Francisco: Chandler Publishing Co., 1965), above and beyond the somewhat unclear distinctions between "plural society" and "heterogeneous society" advanced by M. G. Smith in his article, "Social and Cultural Pluralism," *Annals of the New York Academy of Sciences* 83 Art. 5 (January 20, 1957), 763–77. Ways of operationalizing degrees of enclosure have well developed by Leo Despres to appear in his forthcoming volume on British Guiana. These have also been of immense value in formulating the views expressed here.

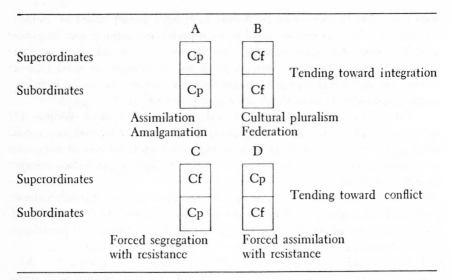

Cp = centripetal
Cf = centrifugal

FIGURE 1 Congruent and Incongruent Orientations toward Centripetal and Centrifugal Directional Movement by Superordinate and Subordinate Groups

box D is especially applicable to the new states of the developing nations where the superimposition of national loyalties upon a "pre-political matrix"[13] is crucial.

There remains the task of conceptualizing the forms of integration-conflict that make up the dependent variables. While there are important clues in this area, there are no more than tentative solutions. Perhaps the most promising lead is that of Werner Landecker who suggests various types of integration and what they imply. First is *cultural integration* which refers to the degree of consistency among cultural standards; second is *normative integration* that denotes the degree of conformity to cultural norms; third is *communicative integration* where there are greater or lesser exchanges of meanings between members of groups; and fourth there is *functional integration* in which the functions exercised by members of different groups constitute mutual services to a greater or lesser degree.[14] If appropriate measures can be devised for these types, the interlocking conflict in

[13] Edward A. Shils, "On the Comparative Study of the New States," in Clifford Geertz, *Old Societies and New States* (New York: The Free Press, a Division of the Macmillan Co., 1963). On this problem see also Karl W. Deutsch and William J. Folty, eds., *Nation Building* (New York: Atherton Press, 1963).

[14] Werner S. Landecker, "Types of Integration and their Measurement," *American Journal of Sociology*, 56 (January, 1951), 323–40.

each case could be dealt with by Robert LeVine's,[15] already tested in comparative studies.[16] More preferable would be a construction of types of conflict parallel with Landecker's four types of integration. However, this would not be necessary prior to the research process, since the latter may be expected to reveal forms of conflict yet unexpected. Promising suggestions for such an exploration have been amply proposed by Raymond Mack and Richard Snyder.[17]

This all-too-brief exposition, tentatively advanced, has aimed to show (1) that intergroup research on a comparative basis can contribute to our general sociological knowledge about the ways societies cope with problems of integration and conflict, and (2) that the germinal ideas of polarity and dialectical relations in Simmel's sketch of a general theory can be given methodical application in the exploration of intergroup relations. I can only hope that this translation of such lively and imaginative insights into the focused and mundane forms of investigation demanded in our day may not wholly dim the excitement and the promise of new discoveries still over the horizon.

[15] R. A. LeVine, "Anthropology and the Study of Conflict, an Introduction," *Journal of Conflict Resolution* 5 (March, 1961), 3–15.

[16] D. T. Campbell and R. A. LeVine, "A Proposal for Cooperative Cross-Cultural Research on Ethnocentrism," *Journal of Conflict Resolution* 5 (March, 1961), 82–108.

[17] Raymond Mack and Richard C. Snyder, "The Analysis of Social Conflict Toward an Overview and Synthesis," *Journal of Conflict Resolution* 1 (1957), 212–48.

3

Intergroup Relations in Western Thought

To be ignorant of what happened before you were born is to be ever a child.

Cicero, *Orator*, Sec. 34

What follows in this chapter may not seem exciting or valuable to the reader who wants to change society. The chapter reviews what influential individuals have said about race, human differences, and intergroup relations. It is history—the history of ideas. For some people this kind of history embodies all that is useless and sterile in education. To study intergroup relations seriously, however, it is essential to feel the flow of history, to be aware of the thoughts and feelings of earlier periods, and to understand that today's influential ideas had their origins in earlier experiences.

Such knowledge may be practical too. A person who wishes to correct a particular social evil can be likened to a hunter who sets out to kill a dangerous beast. Before attacking he may circle at a respectable distance to look for a vulnerable spot. A hunter also may learn about his prey from older hunters. By analogy, conductors of a well-conceived study of intergroup relations take a comprehensive view of the subject and consider carefully what has been thought

53

in the past. That is what this chapter is designed to do. It outlines the historical development of several modes of thinking that have affected human behavior,[1] beginning with a point of view that prevailed in much of the ancient world.

Ethnocentrism

We can only guess when human beings first began to speculate about group differences. Archaeological and ethnological records indicate that ancient groups had contacts with peoples whom they considered different from themselves. Although these early relations were not "racial" in the modern sense of the word, many of the characteristics that are associated with intergroup relations today can be detected in ancient records.

Monuments erected by the Assyrians demonstrate that they were very much aware of physical and cultural differences between themselves and their foes. So do Babylonian tablets. Ancient Egyptian records express the same theme. The Hebrew tribes, according to biblical passages, were awed by the physical appearance of the aboriginal peoples of Canaan. Some ancient peoples deliberately tried to keep their blood "pure," frowning upon intermarriage with aliens and strangers. They typically believed themselves to have special status, which gave them advantages over other groups. Herodotus has written that not only Greeks but also Persians in their turn thought themselves greatly superior to the rest of humanity.

How were the differences interpreted? Aristotle, for one, insisted that the differences between free men and slaves were set by nature. Some were destined to mastery and others to slavery, a condition that involved a burden for the master and benefit for the slave. He claimed further that, if a few Greeks were to be put in a barbarous country, in a few months they would be giving the orders and the natives would be obeying. Aristotle's thinking was not full-blown racism, however, because even though he stressed heredity, he also described situations in which both slaves and masters were Greeks.

As a general rule, however, the differences between one's own people and outsiders seemed self-evident, a thing not to be reflected upon. Outsiders and foreigners were considered either subhuman, superhuman, or equally human. The differences in perspectives usually depended upon the in-group's success or failure to exploit the out-group. The study of intergroup relations, however, hardly proceeded beyond simple enumeration of the traits by which outsiders differed from one's own group, and interpretations often were couched in mythological terms (House, 1934; pp. 440–452).

---

[1] I have been influenced by Floyd N. House (1934), who maintained that, so far as the Western world is concerned, ideas of race seem to have passed through five phases, each phase having been predominant in a certain period. House called these phases "naïvely ethnocentric," "religio-ethical," "taxonomic," cultural," and "sociological."

Some writers—Herodotus was one of them—clearly were aware of ethnocentric tendencies in human behavior, as the following statement shows: "For if one were to offer men to choose out of all the customs in the world such as seemed to them the best, they would examine the whole number, and end by preferring their own; so convinced are they that their own usages far surpass those of all others" (Herodotus, 430 B.C., 1963, p. 137). On the whole, however, the ethnocentrism of the ancient world does not seem to have been very self-conscious or deliberate; the sociologist Floyd N. House was probably correct in calling the perspective "naïve ethnocentrism." Ethnocentrism continues to be a factor in contemporary society, probably because it has importance as a mechanism for maintaining boundaries in the formation, development, and persistence of human groups.

Religious and Ethical Formulations

For sixteen centuries of the Chrisian era, very little literature dealing systematically with the subject of intergroup relations was produced. Intergroup relations were usually defined in terms of religious categories: believer-infidel, Christian-Jew, orthodox-heretic. A few old chronicles, however, contain information about peoples whom missionary groups and religious orders sought to convert. The Florentine Codex is an example. It reports on customs, trade, economics, and the political system of the aboriginal peoples who inhabited the valley of Mexico and describes the Spanish conquest (Harvey, 1970, p. 42).

Social distinctions that had a religious basis provided a rationale for exploitation. The history of the ghetto illustrates the point. Ghettos, or Jewish quarters, were first formally recognized in Germany in 1084. Some evidence suggests that the ghettos may have been conceived at first as a humanitarian gesture offered by Gentiles to Jewish groups who wished to practice their customs unmolested. By 1300, however, Christians in Poland were being urged to avoid living in the same neighborhoods with Jews. And in a papal bull (1555) Pope Paul IV declared it absurd for Jews to live openly among Christians, to own real estate, and to employ Christian servants. Thenceforth, Jews were to be compelled to live within enclosures set apart for them (Lestschinsky, 1931, p. 648).

Conceivably, matters could have been worse. If religion, rather than race, is the basis for gaining entrance into the in-group, at least there is one way of escape from stigma and discrimination. An individual can change religious affiliations and thus avoid persecution. In this sense individuals were not irrevocably barred from the privileges of the favored group because of birth. Some Moors and Jews in Spain and Portugal converted to Christianity and were absorbed into both the aristocratic and lower strata of the population. The discriminations of this historical period must thus be viewed as ethnic, rather than racial.

During the Renaissance (the fourteenth, fifteenth, and sixteenth centuries) and the Enlightenment (the eighteenth century), a number of writers began to deal with the subject of human nature itself and the individual's relation to society. The old order was breaking down, and thinkers were prompted to interpret what had been and what should be. Theirs was not social science as we know it, with emphasis on gathering empirical evidence and testing hypotheses, but rather social philosophy. During those centuries, a great deal was being written about customs, morality, and systems of government. Furthermore, it was a period of exploration and expansion. Europeans were coming into contact with diverse peoples, which further stimulated inquiry into the nature of society.

Whenever the topic of intergroup relations was discussed in the writings that appeared between 1300 and 1800, it was generally overshadowed by philosophical, ethical, political, or religious concerns. The scattered literature that did touch on intergroup relations encompassed a mixed bag of ideas, as the following quotations indicate. A sixteenth-century writer, Juan Gines de Sepulveda, spoke of American Indians as irrational creatures: "The Indians are as different from Spaniards as cruelty is from kindness and as monkeys are from men." David Hume, the Scottish historian and philosopher, wrote, "I am inclined to believe that Negroes are naturally inferior to whites." Hippolyte Taine refused to accept the hypothesis of the equality of men (Quoted in Comas, 1951).

Other points of view were well represented. Michel Montaigne writing about Brazilian Indians in the sixteenth century, argued, "There is nothing savage or barbarous about this nation save for the fact that each of us labels whatever is not among the customs of his own people as barbarian" (Comas, 1951). Later, both Voltaire and Jean Jacques Rousseau stressed the oneness of human nature and the equality of all humans.

Taxonomies

By the eighteenth century the physical and biological sciences had begun to develop rapidly. One of the most important developments was the effort to classify plants and animals systematically and in a uniform manner. Carolus von Linnaeus (1707–1778), who was mentioned earlier, devised a system with definite principles for defining genera and species and a uniform naming procedure. *Homo sapiens* was included as a major division of animal life.

For the subdivision *Homo sapiens*, Linnaeus chose skin color as the primary criterion but he also included temperament, customs, and habits. Of the six varieties[2]

---

[2] Linnaeus also included another subdivision, *Monstrosus*, which comprised six varieties: *Mountaineer* ("small, active, timid"), *Patagonian* ("large, indolent"), *Hottentot* ("less fertile"), American ("beardless"), Chinese ("head conic"), and Canadian ("head flattened").

that he described in his *A General System of Nature*, four correspond approximately to the populations of the major continents:

American	Copper-colored, choleric, erect
	Hair black, straight, thick; *nostrils* wide; *face* harsh; *beard* scanty; *obstinate*, content, free. *Paints* himself with fine red lines. *Regulated* by customs.
European	Fair, sanguine, brawny
	Hair yellow, brown, flowing; *eyes* blue; *gentle*, acute, inventive. *Covered* with close vestments. *Governed* by laws.
Asiatic	Sooty, melancholy, rigid
	Hair black; *eyes* dark; *severe*, haughty, covetous. *Covered* with loose garments. *Governed* by opinions.
African	Black, phlegmatic, relaxed
	Hair black, frizzled; *skin* silky; *nose* flat; *lips* tumid; *crafty*, indolent, negligent. *Annoints* himself with grease. *Governed* by caprice. (1802, vol. 1, p. 9)

At about the same time Georges Comte de Buffon, proposed a six-fold classification and Blumenbach a five-fold one. Somewhat later there were other classifiers —Saint Hilaire, Ernest Haeckel, Joseph Deniker, Sergi, George Baron, Cuvier, Carus, and Klemm. They based their systems on physical features, supposed mental or cultural traits, geography, or language.

As for language, scholars had discovered that there are broad similarities among Greek, Latin, German, and Sanskrit. These languages had developed, it was believed, from an ancient one technically called Indo-European. This ancient language was labeled Aryan by a German linguist, Max Müller (1830–1900), on the grounds that the Sanskrit-speaking invaders of India called themselves Arya. The idea gradually took the form of an Aryan myth, a development that will be discussed shortly.

Anatomical features like length of head, width of face, shape of nose, and type of body have been used in several rather widely recognized taxonomies of the twentieth century. One example is the classification of Europeans as Teutonic, Celtic, and Mediterranean by William Ripley (1867–1941).

More recent classifications have been influenced by developments in the field of genetics. One such system that became prominent in the 1940s views races as Mendelian, or inbreeding, populations. Viewed in this way, races are still being formed. This approach is a shift away from the static concept of species that was established by Linnaeus; nine major *geographical races* have thus been delineated at the continental level (Coon, Garn, and Birdsell, 1950): European, Indian, Asian, Micronesian, Melanesian, Polynesian, American, African, and Australian. Approximately thirty smaller intrabreeding populations, called *local races* (like the Basques of the Pyrenees), are included. Then there are also a number of isolated and tightly intrabreeding populations that are called *microgeographical races* (such as the Pitcairn Islanders or American Isolates like the Cajuns of Alabama).

Geneticists brought about still another development in taxonomy in the late 1950s. The approach, called "numerical taxonomy," is based on procedures for quantifying a large number of characteristics that vary in the study population. A coefficient of similarity is calculated. Then the coefficient is used to cluster and to order the most similar aggregates.

One basic problem has vexed the taxonomists: Groupings that are based on the distribution of one physical feature (for example, skin color) are often discordant with groupings based on some other physical feature (like hair texture). This inconsistency leads to a question that should be rather obvious: What does it all mean? Through the years many of the taxonomies that have been proposed have contained no hint of their ultimate purposes. Depending upon one's objective, the category *Homo sapiens* can be subdivided into two, ten, or a thousand. As S. L. Washburn has correctly observed, a classification can be used to understand history, to explain genetic changes in populations, or to predict future trends. Without some clear underlying rationale, however, a taxonomy really makes no sense, for various human populations are more or less open systems that merge with one another (1963, p. 523).

Racial Superiority

Little did the eighteenth- and nineteenth-century linguists and taxonomists, who began with the idea of an ancient Aryan-speaking people know how influential their ideas would become or how frightful would be their consequences. In the nineteenth century, a Frenchman, Count Arthur de Gobineau, elaborated the idea that only the white race is culturally creative. He believed that within the white race Aryans were the finest. Gobineau's ideas were expressed in a four-volume work entitled *Essay on the Inequality of Human Races*:

> I have been able to distinguish on physiological grounds alone, three great and clearly marked types, the black, the yellow, and the white. . . . The negroid variety is the lowest and stands at the foot of the ladder. The animal character, that appears in the shape of the pelvis, is stamped on the negro from birth and foreshadows his destiny. His intellect will always move within a narrow circle. . . .
>
> The yellow race is the exact opposite of this type. The skull points forward, not backward. . . . The yellow man has little physical energy, and is inclined to apathy; he commits none of the strange excesses so common among negroes. . . .
>
> We come now to the white peoples. These are gifted with reflective energy, or rather with an energetic intelligence. . . . They have a remarkable, and even extreme, love of liberty, and are openly hostile to the formalism under which the

Chinese are glad to vegetate, as well as to the strict despotism which is the only way of governing the negro. . . .

Such is the lesson of history. It shows us that all civilizations derived from the white race, that none can exist without its help, and that its society is great and brilliant only so far as it preserves the blood of the noble group that created it, provided that this group itself belongs to the most illustrious branch of our species. (Gobineau, 1915, pp. 205–210)

Gobineau's "racialism" was essentially an aristocratic view of history. He feared the uprising of peasants and other groups that he considered inferior. To sweep aside members of the old aristocracy who had been trained for leadership would surely mean to cause the decline of civilization. His protest, however, was not as well received in France as it was in Germany. Gobineau was introduced to the German public by the composer Richard Wagner, who believed that Aryanism perfectly expressed the German spirit. The idea was carried farther by Houston Stewart Chamberlain (1885–1927), Wagner's son-in-law, who wrote the widely read *The Foundations of the Nineteenth Century* (1912). In that work Chamberlain visualized two powers—Jews and the Teutonic races—as alien forces confronting each other. The Germans were impressed by Gobineau's Aryanism, but they begin to substitute the word Nordic for the word Aryan. At first Nordic included a great many peoples, but gradually it came to be restricted to Germans and Scandinavians.

These intellectual developments prepared the way for the racism of the Third Reich. Adolf Hitler cultivated the ancient prejudices of the masses and exploited the racial and aristocratic views of various scholars, merging both in a kind of state religion. He wrote:

History has shown with terrible clarity that each time Aryan blood has become mixed with inferior peoples the result has been the end of the culture-sustaining race. . . . The result of every racial crossing, to put it briefly, is always as follows: (a) sinking of the standard of the higher race, (b) physical and mental deterioration and the beginning of a slow but certain and progressive chronic ill health. . . . (1943, pp. 311, 437)

In 1925 Hitler paid a personal visit to the aging Chamberlain on behalf of the Nazi party; within a few years Gobinean societies had been established all over Germany. These events confirmed the intellectual link from Gobineau and Wagner to Chamberlain and Hitler and fulfilled a prediction that another Frenchman, Alexis de Tocqueville, had made about Gobineau: "At best," he said, "your fame will be an echo from across the Rhine" (quoted in Snyder, 1962, p. 49).

The United States has produced its share of writings elaborating the idea of group superiority. During the first half of this century several works attracted considerable attention—Madison Grant's *Passing of the Great Race* (1916), Clinton Stoddard's *America's Race Heritage* (1922), and Lothrop Stoddard's *The*

Revolt Against Civilization: The Menace of the Underman (1922). These writers talked a great deal about "races," but their attitudes expressed cultural prejudice more than racial prejudice. They were frightened by the masses of people who were flocking to American shores. Too many of these immigrants could not speak English, too many were not Protestant, and too many leaned toward radical political ideas to be readily assimilated. The writers feared that important parts of American culture were about to be swamped by alien cultures.

Prominent social scientists were caught up in this reaction. The well-known psychologist William McDougal championed the idea of Nordic superiority and warned the nation about the perils of race mixture (Gossett, 1963, p. 378). Ernest Hooten, an anthropologist, was convinced that valid conclusions about the intelligence of races could be drawn from intelligence-test results (Gossett, 1963, p. 378). E. A. Ross, a sociologist, during part of his career, favored the idea of racial superiority (Gossett, 1963, p. 382). The writings of these men should, however, be interpreted in the context of national concern about the consequences of unlimited immigration

The subject of race and intelligence remained more or less dormant until the end of the 1960s, when it became a major issue. This heightened interest was tied to a national concern: what was happening in the public schools. Desegregation had become a reality, but all was not going smoothly. Students from some groups and social classes seemed to be more highly motivated on school tasks than were those from other groups, and they scored higher on widely used intelligence tests. The ensuing debate centered on two questions: Why do these differences exist? What should be done about them?

Prior to this time it was known that individuals of German, Jewish, Chinese, English, and Japanese descent tended to score above or close to, the norm (that of white Americans) and that Blacks, American Indians, Italians, and Mexicans scored below the norm on standardized intelligence tests. But scholars thought that studies by Otto Klineberg (1944) and others, as well as corroborative evidence from many sources, showed that geographical and social-class differences accounted for more of this variation than did ethnic differences. For example, on certain intelligence tests administered by the army, the median scores for Black G.I.s from New York were significantly higher than those of White G.I.s from Georgia. Whites generally scored higher than Blacks in both states, and Whites from New York scored higher than Whites from Georgia. It was thus generally accepted that differences within groups were greater than those between groups.

That interpretation was abruptly challenged by psychologist Arthur R. Jensen, who advanced the view that the generally lower scholastic ability of American Blacks might be owing to genetic, as well as to environmental, factors. At least, so Jensen held, available evidence does not discredit the idea (1969, p. 82).

Jensen defined intelligence as the "capacity for abstract reasoning and problem solving" (1969, p. 19). He emphasized that it is not completely synonymous with *mental ability*, a term that refers to the totality of a person's mental capabilities. He then attempted to separate I.Q. into genetic and environmental components by using certain statistical techniques. Several types of evidence were produced to show both that the heritability of intelligence is high and that social-class and racial variations in intelligence must be attributed partially to genetic differences. Jensen conceded that extreme environmental deprivation could keep a child from performing up to his genetic potential, but he maintained that no enrichment program could push him above that potential. Hence his well-known opening statement: "Compensatory education has been tried and it apparently has failed" (1969, p. 2).

It is not known exactly how much the I.Q. can be boosted in an enriched environment. In the compensatory programs that Jensen discussed, increases of between 2 and 20 points were reported, with an average gain of around 10 points, and increases in academic achievement of from 0.5 to 2.0 standard deviations (1969, p. 97). This 10-point gain is, as Jensen's critics point out, almost as much as the overall I.Q. difference between White and Black school children (about 15 I.Q. points or 1 standard deviation). They rightly charge that Jensen has contradicted himself. Furthermore, his general indictment of compensatory education was so premature as to be irresponsible. Many of the programs Jensen discussed had been underway for only a short while at the time of the article.

As for genetics, it is quite clear that mental ability is determined partly by inheritance. If the basic specifications for the brain and the nervous system are encoded in the genes, then a genetic component for intelligence is to be expected. But how much?[3]

After all the available evidence is in, no matter how the statistics are manipu-

---

[3] To answer this question, evidence has been sought through several kinds of studies, one being that of the I.Q.s of twins. Identical twins are useful for this purpose because heritability is a constant and any differences in test scores are obviously caused by environment. Studies to date show that, on the average, identical twins are separated by about 6 points when reared together and by about 9 points when reared separately. Jensen has concluded from this type of evidence that environmental factors contribute little to total variation.

These studies, however, also suggest that environmental factors conceivably could bring about a great deal of variation, were gross manipulation to occur. In a study of nineteen twin pairs reared separately, the home and school environments were usually quite similar. But in those instances in which environmental differences were considerable, there was often a marked disparity in I.Q. scores (Goldsby, 1971, p. 117).

Jensen and others have estimated that as much as 80 percent of the variance in I.Q. scores is explained by genetic factors. Jencks has written: "Virtually no American study supports the claim that genes account for 80 percent of the variance in test scores. Our guess, based on the disparate sources of evidence . . . is that the heritability of Stanford-Binet scores in the United States is around 45 percent. This estimate could easily be off by 10 percent either way, and it might be off as much as 20 percent either way" (1972, p. 71).

lated, mental ability is partly genetic and partly environmental. We still do not know the exact size of the respective parts. Summing up the evidence, biologist Richard A. Goldsby has written:

> It should be clear that conclusive identification of the factors responsible for racial differences in I.Q. test scores, whether environmental or genetic, will be technically extremely difficult. It is apparent that given the present uncertainties, no decision can be reached. However, subscription to one or the other of the presently competing hypotheses has implications that extend beyond science into areas of social concern. . . . Many who have examined the history of race relations in the United States and around the world feel that of the two alternative hypotheses, neither of which stand proven, subscription to the genetic one carries considerable potential for mischief. (1971, pp. 123, 124)

Not all social scientists would agree with Goldsby's cautious statement that neither of the two hypotheses stands proven. Many feel that the environmental hypothesis already has sufficient evidence to support it.

More recently Jensen has been joined by William Shockley (1972), Richard Herrnstein (1971), and H. J. Eysenck (1971), each of whom believes that ethnic and class differences on intelligence tests have a genetic base. Their concern has not been confined to school problems but extends also to the general area of public-policy formulation. Shockley, cowinner of the Nobel prize in physics for invention of the transistor, relies heavily upon statistical techniques to argue that genetics is a good predictor of I.Q. scores. Furthermore, he has proposed a voluntary sterilization plan under which all people who pay no taxes, regardless of race or sex, would be paid bonuses for being sterilized. The bonus, according to this "thinking exercise," would be calculated on the basis of the seriousness of the recipient's disability. "A moron," Shockley suggests, would be paid $1000 for "each point below 100 I.Q." Shockley's stated concern is with dysgenics—with genetically unfit individuals who reproduce themselves in the population. Knowing that his idea smacks of Nazism, Shockley points out that Denmark has carried out a sterilization program since 1935 with favorable results. And he makes this further comment on his ideas: "My findings do not support a theory of white Aryan supremacy" (1972, p. 304).

Herrnstein believes individual and class differences are highly heritable in contemporary society and are likely to become even more so in the future. Future society will be a true "meritocracy" based upon I.Q. differences. Herrnstein's argument runs thus: To the extent that all youngsters receive a quality education and ethnic barriers are removed in hiring, to that extent does one major source of variation—environmental factors—become a constant; any variation that then occurs can be attributed to genetics. By making environmental factors more nearly equal, we can ensure that heredity will play an even greater role than it now does in making social distinctions.

Eysenck emphasizes the importance of genetics in society, but his interest centers on explanation of group differences, rather than of individual differences. His book *The IQ Argument* advances the idea that American Blacks are probably a nonrandom, lower-I.Q. sample of African populations. Here is a sample of his argument: "White slavers wanted dull beasts of burden, ready to work themselves to death in the plantations, and under those conditions intelligence would have been counter selective. . . . The inevitable outcome of such selection would of course be a gene pool lacking some of the genes making for higher intelligence" (1971, p. 42).

These ideas have not received general support in academic circles. They have gained wide publicity, to be sure, but they are not a dominant element in the intellectual mainstream of contemporary Western thought. A document prepared by social scientists over twenty-five years ago under the aegis of the United Nations Educational, Scientific and Cultural Organization (UNESCO) articulates a view that no doubt would still receive overwhelming endorsement from social scientists today: "According to present knowledge there is no proof that the groups of mankind differ in their innate mental characteristics, whether in respect to intelligence or temperament. The scientific evidence indicates that the range of mental capacities in all ethnic groups is much the same" (1958, p. 93).

Contemporary Social Science

The remainder of this chapter deals with approaches to intergroup relations that have been given recognized status in contemporary social science. Social scientists, like other scholars, are influenced by the prevailing ideas of their particular disciplines. In every discipline certain bodies of knowledge are acknowledged as legitimate. They are the approaches that have been more successful than competing approaches in explaining problems that are relevant to the field (Kuhn, 1962, pp. 10–22).

Anthropology

Work in physical and cultural anthropology has profoundly influenced all of social science and the public as well. Physical anthropologists agree that *Homo sapiens* comprises different populations that can be distinguished from one another on the basis of biological characteristics. For instance, geographic populations vary in distribution of O, A, B, and AB blood types. R-H negative is more frequent among American Whites than among American Blacks and is hardly present at all among Japanese and Chinese. Whorls in fingerprint patterns are more numerous among Mongoloids than among American Whites or Blacks. Some populations are particularly susceptible to certain diseases: Sickle-cell anemia occurs almost exclusively among Blacks, Tay-Sachs disease among Jews. Some diseases are genetically linked to subdivisions of larger populations; (for example, dysautonomia apparently afflicts only the Ashkenazim, descendants of central and eastern European Jews). Differences among populations also exist in tasting ability, respiratory rates, and other characteristics.

Yet even this biological view of race has been abandoned by a growing number of scholars. They claim that the very concept of race suggests artificial distinctions, that it leads to confusion and therefore has no useful place in modern science. Those who believe that the term ought to be dropped entirely, rather than simply clarified, think of human variation as continuous and of populations that incline gradually toward other populations. Populations, as such, are statistical categories, and the slopes of the character gradients are called *clines*. Ashley Montagu has written:

> In short, there are neither four or five races, nor exclusive varieties, on this Earth. Complexions run into each other; forms follow the genetic character; and upon the whole, all are at last but shades of the same great picture, extending through all ages, and over all parts of the Earth. (1964, pp. xvii, 3)

For three decades, the trend in anthropology has been away from the taxonomical approach that was so prominent in earlier years. A university course that once might have been called Human Races today would be entitled Biological Variation in Human Populations.

Some anthropologists, perhaps the majority, would accept the middle position that has been taken by physical anthropologist William S. Pollitzer:

> Can we then speak of "races" of man at all? While the concept of fixed types remains in the popular thinking, many scientists have gone to the opposite extreme and denied the reality of race at all. My own position is an intermediate one in which I liken human populations to the surface of the earth. Here is a small elevation and there, a larger one; here is a single contour and there, a doubled one. Shallow valleys separate some high ground; deep valleys separate others. Who can say, then, what is to be labeled a hill and what is to be called a mountain? Shall we use one name or two names for closely related projections? Where we draw the line—what labels we attach—these are arbitrary decisions; but the rises and the falls in the earth's surface are facts of nature. So it is with human populations. How finely we wish to divide them, how broadly we lump them or the designations we give to them will inevitably vary; but large populations with distinctive features are still recognizable. It is, of course, mating preferences for physical characteristics which govern the collection of genes in so-called gene pools; and it is our culture which determines these choices. In that sense, those physically recognized groupings which we may popularly refer to as

"races" are dependent upon our culture both for their formation and for their definition. (1972, p. 720)

As for cultural anthropologists, their views on this topic generally coincide with those of sociologists, who will be discussed shortly. Under the influence of Henry Maine, E. B. Tylor, and especially Émile Durkheim, an intellectual tradition developed that placed particular emphasis upon culture and relatively little upon biology in accounting for differences among people. The idea gained ground that significant differences among human groups, once assumed to be primarily innate, are cultural differences.

Once it had become conventional to make a distinction between race and culture, particular groups came to be defined not so much by physical characteristics as by normative patterns. Today, instead of thinking in terms of group superiority, an anthropologist argues for a relativism that recognizes the justification for each society's working out patterns functional for its members. This approach is not without its hazards. Notions about cultural relativism that treat every society's adaptation to its environment as necessarily "good" are of doubtful value. A particular group's adaptation, worked out in earlier days within a different environmental context, may be inadequate to meet demands that are made of that society today.

Franz Boas, more than perhaps any other anthropologist, has had the greatest impact on ideas about race and culture. His book *The Mind of Primitive Man* (1911) has been called the "Magna Carta of race equality" (Kardiner and Preble, 1963, p. 135). Boas' position was essentially that races are mixed and unstable, that "primitive" thought processes are not qualitatively different from modern thought processes, and that physical type bears no inherent relation to mentality, virtue, language, or other cultural traits.

Anthropologists, in interpreting group differences, are willing to take genetics into account. But they, like other social scientists, are sensitive to the dangers of using genetics to explain too much. Evidence of this caution is a motion passed by the American Anthropological Association in 1972[4], rejecting the ideas of Jensen and others and censuring several periodicals and journals for propagating their ideas:

> That the American Anthropological Association condemn as dangerous and unscientific the racist, sexist or anti-working class theories of genetic inferiority

[4] The results of the voting were: aye 1,427 (58.53 percent), nay 913 (37.44 percent), no vote 98 (4.01 percent). As a voting member of the American Anthropological Association, the author is in agreement with the thrust of this resolution but does not support the view that journals or the media should be condemned for publishing ideas that some of us may not accept. If we do not wish others to censor our ideas, we should be disinclined to be censors ourselves.

propagated by R. Herrnstein, W. Shockley and A. Jensen. There is no scientific warrant for ascribing to genetic factors the oppressed condition of classes and ethnic groups. We condemn the irresponsible support of unfounded conclusions by *The Atlantic Monthly, Harvard Educational Review* and the *New York Times Magazine* through publication and wide dissemination of them, especially in view of the destructive political uses to which such views are put.

Theories of genetic inferiority of races, sexes or classes facilitate and justify shifting the burden of the present economic crises onto those who are already the most oppressed. They place the blame for unemployment on its victims instead of on its beneficiaries. Such theories attack the legitimate aspirations of oppressed people for a decent life. (1972, p. 12)

Sociology and Social Psychology

If scholarly interest can be measured by the number of books and articles that are produced on a subject, then the widest interest in intergroup relations is in sociology and in social psychology. Probably the most widely read book on the subject—*The Nature of Prejudice*—was written by a social psychologist, Gordon W. Allport.

In sociology's early days, especially under the influence of Herbert Spencer, the Darwinian concepts of competition, natural selection, and species adaptation provided sociologists with a framework for interpreting social phenomena. Within early psychology as well, a biological perspective was apparent in emphasis upon human instincts. Not until the 1920s did a sustained research orientation develop in sociology. "As sociological study approached the status of scientific procedure," Edward B. Reuter has written, "its emphasis shifted. . . . The interest in differences was replaced by an interest in uniformities; the interest in traits, whether inherited or acquired, whether biological or cultural gave way to an interest in relationships" (1945, p. 455).

Shortly after World War I courses in intergroup relations were begun at The University of Chicago by Robert E. Park, Louis Wirth, and Everett Hughes. They were entitled American Minorities and Racial and Cultural Contacts. The former course dealt with the American situation and the latter with intergroup relations in various societies. These courses became models for similar courses that have become a standard part of the sociological curriculum.

As for the more recent work by sociologists and social psychologists, there seems to be no entirely satisfactory way to arrange them for presentation. Investigations often overlap traditional boundaries and reflect diverse research practices so that the lines move in different and seemingly unrelated directions. One researcher requires a nationwide sample of thousands; another considers twenty-five intensive interviews sufficient. One prefers standardized tests, another an interview guide, and still another the Thematic Apperception Test (TAT) or Rorschach prints.

Some avoid all these techniques and use unobtrusive measures. Various scholars go to census volumes, historical archives, tax records, crime reports, or local "knowledgeables."

How one chooses the proper approach is generally resolved in terms of several or all the following considerations: the researcher's ability or imagination, economics, available time, fads of the discipline, nature of the research problem, and preferences of a major professor, project director, or funding agency. One way to present these studies, however, is to outline them in terms of their method and scope.

Attitude measurement During the 1930s, studies dealing with the social-psychological aspects of intergroup relations became increasingly prominent. "It is beliefs and sentiments that give meaning and value to race relations," one writer of the decade observed. "We may congratulate ourselves, therefore, on the efforts which are being made to study the sentiments, attitudes, and prejudices which enter into the relations of the racial groups" (House, 1934, p. 450).

By the 1950s the attitudes of Whites toward Blacks had become perhaps the most conspicuous research interest in American sociology and social psychology. Ironically, the attitudes of Blacks were generally ignored. They became more important during the 1960s, however, though most of the research problems continued to lie along what Herbert Blumer (1966) has called the "prejudice-discrimination axis." This approach is based on the assumption that relations among groups result from, or are shaped by, the feelings and attitudes of individuals toward one another.

Personality studies Interest in the personality dynamics of both dominant groups and minority groups has stimulated a considerable amount of research activity. A number of researchers have attempted to locate the origins of prejudice in a particular personality type, a subject to be discussed in some detail in Chapter 8.

Ecological and demographic studies The term *ecology* is generally used to refer to relations between various populations and the environment. *Human ecology*, a concept that has been used for many years in sociology, deals with the spatial distributions of human population and the forces that have led to their placement and survival. Human ecological studies and demographic studies tend to use research techniques unlike those used in psychoanalytic research and opinion surveys. The underlying rationale of human ecology, especially, is that relatively impersonal processes and forces have important consequences for intergroup relations. Concepts like "succession," "population balance," "symbiosis," "invasion," and theories involving "race-relations cycles" and "natural histories" of groups all derive from the human-ecological tradition. The impact of this tradition is much diminished today, perhaps because biological analogies are no longer in vogue. Demographic studies and studies of migration patterns and residential segregation in particular continue, however, to be important substantive areas.

Macroanalysis   Such large population aggregates as entire societies or major segments of societies are the focus of some research. Some of these undertakings involve little more than learned speculation, but a few have been based upon rigorous and sometimes massive research activities. Some cut across several disciplinary lines in which sociology, economics, psychology, and political science all play a role. Gunnar Myrdal's *An American Dilemma* (1964) belongs in the latter category. Although Myrdal identifies himself as a political economist, his work is regarded as one of the most extensive sociological investigations ever conducted. It is best known for interpreting American intergroup relations in terms of the moral uneasiness that White Americans presumably feel about the discrepancies between their practices and the values expressed in the American creed. This study also demonstrates that American Blacks have been studying intergroup relations in a scholarly way for a number of years. A substantial part of Myrdal's study was based upon the work of Black scholars like Ralph Bunche and St. Clair Drake, who later became well known in their own right.

The work of the Black sociologist E. Franklin Frazier deserves mention here. Several of Frazier's books, like *The Negro Family in the United States* and *Black Bourgeoisie*, are regarded as major contributions. His *The Negro in the United States* (1957) also has had considerable influence, having been cited in the 1954 Supreme Court decision on school integration. Frazier developed the idea that the isolation of Blacks in the United States has produced serious problems in their community and institutional life and, as a result, has affected their self-concepts.[5]

Several reports by U.S. government agencies have incorporated perspectives and research techniques from sociology and social psychology. A 1966 study, by James Coleman and others, on equality of educational opportunity is a notable example. The "Coleman report," as it has come to be called, is the result of a massive research effort that focused upon desegregation and, as a related issue, aspirations and self-concepts. The study found a positive relationship between the proportion of Whites in a particular school and the levels of achievement of both Black and White students; students from both groups achieved at higher levels in desegregated settings.

The work of the late Frantz Fanon illustrates still another approach to societal analysis. Fanon, whose professional affiliation was with psychiatry, used social-psychological concepts to interpret major societal processes, as well as individual dynamics. Two of his works—*Black Skin, White Masks* (1967) and *The Wretched of the Earth* (1968)—have had an enormous impact in the Third World and upon many minority leaders in the United States. In *Black Skin, White*

---

[5] When, in later years, Daniel Patrick Moynihan expanded on this idea in a government report on the status of Black families (1965b), it created a furor and was roundly denounced as a denigration of Black family life in general.

Masks, Fanon described the vicious circle that he wished to eliminate. Whites consider themselves superior to Blacks. Blacks, who internalize a sense of inferiority, try to prove to Whites at all costs the richness of their thought and the equal value of their intellects. Fanon believed that the primary cause of this dilemma is economic. In *The Wretched of the Earth*, he called upon Blacks to stop imitating Europe (and by extension, White America). He believed that the Third World offers an opportunity to abandon the institutions and the inhumanity of Europe— to "work out new concepts, and try to set afoot a new man" (1968, p. 316).

History

Sociology's claim that it has been the single discipline most interested in intergroup relations has another serious challenger—history. The works of Edward Gibbon, Arnold Toynbee, C. Vann Woodward, Herbert Aptheker, Winthrop Jordan, Stanley Elkins, Robert William Fogel, Stanley L. Engerman, and John H. Franklin, to mention only a few, document the fact that the interest of historians in intergroup relations has been a long and productive one. A number of historians have concentrated on the controversial subjects of slavery and Reconstruction. Elkins (1959), for example, has used historical and crosscultural data in an effort to document the much-debated notion that the psychic trauma of slavery lives on in certain personality characteristics of American Blacks today. Historians also have played key roles in unraveling some old myths. Two instances come to mind. First, the notion that the plantations were worked by happy, unambitious, and docile slaves has been challenged by Aptheker, Kenneth Stampp, and others. (It should be mentioned, however, that this view was supported by several earlier historians including Ulrich B. Phillips, 1918.) Second, the idea that Blacks have contributed little more than manual labor to the development of the nation has been demolished by literally hundreds of publications, especially since 1960. Franklin (1969, pp. 10, 11) has traced the beginnings of this scholarly interest to the frustrations of American Black teachers of history who, before 1915, were obliged to use textbooks that seemed always to reflect an exclusively White point of view. In order to correct this deficiency, W. E. B. DuBois and others founded the Association of the Study of Negro Life and History in 1915. One year later Carter G. Woodson and his associates produced the first issue of the *Journal of Negro History*.

The interest of historians in intergroup relations has not been confined to the Black experience. Orientals, Chicanos, and several other ethnic groups have received some attention, though not on a scale equal to that of Black studies. Historians like Oscar Handlin have written major works on European immigration to the United States. More recently, historians interested in Indians have organized the American Indian Historical Society, which publishes the periodical *Wassaja*.

Other Disciplines

Social work, with a long tradition in the area of applied social science, has not neglected intergroup relations. Such an interest would be expected particularly in view of the fact that clients for a number of social services are drawn from minority groups. The publication of a useful compendium of case studies involving minorities is one of several activities that have been conducted under the aegis of the Council on Social Work Education (Rothman, 1971).

No special section has been devoted here to economics or to philosophy, primarily because these disciplines have not produced general and sustained activity in the field of intergroup relations. Not that individual scholars have made no contribution: The economist James Tobin and the philosopher F. S. C. Northrop —to cite only two examples—have been enormously influential. Tobin has shown that sustained full employment, which can be maintained through governmental intervention, is necessary if American Blacks are to improve their social position. Northrop, whose *The Meeting of East and West* (1946) appeared long before "soul" became a subject of academic interest, wrote that the United States would achieve the good society if it managed to draw not only on the Western tradition but also on the American Indian and African traditions. The African and American Indian component of intuition and feeling, as well as the Western approach, which calls for acquisition of knowledge through inference and scientific verification, are both valuable, Northrop wrote, and this country would desert either only to its peril.

Overview

This chapter outlines the development of perspectives that focus on race, ethnicity, and intergroup relations. These modes of thought appear to have become so influential during certain historical periods that they have overshadowed alternative perspectives.

Ethnocentrism, the first of these views to be considered, seems to have been characteristic of the ancient world. It continues to be of considerable importance, probably because of its functional consequences as a mechanism for maintaining boundaries in the formation, development, and persistence of human groups.

It is a long way from the Egyptian and Hebrew taboos on outsiders to contemporary investigations of relations among various groups. In the ancient world differences among peoples seemed so patent that they evoked little more than speculation or myth. During more recent times social philosophies have fluctuated between prevailing views either that human differences are firmly fixed by nature or that human personality is really very plastic.

With the development of the social sciences, biological modes of explanation were quite influential. Consistent with this view, human aggregates were classified and ranked in terms of physical characteristics. Gradually the emphasis changed, however, and social scientists began systematically to study relations rather than group differences. When differences were studied, explanations were generally sought in culture, personality dynamics, or social class.

How can the change be explained? To a certain extent, "creative exhaustion" occurred. It was gradually recognized that little new was being said with biological analogies, and that much of what had been said was either inaccurate or misleading. The general search for new techniques and modes of analysis brought with it a corresponding shift of emphasis in the study of intergroup relations.

Then too the expansion of the social sciences, with more studies underway and more trained researchers available, plus the growth of the mass media, brought new inputs of information. Often the new information simply would not fit into old categories.

Perhaps the most influential event of all was the ideology of the Third Reich. The whole world saw an idea tested, and social scientists were revolted by the sight. Very few social scientists today rely upon race to explain either personality or culture.

On balance, it should be noted that sentimentality has influenced some studies in the field of intergroup relations. Part of this bias can be characterized in Howard S. Becker's phrase "unconventional sentimentality." The unconventional sentimentalist is one who tends to assume that the underdog is always right and that those in authority are always wrong. This perspective has gradually supplanted an earlier perspective in which the existing world was viewed as a "given," to be described and understood, not challenged or attacked.

Scholarly efforts to understand intergroup relations often overlap academic boundaries and reflect diverse research traditions. These activities are classified in this chapter by discipline—anthropology, sociology, social psychology, history, and so on—and by method. At some risk of oversimplifying, it is possible to categorize the methodologies as making up two main streams that meander side by side, now close and now far from each other. One is oriented toward rigorous measurement, quantification, and precision of mathematical language. This tradition is ambitiously "scientific." The other tends to stress wholeness more than specifics and uses such procedures as free-ranging interviews in preference to elaborate statistical analysis.

For Further Reading

Many of the items among the references cited may be considered as recommended reading as well.

Biddis, Michael D. "The Aryan Myth," *Horizon*, 13 (Summer 1971), 97–101.

Cartwright, Walter J., and Thomas R. Burtis, "Race and Intelligence: Changing Opinions in Social Science." In Norval D. Glenn and Charles M. Bonjean (eds.), *Blacks in the United States*. San Francisco: Chandler, 1969. Pp. 168–183.

Dobzhansky, Theodosius. *Mankind Evolving: The Evolution of the Human Species.* New Haven: Yale University Press, 1962.

Fogel, Robert W. and Stanley L. Engerman. *Time on the Cross*, 2 vols. The Economics of American Negro Slavery, vol. I; Evidence and Methods—A Supplement, vol. 2. Boston: Little, Brown, 1974.

Higham, John, "Toward Racism: The History of an Idea." In Norman R. Yetman and C. Hoy Steele (eds.), *Majority and Minority: The Dynamics of Racial and Ethnic Relations*. Boston: Allyn and Bacon, 1971.

Katz, Erwin and Patricia Gurin. *Race and the Social Sciences*. New York: Basic Books, 1969.

Loye, David. *The Healing of a Nation*. New York: Dell, 1971.

Montagu, Ashley (ed.). *The Concept of Race*. New York: Free Press, 1964.

Rose, Peter I. *The Subject Is Race: Traditional Ideologies and the Teaching of Race Relations*. New York: Oxford University Press, 1968.

Snyder, Louis L. *The Idea of Racial*. Princeton: Van Nostrand, 1962.

THE MIND OF PRIMITIVE MAN[1]
FRANZ BOAS

Franz Boas, the anthropologist, has profoundly influenced the ways in which the intellectual community thinks of human differences. In his preface to the revised edition of **The Mind of Primitive Man**, he re-iterates a central thesis of much of his work. Abram Kardiner and Edward Preble have written, "In his famous book, **The Mind of Primitive Man**, Boas probably contributed more than any other person to a general enlightment on the question of race; it has been called the 'Magna Carta of race equality'" (1963, p. 135).

Since 1911, when the first edition of The Mind of Primitive Man was published much work has been done in all the branches of science that have to be considered in the problem with which the book deals. The study of heredity has made important strides and has helped to clear up the concept of race. The influence of environment upon bodily form and behavior has been the subject of many investigations and the mental attitudes of "primitive" man have been studied from new points of view. For this reason a large part of the book had to be rewritten and rearranged.

The first statement of some of the conclusions reached in the book were made in an address delivered by the author as vice-president of the Section of Anthropology of the American Association for Advancement of Science, in 1895. Ever since that time the subject has remained one of his chief interests. The result of his studies has been an ever-increasing certainty of his conclusions. *There is no fundamental difference in the ways of thinking of primitive and civilized man. A close connection between race and personality has never been established.*[1] The concept of racial type as commonly used even in scientific literature is misleading and requires a logical as well as biological redefinition. While it would seem that a great number of American students of biology, psychology and anthropology concur with these views, popular prejudice, based on earlier scientific and popular tradition, has certainly not diminished, for race prejudice is still an important factor in our life. . . .

[1] Italics added.

THE U.S. CENSUS DEFINITION OF RACE

. . . The concept of race as used by the Bureau of the Census does not denote clear-cut scientific definitions of biological stock. Rather it reflects self-identification by respondents. Since the 1970 census obtained information on race primarily through self-enumeration, the data represent essentially self-classification by people according to the race with which they identify themselves.

For persons of mixed parentage who were in doubt as to their classification, the race of the person's father was used. In 1960, persons who reported mixed parentage of white and any other race were classified according to the other race; mixtures of race other than white were classified according to the race of the father.

The category "white" includes persons who indicated their race as white, as well as persons who did not classify themselves in one of the specific race categories on the questionnaire but entered Mexican, Puerto Rican, or a response suggesting Indo-European stock.

The category "Negro" includes persons who indicated their race as Negro or Black, as well as persons who did not classify themselves in one of the specific race categories on the questionnaire but who had such entries as Jamaican, Trinidadian, West Indian, Haitian, and Ethiopian. The term "Negro and other races" includes persons of all races other than white. . . . (U. S. Bureau of the Census, Census of Population: 1970 "General Social and Economic Characteristics")

DECISIVE GENES
H. J. EYSENCK

The scholarly community, before the mid-1960s, looked upon the debate on heredity versus environment as ancient history. Lines of the truce that had been drawn in earlier years were usually respected. The topic itself bore about as much likeness to a live controversy as does a military parade on Veteran's Day to actual warfare. There was a consensus that heredity is all-important in nonhuman orders of life. In **Homo sapiens**, it was thought, the genes provide coding for the basic outlines within which physical and even mental development occur. For mental ability, however, scholars emphasized that the capacities laid down by the genes are rather broad. Three sets of factors are required to explain individual and group variation: genetics, unique individual experience, and culture (and within culture socioeconomic status).

At various times there had been dissenters from this consensus, but their dissent was not regarded as serious or responsible. Toward the end of the 1960s, however, this peace was disturbed by Arthur R. Jensen, and then by Richard Herrstein and academicians from other disciplines. Their challenge might have gone unanswered had they not linked the heredity-environment issue with the idea of racial inequality. Those two ideas in combination provided the fuel for one of the fiercest controversies of the century.

H. J. Eysenck, a behavioral psychologist, takes the position that genetics plays a decisive role in I.Q.

It is widely agreed that social policy should be governed by the interplay between philosophical and ethical ideas on the one hand and scientifically ascertained facts on the other. By themselves, facts are neutral. One's ideals, one's political orientation and the like govern the way one deals with facts.

Unfortunately, we live with many myths that make it more difficult for us to distinguish fact from fiction than it would otherwise be. There are two complementary myths about intellectual differences that contain just enough truth to make them particularly dangerous. Each myth offers a different interpretation of the fact that whenever members of the working class and the middle class are tested on intelligence tests, marked differences are observed.

Those who believe in the first myth argue that, given the distinction between middle-class and working-class people (which does not rule out considerable overlap), intelligence does not determine a person's social class, but rather a person's social class determines his intelligence. IQ tests favor the middle-class child, who is more likely to have a better education and a greater respect for it, better living conditions, better food, more books in the home, more stimulating conversation. By this account IQ tests measure nothing but the effects of environmental influences and do not in principle differ from tests of educational achievement. But this argument for what determines IQ implicitly denies the well-established claim that differences in IQ are largely determined by genetic factors.

And it is here that the complementary myth enters into the picture, one that was brought to the forefront of the discussion by Harvard psychologist Richard Herrnstein. Herrnstein begins from a position exactly opposite from that briefly outlined above. He is convinced by the evidence that IQ is inherited, and he puts his position in the form of a syllogism: if differences in mental abilities are inherited, if success requires these abilities and if earnings and prestige depend on success, then social standing, which reflects earnings and prestige, will be based to some extent on inherited differences between people. He goes on to say that "our society may be sorting itself willy-nilly into inherited castes." The fear that genetic theories imply something like the picture Herrnstein paints has indeed caused many people to shy away from them and to embrace a purely environmental position. Fortunately, nothing of the kind is true.

Let us pay particular attention to a factor whose importance Herrnstein slights: the existence of genetic regression. This well-known effect, which is based on the genetic mechanisms of segregation and recombination of genes, is illustrated in the following chart:

THE REGRESSION OF CHILDREN'S IQ ON FATHER'S IQ

	Father's Mean IQ	Children's Mean IQ
I. Professional	140	140
II. Semiprof.	130	130
III. Clerical	120 / 110	120 / 110
IV. Skilled		
V. Semiskilled	100	100
	90	90
VI. Unskilled	80	80

The figures are taken from a large-scale study by the late Sir Cyril Burt of University College, London; they are typical of many other investigations. The IQ average for the fathers shows the usual differences between social classes. But note the figures for the children born into these classes: the children have regressed toward the mean IQ score of the population, which is 100. Thus fathers with a mean IQ of 140 are likely to have children whose mean IQ is 120, while fathers with mean IQs of about 80 have children with a mean IQ of 90. Such results are impossible to understand on any environmental basis: the children from the most propitious background have much lower IQs than their parents, while children whose parents can furnish only the worst environment show IQs superior to their parents. However, this difference is precisely what a genetic hypothesis would predict, and indeed the argument from regression is one of the most compelling of all those offered by geneticists.

Such a fact makes Herrnstein's position untenable. No fixed "caste" of dull, unemployed people is developing, either because of technological advances or from other causes. There is instead a marked degree of social mobility enabling children to rise from the working class by virtue of a high IQ or drop from the middle class by virtue of a low IQ.

Many have criticized the argument that IQ is strongly based on genetic factors, and particularly calculations suggesting that approximately 80 percent of IQ variance can be accounted for in genetic terms. Earlier formulas often didn't account for important variables such as differences between families and between genes and the environment. But recent theoretical work has produced a formula that enables us to take these and many other factors into account; in particular, the publications of John Jinks and David Fulker of the University of Birmingham in England have given a sound biometrical genetic structure to this whole field. Further, their work seems to have justified the assumptions made previously about the heritability of intelligence. Such assumptions and conclusions are based on estimates from studies of identical and fraternal twins, of identical twins brought up in isolation from each other, of familial intercorrelations, of regression effects and of many other testable connections. All the studies agree on the figure of 80 percent, and since criticism of one particular method of reaching the estimate is not usually applicable to other methods, the figure seems reliable.

There is a curious disproportion between the amount of government money spent on educational research that lacks any proper rationale—as it is based entirely on misguided and demonstrably false hypotheses—and research on biological measures that could in due course achieve at least some of the aims of those who search for greater equality among people. Where over a thousand "Headstart" programs have failed, the next one or two are not likely to succeed. But suppose we were to look at the research literature on the effects of glutamic acid on feeble-minded children; there is good evidence that it increases the IQs of such children to a measurable and useful extent. It is interesting to speculate on why a research program has not been set in motion and why no money has been spent in the experimental studies of this promising and intriguing drug. The answer must surely be the simple one that educators and politicians not only do not regard human beings as biological organisms but also try to disregard our biological essence as an affront to their higher sensibilities. Until this mistaken view is changed there is little hope of finding an answer to the all-important question: How can we best help the deprived child?

INDECISIVE GENES

LEON KAMIN

Leon Kamin, Chairman of the Department of Psychology at Princeton University, challenges Eysenck's view of the heritability of intelligence.

KAMIN: I'm not an educational psychologist. My own work has been in the area of animal learning. But I got interested in the problem of intelligence testing over a year ago, largely as a result of reading Professor Richard Herrnstein's article in *The Atlantic*. In it, he summarized a lot of research purporting to show that something like 80 percent of individual variation in intelligence is hereditary. What I've tried to do is read in detail the old experimental data, which have been accumulating over 50 years or so, on which this consensus is based. And my own impression, after looking as intensively as I possibly could at these data, is that when they're properly analyzed, the evidence for heritability of intelligence test scores simply disappears. I could not disagree more profoundly with the conclusions that Herrnstein, Arthur Jensen, H. J. Eysenck and others have drawn from those data. And I am especially bothered because the social implications that people draw from their work are obviously very distressing.

Q: Have such social conclusions been made throughout the history of research in this area?

KAMIN: Yes. The first really massive use of intelligence tests anywhere was during World War I, when millions of draftees into the American army were given tests. One of the analyses of these tests had to do with the scores made by immigrants from different countries in Europe. In 1917 and 1918 it was discovered that immigrants from Poland, Italy, Russia and southeastern Europe in general had very much lower scores on the intelligence tests than immigrants from northwestern Europe—Scandinavia, England, France, Germany and so on. Psychologists of the time did a host of studies to demonstrate that what they called Mediterranean-Latin-Slavic people, having done much worse on intelligence tests than "Nordics," had to be genetically stupid, and that if they were admitted to this country in large numbers they would lower the national level of intelligence.

Q: Can you cite a specific example of harmful legislation that has come about as a direct result of the pronouncements of scientists in the field of intelligence testing?

KAMIN: The immigration laws of the 1920s are such an example. And let me cite another. I've been reading in the history of sterilization laws, which are interesting social documents. It was seriously believed by the legislators who passed those laws, and by the social scientists who provided them the information, that criminality and drug addiction and pauperism and so forth were hereditarily transmitted. One can go back and read the *Harvard Law Review* and find learned debates in 1916 about "born criminals versus criminals by acquired habit." And the argument ran that born criminals should be sterilized. It seemed perfectly plausible to many people in those days that such things are transmitted by heredity—and it seems perfectly plausible to many people today that intelligence is transmitted by heredity. I think the notion that intelligence test scores have anything to do with heredity will look as ludicrous to our descendants as the sterilization laws look today.

Q: Given the absence of any hard evidence about the origin of intelligence, do you have any theories or hunches about it?

KAMIN: There really are two separate questions involved here: One is what intelligence is all about, and the other is what intelligence test scores are all about. It would not astonish me if there were indeed some abilities we have not been able to measure that might be very largely heritable. What I am arguing, as seriously and as strenuously as I can, is that scores on intelligence tests as they now exist, despite the interpretations most makers of intelligence tests apply, simply cannot fairly and rationally be assumed to be heritable.

The Eysenck article affords an excellent case in point. The article contains a chart said to illustrate "The Regression of Children's IQ on Father's IQ." Where, however, do all these IQ numbers come from? Professor Eysenck indicates only that "the figures are taken from a large-scale study by the late Sir Cyril Burt." We ought to ask: Precisely how was this study performed?

The facts are easily available to anyone who troubles to read Burt's original articles. The 1961 Burt paper from which the "average IQs" have been lifted indicates that "for the children the bulk of the data was obtained from the surveys carried out from time to time in a London borough selected typical of the whole county." Professor Burt was a school psychologist, for whom it was an easy matter to administer tests to school-children. The common English schools, however, contain very few upper-class children; so, for the "highest occupational classes . . . data were collected in the course of work on vocational guidance at the National Institute of Industrial Psychology." That is how the "representative sample" of children was constituted.

But what about the adults? "The data for the adults were obtained from the parents of the children themselves. . . . For obvious reasons the assessments of adult intelligence were less thorough and less reliable." The reasons may not be so "obvious" to the reader, and we shall return to them shortly.

There is only a single comment by Burt about the *number* of people assessed in this "large-scale study." Burt reported that, in the professional class, "the number examined was nearer 120 than 3."

But most important, the reader should recognize that "assessments" are *not* test scores. In 1958 Burt wrote that "the final assessments for the children were obtained by submitting the marks from the group test to the judgment of the teachers . . . where the teacher disagreed with the verdict of the marks, the child was interviewed personally and subjected to further tests, often on several successive occasions."

To sum up: Professor Eysenck presents some apparently firm "IQ" numbers to substantiate statistically the view that IQ is hereditarily determined. We note, however, that the "IQs" were derived from a sample of unknown size and unknown representativeness. In addition, the "IQs" attributed to *adults* turn out to be guesses made in the course of a personal interview—reinforced by something called a "camouflaged test" of intelligence. The interviewer, of course, was aware of the person's social class when he made his guess. The children's "IQs" in turn have been "corrected" by teachers who are also aware of the children's social class, and Professor Burt evidently allowed himself to retest children with "peculiar" scores for an indefinite number of times. Thus, the reader who is confronted with IQ numbers purporting to prove a theoretical point would do well to be profoundly skeptical until he has examined the original articles himself.

Q: What factors, in your opinion, influence differences in test scores?

KAMIN: I think it's so obvious: a test has to depend on the experience a person has had. If you bring a child up in a closet from the day of his birth, take him out for the first time at the age of ten and give him an intelligence test, he will do poorly on it. It does not seem to me at all unreasonable to suppose that in large measure the people who do very poorly on tests nowadays are people who have, in a sense, been brought up in closets, so far as the environmental opportunities that are related to doing well on these kinds of tests are concerned.

Q: So the standardized tests commonly used in this country may measure very accurately what they are designed to measure—which is to say, what schools require children to do and what the dominant culture values and rewards?

KAMIN: Yes—I don't know that I would say they measure very accurately, because they obviously omit questions of motivation and energy and determination and ambition and what have you. But tests do indeed predict something. Clearly, if you find a young child who has an IQ of, let's say, 160 at age 5, and that's all you know about him, you can make a rational bet that when he is 30 years old he will have had more education than most other people, he will be richer, he will be more successful. But the question I'm asking is: What does that have to do with the inheritance of anything?

Q: Do you think standardized tests should be continued with some modifications, or curtailed or abolished?

KAMIN: On balance, I think as they're now used they create more social harm than welfare. I would like to be more optimistic than I really am about the prospects of developing fairer and more predictive tests in the near future. But I'm not optimistic about that happening soon, and I'm very much aware of the incredible abuses of the present standardized tests. So if you're asking if I tend to sympathize with those who feel that tests as they now exist are so badly misused that they haven't any rational place in our society—yes, I tend to share that view.

GENETICS OF RACE EQUALITY
THEODOSIUS DOBZHANSKY

This selection by Theodosius Dobzhansky, a renowned geneticist, presents the position on genetics and environment to which most social scientists would subscribe.

To sum up, the races of man are not integrated biological entities of the sort that biological species are. Race boundaries are blurred by the more or less slow but long-sustained gene exchange. The number of races that should be recognized is arbitrary in the sense that it is a matter of convention and convenience whether one should give names to only a few "major" or also to a larger number of "minor" races. An anthropologist who maintains that there are exactly five or any other fixed number of races or who resolves to cut the Gordian Knot (mankind has no races) is nurturing illusions. On the other hand, there need be nothing arbitrary about race differences; human populations are racially distinct if they differ in the frequencies of some genes, and not distinct if they do not so differ. The presence of race differences can be ascertained, and if they are present, their magnitude can be measured.

The problem that inevitably arises in any discussion of individual and race equality is how consequential the differences among humans really are. Man's bodily structures do not differentiate him very strikingly from other living creatures; it is the psychic, intellectual, or spiritual side of human nature that is truly distinctive of man. Physical race differences supply only the externally visible marks by which the geographic origin of people, or rather of their ancestors, can be identified. The blood types, nose shapes, and skin colors of people whom we meet are much less important to us than their dispositions, intelligence, and rectitude.

The diversity of personalities would seem to be as great, and surely more telling, than the diversity of skin colors or other physical traits. And, though the biological basis of both kinds of diversity is the same in principle, it is different enough in its outward manifestations that the difference constitutes a genuine problem. This is the perennial *nature-nurture problem*. The confusion and polemics with which it was beset for a long time were due in part to the problem having been wrongly stated—which human traits are due to heredity and which to environment. No trait can arise unless the heredity of the organism makes it possible, and no heredity operates outside of environment. A meaningful way to state it is to ask what part of the diversity observed in a given population is conditioned by the genetic differences between persons composing this population, and what part is due to their upbringing, education, and other environmental variables. Furthermore, the issue must be investigated and solved separately for each function, trait, or characteristic that comes under consideration. Suppose one collects good data on the genetic and environmental components of the observed diversity in the intelligence quotients, or of the resistance to tuberculosis. This would not tell us anything about the diversity of temperaments or about resistance to cancer.

Even correctly stated, the nature-nurture problem remains a formidable one. Dogmatic statements abound on both the hereditarian and the environmentalist sides of the controversy, and most of them say much about their authors but not much about the subject at issue. The plain truth is that it is not known just how influential are the genetic variables in psychic or personality traits or how plastic these traits might be in different environments that can be contrived by modern technology, medicine, and educational methods. There is no way in practice to arrange for a large group of people to be brought up under controlled and uniform conditions in order to see how similarly or differently they would develop. The converse experiment—observing identical twins, individuals with similar heredities brought up in different environments—is possible, but opportunities for such observations are scarce.

Some partisans of human equality got themselves in the untenable position of arguing that mankind is genetically uniform with respect to intelligence, ability, and other psychic traits. Actually it is, I think, fair to say that whenever any variable trait in man has been at all adequately studied genetically, evidence has been found of at least some, though perhaps slight, contribution of genetic differences. Being equal has to be compatible with being different, and different in characters that are relevant to the specifically human estate, not alone in "skin-deep" traits like skin color.

The current civil rights movement in the United States has elicited a rash of racist pamphlets that pretend to prove, very "scientifically" of course, that races cannot be equal because they differ in the average brain size, the average I.Q., etc. Now, there is no reason to believe that small differences in the brain volumes are any indication of different mental capacities; the I.Q. tests are not reliable when administered to people of different sociocultural backgrounds, and in any case they cannot be taken as anything approaching a measurement of human worth. Be all that as it may, the striking fact—which not even the racists can conceal—is that the race differences in the averages are much smaller than the variations within any race. In other words, large brains and high I.Q's of persons of every race are much larger and higher than the averages for their own or any other race. And conversely, the low variants in every race are much below the average for any race. This is a situation quite analogous to what is known about race differences in such traits as blood groups and is in perfect accord with theoretical expectations in populations that exchange genes.

It is impossible in an article such as this one to summarize and to evaluate critically the abundant but often unreliable and contradictory data on the nature-nurture question regarding man. It is more useful to consider here some fundamentals that must be kept in mind in dealing with such data. An all too often forgotten and yet most basic fact is that the genes do not determine traits or characters, but rather the ways in which the organism responds to the environment. One inherits not the skin color and intelligence, but only genes which make the *development* of certain colors and intelligence possible. To state the same thing with a slightly different emphasis, the gene complement determines the path that the development of a person will take, given the sequence of the environments that this person encounters in the process of living. Any developmental process, whether physiological or psychological, can be influenced or modified by genetic as well as by environmental variables. The realization of heredity is manageable, within limits, by physiological and social engineering. What the limits are depends upon our understanding of the developmental processes involved. Modern medicine is able to control the manifestations of some hereditary diseases, which not so long ago were incurable. This does not make hereditary defects and diseases harmless or unimportant; even if they can be cured, it is better for the individual and for his society to have no necessity of being cured.

Although the mode of inheritance of physical and psychic traits in man is fundamentally the same, their developmental plasticity—the ability to respond to modifying influences of the environment—is different. There is no known way to alter the blood group with which a person is born; it is possible to modify one's skin color, making it somewhat darker or lighter by sun tanning or by lack of exposure to the sun; the development of personality traits is very much dependent on the family and social environments in which an individual is brought up and lives. The great *lability* of psychic traits is at least one of the reasons why it is so hard not only to measure precisely the role played by heredity in their variations, but even to prove unambiguously that some of these traits are influenced by heredity at all. The more environmentally labile a trait is, the more critical it is for its investigation to have the environment under control; this is difficult or impossible to achieve with man.

The great environmental plasticity of psychic traits in man is no biological accident. It is an important, even crucial, evolutionary adaptation that distinguishes man from other creatures, including those nearest to him in the zoological system. It is by brain, not by brawn, that man controls his environment. Mankind's singular and singularly powerful adaptive instrument is culture. Culture is not inherited through genes; it is acquired by learning from other human beings. The ability to learn, and thus to acquire a culture and to become a member of a society, is, however, given by the genetic endowment that is mankind's distinctive biological attribute. In a sense, human genes have surrendered their primacy in human evolution to an entirely new, nonbiological or superorganic agent—culture. However, it should not be forgotten that this agent is entirely dependent on the human genotype.

A pseudobiological fallacy—dangerous, because it is superficially so plausible—alleges that the differences in psychic traits among human individuals and races are genetically fixed to about the same extent as they are among races or breeds of domestic animals. This overlooks the fact that the behavior of a breed of horses or of dogs is always a part of a complex of characters that are deliberately selected by the breeders to fit the animal for its intended use. A hunting dog with a temperament of a Pekingese, a great Dane behaving like a fox terrier, a draft horse as high-strung as a race horse or vice versa—all these monstrosities would be worthless or even dangerous to their human masters. Man has seen to it that the genes that stabilize the desirable behavior traits in his domestic animals be fixed and the genes that predispose for variable or undesirable behavior be eliminated.

What is biologically as well as sociologically requisite in man is the exact opposite—not to fix rigidly his qualities; he must be able to learn whatever mode of behavior fits a job to be done, the mores of the group of which he happens to be a member, a conduct befitting the circumstances and opportunities. Man's paramount adaptive trait is his educability. The biological evolution of mankind has accordingly so shaped the human genotype that educability is a universal property of all nonpathological individuals. It is a diagnostic character of mankind as a species, not of only some of its races. This universality is no accident either. In all cultures, primitive or advanced, the vital ability is to be able to learn whatever is necessary to become a competent member of some group or society. In advanced civilizations, the variety of function has grown so enormously that learning has come to occupy a considerable fraction of the life span. Even where, as in India, a society was splintered for centuries into castes specialized for different occupations, the ability to learn new professions or trades has been preserved.

Champions of human equality have traditionally been environmentalists, conspicuously distrustful of genetic determinisms. Historically their attitude has been useful in counterbalancing the influence of those racist hereditarians who tried to justify the denial of equality of opportunity to most people on the pretext that the latter were genetically inferior. The environmentalists, however, went too far in their protest. They simply failed to understand that to be equal is not the same thing as to be alike. Equality is a sociological, not a biological, ideal. A society may grant equality to its citizens, but it cannot make them alike. What is more, in a society composed of genetically identical individuals, equality would be meaningless; individuals would have to be assigned to different occupations by drawing lots or in some other arbitrary manner. The ideal of equality of opportunity is precious, because it holds out a hope that persons and groups diverse in their endowments may enjoy a feeling of belonging and of partnership and may work for the common good in whatever capacity without loss of their human dignity. Men must be dealt with primarily on the basis of their humanity and also on the basis of their potentialities and accomplishments as individuals; the practice of treating them according to their race or color is a nefarious one.

Genetic diversity is a blessing, not a curse. Any society, particularly any civilized society, has a multitude of diverse vocations and callings to be filled, and new ones are constantly emerging. The human genetically secured educability enables most individuals of all races to be trained for most occupations. This is certainly the basic and fundamental adaptive quality of all mankind; yet this is in no way incompatible with a genetically conditioned diversity of preferences and special abilities. Music is an obnoxious noise to some, ecstatic pleasure to others. Some have a bodily frame that can be trained for championship in wrestling, or running, or sprinting, or weight lifting. Some can develop phenomenal abilities for chess playing, or painting, or composing poetry. Can anybody develop a skill in any of these occupations if he makes sufficient effort? Possibly many people could, to some extent. The point is, however, that what comes easily to some requires great exertion from others, and even then the accomplishment is mediocre at best. The willingness to strive derives, however, at least in part, from a feeling that the labor is rewarded by the thrill of accomplishment or in some other way. There is little stimulus to exert oneself if the results of the exertions are likely to be pitifully small. And it is also possible that there is such a thing as predisposition to striving and effort.

It is a perversion of the ethic of equality to endeavor to reduce everybody to a uniform level of achievement. "From each according to his ability" is the famous motto of Marxian socialism, and it behooves democracy to grant no less recognition to the diversity of human individualities. This is not an apology for "rugged individualism"; the "ruggedness" amounts often to indifference or even contempt for individualities of others. Equality is, however, not an end in itself, but a means to an end, which can only be the self-actualization of human individuals and the fullest possible realization of their socially valuable capacities and potentialities. Individuals and groups will arrange their lives differently, in accordance with their diverse notions of what form of happiness they wish to pursue. Their contributions to mankind's store of achievements will be different in kind and in magnitude. The point is that everyone should be able to contribute to the limit of his ability. To deny the equality of opportunity to persons or groups is evil, because it results in wastage of talent, ability, and aptitude, besides being contrary to the basic ethic of humanity.

4

Social
Differentiation:
Minority Formation
and Development

Two sets of forces are always present in society. One furthers assimilation and uniformity; the other promotes differentiation and diversity. During certain periods of time, assimilative forces can become so powerful that group boundaries are blurred beyond recognition. At other times differentiating tendencies predominate, and new groups are formed to function either distinctively in the larger unit or to pull away as separate entities.

Differentiation, broadly defined, is a set of processes that result in separateness and specialization. Specifically, a *differentiated* society has specialized parts that are functionally related to the larger unit. Societies that maintain relatively large amounts of social distance among the various units are said to be *segregated*. If those units are ranked on some hierarchy as higher or lower, superior or inferior, the society is said to be *stratified*.

This chapter is concerned with the differentiation process and broadly outlines[1]

[1] The outline used in this chapter is an expansion of material originally published by Robin Williams, Jr., and his associates (1964, p. 19). I am grateful to Professor Williams for his helpful comments on this chapter.

a pattern that is associated with the formation and development of a minority group. As an abstraction, this outline is based upon the histories of several groups and thus does not fit any one specific instance. Its main purpose is to organize information so that regularities can be detected and understood. Even though the sequence of events may vary from group to group, the following developments occur with such frequency that they seem to be part of a "natural history" of minority formation and development: categorization, typing of occupations, value and behavior patterning, heightening of group consciousness, maintenance of boundaries, and systemic linkage and accommodation.

Categorization

Through historical circumstances persons considered to have some important characteristic in common are characterized as being of a kind. Skin color, religious rites, language or geographical location become signs that give the category visibility (Williams, 1964, p. 18).

The use of categories is essential to human thought, speech, and overt action. Language itself implies grouping things and events into categories. Categories enable us to make sense of the myriad objects, sounds, smells, and other stimuli that surround us. They are basic to all patterned human relations because they enable us to identify and selectively to respond to other individuals and groups. "Every man must categorize his fellows in order to interact with them" (Foote, 1951, p. 17). The very business of growing up to be human involves learning a category system that enables us to behave differentially toward various parts of the environment. A great deal of child rearing is concerned with this task. A category system, once it has been learned, becomes one of the insignias of membership in a given group or society.

Social categories are based upon perceived differences. They may be physical features like skin color or shape of eyes, language or dialect, customs, or geography. If geography is the basis, people who live in a particular region or even in one part of a city come to be thought of as belonging to a category.

The historical circumstances that cause one people to categorize others as belonging to an out-group vary considerably. Migration brought on by such events as famine or overcrowding may bring strangers into a new territory. A conquest may force previously separate peoples into a political unit within which they must regularly interact. Dispersion of peoples and accompanying changes in language may produce separate groups that can no longer communicate with one another.

Categories, once they have been formed, can be quite rigid. In Japan, for example, individuals who have had little personal contact with Westerners often consider them "strange creatures," somewhat like animals. Hiroshi Wagatsuma reports an informant's comment:

> When I think of actual Caucasians walking the street, I feel that they are basically different beings from us. Certainly, they are humans but I don't feel they are the same creatures as we are. There is, in my mind, a definite discontinuity between us and the Caucasians. Somehow, they belong to a different world.
> Deep in my mind, it seems, the Caucasians are ·somehow connected with something animal-like. Especially when I think of a middle-aged Caucasian woman, the first thing which comes up to my mind is a large chunk of boneless ham. This kind of association may not be limited to me. As I recall now, once in an English class at school, our teacher explained the meaning of the word "hog" as a big pig. A boy in our class said loudly, "Oh, I know what it is! It's like a foreign (meaning, Caucasian) woman!" We all laughed and I felt we all agreed with the boy. (Wagatsuma, 1968, p. 143)

The cues for a category are often arrived at through a complex series of historic events and, once chosen, may survive for many generations. The American Indians, by and large, seem not to have felt any substantial identity at the time that the Europeans first encountered them in the fifteenth and sixteenth centuries. They did not share a universal language or a known historical experience. In many ways these indigenous tribes were more culturally diverse than were their discoverers. It was these discoverers who applied to them the common name "Indian." The word did not come from themselves, for they thought of themselves and dealt with the invaders almost entirely in tribal terms. "The tribe[2] represented the way of life of the people," writes anthropologist Hazel Hertzberg; "*Indian* was a way of differentiating aborigine from European" (1971, p. 2).

It is not at all clear exactly how the Blacks who were first brought to Jamestown in 1619 were regarded by White colonists. John Rolfe noted simply, "About the last of August came in a dutch man of warre that sold us twenty Negars." The Blacks may well have been treated at first as indentured servants, rather than as slaves. By 1640, however, some Blacks were in fact being treated as slaves; at least they were being held in hereditary lifetime service. After 1660 slavery was written into law.

Of their initial treatment the historian Winthrop D. Jordan has concluded, "There simply is not enough evidence to indicate with any certainty whether Negroes were treated like white servants or not" (1969, p. 73). He points out, however, that early historic documents set the Blacks apart with a distinct name:

> A distinct name is not attached to a group unless it is regarded as distinct. . . . It seems likely that the colonists' initial sense of difference from the Negro was

[2] Many aboriginal groups in America identified with the clan, band, or local community rather than with the tribe.

founded not on a single characteristic but on a congeries of qualities which, taken as a whole, seemed to set the Negro apart. . . . What may have been his two most striking characteristics, his heathenism and his appearance, were probably prerequisite to his complete debasement. (1969, p. 73)

Typing of Occupations

Individuals in a minority group typically participate in occupations that vary from those of other social categories (Williams, 1964, p. 18).

Rarely are minority members proportionately represented in all parts of a society's division of labor. Instead they tend to cluster in specific occupations. Patterns develop through competition, historical accident, or deliberate planning; gradually norms come to indicate what types of work are suitable for certain groups.

In the United States some groups are conspicuously absent from certain occupational categories. According to 1970 census data, about 65 percent of Blacks have blue-collar jobs (manual labor), and about 35 percent have white-collar jobs. The White population distribution is almost the reverse—63 percent have white-collar jobs, and 37 percent have blue-collar jobs. Occupational typing is not hard to find. Practically no Blacks are instrumentalists in symphony orchestras, but they are so disproportionately represented in jazz and rock music that musician has become a stereotypical role. Neither Puerto Ricans nor Blacks are proportionately represented in the professions of law and medicine. At the present time those who do manage to obtain legal or medical training tend to find employment with governmental agencies like the U.S. Public Health Service. Very few non-Whites become electricians or plumbers, but they dominate the bricklaying and plastering trades in several cities. Some American Indians have found employment in the construction trades and in shipbuilding, but they have only very rarely found jobs in other high-paying occupations.

People of Jewish descent are under represented in banking and insurance, but they are well represented in medicine, law, textiles, merchandising, and the performing arts. One survey conducted in New York City reported that 56 percent of the physicians, 64 percent of the dentists, and 66 percent of the lawyers were Jewish. Yet at the time the city's population was about 28 percent Jewish (Allport, 1958, p. 120).

No single factor is sufficient to explain every instance of occupational concentration Sometimes there is open discrimination by the majority group—its members simply deter minority people from obtaining certain jobs. At other times minority members shun certain careers because of associated activities that are inconsistent with their cherished values.

Some occupations are difficult to enter because there is no direct way for "outsiders" to acquire the necessary credentials or skills, which may deter both minority and majority members. The "tricks" of many trades are learned under the tutelage of experienced practitioners who find the role of mentor satisfying. The mentor-apprentice relationship is crucial to success in practically all the prestigious and economically rewarding occupations, even when racial or ethnic considerations are not present. Whenever minorities have been able to make successful incursions into occupations dominated by the core society, mentor-apprentice relationships across group lines have usually occurred.

Andrew F. Brimmer, who in 1972 was the only Black member of the Federal Reserve Board, has cited the need for more intergroup experience as one of the problems of Black-owned banks: "A few years ago the Black banks . . . were facing very serious management problems. . . . Because of a legacy of discrimination and a lack of experience and opportunity; the managements simply had not acquired the skills necessary."

Occupations that incorporate formal apprenticeship systems tend to perpetuate racial or ethnic monopolies. Under such a system an apprentice must be nominated or sponsored by a master craftsman. If the craft or occupation is a desirable one, there will likely be many applicants. Given a choice, a master craftsman probably will nominate a relative, a friend, or a friend's relative. Were the master craftsman to bypass these applicants and choose an outsider, negative sanctions from colleagues would almost surely follow. The discriminatory features of such a system break down only when there are few applicants, either because the job is unattractive or because the general labor market is tight, or when the goverment (through the courts and so on) decrees that particular crafts, unions, or employers must maintain quotas from various groups.

Other reasons for a particular group's clustering in certain occupations may be less obvious than those mentioned so far. In trading relations, members of a minority may excel as merchants because their status as outsiders ensures the social distance necessary to transact business effectively. Social distance in such a situation is functional in that it enables buyer and seller to maximize their respective interests without the intrusion of extrinsic considerations. Close friends, by contrast, usually find it difficult to strike "hard" bargains with each other.

An anthropologist colleague who had resided on the Northern Cheyenne Indian Reservation once described an incident that illustrates this principle. During 1955–1956, an Indian became proprietor of a service station on the reservation. For a time he did a good business, but gradually it declined, and within a year he was forced to close. The problem seems to have been his difficulty in refusing credit and favors to his "brothers." Meanwhile, a nearby service station operated by an Anglo prospered, partly because Indians felt less free to ask a White man for special treatment and the White felt no obligation to give it!

It may be that human societies became heterogeneous, not by accident, but because they "need" to be (Fallers, 1967, pp. 7–16). The stranger—the member

BANK LOOKING FOR JEWS TO FILL TOP JOBS

[Reprinted from yesterd 's late editions]
[N. Y. Times-Chicago Tribune Service]

Philadelphia, Oct. 26 — The first Pennsylvania Banking and Trust company, Philadelphia's largest bank, is actively looking for Jewish applicants who might eventually qualify for top executive positions.

At the same time, the bank has embarked on a program seeking to eliminate "the subtle anti-Jewish atmosphere that the young Jewish trainee thinks he feels."

This was announced tonight by John R. Bunting Jr., executive vice president of the bank, at the annual dinner meeting of the Philadelphia chapter, American Jewish committee, at the Warwick hotel.

Survey Made Public

"We consider it desirable to bring a leading Jewish figure into the power structure of our bank," Bunting said.

On Sept. 1, the national A. J. C. made public the results of a banking survey which showed, the committee said, that 45 out of the 50 largest commercial banks in the United States had no Jews among their senior officers.

Bunting noted in his address that the committee's figures for Philadelphia indicated that only about one half of 1 per cent of the officers of six major commercial banks here are Jewish.

Scarcity Is Noted

In examining the situation in his own bank, he discovered a scarcity of Jewish senior officials, in spite of the bank's non-discrimination policy, he said.

The reason, he said, is that undoubtedly at some point in banking history there has been hostility toward Jewish employes and "the after-effects lingered long after the hostility died."

As a consequence, he added, few Jews of top rank enter banking, and of those that do, a good percentage leave after a few years, not because of hostility but because "the overall environment is discouraging to them."

More Blacks In Textiles

WASHINGTON (UPI) — The American Textile Manufacturers Institute (ATMI) said Thursday Negro employment in the textile industry reached 12 per cent of the work force in 1969, a gain of 24 per cent over the previous year.

Citing figures compiled by the Bureau of Labor Statistics in Washington, ATMI also noted that the percentage of Negro employment in textiles had passed the manufacturing industries aveage of just over 10 per cent. It said the textile industry increase of 24 per cent compares with a four per cent increase in all manufacturing.

The ATMI report also said the textile work force of just under one million employes was 47 per cent female. During 1969, the percentage of Negro women employed by the textile industry was 10.4, an increase of 35 per cent.

of the out-group—serves an important function. As a resident of the community but one who is not totally committed to its values, he can play the role of middle man. The "stranger's" objectivity, as Georg Simmel once described it, is based upon "distance and nearness, indifference and involvement" (Wolff, 1950, pp. 403–405). Because he is *in* the community but not *of* it, the larger group is likely to take an ambivalent (and sometimes hostile) attitude toward him. When ethnic "outsiders" prosper as traders or middlemen, minority communities may become the objects of suspicion, hostility, and violence. Attacks, repression, or expulsion often occur—with strong economic overtones—as, for example, against the Lebanese in Sierre Leone, against the Indians in Uganda, against the Ibo in Nigeria, and against the Chinese in Burma. Anti-Semitism among some urban Blacks is probably also a variation on the same theme.

The relationship between the stranger-trader and his customers is almost always perceived as a narrow economic one. He is often accused of "exploiting" his customers, of being an unproductive parasite, and of being morally corrupt. Lacking certain ties with the local community, the out-group tends to create its own institutions of social control, worship, recreation, and management of external relations (Fallers, 1967, p. 12).

Value and Behavior Patterning

As a consequence of their distinctive social roles, persons in a given category will develop relatively distinctive interests, beliefs, values, and specific modes of behavior (Williams, 1964, p. 19).

Almost always the necessary work in a society includes tasks that are dirty, dangerous, boring, or debilitating. These tasks have been performed historically by immigrants or slaves, mercenaries, the mentally deficient, or indentured servants. If a society permits these people upward social mobility, replacements must constantly be found to fill the low-status slots that they vacate. It simplifies matters considerably when ways can be found to keep low-status individuals—and their children—where they are. "Race" is such a solution.

Coercion alone is rarely sufficient to make such a system work. A belief system must emerge to lend legitimacy to the arrangement. A set of myths enables individuals at all levels of the status hierarchy to feel that what they are doing is natural and right. In the days of slavery the biblical account of Noah's curse of Ham (*Genesis*, 9:20–27) had that effect. As the verses were then widely interpreted, it was the will of God that Blacks be consigned forever to be "servants of servants."

Members of a minority group can develop a distinctive mental life of their own. They may come to believe in a myth that accounts for their status. Black Muslims, for example, tell of an ancient Black scientist named Yakub, who sinned against Allah by producing an inferior breed of mankind (the White man).

Allah's curse was that Black people would be ruled by White people for 6,000 years. The 6,000-year period of punishment is just about over, so the teaching goes, and Blacks soon will assume their former dominant status. This belief explains present misfortunes and nourishes hope for the future.

Typically, values as well as beliefs are involved. As preferences, or orientations toward life, they provide the individual with a "feel" for what is desirable, what is good, what ought to be. Value orientations, by implication, also indicate what is "bad" and undesirable.

Value orientations can be so pervasive in a particular group that group members come to be characterized by them. If, for example, the scholarly person is an esteemed social type in a particular group, group members may heavily emphasize formal education in their child-rearing practices. If the wealthy person is an esteemed type, group members may heavily emphasize acquisitive activities. These two examples suggest that the connections among values, group stereotypes, and actual behavior can be close. The integration of value orientations with the life and history of a particular people is called by some scholars the "pattern of culture" (Benedict, 1934) and by others "national character" (Bell, 1968, pp. 103–120).

Value orientations guide and channel activities in functionally important areas of life. Consider, for instance, the well-known role of the Chinese in the retail trade of Southeast Asia and in certain other parts of the world (for example, Jamaica). So successful have they been at it that certain countries historically have legally restricted their activities. (King Wachirawut of Thailand, who ascended the throne in 1911, wrote a hostile pamphlet on the Chinese, entitled *The Jews of the East*.) Several factors account for their success: their tightly knit business and familial associations, their insecurity as aliens in many countries, and their knowledge of how to turn one dollar into two. But more important, in terms of this discussion, has been their traditional system of beliefs and values, which support economic activity: "If there is any one petition more than any other which is made to the Chinese gods of the household or of the great gods outside, it is the prayer for success, for prosperity, good fortune, luck in enterprise" (Hunter, 1966, p. 42).

Heightening Group Consciousness

Persons who share similar beliefs and values as well as the same life chances may develop a sense of common identity (Williams, 1964, p. 19).

A minority group is not fully formed until it ceases to be simply a potential membership group and develops into a social unit whose members are aware of their common identity and common interests. In this respect, a minority is much like a social class. Karl Marx made such a distinction, calling a potential membership group a *Klasse an sich* (class in itself) and a self-conscious collectivity a *Klasse für sich* (class for itself).

Differential treatment by itself does not automatically produce new groups. It is only when minority members become *aware* of differential treatment that they begin to establish identity on that basis. "Consciousness of kind did not develop among the Eurasians in India until they realized that they would be treated alike regardless of the differences among them" (Shibutani and Kwan, 1967, p. 212). There is a parallel in the Whites' treatment of American Indians. At first, as we mentioned earlier, the various tribes did not think of themselves as Indians. That came later. "Red power" and "Indian solidarity" are the most recent manifestations of heightened group consciousness that transcends tribal boundaries.

The appearance of a group leader can heighten group consciousness. Such an individual can articulate the group's desires, frustrations, and rage and may be able to provide the necessary strength to keep divisive forces to a minimum and thus to sustain group consciousness. Tunisian President Habib Bourguiba once said: "The Arab world was never unified. As soon as Prophet Muhammad died, Muslims began to fight each other" (*Washington Post*, April 1974). The point is, however, that Muhammad kept group consciousness from being dissipated while he lived.

A group leader need not be an articulate spokesman, but he or she must become a symbol, as was apparent in 1937 when Joe Louis knocked out James J. Braddock to become heavyweight champion. Malcolm X called that victory "the greatest celebration of race pride our generation had ever known." Another example comes from India: Jawaharlal Nehru once reportedly said of Mohandas Gandhi, "He gave India an identity." Some observers feel that the California grape workers' strike—*la huelga*, led by Cesar Chavez in 1965–1970—has had a generally unifying impact upon Chicanos.

The mass media have in recent years heightened group consciousness by making group members aware of their heritage and by providing information about discrimination against their fellows. Cornell University researchers found that a sense of common identity was evident in Hometown whenever instances of discrimination against Blacks in other parts of the nation were reported. The researchers concluded that the main channel of communications was the Black press (Williams, 1964, p. 238).

Historical events like war and revolution may heighten group consciousness. There can be little doubt that group identity and pride among Blacks in the United States have been stimulated by the emergence of independent nations in Africa. It has brought about a tremendous interest in all things African. That continent, once an embarrassment to many educated Blacks, has become a rallying point for persons of color.

Group consciousness can center around a people's ancient heritage. Some groups must, however, create a history for themselves. Anthropological literature provides many examples of peoples whose sense of identity is tied to their descent from illustrious ancestors. The Amish have set themselves apart from the outside world on the basis of doctrines that their forefathers first accepted in the seventeenth century. Black consciousness in America has been accompanied by an intense interest in African history. The Lumbee Indians of North Carolina claim descent from various Indian tribes and from white settlers of Sir Walter Raleigh's Lost Colony. The Melungeons—a marginal people of Tennessee and Kentucky—claim that the Phoenecians are their ancestors. Jews are the children of Abraham. Germans, according to the Nazis, are descendants of the Aryans. And so it is that, with or without reliable historical evidence, a group tradition functions to heighten group consciousness.

Group symbols—political, religious, and otherwise—contribute to and sustain group identity. Insignias (like the swastika), statuses (king, queen, *cacique* [kuh-sēē'-keh], religious or political articles (Torah, cross, stool of the Ashanti) all function in this way. A body of cultural symbols with which every member of the group can identify can have enormous consequences for heightening and maintaining group consciousness.

The physical segregation of a people, even their unplanned migration into an urban area, may facilitate a sense of common identity, as it has among American Blacks. Editor Ralph McGill wrote that the boll weevil was responsible for desegregation; he meant that the ruin of the cotton economy of the South caused massive migration of rural Blacks to the cities, where they developed a sense of common identity, as well as political and economic leverage.

Maintenance of Boundaries

Heightened group consciousness generally is accompanied by increased within-group interaction. This closure of interaction will increase the tendency of outsiders to treat minority members as a unit (Williams, 1964, p. 19).

Maintenance of boundaries and some closure of interaction is implied in the concept of group formation. "A dichotomization of others as strangers, as members of another ethnic group," Fredrik Barth writes, "implies a recognition of limitations on shared understandings, differences in criteria for judgment of value and performance, and a mutual interest" (1969, p. 15). Barth further observes that a polyethnic situation always implies a "series of constraints on the kinds of roles an individual is allowed to play, and the partners he may choose from different kinds of transactions" (1969, p. 17).

Groups use a wide assortment of practices to maintain boundaries. Charles P. Loomis (1964, p. 32) has classified these practices as physical (zoning restrictions, political boundaries) and social (life styles of certain groups, preference for endogamy), planned and rationally applied (travel restrictions in certain nations) and spontaneously applied. They may involve group contraction (casting out deviants) or group expansion (when two groups unite against a third, common foe).

Such practices have been conspicuous in the emergence and development of the American isolates—the more than 200 enclaves that have been identified in eighteen states (Griessman, 1972, p. 693). These enclaves consist of people of mixed descent, some of them tracing their lineage to various Indian tribes. Many of the isolates have an ambiguous social position—that of a third people in societies that recognize only two, Black and White. Historically the residents of some of these communities have been categorized by their neighbors as "colored," "issues," or "mulattoes," so that scholars have called them "submerged races," "marginal peoples," *mestizos*, or "middle peoples." This categorization arises in part from the fact that miscegenation between Indians and those legally classified as Blacks is known to have occurred in some of the enclaves. Although these occurrences seem to have been rare, in a society that regards "one drop of Negro blood" as a contamination it has been regarded as sufficient ground for ostracizing entire communities.

In recent years several of these enclaves have reasserted their "Indian-ness," and researchers have had a rare opportunity to study the development. J. Ken Dane and this author (1972, pp. 694–709) studied three enclaves in rural North Carolina and found that their members engaged in several boundary-maintenance activities. They insisted on being called Indians, rather than Blacks. To suggest the contrary was to invite physical violence. Two of the three communities had engaged in costly legal actions to force the state to remove the designation "colored" or "Negro" from drivers' licenses, birth certificates, and marriage licenses. (This action was unnecessary in the third community, for its members had established their legal status as Indians in the years that followed Reconstruction.) In each instance, the courts ruled in the community's favor.

Each community organized separate schools, churches, and social clubs. To be a member, one had to be regarded by the group as Indian, not Black. There were several instances in which people who belonged to a stigmatized group (a type of out-caste called Smilings) were excluded from Indian churches and schools.

Three separate tax rolls—White, Black, and Indian—were kept at the respective courthouses until 1969 (when new Federal guidelines forbade the practice). From that date until the present only one tax roll has been kept. Before 1969 the Indian Club of the area provided the tax assessors with a list of those it considered *bona fide* Indians. As for the ultimate boundary-maintenance practice—endogamy—young people were encouraged to marry Indian or White. Marriage with a Black meant expulsion from the group.

What has happened to the American isolates in microcosm has happened elsewhere among minority peoples. Where the population base has permitted, separate churches, newspapers, businesses, and clubs have appeared. Typically, youngsters in minorities have felt pressure to marry within their groups. Major American minorities generally have had their own social-class divisions, and members of these communities have tended to remain within their own groups and social classes for most of their primary-group relations. Intergroup contacts frequently have been limited to secondary-group levels like employment and politics. Milton M. Gordon has written:

> The United States is a multiple melting pot in which acculturation for all groups beyond the first generation of immigrants, without eliminating all value conflicts, has been massive and decisive, but in which structural separation on the basis of race and religion—structural pluralism as we have called it—emerges as the dominant sociological condition. (M. M. Gordon, 1964, pp. 234, 235)

A group with explicit boundaries eventually produces individuals who have vested interests in perpetuating the group's separate identity. Educators, merchants, ministers, and politicians typically come to depend upon the group's survival for their livelihoods. During the changes that accompanied school desegregation, opposition predictably came from some members of the Black community who vested interests in the existing arrangement. It seems safe to generalize that social change is always resisted partly because someone stands to benefit from existing arrangements. It should be added, however, that group members are sometimes willing to bear personal loss in order that the group may benefit. Many American Blacks who had benefited personally from a segregated system nevertheless accepted and even advocated desegregation.

One further observation: Carefully maintained group boundaries are barriers to effective communication between majority and minority. If there is widespread ignorance about the other on each side, prejudice may increase.

Systemic Linkage and Accommodation

If a group is dependent upon the environing society for a substantial portion of its goods and services, it will protect these vital ties by accommodating itself to the norms of the environing society (Williams, 1964, p. 19).

Even groups with well-kept boundaries are exposed to outside contacts. It is difficult to imagine a more tightly knit minority than the Amish of Lancaster County, Pennsylvania; yet even they are linked to the surrounding society through trade relations, taxation, and so on. These contacts can be visualized as *systemic linkage*—"the process whereby the elements of at least two social systems come to be articulated so that in some ways and on some occasions they may be viewed as a single system" (Loomis, 1964, p. 32).

Types of systemic linkage are of several orders. Some are clearly defined and involve legal contracts or treaties, whereas others are casual and comparatively unstructured. The "silent trade" of the Congo is perhaps the best-known instance of a simple arrangement (Turnbull, 1963). Trading between Bantu Villagers and Pygmies takes place at regular intervals, but very little face-to-face contact occurs. Villagers leave vegetables, fruits, and other articles in specific places near the village where the Pygmies can collect them. In return, the Pygmies leave meat and other items for the villagers. Were the villagers to leave inferior articles, the Pygmies could retaliate by reducing their offerings in later exchanges. Even in this primitive economic arrangement it is thus apparent that links, though subtle, do exist.

This arrangement also highlights the fact that accommodation between groups is rarely a one-way affair. A simple numerical majority does not necessarily give a group of position of dominance. A relatively small, tightly knit group controlling some scarce good or service can sometimes enforce demands upon a larger group. Such a development, however, can be dangerous if the majority group comes to fear the minority because its members "stick together." If the minority is considered valuable to the core society, the application of negative sanctions tends to be based on calculation of how much the minority will tolerate without revolting.

We need not look very far to find instances of minority peoples who have yielded to pressures from majority groups. In many nations Jewish merchants have been required to close their businesses on Sundays. Until a 1972 Supreme Court decision ruled in their favor, Amish parents were forced to send their children to public high schools. The Pueblo Indians have had to create new political positions (the local "governor," for instance) that were not part of their traditional system so that they could deal with the Anglos. This list could be extended to great length, but the point seems clear: Sustained interaction creates pressures for the minority group to accommodate itself to the norms of the majority group.

There is a sense in which this developmental process runs full circle. A newly emerged group, even with well-established boundaries, will find itself drawn to the core society by assimilative processes that are supported by economic, political, and normative interconnections. It is in this vein that Talcott Parsons has written:

"Perhaps the prominence of polarizations in Western history is a feature of the West's greatness as well as a source of its innumerable tragedies. Although polarization implies exclusiveness, a least on one side it may also set the stage for important processes of inclusion" (1968, p. 353).

Overview

Clyde Kluckhohn, in one of his books, describes the way in which an archaeologist goes about studying the surface of an undug site:

He looks at a handful of potsherds and, if they come from a now well-known archeological culture, he can predict not only what other types of pottery will be found on excavation but also the style of masonry, the techniques of weaving, the arrangements of rooms, and the kinds of stone and bone work. He knows the pattern. (1965, p. 49)

Similiarly, individuals who have studied the ways in which dominant groups and minorities relate to each other will be as informed as the archeologist when they begin to learn the particulars of some new situation. They know what to expect; they know the pattern. For example, a student of intergroup relations should not be surprised to learn that Copts (a non-Muslim, Christian minority in Egypt and other nations of the Middle East) have dominated certain occupations like banking, that they have been required to wear distinctive clothing like black turbans, that they have dietary restrictions placed on them, that they often give their children neutral instead of Christian names to avoid attention, and that one characteristic group response is intensified striving. Study of other groups reveals that these developments are typical in intergroup relations. The particulars in the list vary, but the pattern is a familiar one.

Viewed broadly as a developmental process, the formation of a separate people involves activities that typically occur in a kind of pattern: categorization, typing of occupations, value and behavior patterning, heightening of group consciousness, maintenance of boundaries, systemic linkage, and accommodation. Not that there is a rigid, unvarying sequence, but there is a general pattern that applies to a number of situations.

The way in which a particular people comes to be categorized depends upon historic events that may have economic, religious, and political overtones. The categories frequently coincide with society's division of labor. Distinctive occupations and social roles give rise to distinctive interests, beliefs, and values; an awareness of differential treatment by the core society may also heighten group consciousness. Closure of interaction typically follows. Even if maintenance of boundaries is stressed, however, some links with the surrounding society are usually necessary. These links may eventually serve as the basis for assimilation into some larger unit.

For Further Reading

Many of the items among the references cited may be considered as recommended reading as well.

Banton, Michael. *Race Relations.* New York: Basic Books, 1967.
Barth, Fredrik. *Ethnic Groups and Boundaries.* Boston: Little, Brown, 1969.
Boas, Franz. *Race, Language and Culture.* New York: Free Press, 1966.
Benedict, Ruth. *Patterns of Culture.* Boston: Houghton Mifflin, 1934.

Dunn, L. C., and Theodosius Dobzhansky. *Heredity, Race and Society.* New York: New American Library, 1946.

Goldsby, Richard A. *Race and Races.* New York: Macmillan, 1971.

Park, Robert Ezra. *Race and Culture.* New York: Free Press, 1950.

Shibutani, Tamotsu, and Kian M. Kwan. *Ethnic Stratification: A Comparative Approach.* New York: Macmillan, 1965.

Thompson, Edgar T., and Everett C. Hughes (eds.). *Race: Individual and Collective Behavior.* New York: Free Press, 1958.

Williams, Robin M., Jr. *Strangers Next Door: Ethnic Relations in American Communities.* Englewood Cliffs, N.J.: Prentice-Hall, 1964.

THE PLANTATION AS A RACE-MAKING SITUATION

EDGAR T. THOMPSON

Throughout history, certain low status jobs have been performed by immigrants, conquered peoples, the mentally deficient, indentured servants, or slaves. If a given society were to permit these persons or their children to leave their positions, replacements would have to be found. From the viewpoint of the advantaged class, matters can be simplified considerably by keeping these people in their places. The idea of race provides one form of a "solution."

Edgar T. Thompson's studies of plantations have convinced him that this particular social system provides a setting well suited for the formation of an out-group category and an ideology that justifies keeping people in their place. In the following succinct statement, Professor Thompson calls such a phenomenon a **situational imperative.**

The plantation is a form of organization producing staple crops for an outside, usually an overseas, market. Severe international competition has tended to press heavily on production costs, especially labor costs, and plantation labor has been recruited halfway around the world. Almost every plantation society has put some new combination of men to work—generally, but not always, under white planters or overseers. Thus, one characteristic of the plantation is a labor problem which tends eventually to be defined also as a race problem. The plantation is a race-making situation.

When the planter begins to import an industrial army of occupation and to settle it upon the land, the characteristic outlines of the plantation begin to appear. The plantation is first a settlement institution; it is a form of camp capitalism on an island or at the edge of a settlement where free land is to be had but which is still accessible to the market. In the South the planter imported his labor first from England, then from Africa, and did with it about as he pleased without reference to the native mores. In Hawaii, on the other hand, he had to take the wishes of the monarch into account and bring in only what were called peoples "cognate" to the Hawaiian peoples, i.e., Gilbert Islanders and then Chinese. In such places as Hawaii where the planters were unable to continue their original contractual controls over imported laborers, such laborers left the plantations upon the expiration of their contracts and set up intermediate businesses in the towns and cities, businesses too small for members of the planter class to bother with. Their ranks were filled by new importees, perhaps from another country.

In the South there was a succession from white indentured servants from England to African Negroes, but here the succession of ethnics stopped. The

African slave trade was never large enough to satisfy the demand, and after 1808 by provision of the Constitution the legal importation of Negro slaves was forbidden. Under the circumstances the supply of plantation labor had to be maintained, if it was to be maintained at all, by preventing the children of the Negroes from responding to the ordinary opportunities for upward mobility presented by the frontier. Lifelong servitude began with the second generation. Slavery was calculated to keep a Negro in a state of perpetual childhood, to keep him tied to a master wherever the master might go rather than to a particular piece of land, and to keep him and his offspring in their place forever. Slavery was the Southern analogue of Hawaii's labor succession.

Slavery, and other forms of forced labor similar to it, brought with it problems of control which the idea of race measurably solved so far as the planter was concerned. The naked force of the planter is never sufficient to keep men working at low place. There has to develop some kind of myth, like race, which not only those who rule but those who are ruled accept. It was not sufficient to assert the superiority of the white man and the inferiority of the black man; it was much more important to persuade the black man to accept the allegation of his own inferiority. This is what the idea of race achieves. In the situation the idea of race does not exist merely to effect a separation between peoples; it did this incident to its major function of control. As the cultural differences between whites and Negroes receded, visible physical differences loomed larger to become the chief marks around which to organize doctrines and beliefs of deeper biological differences.

Before World War II Japanese plantation authorities and planters in Taiwan [Formosa] had a very low opinion of the Chinese laborers on the large sugar estates there. "They were lazy, they were untrustworthy, they were irresponsible." These are the same statements that white planters in the South make about their Negro tenants and sharecroppers and have long made about Negroes generally. In Taiwan the principal parties were neither white nor Negro. Instead they were people whom we in America are disposed to classify together as Orientals. All this suggests that conceptions of race, under whatever name, are not conceptions necessarily brought to the situation out of the white man's culture and put into force by the white planter. The suggestion is strong here that *the idea of race is a situational imperative*; if it is not there to begin with, it tends to develop in a plantation society because it is a useful, maybe necessary, principle of control. In Virginia the plantation took two peoples originally differentiated as Christian and heathen, and before the first century was over it had made two races.

THE MEANING OF ISRAEL

HARRY GOLDEN

A sense of peoplehood can emerge from and be sustained by several sources—occupational discrimination, war, invasion, religion, territory. Harry Golden discusses the mingling of all these factors in the following selection. His article highlights the fact that the maintenance of a sense of Jewish identity for many centuries has culminated in Zionism and in the creation of the nation of Israel.

There is little in the Israeli countryside to impress the eye or inspire the imagination. A small place, with a few mountain ranges of moderate size, an arid triangle to the south, plains and valleys yielding fair produce, Israel is comparable in size to the state of Massachusetts. It has a population of 2,660,000. Its economic mainstay is agriculture, and much of this, particularly in the south, is practiced with great difficulty on recalcitrant nonsoil. Mineral wealth is negligible and raw materials must be imported in great quantities.

Yet this little strip of ground, with its limited physical assets, has drawn the world's attention for three thousand years. It is the matrix of the great religions of the West, a holy place alike to Jews and Christians; and to Muslim Arabs, who trace their lineage through Ishmael, the nomadic son of Abraham. Israel is the human story in miniature, a microcosm that summarizes within its shifting boundaries man's striving for freedom and his irrepressible quest for a homeland.

It has been a battleground since the time of Joshua. Egyptians, Assyrians, Persians, Romans, Crusaders and Turks have overrun the land that the Hebrew God promised to Abraham: "And I will give unto thee, and to thy seed after thee, the land wherein thou art a stranger, all the land of Canaan, for an everlasting possession." Some of the mightiest armies ever assembled, including the hosts of Alexander and the legions of Rome, have cast giant shadows on Israel's soil. One episode in particular emerges from the past of embattled Israel—the story of Masada, which has received much attention in the past few years, following the discoveries by archaeologists in 1963 and 1965. . . . It will suffice here to say that one of the last stands of the Jews in revolt against the Romans—an occasion of literal self-slaughter—was made here at Masada.

Once it was obvious the revolt would be crushed, a Pharisee named Jochannan ben Zaccai managed to escape from Jerusalem by concealing himself in a coffin that was carried past the Roman guards. Jochannan asked permission of the Roman authorities to set up a school for the study of Hebrew scriptures. So commenced the history of Israel as an idea in the minds of its exiled Jewish sons and daughters, when Jerusalem fell.

Two thousand years later, Zionism began to give Israel concrete form. Jews started to go back to Israel—then called Palestine—in the 1880's. In the beginning they were Russian Jews who had two choices to escape the pogroms of the czar. One was to get to America, an expensive, protracted adventure; the other was to go to Palestine, entering through Rumania or Turkey or sometimes sailing from Italy. In those days it was just a barren, hot place. In the 7th Century the Caliph Omar had stood on Mount Scopus, looked out over Palestine and said, "Not even the birds can live here."

The idea of a Jewish homeland in Palestine began with Theodor Herzl, a Viennese journalist, dandy and dilettante. He had studied law, but he much preferred writing plays, sketches, criticism and stories, all invested with whimsical Viennese delight. Herzl considered himself many things, probably least of all that he was a Jew. He was completely assimilated, as many Viennese Jews were.

But the trial of Capt. Alfred Dreyfus of the French general staff changed that. The Dreyfus affair reminded Europe that Jews were just that, Jews; they were different and defenseless. Anti-Semitism became a responsible profession. Edouard Drumont edited La Libre Parole, an anti-Semitic paper that became one of the most popular in France. In Austria, Karl Lueger became the Mayor of Vienna on a platform promising to impose anti-Semitic regulations. In fact, the professional anti-Semites were an early influence on Hitler when he lived in Vienna. What dismayed and frightened the Jews was that anti-Semitism raged in France, the very nation which under Napoleon had given them their emancipation. This was what shocked Theodor Herzl, a trauma that turned the dilettante into an intellectual and a political prophet. He saw the publicly dishonored Dreyfus led through the courtyard of the Ecole Militaire crying, "I'm innocent." He heard the sinister shout that the crowd chanted back, "Death to the Jews."

Out of Herzl's shock came his book, Der Judenstaadt (The Jewish State), which proposed establishing a Jewish commonwealth in Palestine, a sovereign state for the ingathering of the Jews in the world. Herzl lectured on this, he wrote again and again, modifying, reformulating, reinvigorating his plan. He visited Kaiser Wilhelm II, talked to the Sultan of Turkey, met with the Pope in Rome as well as the King of Italy and the Grand Duke of Baden. He also met with the leaders of the British government. In his time he saw the rise of dozens of Zionist societies and clubs, which first took root in Poland and Russia. His unflagging energy and imagination made modern Israel a possibility, and he never lost heart. In 1897, in a conversation with Dr. Max Nordau, he insisted the ideal was real.

Nordau said, "Plan on three hundred years for its realization."

"No," said Herzl. "It will need thirty."

Twenty years later came the Balfour Declaration. At the end of World War I, Britain received Palestine as a mandated country. Lord Balfour, the British Foreign Minister, wrote a letter to Lord Rothschild, one of the Zionist leaders of Great

Britain, stating: "His Majesty's government view with favour the establishment in Palestine of a national home for the Jewish people and will use their best endeavours to facilitate the achievement of this object, it being clearly understood that nothing shall be done which may prejudice the civil and religious rights of existing non-Jewish communities in Palestine, or the rights and the political status enjoyed by the Jews in any other country."

One reason for the Balfour Declaration was the work of Chaim Weizmann, a Russian-born Jewish chemist who set up a small laboratory at the University of Manchester in 1904. Weizmann was an ardent Zionist dedicated to carrying on the work of Herzl, and an even better chemist. He advanced the development of acetone, a volatile, inflammable liquid, just the substance a country would need for explosives in a monumental war effort. Weizmann gave the patent for acetone to England. David Lloyd George, the Prime Minister, said, "Acetone made me a Zionist." Weizmann became an influential man. He joined the British ministry, and this brought him into closer contact with the leaders of the government. Ceaselessly he argued for a Jewish homeland. It was Weizmann who said, "A good Jew must believe in miracles if he is a realist."

The Balfour Declaration was published on November 2, 1917. Josephus Daniels, Secretary of the Navy in Woodrow Wilson's Cabinet and one of the first Christian Zionists, cabled Lord Balfour: "Oh, what new wonders will come again from those hills of Judea."

Israel needed one last miracle to become a political reality. Let us call that last miracle David Ben-Gurion, Israel's first Prime Minister, an archetypical Israeli. Ben-Gurion was born in Poland and came to Israel in 1906, when he was twenty years old. He farmed in the death valleys of Galilee but he was in essence a political man, and he was soon embroiled in an altercation with the Turkish government, which arrested him and sentenced him to death. At the last minute the Turks commuted the sentence and deported him. He returned from the United States to join the Jewish Legion in World War I, which fought with distinction in the liberation of Palestine. After the war he became one of the leaders in the Palestine Labor Movement. Ben-Gurion formed the Histadrut, an organization similar to our AFL-CIO. During the years of the British Mandate Ben-Gurion built up labor, guided the economic life of the Jewish settlement, and oversaw the formation of the Haganah (defense militia) and the army.

The common characteristic of these three leaders, Herzl, Weizmann and Ben-Gurion, was that all were intellectuals. They were the kind of men who sit over empty coffeecups arguing hour after hour how to turn an idea into reality. In some respects they resembled the men who framed the Declaration of Independence, all of whom, too, were intellectuals in a country where a large majority could barely read a Bible. Israel was brought into being by men of words.

At the end of World War II, two forces persuaded the British it was time to pull out of Palestine. The first was the rise of nationalism throughout the world:

in India, in Africa, in the East Indies, in China. Nationalism was no less a force in the Middle East. The second was the deterioration of Arab-Jewish relationships. Both peoples wanted to live in the same stretch of land. Though the Jews had purchased this land, no rapprochement was possible. The British had entered a period of austerity. They were not inclined to assume the responsibilities of settling this expensive dispute.

Thus the British decided to pull out of Palestine and seek a solution in the United Nations. In deference to the Arabs, they had tried to limit immigration into Palestine. But by now Zionism had taken hold of Jews all over the world. American Jews pressured for immigration. So did British Jews. So did thousands and thousands of Christians, as did thousands of atheists, all of them heartsick over what had happened to the European Jewish community. Already the Jews were smuggling immigrants into Israel; already the Arabs were initiating armed clashes with Jewish defense organizations and the British army. The British realized it was impossible to appease both Jew and Arab. The United Nations formulated several partition plans, not one of which was acceptable to the Arabs. In fact, the Arabs vowed that their armies would occupy all of Palestine. Every Arab state sought to prevent the establishment of a Jewish state in the Middle East.

The United Nations partitioned the State of Israel out of Palestine on May 14, 1948. On that day Pres. Harry Truman recognized Israel. Joseph Stalin of the Soviet Union recognized it three days later. Recognition was headline news in New York City. The garment industry closed and people cheered the New York *Times* newsboard. New York congressmen rushed home to their constituencies to help celebrate. On the next day the Arabs invaded. The war lasted almost two years.

With the invasion, more than two million Arabs fled Israel, most of them being settled in Gaza, a flat hot desert. At the same time more than half a million Jews left their homes in Arab countries and migrated to Israel. But neither Israeli nor Arab has ever come near a solution that might provide some kind of life for the refugees in Gaza and Jordan.

It is important to remember that 250,000 Arabs remained in Israel in May of 1948. Collectively they are the most prosperous Arabs in the world, in terms of infant mortality rates, life expectancy and individual income. Over 200,000 of them own their own farms. They have been taught the agricultural techniques used by the Israelis, with the result that the Arab farms have increased their productivity sixfold in fifteen years. The government has undertaken a special five-year plan to give the Arab villages basic services, up-to-date sanitation, new waterworks, schools and public buildings. Each Arab village has its own mosque, supported—like the synagogues and churches—by the Israeli government.

Haifa is the magnet for Arab labor. There are already 10,000 Arabs there, and more join them daily. The wages are good, the rent cheap. Only the Arabs of Lebanon have a higher standard of living.

At Hebrew University, the trustees have established a chair in Arabic Studies. Each year the Israeli government imports thousands of copies of the Koran from Turkey, which it distributes to the Muslims within its borders. Israel has every intention of preserving the Arabic language, thought, religion and traditions.

The country has no less than 1,000 clinics, 135 hospitals, 650 mother-and-child health centers. For the population of 2,660,000 there are some 5,000 doctors, one for every 420 inhabitants, by far the highest ratio in the world. For the Arabs in Israel this means the highest life expectancy in the Arab-speaking world. Israel is free from the ravaging epidemics of its neighbors—malaria, typhus, typhoid, tuberculosis. An elaborate network of medical facilities has kept the Jewish population in remarkably good health. The nation's youth, most of them toughened by army service, are in demonstrably better physical condition than the great majority of American teen-agers; this in Israel, a Middle Eastern country heretofore filled with peoples to whom death always comes early. The Syrian child does not bother to wave the flies from his face. The Jordanian child has never brushed his teeth. More Egyptian children die in birth than live. Surrounded by semi-invalidism, the Jewish republic is more than an outpost of democracy on the rim of Asia. It is because its economy and the health and welfare of its people continually improve that Israel becomes important to the stability of the Middle East, and to the world.

The troubled spots of the world are the underdeveloped areas: the Congo, Nigeria, the Far East, the American slums. Call them, as does our State Department, "underdevelopia"—we know that these are the areas that can throw this globe into a convulsion. The way to calm these trouble spots is simple enough: teach each population to develop its own resources—but implementing this is indeed difficult. It is for these underdeveloped areas that the United States and the Soviet Union compete, because the developed countries can choose their own sides.

Israel no longer belongs in underdevelopia. It has a near self-sustaining economy. It is the only formerly underdeveloped country that has managed this within a generation. To be sure, it has received large amounts of aid from outside, but some of the other underdeveloped countries have had larger transfusions of American dollars and Soviet rubles and have managed to accomplish nothing.

Twenty-five years ago, it was impossible to imagine that there could be an Israel in the Middle East. Today it is impossible to imagine what the Middle East would be without Israel. That is another way of estimating Israel's importance to the world. None of us, however, has to estimate Israel's importance to Jews.

There is no doubt that Israel owes a great deal to American Jews. American Jews planted the trees that now flourish on the steep and rocky hillsides. The American Hadassahs, the Organization for Rehabilitation and Training, all the fraternal organizations, helped found the hospitals and welfare clinics. The United Jewish Appeal has funneled millions of dollars into the Israeli economy, all charitably donated.

The real question is how much do American Jews owe Israel? American Jews can never repay Israel for what the Israelis have given them—a sense of belonging. Israel has cured the blight of homelessness that plagued post-Biblical Jews in all times and places. Before Israel the American Jew had Poland or Russia or Germany—some nation in which his ancestors felt alien and in almost every way he felt alien too. Now the Jew has Israel—and the Israelis are fighters. The Jew owes his political allegiance to America, and will fight to the death, as many American Jews have done, for its preservation. To Israel he can pledge his senti- mental allegiance. The old stereotype of the Jew as a business man, a merchant, a capitalistic prince may still be partly accurate, but somewhere else in the world Jews farm land, irrigate deserts, harvest fruit, build roads, drain swamps and even assemble a plant to distill fresh water from the sea. And every Jew realizes that Israel saved his brethren. "I am a Jew." These four words are spoken in the United States without self-consciousness or hesitancy, and therein lies the miracle of Israel's contribution to the American Jew.

After World War II, Europe, with the exception of Russia, England and France, was a continent of refugees. Among these were the homeless, disen- franchised, hopeless Jews, the remnants of the Nazi holocaust, which claimed 6,000,000 of them. The healthy members of the world community have stringent laws dictating who may and who may not immigrate. In Australia, in America, in Canada, no one with trachoma is allowed to enter, and no one who is the object of charity. These are minimum requirements, sensible enough, necessary enough. But Israel established a new concept in human relations. "Bring us the stretcher cases first," they said. "Bring us the blind, the lame, the halt, the wretched, the poor. The healthy can come later." The minimum requirement to immigrate into Israel is the declaration, "I am a Jew." The immigrant needs no papers, no testi- monials, no affidavits signed by rabbis, no religious test. Here, for the first time, immigrants may come into a country where they are not punctured with needles or forced to display their teeth.

Israel is also an anomaly among nations. It is the one country whose people move not from the farms to the cities but from the cities to the farms, or rather to the kibbutzim.

Eleanor Roosevelt said that the kibbutz was the greatest example of man's freedom. Living there means living on the principle of all for one and one for all. A kibbutz is a farm, modest by American standards. Some cover 100 acres, some 200, some 300, perhaps a few are larger. Each is equipped with the apparatus of any modern farm—tractors, milking machines, cows, aluminum silos—and little cottages, for the residents. As a family increases, it moves into larger quarters. When a son goes to Tel Aviv to become a journalist, the parents move into a smaller cottage.

Many of the kibbutzim have begun winter industries to work at when the farming season is over. For example the farmers of Ein Hashofet, a kibbutz near the Lebanese border, sell bolts and nails, manufactured in winter, to Bulgaria and Turkey. Another kibbutz reconditions motors.

The kibbutz is now an integral part of the character of Israel, just as a Pittsburgh steel factory or a Ford motor plant is part of the character of America. The kibbutz exemplifies the direction the country has elected, a direction that is probably irreversible.

Moshe Barzalai, a friend of mine in Ein Hashofet, told me he came there from Brooklyn in the 1930's. The one thing he gave up, he says, was his chance to become a millionaire. He exchanged this opportunity for total security. In return for his work, he gets his eyeglasses and yearly physical, his clothes, his housing, education for his children, two weeks' vacation, and his own library for the rest of his life. Back in Brooklyn, Moshe was pretty sure he wasn't going to become a millionaire. He was driving a cab, and it seemed he would always be driving a cab. Today he chops the beaks off chickens lest they peck each other to death. He is an expert egg candler. He is also a good soldier, belonging to the citizen army of Israel.

The Israelis come in all shapes and sizes. In the same kibbutz I met one of those hardy Israeli women soldiers. She carried a flashlight and a Sten gun, and around her shoulders was strung a bandolier. She was a patriotic, loyal citizen, unafraid of the hazards of the border, and what she wanted most of all was to marry an American millionaire.

I ventured once into the orthodox quarter of Jerusalem, Mea Shearim. There are signs there that warn: "Women of Israel: do not come here unless you are fully clothed." In accordance with Biblical injunction the men of Mea Shearim wear beards, forelocks and side curls; the women shave their heads when they marry and wear black stockings lest their beauty distract the husband from his Talmudic studies. These ultra-orthodox Jews think political Zionism futile, believing that Palestine will be restored only after the Messiah comes. They oppose voting. I went into a *shenk* (saloon) to hear these arguments. I bought everybody brandy. I got into an argument with an elderly gentleman about his refusal to vote.

He said, "Palestine is ours only when the Messiah comes."

"How do you know Ben-Gurion isn't the Messiah?" I asked.

"Because he didn't come on a white donkey," the old gent replied. "It says in the Book he will come on a white donkey."

In Tel Aviv I got into a long conversation with a cab driver, Bajalel Katz. Bajalel told me of his difficulties as a young student in Germany and Austria. Everyone made fun of his name. He complained to his father. The father said, "Your name is Bajalel. Bajalel you will live, Bajalel you will die." His fellow students gave him no rest.

"Then I came to Israel," he said. "When the immigration official asked me my name I said, 'Bajalel Katz.' The fellow never even looked up. I knew I was home."

Salvation comes from the Jews. It is a profound truth too often forgotten. To many millions of men today, as it was centuries ago, salvation lies in the belief that we are all children of the same primeval parents and therefore brothers; that we are all creatures of an omnipotent, all-bountiful God Who created the world and Who rules over us and guides our destiny: that we possess an immortal soul destined for eternity. This belief descended from the Jews, expressed first by Jewish prophets, and it was in the language of the Jews that these words first resounded throughout the world to millions and millions of men, be they Jews, Christians or Muslims. This belief has consoled and fortified humanity in its suffering. Salvation dries the tears of widows and of orphans, alleviates the pain of the sick, heartens men in the hour of death and saves them from despair. Israel guards this belief, preserves it.

5

Social
Differentiation:
Castes, Classes,
and Other
Strata

Now, said I, can we devise something in
the way of those convenient fictions we
spoke of earlier, a single bold flight of
invention, which may induce the community in general, and if possible the
Rulers themselves, to accept?

What kind of fiction?

Nothing new; something like an
Eastern tale of what, according to the
poets, has happened before now in more
than one part of the world. The poets
have been believed; but the thing has
not happened in our day, and it would
be hard to persuade anyone that it could
ever happen again. . . . We shall tell our
people in this fable, that all of you in
this land are brothers; but the god who
fashioned you mixed gold in the composition of those among you who are fit
to rule, so that they are of the most
precious quality; and he put silver in the
Auxiliaries, and iron and brass in the
farmers and craftsmen. Now, since you
are all of one stock, although your
children will generally be like their
parents, sometimes a golden parent may
have a silver child or a silver parent a
golden one, and so on with all the
other combinations. So the first and

chief injunction laid by heaven upon the Rulers is that, among all the things of which they must show themselves good guardians, there is none that needs to be so carefully watched as the mixture of metals in the souls of the children. If a child of their own is born with an alloy of iron or brass, they must, without the smallest pity, assign him the station proper to his nature and thrust him out among the craftsmen or the farmers. If, on the contrary, these classes produce a child with gold or silver in his composition, they will promote him, according to his value, to be a Guardian or an Auxiliary. They will appeal to a prophecy that ruin will come upon the state when it passes into the keeping of a man of iron or brass. Such is the story; can you think of any device to make them believe it?

Not in the first generation; but their sons and descendants might believe it, and finally the rest of mankind.

—Plato, *The Republic*
(Cornford, 1945, pp. 106–107

Riding through the mountains one sometimes comes upon a place where the road has cut into a hillside and left bare the outlines of many strata. There exposed is a mantle of old decayed forest greenery underlain by distorted rock strata, all reflecting a geological past of accumulations and pressures. Human societies are somewhat like that—or so it once must have been thought—for the concept of social stratification comes from geology.

Some societies are comprised of distinct peoples which can be ranked in terms of wealth, power, and prestige. The Union of South Africa with its white, coloured, Bantu, and Indian peoples is a good example of such an arrangement. The groups are self-aware and unequal. Other societies do not have such distinct social groupings. They have inequalities of wealth, power, and prestige, to be sure, but the arrangements are more like a geological formation that gradually shades from rock layers at the bottom to the upper soil residuum. Brazilian society has these characteristics; the boundaries among groups are not nearly as sharp as those in the Union of South Africa.

When there are no sharp boundaries among the units of a society, some social scientists question whether or not the word *stratified* should be used. In fact, a few (Wrong, 1964) avoid using the concept entirely when they discuss social inequalities unless the society they are studying comprises distinct, self-conscious classes or groups. Geologists, incidentally, use the term *stratified* in all instances in which there are differences in composition, color or texture, between adjacent units in a sequence. They distinguish the degree or type of stratification that is present. A particular sequence might thus be composed of either "sharply bounded" units or "gradational" units.

A geological analogy can be misleading if we think only of structure and not of process. Actually, stratification in geology is a process, albeit usually a slow one. A bulldozer that cuts down through the outer layer of earth exposes an evolutionary record that can be understood by a skilled geologist. He sees a structure, but the structure implies processes of formation, disruption, and disintegration.

The same is true of societies. Social aggregates are formed, then become self-conscious and self-seeking. At times revolutions or natural disasters modify earlier social configurations in a manner analagous to mountain-building upheavals. Then, too, societal conditions sometimes cause group boundaries to become blurred and indistinct, as in geology when metamorphic rock is formed deep beneath the earth's crust.

Caste and Class

The title of John Dollard's famous study *Caste and Class in a Southern Town* is a convenient starting point for a discussion of social stratification. By means of the concepts caste and class Dollard described the social configurations of a particular town in the South (Indianola, Mississippi, called Southerntown). There were two castes, Black and White. The castes were in turn comprised of several socioeconomic divisions, which Dollard called "classes."

This analytical approach won widespread acceptance in social science, and it became popular to describe intergroup relations in the United States and elsewhere in terms of caste and class. Some scholars, however, vigorously oppose this general use of the concepts. Oliver Cox (1948), for one, has insisted that castes, in the real sense of the word, are found only in societies like India, not in the United States.

Today social scientists tend to avoid this controversy and to put the question a different way. Instead of asking whether or not there are castes in the United States, they ask, "How caste-like is our social system?" That, it seems, is a logical way to proceed.[1]

---

[1] See Lenski (1966) on this point. This chapter draws heavily on Lenski's excellent discussion of stratification as a process. I am particularly grateful for his comments on this chapter.

The caste system of India has been written about at great length. (Several studies are listed at the end of this chapter.) The system, according to Mason Olcott (1944), has five essential features:

1. *Endogamy.* Caste members are required to marry within their castes and within their subcastes.
2. *Religious sanctions.* "To be a good Hindu a man may believe anything or nothing but he must fulfill his caste obligations" (Olcott, 1944, p. 648). The entire caste system is rooted in the ancient Hindu religion.
3. *Hierarchy based on birth and reincarnation.* Of the major divisions—Brahmans (priests and teachers), Kshatriayas (secular rulers and warriors), Vaisyas (merchants and farmers), and Sudras (servants)—only the Brahmans have reached the pinnacle of perfection. If a person is born a lowly Sudra, he may be reborn in a higher caste in the next life as a result of duty and service, devotion, and knowledge in this life. If an individual violates caste obligations, he may be punished by being reborn in the next life as a beast or even as an insect.

    The original caste divisions have proliferated so that literally thousands of subcastes exist throughout India. Only a few castes or subcastes will be represented in one particular village, however.
4. *Socioeconomic interdependence.* Even were an individual to reject the caste system, he would find it difficult to break the tight network of dependencies and expectations, especially in the rural areas and in the small towns. A person born into a carpenter's family, for example, is expected to become a carpenter. He, in fact, inherits a clientele made up of customers whose families have depended upon his family for carpentry services through several generations.
5. *The outcaste substratum.* In 1931 an estimated 40–70 million persons categorized as outcastes, depressed classes, and untouchables were forbidden to use schools, temples, hotels, theaters, and even tax-supported roads. They were mainly descended from ancient peoples that had inhabited India before invasion by Mediterranean and Aryan-speaking peoples. Today, it is unlawful to discriminate against peoples from these groups, but old customs persist, especially in remote villages.

How similar is the caste system of India to intergroup relations in the United States? At the time when Dollard wrote about Southerntown, it was quite similar. The Black-White divisions that he described, like castes in India, were endogamous. True, there were sexual relations between Blacks and Whites in Southerntown and probably between members of different castes in India too, but there were essentially no marriages.[2] The laws and the mores saw to that. Religion and

---

[2] Marriages across caste lines are mentioned in ancient Indian scriptures like the *Puranas* and *Dharamshastras*, but they seem to have been the exception, rather than the rule. Apparently such marriages did not usually carry positive social sanctions.

the mores sanctioned the system—at least in Mississippi in the 1930s and certainly in India at the time. Both systems were eventually challenged on moral and religious grounds. The fight against segregation in the United States was to be endorsed by clergymen and led by a minister, Rev. Martin Luther King, Jr. In India the untouchables and other "scheduled castes and tribes" were also befriended by a religious man, Mohandas Gandhi. Gandhi did not challenge the caste system per se, but he did oppose discriminatory practices against untouchables.

Other similarities were apparent, especially in the 1930s. Blacks, like the outcastes of India, were barred from a great many public and private facilities like restaurants, theaters, hotels, schools, and hospitals. In India social distance was maintained between Brahman and untouchable to the extent that an untouchable's very shadow passing over a Brahman rendered him ritually unclean. Social distance between Blacks and Whites never became that wide or ritually enforced, but it was commonly believed in the United States that Blacks should not use white restrooms, drinking fountains, eating utensils, and so on. Belief in reincarnation gave lower-caste Indians hope for betterment in the next life. In the United States also, organized religion tended to emphasize heavenly rewards in preference to earthly ones. An Indian was assigned his occupation by means of caste. That was perhaps not as strictly true of the Black-White division in the 1930s, as it was of Indian society. But group typing of occupations was certainly a fact of life when Dollard wrote, and it still is.

Each caste in Southerntown had its class divisions. It is customary in social science, following Max Weber, to make a distinction among *class, status,* and *party* (or power). A person's *party* reflects affiliations made in order to further his interests. *Status* refers to prestige, not so much individual prestige as the prestige associated with a particular position. An individual's *class* determines his economic and material opportunities. In a modern society, class is usually based upon occupation (Eisenstadt, 1971, p. 81).

An individual who is ranked high by one set of criteria may also be ranked high on the other two. A ruling group with great power tends also to be a privileged group economically. Power and wealth tend to give rise to a life style that is prestigious. But not always. A person or group may have much wealth but little prestige or power. (The concepts used to describe these phenomena are "status congruence" and "status incongruence.") In Southerntown there was status congruence: middle- and upper-class whites had wealth, power, and prestige. To a considerable extent, this congruence still exists today.[3] Nor are such arrangements restricted to small towns in the South, though there it has been more obvious and more institutionalized (see Knowles and Prewitt, 1969).

[3] A number of students who were reared in small towns of the Deep South have commented, upon reading Dollard's book, that his four-decade-old account is remarkably accurate today.

The Basis of Ethnic and Racial Stratification

Some writers hold that a system of ethnic or racial stratification depends upon three essential conditions: ethnocentrism, competition, and differential power (Noel, 1968, pp. 157–172). These variables seem to have been important in the development of the slave trade in the seventeenth-century English colonies. This observation also squares with evidence that Fredrik Barth (1969) has cited from Western Sudan and Afghanistan to the effect that stratification occurs when one group controls the means of production used by another group. But, when groups use different niches or have access to them independently of one another, stratification often does not occur. In Southerntown, to return to Dollard's study, Whites were ethnocentric (Dollard has an entire chapter on "defensive beliefs"); they competed with Blacks for scarce goods and services, and they had power.

The emphasis upon differential power, and especially on conflict, in many interpretations of stratification needs some qualification. "Only after repeated unsuccessful attempts to apply this interpretation universally to ethnic relations throughout the world," R. A. Schermerhorn has written, "have I been driven to the conclusion that the framework is insufficient" (1970, p. 53). Instead he has turned to a more dialectical view, one in which conflict and order are seen as complementary. He reports that his thinking was influenced by reports, especially from Africa, in which conflicts between groups with unequal power produced new integrative relationships that had system characteristics.

It should be remembered that stratification is a process—a process in which privilege, power, and prestige are distributed unequally (Lenski, 1966). Under certain circumstances the process results in rigidly segregated endogamous groups, which may persist as identifiable units of the population over long periods of time. These units are the castes. The distribution process also may produce self-conscious groups with similar economic interests that cut across caste divisions. These units are the classes. At given times units with differential power may be formed and may even cut across class and caste lines. They are parties. Finally, the distribution process may result in a continuum of unequal statuses in which class or caste lines are blurred and indistinct (Wrong, 1964). In the United States the distinction between the very rich (upper-uppers) and the very poor (lower-lowers) is conspicuous and distinct, but between these extremes the divisions are less sharply defined. Stratification in the United States, to take a term from geology, tends to be gradational, rather than sharply bounded.

We should not receive the impression from this discussion that ethnic differentiation is more important than economic differentiation. Economic considerations often lead to the original setting apart from a group that then gradually becomes caste-like. Economic factors also help perpetuate caste distinctions.

Valid and reliable measures of social class, or "socioeconomic status" (SES), are not easy to come by. In order to obtain approximate measures, social scientists customarily use a respondent's income, occupation, and formal educational attainment as basic indicators of SES. A great many studies using these indicators show general similarities among individuals of the same SES, even though these individuals belong to different racial or ethnic groups. Studies that show significant differences among racial and ethnic groups on variables like crime statistics, mortality rates, illegitimacy rates, career aspirations, and political preferences also report that the differences are minimal or disappear when the researcher uses SES as a control variable.

Some groups develop distinctive value orientations and life styles, to the point that some researchers say that these groups have "subcultures" or even "cultures." Still, numerous studies of a wide range of behavior suggest that SES "explains" as much or more of the variation than does group membership. The behavior and value orientations of middle-class Japanese in the United States, for example, are remarkably similar to those of middle-class Whites. Japanese-Americans—in George Kobayashi's words—have "outwhited the whites." The same observation has been made of middle-class Blacks whose mode of individual adaptation has tended to be scrupulous conformity. General similarities between minority and majority members of lower SES and upper SES are known to exist as well. Not that lower-class Blacks identify with lower-class Whites more than they do with other classes of Blacks. Historical circumstances have been such that, despite similarities between Blacks and Whites of the same social class, the life chances of individuals and their identities have been linked with their respective groups. Black and White individuals of the same social class have characteristics in common, but, as Andrew Billingsley (1968) has correctly noted, they do not share the same sense of "peoplehood."

The distribution of wealth and power in a society determines the class composition within a particular group of that society. If discrimination against a particular group is extreme, that group's upper class will tend to be small or even nonexistent and its lower strata relatively large. This distribution has been common among many minorities.

Specific class configurations vary from community to community and from region to region. Nationwide, Billingsley (1968) estimates that about 10 percent of Black families can be considered of the upper class in the sense that they are well educated, earn high incomes, have secure occupational careers, and live in comfortable surroundings. The upper class is comprised of two categories—old wealth and new. Billingsley estimates the middle class to be about 40 percent of the Black population. It is subdivided into the upper middle class, the "solid middle class," and the "precarious middle class." (The most exhaustive studies of the middle class are those of E. Franklin Frazier.) The lower classes represent, in Billingsley's estimate, about 50 percent of the Black population. He subdivides this category into the "working nonpoor," the "working poor," and the "nonworking poor." Working nonpoor families are headed by persons who have secure, usually semiskilled jobs. The working poor families have heads who work in unskilled and service occupations and receive marginal incomes. It is the largest category of lower-class families. The nonworking poor represent about 12 percent of all Black families and are the category that has contributed disproportionately to the stereotypes that many majority-group individuals hold. Those who make up this category are unemployed or intermittently employed and supported by relatives or by welfare (Billingsley, 1968).

Other Strata and Divisions

Cleavages often run deep within the minority group itself, a fact sometimes overlooked by the casual observer. It seems that members of a group can always find ways to create an out-group, even if it must be formed within the group itself. Ridding a geographical area of one particular out-group thus does not necessarily eliminate conflict or stop social differentiation from occurring. In Haiti practically all the whites were driven out or killed in a revolution that occurred in 1791, and those who survived were forbidden to own land. Their absence, however, left the Blacks and the Coloreds locked in a rivalry that has grown fiercer through the years (Lowenthall, 1968, p. 335).

Color

Haiti is only one of many places where differentiation within groups is based on shadings of skin color. Among some Blacks in the United States this kind of distinction still lingers as a kind of "contemporary status symbol" that is important in the choice of a marriage partner, in certain occupations and club memberships, and so on (Freeman, 1966, 365–374). Malcolm X, recalling his childhood, has declared: "Most Negro parents in those days would almost instinctively treat any lighter children better than they did the darker one. It came directly from the slavery tradition that the 'mulatto,' because he was visibly nearer to white, was therefore 'better'" (quoted in Haley, 1966, p. 4). Actually, this type of discrimination has a double edge, so that those with relatively light skins, as well as those with dark skins, are sometimes stigmatized.

In India members of higher castes within a particular region generally have lighter skins than do members of lower castes. In northern India, however, members of lower castes often are lighter-skinned than are higher-caste individuals from southern India. Skin color is still a consideration in contemporary India, as is evident by a characteristic of big-city newspapers, which carry marriage advertisements in the personal-announcement columns. These announcements typically include mention of skin color.

Brazilians, who are widely extolled for their tolerance, nonetheless manifest considerable sensitivity to shadings of color. They too have developed a nomenclature to designate varying combinations of skin colors, facial features, and hair textures. The more common terms are *branco, branco do Bahia, cabra, cobo verde, mameluco, caboré, mazombo, muleque, moreno, mina, preto, pardo, caboclo, mulato, preto retinto, escuro,* and several others. These words do not usually describe well-defined groups, however, and their usage varies from region to region (Van den Berghe, 1967, p. 71).

Religion

In many instances religion divides minority groups from the larger society. If the group is composed of immigrants, some members may convert to the major religion of the host society, a process usually accelerated whenever marriages between the two groups begin to occur. Schisms within the minority group's own religious structure also occur. Even though American minorities tend to be either predominantly Protestant or Roman Catholic, subdivisions and other distinctions within denominations are present. These subdivisions usually reflect social-class distinctions and life styles, but they sometimes convey intergroup nuances as well. One of my students, himself a member of an African Methodist Episcopal church (A.M.E.) in a metropolitan area, has reported that some Black churches are labeled "White" by some Black nonmembers. They tend to be upper-class or upper-middle-class churches, with formal services and elaborate rituals, and they do not encourage the uninhibited expression of religious feelings that is permitted in other churches even of the same denomination (see also Rohrer and Edmonson, 1964, pp. 32–34).

In India conversions from Hinduism to Buddhism by lower-caste Indians have been increasing in recent years. Since the 1950s it is estimated that as many as 2 million untouchables have converted to Buddhism, which, unlike Hinduism, is casteless and emphasizes the present life, rather than the hereafter. Two villagers who in 1973 made the trip to New Delhi to take their vows as Buddhists made these comments:

> "One leaves the village as an untouchable cobbler and returns to the same village with the same people as a touchable Buddhist."
> "Maybe life will not change for me. But I will *feel* equal." ("The Touchables," *Newsweek,* 1973, p. 88)

On an American Indian reservation an individual may give allegiance, or at least lip service, to his own native religion, as well as to a Christian denomina-

Religious festival in Cochiti Pueblo, N. M. Elements of tribal religion and Catholicism are both present in the ceremonies.

tion. In Cochiti (pronounced kō' che tē') Pueblo, for instance, the residents participate in the ceremonies of both the native religion and the Roman Catholic church. Even though certain rituals combine features of both religions—instances of religious syncretism—there are still deeply felt religious differences in the community.

Age

Age differences figure in the organization of all human societies, but they frequently take on added importance within minority groups. Among immigrant populations, members of the first generation and those of the second and third generations may cope with the world in strikingly different ways. The author's own interviews in 1962 with second- and third-generation Italians in New Orleans highlighted a generation gap on such matters as dating practices, "proper" relations between the sexes, participation in Italian clubs and fraternities, and attitudes toward debt and religion. At the time of the study, extended family ties and a sense of ethnicity were still viable forces in community life.

Politics

Differences within the minority group along the political dimension may run no deeper than individual alignments with particular major political parties. Fierce debates, however, often rage within a minority group about how the group can best cope with its problems. These conflicts may lead to bitter internecine strife and to the formation of splinter groups organized as conservatives, moderates, gradualists, or militants. This pattern has characterized American Indians. Rarely have they been able to surmount old tribal identifications to form viable political organizations. Some ethnic groups like the Irish in the United States have, however, been able to close ranks and to become powerful political forces in certain locales. This general characteristic of minorities is discussed further in Chapter 7.

Old Residents and Recent Immigrants

Whenever a minority group migrates to one geographical area over a comparatively long period of time, differences may develop between new arrivals and older residents within the group. This pattern has been observed in northern and western cities of the United States, where older Black residents have viewed with contempt and apprehension the more recent arrivals from the rural South. Claude Brown recalls how, as a Harlem youngster, he welcomed a visiting relative from Dixie.

> I had realized that this was just another one of those old crazy-acting, funny-dressing, no-talking people from down South. As I stood on the other side of the room looking at her, I was wondering if all the people down South were crazy like that. I knew one thing—I had never seen anybody from down there who looked or acted as if they had some sense. Damn, that was one place I never wanted to go to. It was probably eating corn bread and biscuits all the time that made those people act like that. (1965, p. 38)

The history of Jewish immigration to the United States affords an example of the differences that can exist within a single ethnic group. Those who immigrated in colonial times, according to a study by Mannheim Shapiro (1963, pp. 97, 98), were mainly descended from Jews who had originally lived in Spain and Portugal (Sephardic Jews) and who had been forced to leave those countries in 1492. The lives of these people revolved largely around the synagogues, where they could worship with their brethren and obtain help when needed. By contrast, Jewish immigrants from the German-speaking countries during the first half of the nineteenth century were accustomed to mingling freely and to speaking the languages of their Gentile neighbors. They tended to look upon themselves as part of the total community. "Discrimination against them was virtually unknown" (Shapiro, 1963, p. 98). The immigrants who came from Germanic countries from the mid-nineteenth century on usually came as families, rather than as individuals. They were likely to settle in the same towns, form various Jewish organizations, and participate in the development of community life. In the late nineteenth and twentieth centuries thousands of immigrants came from eastern Europe and Russia. They brought with them the ideologies, group loyalties, and attitudes that were common among east European Jews, various types of Zionism, and Yiddish literature and folklore. Many of these newcomers were very poor and very unconventional; consequently, they were a source of embarrassment to the older, established Jewish community (Shapiro, 1963, pp. 97, 98).

Chinese-American communities have similar divisions. The relaxation of immigration barriers in 1965 led to an influx from Taiwan, Hong Kong, and Macao. Those who were fresh off the boat (F.O.B.s) tended to be young, unskilled, without family connections, and unable to speak English fluently. Most of the jobs open to them paid poorly and were controlled by American-born Chinese (A.B.C.) family associations called "tongs." This Chinatown conflict has erupted into gang warfare and has claimed several victims in San Francisco and New York ("The Gangs of Chinatown," *Newsweek*, 1973, p. 22).

Overview

A slogan from Orwell's *Animal Farm*—"Some are more equal than others"—tells a great deal about social existence. An enormous amount of human energy has been devoted to establishing various kinds of hierarchies and trying to keep people satisfied with the resulting arrangements. In some societies the hierarchies and inequalities are more obvious and more resistant to change than in others. Drawing an analogy from geology, we can say that some societies have sharply bounded strata, whereas others are gradational. Various aggregates, arranged in terms of their degree of "equality," are called "castes" and "classes" by social scientists. A system of racial and ethnic stratification seems to require at least three essential factors: ethnocentrism, competition, and differential power.

Many societies have caste-like characteristics similar to those of the stratification system that has existed in India. The basic features of that caste system are endogamy, religious sanctions, a hierarchy based upon birth and reincarnation, socioeconomic interdependence, and an outcaste substratum.

The framework of caste and class has gained widespread acceptance as a useful way to describe intergroup relations in the United States. The two castes— Black and White—have their own respective classes. A person's class denotes his or her economic and material opportunities; status denotes the prestige he or she possesses, usually by virtue of some position that he or she occupies in the society. In modern nations like the United States, an individual's class, or socioeconomic status (often designated as SES) is usually determined by occupation.

Social scientists who study intergroup relations have given considerable attention to "status congruence," that is, the degree to which powerful groups and individuals also have wealth and prestige. In Southerntown, the site of Dollard's famous study, there was a considerable degree of status congruence: upper-class Whites had prestige, wealth, and power.

Ethnic and racial groups have other internal divisions in addition to their social classes. They often include skin color, religion, politics, and distinctions based on length of residence and age.

For Further Reading

Many of the items among the references cited may be considered as recommended reading as well.

Dollard, John. *Caste and Class in a Southern Town.* New Haven: Yale University Press, 1957.

Frazier, E. Franklin. *Black Bourgeoisie: The Rise of a New Middle Class.* New York: Free Press, 1957.

Ghurye, G. S. *Caste and Class in India.* Bombay: Popular Book Depot, 1957.

Hutton, J. H. *Caste in India.* New York: Oxford University Press, 1963.

Lenski, Gerhard E. *Power and Privilege: A Theory of Social Stratification.* New York: McGraw-Hill, 1966.

de Reuck, Anthony, and Julie Knight. *Caste and Race: Comparative Approaches.* Boston: Little, Brown, 1967.

Rohrer, John H., and Munro S. Edmonson *et al.* *The Eighth Generation Grows Up: Cultures and Personalities of New Orleans Negroes.* New York: Harper & Row, 1960.

Shibuntani, Tamotsu, and Kian M. Kwan. *Ethnic Stratification: A Comparative Approach.* New York: Macmillan, 1967.

Van den Berghe, Pierre. *Race and Racism: A Comparative Perspective.* New York: Wiley, 1967.

THE CODE OF ALABAMA

Intermarriage between Blacks and Whites in the United States has not been left to chance or the decisions of individuals. Instead, laws in many states have strictly forbidden such marriages. Gunnar Myrdal reported eighteen southern and border states with laws prohibiting intermarriage (1962, p. 1072).

In 1967 the State of Virginia's miscegenation laws were ruled unconstitutional by the U.S. Supreme Court. On the basis of that decision, Alabama's laws were ruled in violation of the Fourteenth Amendment of the U.S. Constitution.

The following selection from **The Code of Alabama** is representative of similar laws in other states. The particular publication from which it is excerpted is prepared primarily for the general use of the courts and the legal profession. The selection contains the text of the law itself, as well as summaries of prior decisions on relevant questions.

Miscegenation

Sec. 360. Marriage, adultery, and fornication between white persons and negroes.
Sec. 361. Officer issuing license or performing marriage ceremony.

360. Marriage, adultery, and fornication between white persons and negroes.—If any white person and any negro, or the descendant of any negro intermarry, or live in adultery or fornication with each other, each of them shall, on conviction, be imprisoned in the penitentiary for not less than two nor more than seven years. (1927, p. 219.)

Editor's note.—This section was amended by Acts 1927, p. 219. Prior to this amendment only persons descendant from negroes through the third generation were classed as negroes, but now one drop of negro blood seems to be sufficient to create the offense of miscegenation, when there is marriage, adultery or fornication.

For case decided prior to the amendment of 1927, concerning marriage of octoroon with white person, see Weaver v. State, 22 Ala. App. 469, 116 So. 893.

History of section.—See Jackson v. State, 37 Ala. App. 519, 72 So. (2d) 114.

Strict construction.—This section is of course penal in nature. Likewise § 2 of Title 1, defining "negro," is in derogation of the common law. Both statutes must therefore be strictly construed, and neither, under elemental rules of statutory construction can be broadened by analogical extension. Agnew v. State, 36 Ala. App. 205, 54 So. (2d) 89.

This section manifests a public policy to prevent race amalgamation and to safeguard the racial integrity of white and negro peoples. Dees v. Metts, 245 245 Ala. 370, 17 So. (2d) 137.

And does not violate 5th or 14th amendment.—See Jackson v. State, 37 Ala. App. 519, 72 So. (2d) 114. . . .

The offense is a felony.—Under this section the offense of miscegenation, being punishable by imprisonment in penitentiary, is a felony. Williams v. State, 24 Ala. App. 262, 134 So. 34.

The punishment does not constitute an unconstitutional discrimination.—The fact that the punishment affixed to the offense of living in adultery or fornication, when committed by a white person and a negro together, is different from that affixed to that offense when committed by two white persons or two negroes, is not a discrimination in favor of or against either race, and is not violative of the 14th Amendment of the Federal Constitution. Pace v. State, 69 Ala. 231, 44 Am. Rep. 513.

Statute applies to person who is part Indian.—The contention that a person who is part Indian should be considered as of the Indian race, and therefore not subject to the operation of the miscegenation statute, is without merit. Agnew v. State, 36 Ala. App. 205, 54 So. (2d) 89.

The elements are the same as in adultery and fornication with exception of racial feature.—With the exception of the racial feature, the constituent elements of miscengenation are the same as in ordinary cases of adultery and fornication. As has been often explained, the statute is directed against a state or condition of cohabitation which the parties intend to continue so long as they may choose, as distinguished from a single or occasional act of illicit sexual intercourse. Jones v. State, 156 Ala. 175, 47 So. 100, 101; Bailey v. State, 29 Ala. App. 161, 193 So. 871. . . .

Actual proof of intercourse is unnecessary.—The act of intercourse is not necessary to prove an offense denounced by this section; if the two persons are seen nude, in bed together and in each other's arms, that is sufficient proof of the corpus delicti to admit in evidence a confession made by one of the defendants. Jones v. State, 156 Ala. 175, 47 So. 100.

Both defendants charged with miscegenation are equally guilty or equally innocent. Jackson v. State, 23 Ala. App. 555, 129 So. 306. But, under this section a defendant is not entitled to discharge on habeas corpus while serving sentence for miscegenation, on ground that codefendant received lesser punishment. State v. Ham, 24 Ala. App. 147, 133 So. 60.

But acquittal of one is not necessarily acquittal of other.—But acquittal of one of two defendants on charge of miscegenation committed by them jointly does not necessarily work an acquittal of the other defendant. Bailey v. State, 29 Ala. App. 161, 193 So. 871.

The Bailey case, supra, overrules Reed v. State, 20 Ala. App. 496, 103 So. 97, wherein it was held that when two persons are jointly indicted for an offense denounced by this section one cannot be convicted and the other acquitted, as the acts constituting the offense must ex necessitate be joint and both are equally innocent or guilty.

Nor does conviction of one necessarily justify conviction of the other.—Gore v. State, 58 Ala. 391, cited in Bailey v. State, 29 Ala. App. 161, 193 So. 871.
The race of each offender must be proven.—To sustain a conviction under this section the evidence must show adultery, fornication or marriage, between persons of the white and negro race. The race of each offender must be established; proof that one of them is negro without proving the other to be white is not sufficient. The appearance of defendant as a witness in a trial for miscegenation is sufficient to authorize the finding that she is of the negro race. Metcalf v. State, 16 Ala. App. 389, 78 So. 305.

In prosecution for miscegenation, under this section, prior to amendment by Acts 1927, p. 219, witness was held competent to testify that man was negro or white man if he knew type and was not testifying to mere conclusion, but when there was admixture of white and negro races, witness was not competent to testify to his conclusion that man was negro within third degree. Weaver v. State, 22 Ala. App. 469, 116 So. 893.

Proof that defendant's grandfather had kinky hair, which is one of determining characteristics of negro, and questions involving nose and other features of grandfather were properly admitted. Weaver v. State, 22 Ala. App. 469, 116 So. 893.

But proof of man's race may be made by his admissions, either verbally or by conduct in associating with negroes, attending negro churches, sending children to negro schools, and otherwise voluntarily living on terms of social equality with them. Weaver v. State, 22 Ala. App. 469, 116 So. 893.

Living together in adultery for a single day is sufficient, though no agreement to continue sexual intercourse is established. Linton v. State, 88 Ala. 216, 7 So. 261.

But evidence merely disclosing single act of intercourse without intention to continue illicit relations was insufficient to establish offense of miscegenation. Jackson v. State, 23 Ala. App. 555, 129 So. 306.

The conviction of miscegenation cannot be had on testimony of accomplice, unless corroborated by other evidence tending to connect defendant with offense. Jackson v. State, 23 Ala. App. 555, 129 So. 306.

Statutory marriage.—Where there was no evidence that defendants lived together in fornication or adultery, and state in prosecution for miscegenation, under this section, relied solely on statutory marriage for conviction, instruction that if jury believed evidence it could not convict defendant for living in adultery or fornication held not error. Williams v. State, 23 Ala. App. 365, 125 So. 690.

Guilt of white man cannot be predicated on state of feeling between his wife and the other alleged particeps criminis.—Where defendant, a white man, and negro woman, who had been hired to attend the ill wife of defendant, were charged with miscegenation, testimony that upon the occasion of the moving of the negro woman into defendant's house the wife of defendant said in the woman's presence, "I don't want you to move her in," and that defendant said "I love her better than anything in the world and I have been going with her sixteen years," was inadmissible against defendant, since his guilt could not be predicated upon the state of feeling existing between his wife and the other alleged particeps criminis, and was inadmissible as "hearsay" as to the negro woman. Jordon v. State, 30 Ala. App. 313. 5 So. (2d) 110. . . .

Am. Jur. and ALR references.—36 Am. Jur., Miscegenation, § 1 et seq.

Criminal prosecution for seduction as affected by statute prohibiting marriage between persons of different races. 85 ALR 126.

Interracial bar as ground for attack on validity of marriage after death of party thereto. 47 ALR2d 1405.

361. Officer issuing license or performing marriage ceremony.—Any probate judge who issues a license for the marriage of any persons who are prohibited by section 360 of this title, from intermarrying, knowing that they are within the provisions of that section; and any justice of the peace, minister of the gospel, or other person by law authorized to solemnize the rites of matrimony, who performs a marriage ceremony for such persons, knowing that they are within the provisions of such section, shall each, on conviction, be fined not less than one hundred nor more than one thousand dollars, and may also be imprisoned in the county jail, or sentenced to hard labor for the county for not more than six months.

This section is not unconstitutional as violative of the 14th Amendment to Federal Constitution. Green v. State, 58 Ala. 190, 29 Am. Rep. 739, overruling Burns v. State, 48 Ala. 195, 17 Am. Rep. 34.

THE CODE OF ALABAMA

The following selection reflects basic changes that have occurred in the law since 1966.

Miscegenation

360. Marriage, adultery, and fornication between white persons and negroes.

Constitutionality.—There are still forty-four sections of the Alabama Code devoted to the maintenance of segregation in schools, public utilities, mental institutions, nursing, penal and correctional institutions, pauper care, and the marriage choice. All these statutes under decisions of the United States supreme court may now be unconstitutional. United States v. Alabama, 252 F. Supp. 95 (M.D. Ala. 1966).

This section is violative of the fourteenth amendment to the Constitution of this country. United States v. Britain, 319 F. Supp. 1058 (N.D. Ala. 1970).

361. Officer issuing license or performing marriage ceremony.

Constitutionality.—This section is violative of the fourteenth amendment to the Constitution of this country. United States v. Brittain, 319 F. Supp. 1058 (N.D. Ala. 1970).

Attorney general to advise of invalidity of this section.—The attorney general of the state of Alabama is required to advise the judges of probate of the several counties of Alabama of the invalidity of this section. United States v. Brittain, 319 F. Supp. 1058 (N.D. Ala. 1970).

FREE JOE AND THE REST OF THE WORLD

JOEL CHANDLER HARRIS

Joel Chandler Harris, the author of this selection, is best known for his Uncle Remus stories. Harris was himself a kind of outsider—the son of an immigrant and a Roman Catholic in a predominantly Protestant society. He was an acute observer, he listened well, and he criticized much of what he saw and heard, putting his comments in the speeches of unthreatening characters: Uncle Remus, Br'er Rabbit, Br'er Fox, and, in this selection, Micajah Staley and Free Joe. The author's use of regional dialects makes reading difficult in places, but it is worth working through his narrative to learn what he observed. "Free Joe" is important because it describes the irony of slavery, the social distance between the Black world and the White, the class distinctions within the two worlds, and the relations of Free Joe, first with his White master and later with poor Whites.

The problems of one generation are the paradoxes of a succeeding one, particularly if war, or some such incident, intervenes to clarify the atmosphere and strengthen the understanding. Thus, in 1850, Free Joe represented not only a problem of large concern, but, in the watchful eyes of Hillsborough, he was the embodiment of that vague and mysterious danger that seemed to be forever lurking on the outskirts of slavery, ready to sound a shrill and ghostly signal in the impenetrable swamps, and steal forth under the midnight stars to murder, rapine, and pillage,—a danger always threatening, and yet never assuming shape; intangible, and yet real; impossible, and yet not improbable. Across the serene and smiling front of safety, the pale outlines of the awful shadow of insurrection sometimes fell. With this invisible panorama as a background, it was natural that the figure of Free Joe, simple and humble as it was, should assume undue proportions. Go where he would, do what he might, he could not escape the finger of observation and the kindling eye of suspicion. His lightest words were noted, his slightest actions marked.

The name of Free Joe strikes humorously upon the ear of memory. It is impossible to say why, for he was the humblest, the simplest, and the most serious of all God's living creatures, sadly lacking in all those elements that suggest the humorous. It is certain, moreover, that in 1850 the sober-minded citizens of the little Georgian village of Hillsborough were not inclined to take a humorous view of Free Joe, and neither his name nor his presence provoked a smile. He was a black atom, drifting hither and thither without an owner, blown about by all the winds of circumstance, and given over to shiftlessness.

Under all the circumstances it was natural that his peculiar condition should reflect itself in his habits and manners. The slaves laughed loudly day by day, but Free Joe rarely laughed. The slaves sang at their work and danced at their frolics, but no one ever heard Free Joe sing or saw him dance. There was something painfully plaintive and appealing in his attitude, something touching in his anxiety to please. He was of the friendliest nature, and seemed to be delighted when he could amuse the little children who had made a playground of the public square. At times he would please them by making his little dog Dan perform all sorts of curious tricks, or he would tell them quaint stories of the beasts of the field and birds of the air; and frequently he was coaxed into relating the story of his own freedom. That story was brief, but tragical.

In the year of our Lord 1840, when a negro-speculator of a sportive turn of mind reached the little village of Hillsborough on his way to the Mississippi region, with a caravan of likely negroes of both sexes, he found much to interest him. In that day and at that time there were a number of young men in the village who had not bound themselves over to repentance for the various misdeeds of the flesh. To these young men the negro-speculator (Major Frampton was his name) proceeded to address himself. He was a Virginian, he declared; and, to prove the statement, he referred all the festively inclined young men of Hillsborough to a barrel of peach-brandy in one of his covered wagons. In the minds of these young men there was less doubt in regard to the age and quality of the brandy than there was in regard to the negro-trader's birthplace. Major Frampton might or might not have been born in the Old Dominion,—that was a matter for consideration and inquiry,—but there could be no question as to the mellow pungency of the peach-brandy.

In his own estimation, Major Frampton was one of the most accomplished of men. He had summered at the Virginia Springs; he had been to Philadelphia, to Washington, to Richmond, to Lynchburg, and to Charleston, and had accumulated a great deal of experience which he found useful. Hillsborough was hid in the woods of Middle Georgia, and its general aspect of innocence impressed him. He looked on the young men who had shown their readiness to test his peach-brandy, as overgrown country boys who needed to be introduced to some of the arts and sciences he had at his command. Thereupon the major pitched his tents, figuratively speaking, and became, for the time being, a part and parcel of the innocence that characterized Hillsborough. A wiser man would doubtless have made the same mistake.

The little village possessed advantages that seemed to be providentially arranged to fit the various enterprises that Major Frampton had in view. There was the auction-block in front of the stuccoed court-house, if he desired to dispose of a few of his negroes; there was a quarter-track, laid out to his hand and in excellent order, if he chose to enjoy the pleasures of horse-racing; there were secluded pine thickets within easy reach, if he desired to indulge in the exciting pastime of cock-fighting; and various lonely and unoccupied rooms in the second story of the tavern, if he cared to challenge the chances of dice or cards.

Major Frampton tried them all with varying luck, until he began his famous game of poker with Judge Alfred Wellington, a stately gentleman with a flowing white beard and mild blue eyes that give him the appearance of a benevolent patriarch. The history of the game in which Major Frampton and Judge Alfred Wellington took part is something more than a tradition in Hillsborough, for there are still living three or four men who sat around the table and watched its progress. It is said that at various stages of the game Major Frampton would destroy the cards with which they were playing, and send for a new pack, but the result was always the same. The mild blue eyes of Judge Wellington, with few exceptions, continued to overlook "hands" that were invincible—a habit they had acquired during a long and arduous course of training from Saratoga to New Orleans. Major Frampton lost his money, his horses, his wagons, and all his negroes but one, his body-servant. When his misfortune had reached this limit, the major adjourned the game. The sun was shining brightly, and all nature was cheerful. However this may be, he visited the court-house, and executed the papers that gave his body-servant his freedom. This being done, Major Frampton sauntered into a convenient pine thicket, and blew out his brains.

The negro thus freed came to be known as Free Joe. Compelled, under the law, to choose a guardian, he chose Judge Wellington, chiefly because his wife Lucinda was among the negroes won from Major Frampton. For several years Free Joe had what may be called a jovial time. His wife Lucinda was well provided for, and he found it a comparatively easy matter to provide for himself; so that, taking all the circumstances into consideration, it is not matter for astonishment that he became somewhat shiftless.

When Judge Wellington died, Free Joe's troubles began. The judge's negroes, including Lucinda, went to his half-brother, a man named Calderwood, who was a hard master and a rough customer generally,—a man of many eccentricities of mind and character. His neighbors had a habit of alluding to him as "Old

Spite;" and the name seemed to fit him so completely, that he was known far and near as "Spite" Calderwood. He probably enjoyed the distinction the name gave him, at any rate, he never resented it, and it was not often that he missed an opportunity to show that he deserved it. Calderwood's place was two or three miles from the village of Hillsborough, and Free Joe visited his wife twice a week, Wednesday and Saturday nights.

One Sunday he was sittting in front of Lucinda's cabin, when Calderwood happened to pass that way.

"Howdy, marster?" said Free Joe, taking off his hat.

"Who are you?" exclaimed Calderwood abruptly, halting and staring at the negro.

"I'm name' Joe, marster. I'm Lucindy's ole man."

"Who do you belong to?"

"Marse John Evans is my gyardeen, marster."

"Big name—gyardeen. Show your pass."

Free Joe produced that document, and Calderwood read it aloud slowly, as is he found it difficult to get at the meaning:—

"To whom it may concern: This is to certify that the boy Joe Frampton has my permission to visit his wife Lucinda."

This was dated at Hillsborough, and signed *"John W. Evans."*

Calderwood read it twice, and then looked at Free Joe, elevating his eyebrows, and showing his discolored teeth.

"Some mighty big words in that there. Evans owns this place, I reckon. When's he comin' down to take hold?"

Free Joe fumbled with his hat. He was badly frightened.

"Lucindy say she speck you wouldn't min' my comin', long ez I behave, marster."

Calderwood tore the pass in pieces and flung it away.

"Don't want no free niggers 'round here," he exclaimed. "There's the big road. It'll carry you to town. Don't let me catch you here no more. Now, mind what I tell you."

Free Joe presented a shabby spectacle as he moved off with his little dog Dan slinking at his heels. It should be said in behalf of Dan, however, that his bristles were up, and that he looked back and growled. It may be that the dog had the advantage of insignificance, but it is difficult to conceive how a dog bold enough to raise his bristles under Calderwood's very eyes could be as insignificant as Free Joe. But both the negro and his little dog seemed to give a new and more dismal aspect to forlornness as they turned into the road and went toward Hillsborough.

After this incident Free Joe appeared to have clearer ideas concerning his peculiar condition. He realized the fact that though he was free he was more helpless than any slave. Having no owner, every man was his master. He knew that he was the object of suspicion, and therefore all his slender resources (ah!

how pitifully slender they were!) were devoted to winning, not kindness and appreciation, but toleration; all his efforts were in the direction of mitigating the circumstances that tended to make his condition so much worse than that of the negroes around him,—negroes who had friends because they had masters.

So far as his own race was concerned, Free Joe was an exile. If the slaves secretly envied him his freedom (which is to be doubted, considering his miserable condition), they openly despised him, and lost no opportunity to treat him with contumely. Perhaps this was in some measure the result of the attitude which Free Joe chose to maintain toward them. No doubt his instinct taught him that to hold himself aloof from the slaves would be to invite from the whites the toleration which he coveted, and without which even his miserable condition would be rendered more miserable still.

His greatest trouble was the fact that he was not allowed to visit his wife; but he soon found a way out of this difficulty. After he had been ordered away from the Calderwood place, he was in the habit of wandering as far in that direction as prudence would permit. Near the Calderwood place, but not on Calderwood's land, lived an old man named Micajah Staley and his sister Becky Staley. These people were old and very poor. Old Micajah had a palsied arm and hand, but in spite of this, he managed to earn a precarious living with his turning lathe.

When he was a slave Free Joe would have scorned these representatives of a class known as poor white trash, but now he found them sympathetic and helpful in various ways. From the back door of their cabin he could hear the Calderwood negroes singing at night, and he sometimes fancied he could distinguish Lucinda's shrill treble rising above the other voices. A large poplar grew in the woods some distance from the Staley cabin, and at the foot of this tree Free Joe would sit for hours with his face turned toward Calderwood's. His little dog Dan would curl up in the leaves near by, and the two seemed to be as comforatble as possible.

One Saturday afternoon Free Joe, sitting at the foot of this friendly poplar, fell asleep. How long he slept, he could not tell; but when he awoke little Dan was licking his face, the moon was shining brightly, and Lucinda his wife stood before him laughing. The dog, seeing that Free Joe was asleep, had grown somewhat impatient, and he concluded to make an excursion to the Calderwood place on his own account. Lucinda was inclined to give the incident a twist in the direction of superstition.

"I 'uz settin' down front er de fireplace," she said, "cookin' me some meat, w'en all of a sudden I year sumpin at de do'—scratch, scratch. I tuck'n tu'n de meat over, en make out I ain't year it. Bimeby it come dar 'gin—scratch, scratch. I up en open de do', I did, en, bless de Lord! dar wuz little Dan, en it look like ter me dat his ribs done grow tergeer. I gin 'im some bread, en den, w'en he start out, I tuck'n foller 'im, kaze, I say ter myse'f, maybe my nigger man mought be some'rs 'round'. Dat ar little dog got sense, mon."

Free Joe laughed and dropped his hand lightly on Dan's head. For a long time after that he had no difficulty in seeing his wife. He had only to sit by the poplar-tree until little Dan would run and fetch her. But after a while the other negroes discovered that Lucinda was meeting Free Joe in the woods, and information soon reached Calderwood's ears. Calderwood was what is called a man of action. He said nothing; but one day he put Lucinda in his buggy, and carried her to Macon, sixty miles away. He carried her to Macon, and came back without her; and nobody in or around Hillsborough, or in that section, ever saw her again. . . . How many long nights Free Joe waited at the foot of the poplar-tree for Lucinda and little Dan, no one can ever know. He kept no account of them, and they were not recorded by Micajah Staley nor by Miss Becky. The season ran into summer and then into fall. One night he went to the Staley cabin, cut the two old people an armful of wood, and seated himself on the door-steps, where he rested. He was always thankful—and proud, as it seemed—when Miss Becky gave him a cup of coffee, which she was sometimes thoughtful enough to do. He was especially thankful on this particular night.

"You er still layin' off for to strike up wi' Lucindy out thar in the woods, I I reckon," said Micajah Staley, smiling grimly. The situation was not without its humorous aspects.

"Oh, dey er comin', Mars Cajy, dey er comin', sho," Free Joe replied. "I boun' you dey'll come; en w'en dey does come, I'll des take en fetch um yer, whar you kin see um wid you own eyes, you en Miss Becky."

"No," said Mr. Staley, with a quick and emphatic gesture of disapproval. "Don't! don't fetch 'em anywheres. Stay right wi'em as long as may be."

Free Joe chuckled, and slipped away into the night, while the two old people sat gazing in the fire. Finally Micajah spoke.

"Look at that nigger; look at 'im. He's pine-blank as happy now as a killdee by a mill-race. You can't 'faze 'em. I'd in-about give up my t'other hand ef I could stan' flat-footed, an' grin at trouble like that there nigger."

"Niggers is niggers," said Miss Becky, smiling grimly, "an' you can't rub it out; yit I lay I've seed a heap of white people lots meaner'n Free Joe. He grins,— an that's nigger,—but I've ketched his under jaw a-trimblin' when Lucindy's name uz brung up. An' I tell you," she went on, bridling up a little, and speaking with almost fierce emphasis, "the Old Boy's done sharpened his claws for Spite Calderwood. You'll see it."

"Me, Rebecca?" said Mr. Staley, hugging his palsied arm; "me? I hope not."

"Well, you'll know it then," said Miss Becky, laughing heartily at her brother's look of alarm.

The next morning Micajah Staley had occasion to go into the woods after a piece of timber. He saw Free Joe sitting at the foot of the poplar, and the sight vexed him somewhat.

"Git up from there," he cried, "an' go an' arn your livin'. A mighty purty pass it's come to, when great big buck niggers can lie a-snorin' in the woods all day, when t'other folks is got to be up an' a-gwine. Git up there!"

Receiving no response, Mr. Staley went to Free Joe, and shook him by the shoulder; but the negro made no response. He was dead. His hat was off, his head was bent, and a smile was on his face. It was as if he had bowed and smiled when death stood before him, humble to the last. His clothes were ragged; his hands were rough and callous; his shoes were literally tied together with strings; he was shabby in the extreme. A passer-by, glancing at him, could have no idea that such a humble creature had been summoned as a witness before the Lord God of Hosts.

PIG AND POLICY: MAINTENANCE OF BOUNDARIES BETWEEN HAN AND MUSLIM CHINESE*

BARBARA KROLL PILLSBURY

Partly because of the United States' almost exclusive preoccupation with things Western and partly because of the inaccessibility of mainland China to outsiders in recent years, our knowledge of social processes among one fourth of the world's inhabitants is woefully lacking. In terms of intergroup relations, it is known that minorities have long been present in China and that relations between various minorities and the dominant Han Chinese have been a source of continuing difficulty.

One of the most important of these minority groups is the Muslims. Barbara Kroll Pillsbury, an anthropologist at San Diego State University, has been investigating this large group for several years, beginning in Cairo, Egypt, where she studied Muslim culture in general. There she became interested in the Chinese Muslims, a minority that has claimed as many as 48 million members in mainland China alone. Later she was able to do resident research on Taiwan among Chinese Muslims living there. This study is based on interviews, previous studies, and historical data. She focuses on the way in which a food taboo—in this instance, abstinence from pork—serves as a social boundary.

* Research on which this study is based was carried out on the Chinese island province of Taiwan from 1970 to 1972. I am indebted both to the Hui of Taiwan for their hospitality and cooperation and to Professors Conrad Arensberg, Myron Cohen, Morton Fried, Margaret Fried, Margaret Mead, and Abraham Rosman of Columbia University for their advice and guidance. My fieldwork was carried out under a grant from the National Institute of Mental Health and the sponsorship of the Academia Sinica in Taipei.

Acculturation, assimilation, and interethnic relations have long been subjects of study among cultural and social anthropologists. More recently, however, many anthropologists have turned their attention away from the melting down of ethnic differences to focus instead on the perpetuation of those differences and the maintenance of social boundaries among ethnic groups.

The mere fact that members of a minority have "learned" many traits of the culture of the dominant majority does not automatically imply assimilation. As the anthropoligist Fredrik Barth emphasizes in his book *Ethnic Groups and Boundaries: The Social Organization of Cultural Difference*, the critical feature of ethnicity should be the characteristic of self-ascription (and ascription by others), rather than the sharing of certain traits of a given culture. The importance of this criterion of ascription is well illustrated by the Muslims of China who regard themselves—and are regarded by non-Muslim Chinese—not as a separate religious group but as a separate minority people. the *Hui*.[1]

Most Hui today speak virtually the same language and display generally the same physical features as the Han, the dominant and ethnically Chinese majority in China. But, although they share these traits and although the Hui now acknowledge that they are citizens of China, they nevertheless vehemently insist that they are not ethnically Chinese. Research on the nature of the relations between Hui and Han, both in the past and in the present, reveals that two factors have been critical in perpetuatng this sence of ethnic separateness. First is the Islamic injunction against eating pork, and second is the policies that the governments of China have pursued with respect to minorities. Whether on present-day Taiwan, the present-day Chinese mainland, or the pre-Communist mainland, these two factors —pig and policy—have been instrumental in creating and maintaining boundaries between the Hui minority and the encapsulating Han majority.

Historical Background

The Hui, estimated at mid-twentieth century to number as many as 40 or 50 million, or almost one-tenth of the entire population of China, trace their ancestry to Arab, Persian, and Turkic merchants and mercenaries who settled in China, some as early as thirteen centuries ago.[2] Islam—like Buddhism, Christianity, and Judaism —was a "foreign" religion imported into China. It followed two routes to China, traveling first by sea and later by land.

---

[1] *Hui* sounds like "whey" in "curds and whey"; *Han* rhymes with "on."

[2] By 1937 the *China Handbook*, an official fact book, was reporting a Muslim population of 48 million distributed through all China's provinces—along with 45,000 mosques (thirty-five located in Peking alone). Caution must be exercised, however, in accepting Chinese census figures. There is considerable disagreement on the number of Muslims in China both in the past and at present.

In A.D. 622, the year in which the Prophet Muhammad made his famous pilgrimage from Mecca to Medina in Arabia, there already existed in Canton and other ports of China sizable communities of Arab traders. Arab merchant ships had been plying the seas between the Middle East and the Middle Kingdom for some two centuries and, within a few decades after the rise of Islam in Arabia, were carrying not only medicinal herbs, spices, and gems but a new religion as well. By about the tenth century Islam was proceeding steadily along a second pathway to China: the fabled Silk Road across central Asia into Turkestan. It was carried along the caravan routes primarily by Persian and Turkic peoples, who penetrated as far east as Peking. Its greatest impact was felt during the Mongol conquests of the thirteenth century.

Throughout their first seven centuries in China, Muslims were considered foreigners (literally, "barbarian guests") and were set apart by dress, language, dietary laws, and religious customs. In cities like Canton special Muslim neighborhoods were established, in which *qadis*, Islamic legal authorities, were responsible for maintaining law and order. In many rural districts Muslims lived in separate villages called *ying*, or "barracks," reflecting the large number of Muslims in military professions. Those Chinese women who married into Muslim households became Muslims themselves and raised their children as Muslims, reportedly designated by the term "China-born barbarian guests."

The Chinese emperors of the Ming dynasty (1368–1644), however, prohibited foreign dress and the use of foreign languages and foreign names. With the cessation of migration to China and the lessening of foreign influence in general, the Muslims in China slowly began to lose their alien status. A Hui scholar outlines the sinification which took place among Muslims of China proper as adoption of Chinese surnames, Chinese dress, Chinese eating habits (like use of chopsticks), and Chinese local dialects in place of Arabic and Persian as the means of communication not only between Muslim and Chinese but as the *lingua franca* for Muslims as well (Ting 1958, pp. 349–350). For approximately the next five centuries the vast majority of Muslims in China remained completely isolated from the rest of the Islamic world.[3] It was during this period that they came to be designated as Hui rather than as Arab, Persian, or "barbarian guest."

Sinification during these centuries meant for the Hui, however, not assimilation—as in the instances of the early Christians and the Chinese Jews—but rather only acculturation. It clearly appears that Hui had, by the twentieth century, *learned* Chinese ways, but had nevertheless refused to adopt and internalize them as their own. The social boundaries that existed between the Muslim Hui and the

[3] A few Chinese Muslims (for example, the Hu Teng-chou, Ma Ming-hsin, and Ma Fu-ch'u) did make their way to Arabia and Turkey during this period, but reforms that they attempted to initiate upon return to China were not successful in bringing the Hui back into the mainstream of Islam.

Chinese Han on the pre-Communist mainland are reflected in this passage from a 1943 government publication:

> The Mussulmans, true to their own ways and ideas, wherever they might be, formed their own community apart from the Chinese. The Mohammedans to whom pork is taboo never share the same table with Chinese. Nor do they inter-marry with unbelieving Chinese. For such populace of unyielding temper the Chinese naturally never had love to lose. It was not surprising that disputes between Moslem and native populations were often bitter. (*China Annual*, 1943, p. 68)[4]

Here in a nutshell are the basic social facts that determined or characterized the Hui-Han dichotomy on the pre-1949 mainland, that explain to a large extent why Hui were not assimilated during their thirteen centuries in China, and that permit an understanding of the present social boundary between the Hui minority and the dominant Han Chinese majority. These facts (admittedly generalizations) may be summarized: First, wherever the Muslims may be, they form their own communities apart from the Chinese; second, pork is taboo, and Muslims do not share the same table with Chinese; third, Muslims do not freely intermarry with Chinese; and, fourth, disputes between Muslims and Chinese have often been bitter. Hui also emphasize that they, unlike the Chinese, do not and have never worshiped their ancestors.

The Hui Community on Taiwan: A Case Study

Twice in its history the Chinese island province of Taiwan has provided refuge for Chinese fleeing from anticipated oppression at the hands of a new regime on the mainland. The first time was in 1661, when China passed into the hands of the Manchus; the second was in 1949, when the mainland came under Communist control. In both instances, large numbers of Muslims were among those who settled on Taiwan. The present government currently reports a population on the island of 40,000 Hui.

Among this group the Taiwanese descendants of Muslims who fled to Taiwan in the 1600s number approximately 20,000. They are concentrated primarily in small coastal towns, where, like other Indigenous Taiwanese, most make their living by farming or fishing. All retain vestiges of "Hui culture," but only a few dozen elders actually continue to identify themselves as Hui. Most of these so-called

---

[4] "Mussulmans" and "Mohammedans" are but two of the diverse—and often ridiculous—labels pinned on Chinese Muslims by American and European geographers, journalists, missionaries, travelers, and military and diplomatic personnel. Only "Muslim," "Hui," and (with reservation) "Hui-hui" are now acceptable English usage.

"Taiwanese Muslims" no longer consider themselves Hui, for, they say, "we have ruined our mouths"—that is, they now eat pork.[5]

Mainlander Muslims on Taiwan—those who arrived in or shortly after 1949—are concentrated chiefly in Taipei and other urban centers. Like other mainlanders, but in contrast to the Taiwanese of Muslim ancestry, the majority earn their livelihood as career military personnel, civil servants, and small businessmen. A disproportionate number are engaged in the restaurant business (as was also true on the mainland). Only a few earn a living from the land and none from the sea.

Opinion, both Chinese and Western, has long been divided on whether "Hui" signals a racial or only a religious distinction. Some writers have stated that it means, simply, a Chinese who believes in Islam (traditionally referred to in China as—tautologically—"the religion of the Hui"). Others have maintained the contrary, that the Hui are "not merely Chinese with a different religion [but] . . . a distinct race" (Cressey 1934, p. 194). Much of this confusion arises from the difficulty of translating between Chinese and English. In Chinese Hui designate themselves and are generally designated by others as a *mintsu*, a term often mistakenly translated into English as "race" but that, more accurately, is translated "a people," in the sense of the English expression "ethnic group."[6]

The 20,000 mainlanders on Taiwan who identify themselves as *Hui-min*, or "Hui people," include three subgroupings. One consists of Turkic-speaking *Hui-hui* from Sinkiang province, who are either Uighur, Tartar, or Kazakh in ancestry and physically unlike the Han Chinese. A second subgrouping consists of the so-called *Han-hui* of China proper. Because so many of their Arab and Persian ancestors of more than a thousand years ago took native Han Chinese wives, the majority of the *Han-hui* look and speak almost the same as Han Chinese of their native regions. The third subgrouping, the Hui of northwest China (Chinghai, Kansu, Ninghsia, and Shensi provinces), represents a type intermediate between the first two in physical appearance and sometimes in speech as well.

Overt differences among members of the three subgroupings have not impaired the Hui image of themselves as a distinctive ethnic unit with a shared culture and unambiguous boundaries. Rather, it is adherence to the "Hui culture" and the special "way of life" it dictates that continues on Taiwan to draw individual Hui together while setting them apart from Han Chinese. In the words of Barth, "To the extent that actors use ethnic identities to categorize themselves

---

[5] It is significant that these Taiwanese, who are descended from Muslims, eat pork themselves but do not—unlike other Taiwanese—include it in food offerings to their ancestors. They feel it would be unfilial to do so. "Our parents and ancestors were Hui and did not eat pork," they explain. "It would be a shame to ruin their mouths now after all their centuries of abstention."

[6] The standard translation of *mintsu* in publications of the People's Republic of China is "nationality." *Mintsu* is pronounced "min- (rhyming with "win")-zoo."

and others for purposes of interaction, they form ethnic groups in this organizational sense" (1969, pp. 13–14).

Should it be implied to Hui that they may really be "just Han with a different religion," virtually all respond—some even angrily—that "We are not Han, and our culture is not Han." They typically insist that, though isolated for many centuries from the heartland of Islam, they never did enter into the sociocultural mainstream of the Han. In their eyes, Hui culture remains a well-defined body of beliefs and practices distinct from that of any other *mintsu*, or "people," of China.[7] Hui cite, for example, the obligation deriving from Arab desert society to offer hospitality (food and accommodations) to other Hui, friends, or strangers who are away from their own homes.

Cultural diversities observable among Hui from different mainland communities thus have not presented a barrier to Hui interaction. There are numerous examples, for instance, of Hui men and women who have married on Taiwan, despite the fact that, coming from different parts of China, they did not even speak mutually intelligible languages or dialects.

What actually does present a barrier to interacting and forming new relationships is whether or not an individual is a pork eater—and it is assumed that all Han are. So strong is the connection between pigs and Han in the minds of most Hui that they often refer to pork as "Han religion meat," despite the fact that no such thing as "*the* Han religion" actually exists.

Pig: The "Black Worm"

Eating is fundamental to Chinese social life. To issue invitations back and forth for meals is virtually indispensable to establishing friendly relations. Rarely does one enter a Chinese home without being offered food or drink. To participate in the continuing reciprocity of offering food and invitations to eat, one must eat the same food. Han and Hui do not. Hui eat beef and lamb; Han eat pork, the "flesh of the black worm," as it is called by those Hui who observe the old taboo against even uttering the word for pig. It is no small distinction in a country where the pig is not only the chief source of animal protein but also a key ingredient in a highly agrarian economy.

"There is absolutely no way for us to be friends with ordinary Chinese," states a certain Hajji Suliman. "We eat beef; they eat pork. With the other minorities, yes. Border people like the Tibetans and Mongolians are accustomed to

[7] The Hui culture is what anthropologist Max Gluckman has called an "endoculture"— the culture of a group as perceived by members of that group. An endoculture, he points out, is usually quite different from the culture of the same group as described by a social scientist (1959, p. 57).

eating beef and lamb. But the Han, impossible! They won't give up their pork for anything!" "No people in the world love pork more than the Chinese Han," concluded an *imam* from Chinghai province with the perspectives gained from a recent pilgrimage to Mecca.

The primacy of the pig in the Chinese diet and economy is indicated in an article titled simply "Pigs": "The importance of pigs in China . . . cannot be exaggerated. Pork is the standard meat. . . . The pig is a good source of manure. . . . Each pig is a small organic fertilizer factory. . . . The pig is a national treasure" (1969, pp. 1–6).

According to one scholar, "Perhaps the best illustration of the importance of the pig in China is the fact that the Chinese ideograph meaning 'home' consists of the signs for 'roof' and for 'pig' " (Simoons, 1961, pp. 26–27).

These evaluations stand out in bold contrast to appraisals of Hui attitudes toward the pig: "With them pork is taboo: they look upon the pig and its meat as abominations. Not only do they not eat pork, but they even abhor any reference to it. Many are the instances of . . . troubles with Chinese on account of this habit" (*China Annual*, 1943, p. 106).

Indeed, "troubles with Chinese on account of this habit" have been many. Chinese have traditionally taunted Hui with the nicknames "Pig Snout," "Pig Egg," "Pig Tail," and "Pig Baby"—hardly behavior designed to pave the way for smooth social relationships. Many Chinese still delight in telling tales of how all Muslims are descended from a pig or how Hui all worship a pig instead of human ancestors. Publication of such accounts has led in certain instances to closing of bookstores, firing of editors, and forcing of periodicals out of publication.

Hui who traveled in the Arab world, as well as Arab Muslims who have lived among the Hui, both believe that Chinese Islam deviates most radically from Islam in the Middle East in that it is upon the avoidance of pork that maintenance of Hui identity has come to be based. "We Hui," admits Hajji Abdulla Ma, "have turned Islam upside down. 'Don't eat pork' is not even one of the five duties of Islam, but to us it is more important than the duty of prayer!"

It is important not only in the eating habits of an individual Hui and consequently in determining with whom he socializes but also in determining whom he marries. Membership in the Hui minority is determined by rule of descent (being born into the community) and enforced by endogamy (marrying within the community). Unless a Han is willing to undergo the rituals of conversion and to attempt to forgo pork, a Hui cannot marry him.

"Not eating pork is probably the reason that we Hui have survived for more than a thousand years and not been absorbed by the Han," acknowledges Hajji Abdulla. Today many Hui on Taiwan think that they can avoid assimilation by the Han by avoiding pork and only if government policies permit preservation of minority cultures.

Government Policy

Regimes attempting to extend or consolidate power over China during the past century have pursued various policies toward the non-Han peoples. Several alternative strategies can be isolated; all have had the largely unintended consequence of further emphasizing the separateness and distinctiveness of the Hui.

During the latter part of the Ch'ing dynasty (ended 1911), policies pursued by the Manchu emperors included that of divide and rule. Forbidding Hui to own land or reside within the walls of a city was but one of the many measures designed to segregate and to make difficult communication between Hui and Han. The various oppressive Manchu policies led to (and were also a reaction to) a series of rebellions in Yunnan province and northwest China—going back more than a century—which took several million Hui and Han lives and embittered each against the other. Hui themselves (see, for example, Fu, 1940, p. 166; Pai, 1953) emphasizes that these battles were perceived as ethnic confrontations between the Han and Hui nationalities (*mintsu*), not as religious wars between Buddhists and Muslims.

Following the collapse of the Manchu regime in 1911 and the founding of the Republic of China, a creed of equality was promulgated and a new national flag designed. The flag was composed of five horizontal stripes of equal width, one each for the "five great *mintsu*" of China. One was white for the Hui. The equal width of the stripe symbolized that, thenceforth Han, Manchu, Mongol, Hui, and Tibetan peoples would be equal. The creed of equality was formalized for the Hui by the insertion into the constitution of a special clause designating the Muslims as a "*mintsu* with special living habits" and guaranteeing them a minimum number of seats in the National Assembly and other organs of the central government. Despite cultural, linguistic, and geographic distinctions, the Muslims of all China were formally identified as one people, the Hui.

During the Chinese war of resistance against Japan in the 1930s and 1940s, however, this policy was altered, and thereafter the Hui in Nationalist China were formally identified not as a separate people per se but as part of the Chinese people following a religion separate from that of the Han majority. The reasons for this shift were complex but were related in large part to Japan's attempts to infiltrate the Hui, arising from desire to enhance its position in China by proclaiming itself a champion of greater political autonomy for the Hui than they had under the Han regime. Although Nationalist policy on Taiwan has remained basically the same, the Hui have derived a sense of security from the fact that several of their number have achieved high government and military positions, including that of minister of defense.

Policies on the Communist mainland, having gone through similar shifts, emphasize Hui separateness in yet other ways. There the Hui were first sorted out according to distinctions most clearly identifiable as linguistic. Second, the meaning of "Hui" separated into two elements—religion and "nationality," each thereafter to be dealt with according to two separate bodies of policy. Religious matters were placed under the rubric of "Islam," rather than "Hui," and dealt with according to policies formulated for Buddhism, folk religion, Christianity, and other religious beliefs. The "Hui nationality" was generally defined to include only the Hui of China proper, the group identified earlier as physically and linguistically similar to the Han. As "nationalities" the Hui, Uighurs, Tatars, and Kazakhs are dealt with according to minority policies formulated for such other peoples as the Tibetans and Mongolians. In general it may be hypothesized that Muslims in Communist China have fared better as members of minority nationalities than as adherents of Islam.

Both on Taiwan and on the mainland, however, Muslims have found themselves an important ingredient in foreign policy. Both regimes, for example, have selected and financed delegations of pilgrims to Mecca (where there is a resident community of some 20,000 Chinese Muslims), and both welcome to their mosques Islamic delegations from other countries. Chinese Muslim graduates of al-Azhar University in Cairo have for several decades served in Middle East embassies of the Republic of China. A large Arabic-style mosque was constructed in Taipei in the early 1960s with financial contributions from King Faisal of Saudi Arabia, King Hussein of Jordan, and Reza Shah Pahlevi of Iran. For more than ten years Saudi Arabia has provided fellowships for Chinese Muslims from Taiwan to study at the Islamic University in Medina, and the present number-one imam of Taiwan's largest mosque is a Saudi citizen sent to Taipei and serving there on salary from his government.

In conclusion, both the Islamic injunction against pork and the policies pursued by the governments of China have been instrumental up to the present in heightening the Hui sense of ethnic separateness and in maintaining social boundaries between Muslim and Han Chinese. Sentiments of the Hui and other Muslim peoples in the People's Republic of China toward their present and future status remain matters of much speculation. Hui on Taiwan, however, fear that fellow Hui on the mainland will be assimilated as the national minorities there are led down the socialist road. Many on Taiwan have also come to perceive themselves as increasingly threatened by the Han and point to the ways in which other minorities—the Chinese Jews, the Manchus, and more recently the Taiwanese of Muslim ancestry— have been absorbed by the Han. The Hui on Taiwan look upon the pig as filthy and foe, upon King Faisal as a friend, benefactor, and spiritual head. But they identify both as extremely important in staving off assimilation. The first enforces endogamy; the second provides leadership. Together they are viewed as essential to what the Hui consider preservation of their culture and what the social scientist calls maintenance of ethnic boundaries.

References

Barth, Fredrik. "Introduction." In *Ethnic Groups and Boundaries: The Social Organization of Cultural Difference*. Boston: Little, Brown, 1969. Pp. 9–38.

China Islamic Association (Chung-kuo I-ssu-lan Chiao Hsieh-hui). *Chung-kuo ti Mu-ssu-lin (Chinese Muslims)*. Peking: Foreign Language Press, 1955.

Cressey, George. *Land of the 500 Million: A Geography of China*. New York: McGraw-Hill, 1955.

Fu T'ung-hsien. *Chung-kuo Hui-chiao Shih (A History of Chinese Islam)*. Taipei: Commercial Press, 1969 (originally published, 1940).

Gluckman, Max. *Analysis of a Social Situation in Modern Zululand*. Manchester: Rhodes Livingstone Institute, 1958 (originally published, 1940–1942).

Pai Shou-i, (ed.). *Hui-min Ch'i-i (The Muslim Rebellions)*. Shanghai, 1953.

"Pigs," *China News Analysis*. 778, 1969, 1–7.

Pillsbury, Barbara. Cohesion and Cleavage in a Chinese Muslim Minority. New York: Unpublished doctoral dissertation, Columbia University, Ann Arbor: University Microfilms, 1974.

Simoons, Frederick. *Eat Not This Flesh: Food Avoidances in the Old World*. Madison: University of Wisconsin Press, 1961.

Ting, Dawood C. M. "Islamic Culture in China." In *Islam—The Straight Path: Islam Interpreted by Muslims*, ed. by Kenneth Morgan. New York: Ronald Press, 1958.

6

Assimilation

In their early days the Normans borrowed no manners and few customs from
the Islanders. The only culture was
French. Surviving Saxon notables sent
their sons to monasteries of France for
education. The English repeated the experience of the ancient Britons; all who
could learnt French, as formerly the con-
temporaries of Boadicea had learnt Latin.
At first the conquerors, who despised
the uncouth English as louts and boors,
ruled by the force of sharpened steel.
But very soon in true Norman fashion
they intermarried with the free population and identified themselves with
their English past.

—Winston S. Churchill
(1964, pp. 34, 35).

The history of civilization is plentifully supplied with records of intergroup
contacts that eventually resulted in various forms of alliances, mergers, and fusions
of peoples. Our term Anglo-Saxon, for instance, indicates that once two peoples
met and eventually became one. The concepts most widely used to discuss these
events are *assimilation, acculturation, integration,* and *syncretism.* All have to do
with processes in which diverse peoples come to interact in the life of a larger group.

It was mentioned earlier that differentiating forces, as well as assimilating
forces, are present in all human societies. These opposing sets of forces have manifested themselves in American society during recent years in several ways. Differentiating forces have been evident in the flourishing of ethnic-identity organizations,
the widespread discussion of cultural pluralism as a national goal, the growing

number of segregated private academies, resegregation in the public schools, and the emergence of Black nationalism. At the same time the effects of assimilative forces are apparent in the desegregation of previously segregated schools and churches, the Supreme Court's ruling against miscegenation laws, and the entrance of minority members into jobs previously closed to them.

These varied events involve too many important details for us to say simply that assimilation is or is not taking place. It is more important to show what kind of assimilation is taking place and to what extent. In order to make the necessary distinctions, social scientists conceptualize assimilation as a comprehensive process that includes several subprocesses. At first this statement may sound like jargon—a few more terms to bandy about. Actually, however, the terms enable us to describe what is occurring with greater precision than would otherwise be possible. These subprocesses of assimilation are acculturation, structural assimilation, identificational assimilation, civic assimilation, and intermarriage.[1]

Acculturation

Some cultural exchanges are virtually unavoidable whenever different groups come into contact with one another. It is not easy, however, to predict which way change will go or, for that matter, exactly what parts of the respective cultures will be affected. In some instances one culture will virtually eclipse another, but in others parts of both cultures will be adapted along new lines. *Acculturation* is usually defined as the modification of the culture of a group through contact with other groups. It implies the acquisition or exchange of cultural traits.

Acculturation is typically the first of the assimilative subprocesses to occur, as is illustrated by immigrants' experience in the United States. The millions of people who came to this country during the early part of this century generally learned enough English to get by, acquired new work skills whenever necessary, and adopted many local behavior patterns. The rate of acculturation accelerated in the second generation. Perhaps the most noticeable aspect of the acculturation of immigrants in the United States was the fluency with which many second-generation people learned to speak the English language.

Almost always, learning the language is a first step in acculturation.[2] A

---

[1] Milton M. Gordon's analysis of assimilation (1964) is the most satisfactory conceptual scheme yet proposed for interpreting assimilation. The present chapter is organized around a modification of his conceptual scheme. Gordon suggests two additional subprocesses—absence of discrimination and absence of prejudice—which will not be treated separately in this chapter.

[2] Actually, elements of a group's technology may be diffused more rapidly and more widely than its language. W. F. Ogburn introduced the concept of "culture lag" to describe the phenomenon in which some parts of culture change more rapidly than others.

language permits transactions to take place. It shapes and molds ideas by means of the categories that it provides. It facilitates a sense of unity in a society and paves the way for further cultural interchanges. The Inca empire, for example, consisted of more than 6 million subjects and included many distinct cultures and languages. At its peak the empire stretched from Ecuador in the north to Chile in the south—in all, an area larger than Europe. A common language, Quechua (ketch-u-ah), became the official idiom of the empire and helped to unify the society. When the Spanish came, Quechua was adopted as a second tongue. Today, three centuries after the Spanish conquest, it is still spoken by the majority of the peoples of the Andes.

In the Roman empire, too, conquests were only partially the result of military might. Roman officials encouraged and rewarded the acquisition of Roman culture, customs, manners, and especially mastery of the Latin language. Only isolated mountainous regions and other remote spots of the empire escaped the full thrust of this policy.

The rate and degree of acculturation are usually slower when the peoples affected are geographically isolated. In the United States this slowness has been observable among the Amish in Pennsylvania and American Indians still on reservations. It seems clear, however, that their isolation has tended only to delay the final impact of acculturation. On Indian reservations today the mass media, especially television, are spanning physical distances and reducing cultural differences. The Amish, too, are feeling the impact of the outside world. Reports persist that many Amish youths, restive in their plain life, surreptitiously seek excitement in the nearby towns and cities when they can.

Acculturation takes place even in hostile contacts between peoples. Mutual borrowing between Europeans and American Indians occurred, despite frequent eruptions of violence. It seems that cultural exchanges result from practically any kind of contact.

The coming together of peoples may result in one set of culture traits' being replaced by another. Or cultural elements from the different societies may be recombined into something new. This process is called *syncretism.* Instances of syncretism have been reported from virtually every geographical region of the world. It may involve religious customs, economic practices, language, and even eating habits.

The Japanese dish *sukiyaki* is an interesting case in point. Actually *sukiyaki* is neither typically nor originally Japanese. It was introduced to Japan in about the sixteenth century from Portugal or Holland. At first it consisted of pan-broiled meat and vegetables, but around 1700 the Japanese added a local sauce. The dish became popular among Westerners who at that time found meat hard to obtain in Buddhist Japan. After foreign influence led to the acceptance of meat, the Japanese began to treat themselves to *sukiyaki* on special occasions. In Japan today each province has its own variety of *sukiyaki.* The dish is usually made with beef or chicken and vegetables: onions, bamboo shoots, watercress, mushrooms, bean curd, yam noodles, all cleaned and arranged on a platter. These ingredients are cooked one by one at the table in soy sauce mixed with sweet Japanese rice wine, soup stock, and sugar (Norman and Tatsumara, 1969, p. 59). What marvels culture contact hath wrought!

Acculturation may result from structural variables. In a conquest state, acculturation of the dominant group is likely if the conquerors lose touch with one another. The maintenance of a particular culture depends upon a nucleus of individuals who associate with one another.

One characteristic of conquerors is that they often are reluctant to care for their own children. This task is usually delegated to members of the subject group. In the process of socialization the children are exposed to the culture of the conquered people at an impressionable age. This fact may spell the destruction of the conquerors as an integrated social unit. The Norman experience in the British isles illustrates the principle. After a few generations, those who had settled in England had lost their identity as Normans and had become English, those in Scotland were Scottish, and those in Ireland had become very Irish, hating Englishmen with patriotic fervor (Linton, 1964, p. 246).

Acculturation can be the key to technological development. The fact that a particular society has not advanced economically or technologically is sometimes erroneously attributed to its racial composition. In reality, underdevelopment may result from lack of raw materials, harsh climate, a value system that is incompatible with economic development, or, very important, cultural insulation. Lack of "creative borrowing," to use Eric Hoffer's expression, typically results in communities that are in-grown and lethargic (1969, p. 12).

Few parts of the world today are insulated from Western technology. In the Middle East, people originally accepted the techenology of the West with little resistance, partly because technology did not occupy a focal position in their own culture. Switching to new machines and gadgets was viewed as a minor change. Raphael Patai has written,

> Only later, in fact when it was too late, did it dawn upon them that the admittance of even a single Western culture element inevitably brought in its wake more and more new elements with more and more changes, resulting in serious disturbances in the vital texture of their traditional culture. (1971, p. 370)

Structural Assimilation

Whenever minority peoples are incorporated into the institutional structures, clubs, cliques, and primary groups of the core society, structural assimilation is said to have occurred. Because society is a "group of groups," inclusion in the basic groups of a society is necessary in order for a people to share in the common life of that society. It is possible for a people to acquire the language, technology, and values of the core society—to be culturally assimilated—but to be excluded from intimately and fully sharing in societal experiences. American Blacks, for example, have acquired many of the cultural traits of the core society, even though they have been segregated economically and socially. Blacks have accepted the Christian religion to a degree that exceeds that of the general population. They have acquired the English language, and surveys show that they generally support political ideals congruent with those of Whites. This pattern is in marked contrast to that of nations like India in which peoples are set apart by fundamental barriers of religion, caste, and language.

Yet this cultural resonance between American Blacks and Whites has not been accompanied by a large degree of structural assimilation. "We have remained marginal members of this civilization," Louis E. Lomax has stated, "because only doors on the periphery have been opened to us" (1963, p. 20). The fact that Blacks have participated on a face-to-face basis with Whites, especially in the South, has not proved effective in gaining them membership in important basic units of the society. True, they have often been physically present in the homes, in the club rooms, and at the political caucuses of the dominant group; but they have not been there as equal members. They have most often been there as domestics, as chauffeurs, as functionaries.

Many accounts describe attempts by dominant groups to keep minority persons out of the inner groups of the core society. These documents reveal that it is usually not enough for an individual simply to desire membership in such groups. For example, off-campus teen clubs, according to a 1973 report by the Florida State Education Commission, have hampered school desegregation in several cities and may have contributed to increased intergroup tensions in the public schools. High-school sororities and fraternities, which were banned in the 1950s because they emphasized snobbishness, have reappeared in the 1970s as clandestine groups with racial or ethnic overtones (Associated Press, June 14, 1973).

The roles that minority-group members are permitted to play and the facilities offered to them for performing these roles may be of a special kind. The dominant group may put pressure upon minority-group members to change some of the habits and customs that they wish to retain. Or there may be disjunctions between role expectations and demands: Minority-group members may want to attain only economic roles, but the core society may attach political demands to these economic roles (Eisenstadt, 1954, p. 10).

Entering the clubs, cliques, and other primary groups of the core society permits the initiate to observe and probably to imitate new behavior patterns. The widespread practice of initiation and adoption of newcomers among primitive peoples bears out the truth of this idea. These practices serve the function of inducting aliens and outsiders into intimate group contact. An initiate is likely to view the adopting group as an important referent.

After World War II, Zuñi and Navaho young men who had served with the American army faced special problems when they returned home. While in the armed forces, they had been removed from the influence of their own societies and had been compelled to acquire many new forms of behavior. Upon returning, these veterans were regarded with suspicion by older, conservative members of the tribes. Doob has described the efforts that were made to reabsorb these young men into the traditional ways of the tribe: Ceremonials and rites of purification were staged, in order symbolically to remove some of the outside contaminations. Whenever the veterans displayed Anglo ways, they were made to feel conspicuous and uncomfortable through gossip, rumor, and ridicule. The attitudes of other members of the group thus had important implications for the veterans' own attitudes toward assimilation into the core society (1960, pp. 131, 132).

In modern nations, important key groups afford their members strategic access to scarce goods, services, contacts, and vital information, For example, in the United States millions of dollars in business contracts are negotiated on golf courses and in club rooms. These contacts are considered so important that many corporations pay the club dues for top employees. A recent survey of Black-owned banks highlighted this consideration. It was found that the really large industrial corporations and investors do not deposit funds or use the services of these banks. Prejudice against Blacks and failure of the banks to provide needed services were among the reasons given. Lack of personal contacts, however, turned out to be an important consideration. One Black banker commented: "It doesn't hurt when the banker and the biggest manufacturer in town golf together or are old frat brothers. Blacks simply do not have those contacts" (Garnett, 1972, p. 3).

The best index of full assimilation, sociologist S. N. Eisenstadt believes, is "institutional dispersion"—the complete loss of identity of minority groups within the absorbing system. Eisenstadt maintains that full assimilation does not take place until the minority group ceases to have a separate identity within the social structure. Otherwise, vestiges of the minority-group status may serve as a rallying point for separatist tendencies and for particularist group identifications, which may, in turn, become foci of intergroup tensions (1954, p. 13).

Sometimes the outcome is not the obliteration of minority entities but, instead, the development of a pluralistic structure. A pluralistic structure comprises two or more groups that maintain certain distinctive features but participate as partners in one social system. Paradoxically, pluralism often aides further assimilation because those involved do not feel obligated by the core society to drop certain cherished beliefs and customs. This sense stimulates a receptive attitude toward the environing society.

Structural assimilation may be retarded by attitudes of the minority-group members. Numerous instances can be cited in which the core society wished to assimilate various smaller groups, only to have its overtures rejected. In the United States, a number of ethnic groups have tended to turn to their own groups and social classes for a large proportion of their primary group relations. This insularity arises partly from the fact that the major religious groupings have their own networks of cliques, clubs, organizations, and institutions, which tend to confine the primary-group contacts of their members within the group.

If structural assimilation becomes widespread, either simultaneously with or subsequent to acculturation, all the other types of assimilation are likely to follow. This prediction is based on the observation that, when individuals are widely admitted to primary groups and relationships are direct and personal, other aspects of assimilation are likely to occur. For this reason structural assimilation has been called the "keystone of the arch of assimilation" (M. M. Gordon, 1964, p. 81).

Identificational Assimilation

Complete assimilation involves more than acquiring the language, the moral and religious ideas, and the customs of the dominant group. A subjective element is involved—a feeling of identity with the core society. When this feeling occurs, individuals not only act out the traditions of the society but they identify with those traditions as well. Stated another way, identificational assimilation occurs when the core society becomes an important positive referent for members of the minority group.

Identificational assimilation is perhaps most apparent in the experience of an immigrant to a new country. The immigrant's system of values may have to be revised in terms of the values that are accepted by the new society. In many ways this resocialization is similar to an individual's initial socialization, except that an immigrant starts from an already existing social base (Eisenstadt, 1954, p. 7).

Identificational assimilation is both *cognitive* and *affective*. In its cognitive aspect it involves a change of perspective. Minority members are assimilated to the extent that they *see* themselves from the point of view of individuals in the core society and to the extent that members of the core society view them as fellow members. In its affective aspect minority members *feel* that they belong to the larger society; a reciprocal feeling may exist in the dominant group. When identificational assimilation is complete, members of all interacting groups identify with one another as being of a kind.

Minority members who conform to the norms of the core society may simply pretend to agree with members of the dominant group. Sometimes, of course, minority members do agree with the dominant group and see their own group from the dominant group's perspective. Even so, they may be barred from structural and marital assimilation.

Actually the overlapping of group affiliations need not lead to psychological difficulties and may cause little concern. As members of complex societies, all of us regularly learn to compartmentalize our lives, at least to some degree. We tend not to reflect upon incompatible identifications until we find ourselves in situations that present conflicting demands. The same type of conflict occurs when individuals are caught between two divergent cultures, except that the pressure is likely to be more intense.

Identificational assimilation and the tendency toward conformity that is associated with it lead to elimination of diverse elements in a population. Conceivably, minority members may continue to think of themselves as belonging to a distinct group while at the same time identifying with the larger society. Put another way, identificational assimilation can occur in a pluralistic setting. In Switzerland, for example, a citizen of that country identifies with his canton (state) and speaks the language of that canton. But he thinks of himself as Swiss.

Identificational assimilation is Janus-faced. In order for it to occur, members of both the dominant group and the minority must come to think of each other as "we." Chronologically, there are three possibilities: A dominant group may identify with a minority at about the same time that the minority identifies with it, later, or earlier. It is at the point when both the majority and the minority begin to think and feel as one that identification assimilation can be said to have occurred.

Civic Assimilation

The term "civic assimilation" refers to the elimination of power conflicts based on racial or ethnic identifications. As a concept, it includes all the mechanisms that result in incorporation of heterogeneous elements into one comprehensive political unit. Some conquest states in the past have attempted to achieve civic assimilation by offering formal membership in the ruling group to selected individuals or categories of individuals among the conquered. The effect of such a policy has been to unify the state and at the same time to reduce the number of those who might join with outside foes in an attack. The advantages of membership in the dominant group have often been sufficient to ensure acceptance, and refusal has generally been considered a disloyal act.

In Roman times the extension of citizenship to residents of favored cities, as well as to selected individuals, is an illustration of the way in which people of diverse backgrounds can be incorporated into one political unit. S. Dill claims:

> The Empire was not an object of hatred to the barbarians. Indeed, they were eager to be taken into its service, and many of their chiefs, like Alaric . . . had no higher ambition than to be appointed to high military command. On the other

hand, there was a corresponding readiness on the Roman side to employ barbarian forces in war. (1925, p. 29)

The great Roman generals—Pompey, Caesar, Antony—were very free in conferring Roman citizenship upon provincials who had aided them conspicuously. Citizenship involved economic and financial privileges, legal rights, and social distinction, all of which were hereditary, and it was therefore much sought after. The possessors of Roman citizenship came to form a new aristocracy devoted to Rome. The civic unity thus formed became an essential part of the foundation upon which was built the Augustan age (Swain, 1950, p. 391).

Civic assimilation involves free participation in the political life of a nation on a footing of equality. When we view the question this way, we notice a great variation in the policies of modern nations. In the Caribbean, for example, Great Britain generally maintained an exploitative attitude toward its possessions, whereas France was more inclined to assimilate them into the mother country, not only politically, but economically, socially, and culturally as well. "With its roots in humanitarian and Enlightenment ideals," Arvin W. Murch observes, "France's assimilationism apparently led to a greater spread of human rights in the Antilles than did British policies in the West Indies" (Murch, 1968, p. 559).

Civic assimilation in the United States has been an uneven and painful process, but, viewed historically, the trend has been toward increased participation by minorities in the nation's political life. Riots against the Irish are a thing of the past. Discrimination against Scandinavians has largely disappeared, and their group boundaries have become blurred. For Blacks, American Indians, Orientals, and Mexican-Americans, the barriers to governmental participation have been removed more slowly and usually more grudgingly. In many localities it has been only within the past few decades that minority members have voted, served on juries, attended predominantly White state schools and colleges, or held office.

During the 1960s statements like the following began to be incorporated in such documents as research proposals and contracts authorizing federal funds:

Discrimination Prohibited—Title VI of the Civil Rights Act states: "No person in the United States shall, on the ground of race, color, or national origin, be excluded from participation in, be denied the benefits of, or be subjected to discrimination under any program or activity receiving Federal financial assistance."

Debate about how civic assimilation can be achieved—or whether or not it is even desirable—has been bitter. The classic liberal position presupposes a government that is "color blind." Traditionally, liberals have emphasized the values of individual achievement and equality. Their activities have focused on removing handicaps in order that *individuals*—whatever their group affiliations—may compete successfully. Short of that ideal, they have attempted to repair the damage done by discrimination. The ultimate aim has been a society in which individuals freely vote, campaign, debate, and participate in the governmental process.

That approach has been branded by some strategists as naïve, hypocritical, and ineffective. Minority members as individuals—it is argued—have too little power to affect society. In view of this consideration, some writers have urged a policy that is admittedly group-conscious and color-conscious. "Racial integration is not regarded as a matter of immediate, high priority," Charles V. Hamilton has written, "because it is recognized that before any group can enter the open society it must first close ranks" (1969, p. 30).

The Soviet Union's experience with its numerous minorities has been a torturous one. With approximately 130 language and dialect groups, three major religions, and numerous sects and denominations to deal with, the task of sustaining a workable political union could not possibly be easy. Some of the languages, like Ukrainian and Byelorussian, are spoken by millions of people. The cultures of some groups, like the Armenians and Georgians, are old and highly developed. Even in terms of population size, non-Russians slightly outnumber Russians.

During the days of the Russian empire, enforced Russification was the policy. The official stance was embodied in the slogan "One Faith [Orthodoxy]! One Ruler [Autocracy]! One Language [Nationality—Russian]!" Russian was used exclusively in government schools; other languages were suppressed, and Russians were placed in official positions in every region. Minority populations received little formal education because it was believed that they would be easier to govern if they were ignorant.

When the Soviet government came to power in 1917, many of these russification policies were reversed. Every population was permitted to use its own language for daily activities and for proclamations within its regional boundaries. This liberal policy, however, was followed by waves of reaction between 1930 and 1938, when national cultures were again systematically repressed. The literacy and artistic élites in the Ukraine, Armenia, and Turkestan were wiped out. This period was followed by one of relative freedom for nationalities that has continued into the 1970s.

Through all this change the Russian language has retained high prestige in the Soviet communications network and, though it is no longer imposed, it is the *lingua franca* of the entire nation. It seems generally understood that an individual's chances for advancement in Soviet society, especially in central Asia, are greatly enhanced if he or she can speak Russian.

A policy of ethnic democracy was written into the 1936 constitution. Article 123 states:

> Equality of rights of citizens of the U.S.S.R., irrespective of their nationality or race in all spheres of economic, state, cultural, social, and political life is an indefeasible law. Any direct or indirect restriction of the rights of, or, conversely, any establishment of direct or indirect privileges for any citizens on account of

race or nationality, as well as any advocacy of racial or national exclusiveness or hatred is punishable by law.

Nikolai Lenin's contribution to the solution of the "national" problem is held to be the principle of self-determination for all national groups, with the proviso that the interests of socialism remain paramount. Nationalities are free to pursue those goals that do not conflict with larger socialist objectives.

It is difficult for Western observers accurately to assess the gap between official policy and public response in the Soviet Union. Reports of anti-Semitism, persecution of various religious groups, and clashes between various groups appear from time to time. It seems that neither the Soviet Union nor the United States is the "promised land" for minorities, the official policy of both nations notwithstanding.

Intermarriage

> "Intermarriage" itself is resented because it would be a supreme indication of "social equality," while the rationalization is that "social equality" is opposed because it would bring "intermarriage." (Gunnar Myrdal, 1962, p. 591)

Complete assimilation implies intermarriage between members of originally separate groups. Intermarriage is an extension of structural assimilation, inasmuch as it incorporates minority members into primary groups of the society. This function is relatively obvious in societies in which extended families predominate or in which marriages are arranged by families. Yet even in our own society, in which romantic love and individual choice are emphasized, it is a rare marriage that does not bring bride and groom into a network of kinships and family-related friendships.

Some intermating, or miscegenation, almost always occurs whenever two groups are in contact. Contact between two groups may, in fact, be virtually limited to casual sexual relationships, as was true of European sailors who were periodically given shore leave at various islands of Oceania; yet no large-scale assimilation occurred. Intermarriage, sometimes called *marital assimilation* or *amalgamation*, is thus a concomitant of structural assimilation. When it occurs, the minority group gradually loses its visibility in the larger society. Prejudice and discrimination on the basis of prior affiliations gradually subside as descendants of the original minority group become virtually indistinguishable from the core population. Group relations facilitated by marriage tend to foster an "in-group" feeling, which encloses all members of the group.

Intermating, even when not positively sanctioned, may eventually lead to assimilation. When women of minority status are either exploited or voluntarily associate with men of the dominant group, their offspring frequently receive favorable treatment. Even when these children are not fully accepted in the dominant group, their fathers sometimes provide them with education and other advantages that furnish opportunities to move up the economic ladder. Children of mixed descent may even be given privileged status in the society. During the colonial era in Mexico, for example, *mestizos* were exempted from the tribute exacted of Indians (Shibutani and Kwan, 1967, p. 191).

Intermarriage is sometimes promoted as a political strategy. When the British first extended their economic interests into India, they encouraged intermarriage with the local people. From this contact the Anglo-Indian, or Indo-European, population developed. The Court of Directors of the East India Company, in 1687, declared that the marriage of their soldiers to the native women was "a matter of such consequence to posterity" that it was to be encouraged at some expense. When the Anglo-Indians became numerous and threatened to outnumber the Europeans and when the competitive demand for positions became pronounced, the policy changed (C. S. Johnson, 1939, pp. 271–291, 302–303).

Status is all-important in a consideration of intermarriage. If the economic or power gap between the two groups is great, positively sanctioned intermarriage is not likely to occur, though "illegitimate" liaisons may be frequent. In the instance of American Blacks and Whites, it probably has not been so much a question of mutual attractiveness as of the difference in status that has prevented intermarriage from occurring more frequently.

One of the few places in the United States where Chinese have intermarried with other groups is in the Mississippi Delta area around Greenville, Mississippi. The first Chinese in the area migrated from New Orleans and began to work as tenant farmers. Gradually they saved their money and became grocers. Even though these Chinese catered to the Black community, they themselves seem to have been regarded at first as non-Black. Chinese were admitted to White schools and churches in a few small towns of the Delta. During the first generation, however, a few of the Chinese took Black women as wives (usually common-law wives). Two factors seem to have led to this choice. First, eligible females were not available, primarily because our laws generally prohibited Chinese females from immigrating to this country. Second, both the Chinese and the Blacks had approximately the same social status.

Partly as a result of such intermarriage with Blacks, Whites began to exclude Chinese from their schools and churches. In the course of time, however, the Chinese merchants became more affluent. This new wealth and somewhat relaxed immigration laws permitted parents to arrange marriages for their children with Chinese in California, China, and Taiwan. In addition some intermarriage occurred between Chinese and Whites. With these developments came more general acceptance by Whites. Recently the Chinese community has become divided over whether or not it ought to shun Blacks and associate exclusively with Whites. Some of the older Chinese feel that this choice would be disloyal to their one-time friends. Others think that it would be foolish to lose the advantages of association with Whites because of friendship for Blacks (Loewen, 1971).

In the Delta intermarriage between Chinese and Blacks began to decline when the economic and status gap between the two groups widened. A different set of circumstances has prevailed in Hawaii. There intermarriage has been much more frequent, even among groups like the Japanese, who traditionally have avoided exogamy.

Conditions in Hawaii were favorable for intermarriage from the earliest contacts. As early as 1778 King Kamehameha I gave two of Captain James Cook's seamen Hawaiian women of high social rank in marriage. This royal approval paved the way for marriage between Hawaiian women of all social ranks and foreign men of various ancestry (Cheng and Yamamura, 1957, p. 77).

Eventually large numbers of Portuguese, Americans, Chinese, and Japanese migrated to the islands, and many of them intermarried. The Japanese, however, were more endogamous than other ethnic groups. Between 1910 and 1920, only 0.5 percent of the Japanese grooms and 0.2 percent of the Japanese brides married partners other than Japanese. Several explanations have been given (Lind, 1967, p. 108): First, marriage was arranged by the parents, and choice of someone from another group was not likely to occur; second, the Japanese government arranged for sufficient women to be included in each shipment of immigrants.

Even so, the pressures toward exogamy were too great to resist. The Japanese parents in Hawaii, though mistrusting American ways, recognized that their children would eventually become Americans, and they adjusted to the situation. In many instances they began by trying to enforce the old Japanese marriage customs but ended by yielding to the wishes of their children.

World War II was the catalyst for this evolving attitude. During the war years considerable dating occurred between American servicemen and Japanese women. Even after the military population declined at the end of the war, a lasting impression was left on the courtship patterns. It seems that the Japanese group, which was large enough to maintain its identity for many years and was slow to intermarry, became involved in the life of the surrounding community to the point at which, even in marriage, association with the larger society became more important than loyalty to the past (Hormann, 1948, p. 70).

Intermarriage may not take place because it is illegal. At one time, many states enacted and enforced miscegenation laws that provided stiff penalties for offenders. "Until 1948, the marriage of a Chinese man to a white woman was prohibited by California law" (Gold, 1973, p. 6). Not only the bride and groom but also the clergyman (or other official) who took part in such proscribed activities faced severe sanctions in most states.

This situation still prevails in the Union of South Africa. The Immorality Act, passed in 1950 by the ruling National party, forbids sex between persons of different groups. More than 7,600 people have been convicted since its enactment

("Shame City," 1971, pp. 25, 28). A countertrend is apparent in the United States. One by one the miscegenation laws of the various states have been repealed, and those that remained in force in 1967 were, in effect, nullified by the Supreme Court decision of Loving *et ux. v.* Virginia. In that decision the court held that Virginia's statutory scheme to prevent marriages between persons solely on the basis of racial classifications violated the equal protection and due-process clauses of the Fourteenth Amendment. (See pp. 129, 130.)

Intermarriage may not occur because it violates the mores. When that is so, then even when laws actually permit intermarriage it will still not occur very often. Members of a particular group may believe that intermarriage outside the group is degrading or sinful, and such a belief has the effect of maintaining group solidarity, particularly among religious minorities.

A prohibition against intermarriage is often economically advantageous for a wealthy group. Whenever custom and tradition have it that dirty, poor-paying jobs are to be assigned to members of a particular ethnic group, intermarriage confuses matters and threatens the position of the wealthy group.

The Rate of Assimilation

Robert Ezra Park believed that an "apparently progressive and irreversible" cycle characterizes the relations between unlike peoples—contact, competition, accommodation, and eventually assimilation (1926). Social scientists today agree that strong assimilative forces may be present in such situations, but they do not generally accept the claim that the process is always progressive and irreversible. It is clear that some individuals and groups tend to be more readily assimilated than do others. Certain conditions in society and certain group and personal characteristics affect the rate of change. Several writers (Simpson, 1968. I, 439ff; Berry, 1965: 263–271) have described key variables, of which the following seem to be the most important.

Cultural Similarity

When there is congruence between the culture of the minority and the culture of the core society, the minority will tend to be more rapidly assimilated than when there is little congruity between the cultures. Differences in important cultural elements—language, religion, dietary taboos, style of dress—typically slow the rate of assimilation.

Studies of marriage and religious affiliation illustrate the point. Before the 1940s the "melting pot" concept was an essential part of the American view of things. It was widely believed that it was only a matter of time until the diverse peoples of the United States would be merged into "true" Americans. In 1944, however, Ruby Jo Reeves Kennedy published research that challenged this idea. She reported, after studying intermarriage rates in New Haven from 1870 to 1940, that there was instead a "triple melting pot" (1940, pp. 331–339). By this phrase, Kennedy meant that intermarriage was taking place across nationality lines but that these marriages tended to take place within the boundaries of three major religious groups: Protestant, Roman Catholic, and Jewish.

Any culture includes a great many elements, some of which are valued more than others. In the example just described, the part of culture most emphasized was religion. In other situations the interacting groups may attach great importance to language (for example, the Ainu in Japan were forced to learn Japanese), clothing (like the "plain" clothes of the Amish), diet (as in Hindu prohibitions on eating beef), or family organization (the extended family or the nuclear family, monogamy or polygyny).

Demography

The size and composition of a group will affect the rate of its assimilation. Youthful immigrant groups generally assimilate more readily than do those composed largely of older people. In Hawaii there has been a stronger tendency for members of numerically small groups to marry outside their own groups than for those of larger groups to do so (Cheng and Yamamura, 1967, pp. 77–84).

The rate of entrance of a minority group will affect the rate of assimilation. One underlying reason is that a large unassimilated group is more visible and is likely to be singled out for prejudice and discrimination. Also, a sudden influx of immigrants often alarms older, established peoples and tends to disturb earlier relationships. This reaction occurred in Great Britain when the number of Black immigrants from the West Indies increased rapidly following World War II. The Indian refugees who fled East Africa in the 1970s further exacerbated the problem, so that for the first time in many years intergroup tension became a domestic issue in Great Britain.

When a minority group is concentrated in one geographical area, assimilation is less likely to occur than when it is widely dispersed. Ecological islands of minority peoples provide security for new arrivals and tend to isolate them from the mainstream of the larger society. A numerically small, widely dispersed minority poses no threat to the dominant group. In addition, such groups are unable to sustain those organizations that facilitate group preservation (separate schools, churches, and the like).

Physical Features

When individuals speak a different language, they can be readily identified as different from those around them. But, if they become facile in the national language, it is more difficult to recognize them as outsiders. Physical features—like skin color, shape of eyes, and hair texture—are another matter because they are permanent and noticeable. For this reason physical features often are the "role signs" or insignias for discrimination in various societies. In given situations, however, physical differences may be ignored. Persons with red hair, for example, have never been the objects of systematic discrimination in American life. Red hair is a real physical difference, but it has not become socially defined as a criterion for discrimination. For reasons discussed previously, skin color, shape of nose, and texture of hair have been so defined. Studies using the Bogardus social-distance test between 1926 and 1966 have revealed that groups whose physical characteristics diverge most from those of the English and White Americans—Japanese, Turks, Koreans, Mexicans, Blacks, and American Indians—have received the highest social-distance scores (Bogardus, 1966).

Permanence of the Group

Assimilation is not likely to occur when members of a group feel that they are transients. Historically, a rather large number of groups have produced individuals with "sojourner" or "pilgrim" mentalities. People with such a perspective, especially those in religious minorities, take the attitude that it is not really worth the time and effort to learn the language and customs of the environing society. Overseas Americans tend to adopt a similar attitude, though it usually has a secular basis. Because they know that they will one day return to "the States," they often do not bother to learn the language well, they tend to be careless about local customs and etiquette, and they are usually clannish. Rarely do they give up their citizenship. Neither acculturation, identificational assimilation, civic assimilation, nor intermarriage occurs to any great extent. Intermating has been known to occur!

Economic Factors

Minorities tend to be assimilated when there are substantial economic advantages to be derived from merging. The observance of various customs like religious holidays and food taboos (which often serve as symbols of a group's identity) may gradually come to be ignored if they result in serious economic disadvantages.

Broad similarities in the life styles of those who engage in production, whether industrial, agricultural, or pastoral, provide a basis for understanding and assimilation. Conversely, marked differences in the technology of the interacting groups retard assimilation. It may take many years for an industrialized society to assimilate a peasant people. The nation of Israel has experienced this problem with its immigrants, some of whom come from industrialized nations like those of western Europe and others from the agrarian societies of the Middle East and Africa.

If a group is economically self-sufficient, its prevailing attitude is likely to be ethnocentric. Among the Hutterites in Canada, residents of large, self-contained communities are more ethnocentric and are less friendly toward outsiders than are residents of small, economically dependent communities.

Attitudes

Some groups fear assimilation and resist it vigorously, whereas other groups seem obsessed with the desire for acceptance by the core society. The mere desire to maintain a traditional culture is not in itself an all-sufficient barrier to assimilation. The Amish have had considerable success, but some ethnic groups like the Russian Molokans in California have found the task of preserving old ways too great (Berry, 1965, p. 267).

The Social Structure of the Group

A highly integrated community is likely to resist assimilation if it provides many satisfactions for its members. A highly disintegrated ethnic community, however, may be rejected by the host community and forced into a marginal position. In between apparently lies maximum likelihood of successful assimilation (Williams, 1964, p. 303).

The Time Factor

Assimilation often cannot be promoted directly but only indirectly, that is through supplying the conditions that make for joint participation. It has been observed that only life itself can erase the minority group's memory of its past. Time is also required for individuals in the core society to forget that individuals with certain physical features or family surnames once belonged to a separate and distinct group.

Overview

Several subprocesses are involved when unlike peoples meet and eventually become one—acculturation, structural assimilation, identificational assimilation, civic assimilation, and intermarriage. Usually acculturation is the first of these subprocesses to occur. Learning the language, customs, beliefs, and etiquette of the core society becomes the basis for further integration. Structural assimilation involves the incorporation of minority members into the clubs, cliques, and primary groups of the core society. One of the assimilative subprocesses may occur without the other, however. In the United States, for example, Blacks have become acculturated, but there has been relatively little structural assimilation. Identificational assimilation involves the subjective experience by which the individual comes to feel an identity with the core society. When identificational assimilation is complete, members of all interacting groups identify with one another as being of a kind.

Civic assimilation involves the elimination of power conflicts based on minority-majority relations. Historically, civic assimilation has been a deliberate strategy of many governments. The Roman empire made Roman citizenship available to numerous categories of individuals in the provinces.

In the United States civic assimilation has been uneven and painful, but the long-range trend has been toward increased participation by minorities in the nation's political life. The Soviet Union, with its many language and dialect groups, predictably has experienced many difficulties in incorporating its heterogeneous peoples into one viable political system. In many developing nations allegiance to the tribe or people rather than to the nation has been the rule, not the exception, and it continues to be one of their major domestic problems.

Widespread intermarriage lowers the visibility of a minority and accelerates the other assimilative subprocesses. Intermarriage, in contrast to miscegenation without societal approval, is actually a form of structural assimilation. Some societies have prevented its occurrence through legal means, like the miscegenation laws of the United States, or through the mores.

Most social scientists foresee a heterogeneous American society for a long time to come. George Simpson has written:

> If the ultimate test of complete assimilation is large-scale intermarriage, that state will not be reached in the United States in the near future. Changes will occur in the relations between members of diverse racial and ethnic groups, but these changes will consist mainly of a closer approximation to equal education and economic opportunities, increased political participation and an acceleration of desegregation in schools and places of public accommodation. (1968, p. 444)

For Further Reading

Many of the items among the references cited may be considered as recommended reading as well.

Downs, James F. *The Two Worlds of the Washo: An Indian Tribe of California and Nevada.* New York: Holt, Rinehart and Winston, 1966.
Fitzpatrick, Joseph P. *Puerto Rican Americans: The Meaning of Migration to the Mainland.* Englewood Cliffs, N.J.: Prentice-Hall, 1971.
Gist, Noel P., and Anthony Gary Dworkin (eds.). *The Blending of Races: Marginality and Identity in World Perspective.* New York: Wiley, 1972.

Gordon, Milton M. *Assimilation in American Life: The Role of Race, Religion, and National Origins.* New York: Oxford University Press, 1964.

Grebler, Leo, Joan W. Moore, and Ralph C. Guzman. *The Mexican-American People.* New York: Free Press, 1970.

Handlin, Oscar. *The Newcomers: Negroes and Puerto Ricans in a Changing Metropolis.* New York: Doubleday, 1962.

Handlin, Oscar. *Race and Nationality in American Life.* New York: Doubleday, 1957.

Herberg, Will. *Protestant—Catholic—Jew.* New York: Doubleday, 1955.

Levine, Stuart, and Nancy O. Lurie (eds.). *The American Indian Today.* Baltimore: Penguin, 1970.

Mead, Margaret, *New Lives For Old.* New York: Dell, 1968.

Meier, August, and Elliott M. Rudwick. *From Plantation to Ghetto: An Interpretive History of American Negroes.* New York: Hill & Wang, 1966.

ETHNIC MINORITIES IN THE SOVIET UNION

ERICH GOLDHAGEN

Very few Americans realize how complex and sensitive the minority situation in the Soviet Union really is. Civic assimilation in the U.S.S.R. has been a tortuous and painful experience. The following article outlines the more prominent dimensions of the problem.

Few aspects of Soviet society have been the object of such divergent opinions and impassioned disputes as the condition of the numerous ethnic minorities inhabiting the Soviet Union. On the one hand, some Western writers have denounced the Soviet Union as a colonial oppressor that has subjugated the non-Russian peoples, subjected them to severe treatment, and endeavored to divest them of their native cultures by imposing upon them Russification. And in the case of some minorities, so the indictment runs, the treatment was so severe that it may be said to border on genocide. On the other hand, in sharp contrast to this dark picture, the Soviet Union has presented to the world a radiant image. In it, the numerous nationalities form a fraternal and harmonious union of which the Russian people are an unprivileged member; their separate cultures are protected and fostered in equal measure; enmity and even discord among them have evaporated under the enlightenment of Communism; and no Soviet citizen suffers discrimination because of his ethnic origin. In short, in Soviet parlance, the national problem has been solved in the Soviet Union. This solution, though an unprecedented historical achievement, will however be supplanted by a still more perfect consummation whose beginnings are already discernible. In the future, all nationalities will gradually and voluntarily shed their distinctive identities, abandon their respective languages for Russian, the lingua franca of the Soviet Union, and merge into a common body from which all ethnic differences will disappear—a Russian-speaking cosmopolis.

Confronted by these sharply contrasting pictures one might be tempted to dismiss them as figments of partisan imaginations. Indeed, the truth is neither as black as some Western writers paint it nor the pastoral idyll drawn by Soviet propagandists. The condition of the ethnic minorities in the Soviet Union is complex and many-hued, a unique and novel phenomenon defying the labels of political polemics. It is the purpose of this volume to unfold before the reader the complex and unique fate of the major non-Russian peoples under Soviet rule.

The Bolsheviks began their rule with a noble promise to the nationalities. They proclaimed the right to self-determination, which meant the right of each nation to secede from the Russian empire and constitute itself as an independent state. Not that Lenin regarded self-determination as a desirable goal. On the contrary, he viewed it as detrimental to socialism, for it would produce a multitude of states hindering the creation of large-scale socialist economies essential to the flourishing of a socialist society. He believed, however, that the striving for national independence could best be checked by announcing that no obstacles stood in its way. If, out of concern for the future of socialism, one denied the right to self-determination, one would stir resentment among the nationalities and increase the desire for independence. But by leaving the door to secession wide open one would blunt the desire for it, since the nationalities, recognizing the benefits to be derived from a large socialistic commonwealth, would choose to remain within the union rather than to withdraw into the constricting framework of small statehood and a precarious, and in many cases penurious, existence. In Lenin's view the right to self-determination was to be promulgated in order to nip the desire for it in the bud.

But when, amid the turmoil of revolution and civil war, independence movements sprang up among the nationalities, rending asunder the empire, the Bolsheviks threw the promise of self-determination unhesitatingly and remorselessly to the wind and set out to subdue the national minorities that refused to submit to their authority; within a few years after the Revolution, aided by small Communist minorities within each of the nationalities, they succeeded in recapturing all of the Asian provinces and a great part of the European domain of the Czarist empire, welding them into a Communist state.

Although honored in the breach, the right to self-determination has ever since remained an article of the official creed, as though it had never been violated; and it was solemnly enshrined in the Soviet constitution—a stillborn, decorative right of which one is free to boast in the Soviet Union but which it would be dangerous to claim.

Unlike the Czarist regime—which, though desiring to Russify the whole of the empire, did not reach deeply into the internal life of any of the non-Russian peoples under its rule, except in those cases in which it felt threatened by native recalcitrance—the Soviet regime set out to transform the lives of the nationalities in accordance with the precepts of its ideology and the requirements of industrialization and modernization which it sought to effect. It viewed the nationalities not only as inhabitants of territories rich in resources, or of strategic value, but also as backward and "feudal" peoples to be radically reshaped in the socialist image. Moreover, the Bolshevik leaders of the early days were imbued with a strong sense of internationalism. They were for the most part free from ethnic prejudice; and although the Bolshevik party, composed predominantly of Russians, may have appeared to the nationalities as the heir of the Czars, the Bolsheviks thought of themselves as builders of a new society whose hallmark would be the equality of all. In the 1920's, in order to placate national sentiments and to give a native flavor to its rule, the Communist dictatorship granted to the major nationalities formal autonomy in the shape of constituent republics of a federal Soviet

Union. This autonomy has ever since been spurious, for all power has remained in the hands of the central authority in Moscow, where all major decisions affecting the destinies of the minorities are taken.

Yet one should not underestimate the symbolic satisfaction that the trappings of autonomous "statehood," however insubstantial, have given to the ethnic pride of the minorities. Beyond this, the Communist regime during the 1920's encouraged the use of the native languages in local administrations and in the schools. It greatly expanded the educational systems of the minorities and launched a campaign to abolish illiteracy, widespread among most of them. It devised alphabets for unlettered peoples whose languages had never been written down. In short, it began to equip each of the non-Russian peoples with a cultural apparatus intended to transmit to them scientific knowledge and technical skills, as well as to serve as a means by which the new ideology could be implanted in the minds and hearts of its people. The statistics on the growth of schools, the increase of literacy, the numbers of educated persons and of trained engineers, scientists, and holders of academic degrees offer an impressive picture of cultural ascent of the minorities under Communist rule. The Soviet dictatorship surrounded the nationalities with an iron hedge, ruthlessly suppressing all endeavor for independence, but within these confines the national identity was given considerable freedom of scope. The dictatorship arrogated to itself, however, the right to be the arbiter of what was permissible and impermissible, which part of the national culture could be fostered and which was to be subdued or discarded. Yet whatever the intentions of the regime may have been, the cultural institutions it created among the non-Russian peoples, together with the symbols of autonomy it conferred upon them, had the unintended effect of strengthening their national consciousness, especially among the nationalities in whom it had been but feebly developed.

After the great change of the early 1930's, under Stalin's iron rule, the minorities were subjected to far sterner dispensation. The new period was characterized by the elevation of the Russian people and things Russian to a position of preeminence, and by the endeavor to draw the minorities into the orbit of Russian culture with an ultimate view to Russification and, as a corollary, the constriction of the scope and content of native cultures. It was a period in which the Russian language was exalted, the heroes of Russian history (even those who had hitherto been treated as reactionaries) celebrated, and the symbols of Russian nationhood revered. Conversely, many of the heroes of the national minorities were dethroned, many of the ethnic symbols tabooed or subdued, and every institution or person that strove or appeared to strive to protect native identity against the encroachment of Russian culture denounced as a promoter of "bourgeois nationalism," one of the chief heresies in the Soviet canon. There is scarcely a nationality that escaped the heresy hunt, and innumerable non-Russians, Party members, writers, and common people paid with their freedom or with their lives for the real or imagined sin of bourgeois nationalism.

Six ethnic groups were treated so severely that their very existence as coherent, viable entities was endangered: the Ingush, the Chechens, the Crimea Tartars, the Kalmyks, the Karachai, and the Balkars. Each of these groups had incurred the wrath of Stalin, who held all of its members accountable for the collaboration of some in their midst with the German invaders during World War II. The sins of the few were visited upon the whole community. Each group in its entirety was banished from its native land to a remote place under conditions of extreme privation, causing widespread suffering and death; and its name was expunged from the public records of the Soviet Union as though it had ceased to exist. After Stalin's death, the Soviet Government pronounced the deportation of these nationalities a "gross error" and rehabilitated them. According to Krushchev, Stalin was tempted to mete out similar punishment to the Ukrainians, but their numbers made banishment impracticable. The experience of these groups shows that the fate of ethnic minorities, like that of other social groups, was determined not only by ideological and political considerations but also by the capricious, vengeful temper of the dictator and the irrational vagaries that marked his rule.

In exalting things Russian and in glorifying Russian nationalism, Stalin and successive Soviet leaders were moved not by chauvinistic impulses but by considerations of totalitarian *raison d'état*. They appealed to Russian national feelings because the Russians were the most numerous and the most important of all the nations of the Soviet Union and their support was necessary if Communism was to succeed. Moreover, it is easier to rule an ethnically homogeneous state than a multinational realm, which is a perpetual breeding ground of recalcitrant national feelings and aspirations. Also, insofar as the Soviet leaders were still needful of Marxian rationalizations, they could justify to themselves their policy to make the minorities surrender to Russian culture—the process they euphemistically call the "fusion of nations," or "internationalization"—as a progressive endeavor: the undoing of *Kleinvölkerei* as a step toward the creation of a universal socialist society.

Whatever the motives of the Soviet leaders, it is clear that for them the preservation of the separate identities of the ethnic minorities is not a desirable goal, and that their aim is to bring about the "fusion of nations." Every pronouncement by the Soviet leaders dealing with the future of ethnic minorities professes that aim. One such utterance by a Soviet leader, chosen almost at random, may be given here as an example. In a speech before the Twenty-second Party Congress, Khrushchev said:

> One cannot fail to note the growing striving of the non-Russian peoples to acquire the Russian language which has become in effect the second native language for the peoples of the U.S.S.R. . . . The process actually now taking place of voluntary study of the Russian language is of positive significance for the development of cooperation between nations. A process of bringing nations

closer together is taking place in our country; their social homogeneity is being strengthened.

Every sign of Russification is acclaimed and every resistance to it denounced as an ignorant balking of historical progress or, worse, as a conscious or unconscious service to the enemies of the Soviet Union. Thus *Izvestiia* reported the exultation of a Caucasian poet at having been penetrated by Russian culture: "A son of the mountains I am in spirit, and in mind a Russian man. Without the Russian language, without the Russian environment, nothing in life is close to me."*

How successful has the policy of "fusion" been? If the degree of displacement of the native languages by Russian is taken as an indicator, then the inroads of Russian culture into the ethnic fabric of the minorities have not been very deep. The census of 1959 revealed that most minorities cling to their languages, and even in the case of the Jews, who have undergone a high degree of linguistic Russification, the sense of ethnic consciousness and apartness has remained alive. Fifty years after the Bolshevik Revolution, the goal of Russification must seem more remote to the Soviet leaders than it did during the 1920's or the 1930's, when the Bolshevik mind was less tempered by the complexity of reality, when it seemed that the social world was but clay in the hands of the Bolshevik potters.

If in the political and cultural sphere the Soviet Union has grossly departed from its original promise of self-determination, in the economic and social treatment of the minorities it has remained more faithful to its professed creed. The services provided by the Soviet state, such as pensions, medical treatment, holidays, etc., are more or less equitably dispensed to all Soviet citizens irrespective of their ethnic origins. Although Vsevolod Holubnychy, casts doubt on the belief that economic resources are equitably distributed among the various republics, one cannot call the Soviet economic policies in regard to minorities "colonialist," unless one assigns to that word a meaning quite different from its usual sense.

In any discussion of ethnic minorities in the Soviet Union, the movement of polycentrism sweeping over the Communist world, fragmenting the former monolithic unity of which it had boasted and which had for so long seemed unshakable, comes to mind. Underlying that movement is the doctrine that the will of the Soviet Union can never again be, as it was in the days of Stalin, a command for other Communist parties and states. The primacy of the Soviet Union must be replaced by the recognition of the sovereign right of all members of the Communist camp to follow their own course both in their internal affairs and in the world at large. This doctrine has been militantly asserted in many parts of the Communist world and reluctantly accepted by the Soviet Union. It might hold a perilous attraction for the leaders of some nationalities of Soviet Russia. Surely, they might argue, why should, say, Georgia and the Ukraine be entitled, if not to

* *Izvestiia*, December 5, 1961.

the full measure of sovereignty granted Poland and Rumania, at least to a greater measure of genuine autonomy within the framework of the Soviet Union? There are signs that the Soviet leaders are conscious of the danger that the spirit of polycentrism may penetrate into their own domain to inflame national feelings and stir national aspirations that could lay claim to doctrinal legitimacy. They have recently displayed a heightened alertness to the manifestations of nationalism, and a note of profound disquiet is audible in the official pronouncement on the theme. "In nationalism," *Pravda* observed on February 7, 1968, "lies the greatest danger to the fighting capability and ideological power of the Communist movement. . . . It must not be reconciled with the ideology of Marxism-Leninism." This disquiet is mingled with perplexity at a phenomenon for which Marxist theory cannot account. According to the Marxian prophecy, nationalism would wane with the advance of Communism. Yet the opposite has occurred—it has been growing. Unable to admit in public, or even to themselves, that the ideology upon which their claim to power rests has proved to be so profoundly mistaken, they have sought to persuade themselves and others that the spread of nationalism in the Communist camp is an unnatural and transient aberration. Yet as they watch the powerful currents of nationalism coursing through their camp they are overcome by worry. Never before in the history of the Soviet Union has the danger of nationalism so intensely and so anxiously preoccupied its leaders as it does today.

The verdict of the objective student on the historical performance of the Soviet Government in the treatment of ethnic minorities under its rule cannot be rendered in clear-cut and unicolored terms. The Soviet Government appears here in a manifold role. To the Asian peoples under its sway, it was the great Westernizer of their societies, imparting to them the skills and attitudes of modernity and raising them to a level of economic development which compares favorably with that of the adjacent Asian countries. In the cultural realm, however, it has been the high-handed tamperer with their cultural legacy, suppressing or curtailing many parts of their tradition. To the six nationalities that were deported, the Soviet Government appeared as the brutal assailant upon their very lives, and, to the Jews, as the enemy of the whole of their cultural legacy, excepting an emasculated and shrunken Yiddish literary estate. To the Baltic peoples, to the Ukrainians and Georgians, the Soviet Government is the undoer of their independent statehood, however short lived and imperfect it may have been, and the arbitrary manipulator of their art, literature, historiography, and the sanctities of their nation. Among most minorities material achievements, impressive as they are in many cases, have been attended by intellectual and cultural constrictions and the tailoring of their identities, and all have been exposed to the pressures of Russification. Yet all we know about the Soviet minorities suggests that their ethnic personalities are alive and that their muteness is a tribute to the efficiency of the totalitarian Leviathan rather than a sign of the absence of collective aspirations. If the incipient, feeble, and struggling trend toward pluralism in Soviet society increases, then these aspirations may assert themselves and profoundly affect the shape of Soviet society. But in any case it is doubtful whether the national minorities will conform to the blueprint of the "fusion of nations" nourished by the Soviet leadership. History may yet assign to the national minorities a role in the future of Soviet Russia quite different from that reserved for them by Lenin and Stalin in their visions of the future.

NATIONAL LANGUAGES
AND THE LANGUAGE
OF INTERLINGUAL COMMUNICATION

YURI DESHERIYEV

This article originally appeared in the magazine **Communist.** It is particularly useful for the study of intergroup relations because of its candid description of the problems associated with acculturation and civic assimilation. What is of particular interest to the social scientist is that the article is written from the point of view of a government wrestling with the difficulties that seem always to be present in multigroup nations.

The peoples inhabiting the Soviet Union speak almost 130 languages. Prior to the October 1917 Revolution any attempt to develop non-Russian cultures and languages was crushed. Czarist ideologists wrote in alarm: ". . . Strengthen any language by providing it with an alphabet; give it a certain amount of literary form; set forth its rules of grammar; introduce it into school teaching, and you thereby [*horribile dictu!*—Y.D.] strengthen and develop the corresponding national minority."* The Russia of the bourgeoisie and the landowners left an evil heritage. The inhabitants of most of the non-Russian border regions were illiterate. According to the first All-Russia Census of 1897, 21.2 percent of the inhabitants of the Russian Empire were literate, while for Turkestan (today's Soviet Central Asian republics) the percentage ran between one and five. It is noteworthy that the following decade literacy in European Russia rose by an average of 42.2 percent, as against 1.1 percent in the Caucasus, 1.3 percent in Siberia and 0.4 percent in Central Asia. At this rate, to achieve universal literacy would have taken 120 years in European Russia, 430 years in the Caucasus and Siberia, and 4600

* Journal of the Ministry of Public Education, 1887, February, p. 37.

years in Turkestan! The other non-Russian outlying areas of the czarist empire were in no better condition.

The October Revolution ushered in fundamental social and economic changes, among them application in practice of the Leninist national policy calling for the emancipation of the peoples from all forms of social and national oppression and for the development of their cultures and languages. There was an acute shortage of literate men and women in the non-Russian areas. A purposeful and comprehensive program of education for adults was essential, and such a program was adopted in 1921 by the Tenth Congress of the party. The historic decision declared that it was the task of the party to help the working masses develop and strengthen the Soviet state in ways that conformed to the specific national conditions of a given area; to create courts of law, legislative, administrative and economic bodies, a press, theater, general and vocational schools—all using the language of the area—in order to accelerate the training of local personnel.

For the first time in the history of the world alphabets were created for dozens of languages widely different in structure.

The Presidium of the All-Russia Central Executive Committee formed a Central Committee for New Alphabets and a Committee for a New Alphabet for the Peoples of the North; language and cultural institutions were established under the Councils of People's Commissars of the union republics. All these measures were applications of the Soviet policy on language.

In the twenties schools with instruction in the local languages were set up all over the country, spelling and terminology were evolved and textbooks compiled. Certain ancient alphabets were replaced by modern systems of writing. As a result, over 40 national groups acquired scientifically grounded alphabets.

Many such languages did not even have terms for concepts that we consider elementary today: letter, alphabet, writing, book, blackboard, classroom, teacher, pupil and the like. Neither did they have grammatical terms, indispensable in teaching the language.

An end to illiteracy and semiliteracy for the vast majority of the population was the prime educational target in the first decade after the Revolution, for, as Lenin pointed out, "A communist society cannot be built in an illiterate country."

Matters were complicated by the fact that there were practically no teachers of Kirghiz, Kazakh, Tajik, Uzbek or Turkmen nationality. The main burden of training local teachers fell on Russian educators.

Training teaching personnel and creating alphabets went hand in hand. To decide which dialect should provide the foundation for a system of writing for a particular people, Soviet linguists researched the phonetic systems, grammatical structures and lexical stock of the languages in question, and ascertained the links between cognate languages and dialects. Teams of scholars were sent to study languages that had been either wholly neglected or insufficiently studied. The following requisites were proposed to determine the dialects to be chosen as the basis of the respective languages: whether they were used by the bulk of the given population, whether the phonetic system, the grammar structure and the lexis of the dialect reflected the main features of the language for which the alphabet was being created. Also taken into account were the historical traditions in the use of a particular dialect by speakers of other dialects as a means of communication.

A comprehensive solution had to be found to numerous problems of major social, governmental and scientific significance: the establishment, in the areas where new systems of writing had been introduced, of schools at all levels, research institutes, academies of sciences, theaters, clubs, a periodical press; the determination of principles in choosing the languages for which writing systems were to be created; research on the social functions of languages; the establishment of the phonological and visual basis of alphabets, and the like. Language development was generously financed by the state. In those very difficult days for the new Soviet Republic, Lenin spoke of the need to allot the money for "wiping out illiteracy, and for reading rooms."

There were, of course, shortcomings, miscalculations and errors. Alphabets and systems of writing were devised for very small nationalities and ethnic groups, only to be later rejected by them in favor of the languages of the larger nations in which they lived. There was unjustified preference for artificial and abstruse terms instead of those accepted internationally and in the USSR. There were archaic terms. But the development of national languages helped stamp out illiteracy and semiliteracy in an astonishingly short period.

Mutual Influence and Enrichment

Today such languages as Armenian, Azerbaijani and Georgian are used in every area of life in the respective republics. The use of newly alphabetized languages (Abkhazian, Avar, Balkarian, Ingush and others) has expanded to such a degree that novels, poetry, and social and political literature are now published in them, and they are used in teaching and in mass media.

The use of the languages of many of the non-Russian nationalities has expanded enormously. This applies especially to Ukrainian, Byelorussian, Uzbek, Kazakh, Lithuanian, Georgian, Azerbaijani, Kirghiz, Moldavian, Latvian, Tajik, Armenian, Turkic, Estonian, Tatar and others. Publication in these languages of novels and poetry, of social, political, scientific and technical literature is rising by leaps and bounds. Thus, while not a single book was published in Tajik in 1913, the totals in 1950 and 1970 were 2,313,000 and 4,100,000 copies respectively in this small republic.

Most of the newly alphabetized languages used in the various autonomous republics, regions and national areas have begun to function as literary languages.

Not only are novels and poetry, both in the original and translation, as well as social, political and educational literature, published in these languages, but they are used on the stage, on radio and television, as well as in the very popular amateur art activities.

Cultural exchange is continuous, promoted by the practice of regular festivals of national literature and art held in Moscow, Leningrad and the various republics, regions and areas. Works by writers and poets in Russian and other world languages are widely published in the languages of the non-Russian Soviet republics. The works of writers not only in the union republics but also those belonging to the smaller nationalities are translated into other Soviet languages. The Abkhaz Dmitri Gulia, the Avar Rasul Gamzatov, the Balkar Kaisyn Kuliev, the Kabardinian Alim Keshokov, the Adyghe Tembot Kerashev, the Ingush Idris Bazorkin, and the Chechen Magomet Mamakayev have been translated into many Soviet and foreign languages.

An important socially conditioned factor in the development of languages in the Soviet Union is their interaction and mutual enrichment. True, before the Revolution there was some interaction, but under those conditions the languages used by the oppressed peoples were generally replaced or suppressed. The almost total illiteracy of the masses was the greatest deterrent to any of the possible values of interaction.

The mutual enrichment of languages has made great advances in Soviet times. This, of course, does not mean that languages have discarded their national elements or that they have been assimilated. Development and mutual enrichment have not prevented them from preserving their vital national characteristics. The Russian language is perhaps the best case in point. At all stages of its historical development, Russian has been a source of enrichment for all the other languages spoken in our country and has itself grown richer by borrowing from them.

Russian is one of the main sources for the enrichment and development of the newly alphabetized languages of the Soviet peoples. Between 70 and 80 percent of all their sociopolitical, scientific and technical terms come from Russian and, through Russian, from other languages. Words taken from Russian figure in all the languages of the Soviet peoples without exception.

Still, not one of them has done so much borrowing as Russian, since it has interacted, to a greater or lesser degree, with all the other languages in our country, a process which continues.

Prior to the Revolution, words taken from the other languages of Russia were limited to so-called ethnologisms. In Soviet times, with the development of art, literature, and scientific and technical disciplines in the non-Russian languages, Russian has had more sources of enrichment to draw upon. Thus, such new terms have appeared in Armenian from international models as nairite, ditilen, tangleron, sevanite, erevanite and the like. These have become part of the Russian literary language and of the international terminology of the appropriate branch of knowledge. Similar processes of mutual enrichment are also taking place in other of our literary languages. It was Alexander Pushkin, the founder of modern literary Russian, who said that Russian is "receptive and hospitable in its relations with other languages."

The vast majority of borrowed words reflect elements of the customs and cultures of the peoples inhabiting the Soviet Union.

Many new elements in the development of the non-Russian languages derive from the formation of a common vocabulary in the Soviet languages, first and foremost from such international and Soviet words as socialism, communism, Soviet, kolkhoz, sovkhoz and the like. In most of our literacy languages, spelling and pronunciation norms for borrowed words often conform to models provided by words belonging to the common vocabulary—party, Komsomol, philology, philosophy, cosmos and so on.

Interlingual Communication

Russian has become the common language of communication among the Soviet peoples. As was noted by the Resolution of the CPSU Central Committee on preparations for the fiftieth anniversary of the formation of the USSR, "All nations and nationalities of the USSR have voluntarily chosen the Russian language as their common tongue. It has become a powerful instrument for the relationship and cohesion of the Soviet peoples, the medium of their association with the finest achievements of their country's culture and world culture." History has given that function to the Russian language.

In the first place, Russian is the mother tongue of over half the inhabitants of the Soviet Union; secondly, it is used by a considerable part of the non-Russian population of the country; thirdly, a definite role has been played by tradition, the great and beneficent influence of Russian culture and science on the development of the languages and cultures of the peoples of the USSR; fourthly, the Russian people, who led the heroic struggle to liberate the country from the yoke of the czarist enslavers, have given systematic and fraternal aid to all the Soviet peoples in their political, economic and cultural development.

Although school instruction at all levels, the publication of scientific and technical literature, and the training of scientific personnel are carried on in dozens of languages used by the peoples of our country, a fluent knowledge of Russian is still necessary, both for communication within the country, and for communication with other countries. Russian is one of the official languages of the United Nations. Besides, it is the country's most complete source of scientific and technical information on current development in all branches of knowledge. The growing cultural needs of Soviet people cannot be met fully unless the non-Russian inhabitants of our country know Russian. That is why a fluent knowledge of Russian, side by side with the mother tongue, has become common in our country.

Bilingual courses of study in secondary and higher education are general in the Soviet Union. For many years such courses have been given at secondary and higher schools in Abkhazia, Adygei, Daghestan, Karachayevo-Circassia, Kabardino-Balkaria and North and South Ossetia, wherever it was deemed necessary by the local population. Bilingual courses of study are also in use, to one degree or another, in other non-Russian areas of the country.

In the early years of Soviet power, Lenin condemned and rejected all proposals calling for the introduction of Russian as the official language in the non-Russian areas on a compulsory and exclusive basis. But Lenin also foresaw that Russian would become the common language of communication, cooperation and mutual aid for the peoples of our country.

MAORI ATTITUDES TOWARD INTEGRATION*

THOMAS K. FITZGERALD

Between 1967 and 1969, a study was conducted in New Zealand to measure the attitudes Maori (mā'oree) University graduates held toward "integration." The Maori, a Polynesian people, have retained much of their traditional culture while maintaining a workable relationship with the white-controlled society. The following selection documents some of the feelings that minority people in situations of rapid change and multi-cultural choice have about themselves, their culture, and the environing society.

"Integration" is a highly emotive term in New Zealand, primarily because it is associated with a government policy that is interpreted as the opposite of "true" integration. The big problem seems to be in the rather slipshod way that the concept is employed. Rarely is the term ever qualified. Consequently, sometimes one speaks of *cultural* integration, again of socio-economic integration, but more likely of biological or "racial" assimilation.

Because of the government's equation of integration with cultural assimilation, the Maoris naturally suspect it: "Integration means the big fish swallowing the

* Field research for this study was carried out in New Zealand, and assisted by a grant from the National Institutes of Health (MH 19560). The study is based on 106 questionnaires and 48 intensive interviews with Maori college graduates.

little fish" or, as another graduate described the fear, "Integration is me, a Maori, fitting into the Pakeha way of life and not the Pakeha fitting my Maori way of life!" Obviously, then, just labeling a process of acculturation "integration" does not lessen dread that the majority culture will absorb the minority culture, rather than meeting it part way.

Maoris often talk as if they would like more than anything else to achieve an "integrated" society, one in which Maori and Pakeha ("Europeans") would share a common culture. The focus of our research was on "acculturation and identity" among Maori university graduates, but also we were secondarily interested in the question of "race relations" in New Zealand generally. Using a simple sentence-completion "test," a group-aspirations measure,[1] and formal and informal interviews, we attempted to gauge the Maori graduate's reactions to such emotionally loaded concepts as "integration," "race relations," and "cultural understanding." The conclusions are interesting in themsleves, but they may also have special relevance for comparison.

We have found that the idea of integration as a fusion of two elements was only vaguely comprehended. Informants sometimes referred to integration as a "blending of two cultures," but there was almost no explanation of how it might come about. Much more popular was the stress on unity in diversity, what we might call "democratic cultural pluralism." True integration was defined as the cooperation of two "cultures," rather than an amalgamation or assimilation of one or the other. This emphasis on "enlightened provincialism" was summed up concisely by a young female graduate: "Integration means you accept me as such and I do the same for you."

Thus, integration as total fusion was not found to be an altogether adequate solution, at least not with this sample. To quote an informant: "Integration means one culture—but who needs it? Pakehas would rather be Pakehas and Maoris would rather be Maori, so true integration in this sense is undesirable."

The ultimate threat of an integrated society is the loss of a viable culture or ethnic identity. Maoris believe there is something culturally different about themselves that distinguishes them from European New Zealanders; this distinctiveness they sometimes call Maoritanga. The common denominator of Maoritanga is not always culture per se but a sense of cultural identity; in general, a sense of belonging to and sharing in an historically rooted subculture; in particular, an ascribed identity with an extended kin group, or, as is often the case, a substitute kin group. This microculture (subculture) is perceived as highly supportive and deeply satisfying. Most Maoris, then, find the retention of a cultural identity incompatible with a totally integrated society and therefore shy away from any notion of complete integration in New Zealand.

[1] Parts of Hadley Cantril's measure for aspirations and strivings were borrowed but considerably modified to meet the requirements of this research (1965, pp. 22–24).

Maoris in New Zealand show some evidence of achieving a kind of cultural integration—at least, at the national level (New Zealand macroculture) and New Zealand society is remarkably successful in giving the Maori room for such cultural expression. At the microcultural level, however, they seem to prefer democratic pluralism, an amicable coexistence with the dominant Europeans. Integration at this level, they fear, could destroy their cultural integrity and hence the basis of their ethnic identity.

Despite a fair amount of "racial" goodwill in New Zealand, there is still some evidence of intercultural conflict, owing largely to discontinuities in cultural values. It boils down to the failure of the government and educational system to grapple adequately with bicultural reality. As a Maori social worker stated the issue: "Cultural understanding is biased in New Zealand. The Pakeha, despite good intentions, foists his own attitudes upon the Maori who unsuspectingly adopts them." Cultural integration, after all, is a two-way process. If the Maori subculture is to contribute anything to the New Zealand national society, then Pakehas must be educated to what Maori culture really is. And, insofar as the educational system does *not* fully recognize divergent cultural traditions, "education" for such minority groups can result only in cultural assimilation. Such is the fear of most Maori graduates, and it is this fear that undermines so-called "good race relations" in New Zealand.

The concept of "race" (narrowly defined as "genetic identity," that is, in biological terms) is almost totally alien to modern New Zealand society. In fact, the egalitarian emphasis in New Zealand makes even a residual racism highly suspect. Maori graduates see the racial situation as "comparatively good," but substantially indifferent.

The significant conclusion suggested by our data was that there are—at least from an analytical perspective—three rather distinct, though overlapping, components to consider under the concept of "race": color, class, and culture. These components are, of course, not static entities and therefore vary according to circumstances and historical trends.

It is our conclusion that, at present, biological factors, as a group phenomenon, figure little, if at all, in "racial consciousness" in New Zealand. It is possible, however, that social-class factors will gain some ascendancy in defining major lines of cleavage in New Zealand. Although, the "revolution of rising expectations," so characteristic of other countries, may be to some extent mitigated by the overall equal standard of living found in New Zealand, the class factor will nonetheless remain significant as long as the socioeconomic position of the average Maori is lower than that of the European.

The cultural component, then, figures most prominently in the sentiments expressed by Maori graduates. Here the picture is complicated by assimilative pressures. In New Zealand there is often a confusion of race and culture—a serious misconception considering that the government, in a defensive position in face of world opinion, feels that it will encourage a "racial" situation by recognizing any *cultural* realities. In order to avoid this perceived racial threat, it has recently passed legislation undermining Maori cultural values, and hence the subculture itself.

In our study, we found practically no evidence for a firm racial identity among Maori university graduates. If the government persists in its present policy of cultural assimilation, however, it may well precipitate the very problem that it has tried to avoid. We are suggesting that a policy of "forced acculturation" may lead to an exaggeration of biological ("racial") symbols for purposes of identification, in order to compensate for the loss of cultural symbols. At any rate, it is obvious that the government's notion of integration and that of the Maori are quite different, and these divergent views underlie the quality of race relations in New Zealand.

In summary, Maoris often *say* they want "integration," yet they clearly do not envisage an end to the Maori microculture or to their separate cultural identity. Although change per se is not resisted, many people feel that Maoris stand to lose many valuable things under the magic word "integration."

THE ONE HUNDRED PERCENT AMERICAN

RALPH LINTON

In 1937, when Ralph Linton published "The One Hundred Percent American," an isolationist outlook pervaded the American political scene. Almost by definition, **outside** influences were **alien** influences. Patriotism involved an almost facile sense of self-sufficiency. World War II had the effect of abruptly pulling the nation back into international affairs as a world power, a role that it has self-consciously, unwillingly, and too often ineptly played ever since. Even though the original setting for Linton's statement has been greatly altered during the succeeding four decades, his essay is particularly helpful today because it indicates the extent of our borrowing. The piece no longer reads as a response to nativistic ideology; it reads more as an acknowledgment of a debt to many peoples far-flung in space and time.

There can be no question about the average American's Americanism or his desire to preserve this precious heritage at all costs. Nevertheless, some insidious foreign ideas have already wormed their way into his civilization without his realizing what was going on. Thus dawn finds the unsuspecting patriot garbed in pajamas, a garment of East Indian origin; and lying in a bed built on a pattern which originated in either Persia or Asia Minor. He is muffled to the ears in un-

American materials; cotton, first domesticated in India; linen, domesticated in the Near East; wool from an animal native to Asia Minor; or silk whose uses were first discovered by the Chinese. All these substances have been transformed into cloth by a method invented in Southwestern Asia. If the weather is cold enough he may even be sleeping under an eiderdown quilt invented in Scandinavia.

On awakening he glances at the clock, a medieval European invention, uses one potent Latin word in abbreviated form, rises in haste, and goes to the bathroom. Here, if he stops to think about it, he must feel himself in the presence of a great American institution; he will have heard stories of both the quality and frequency of foreign plumbing and will know that in no other country does the average man perform his ablutions in the midst of such splendor. But the invidious foreign influence pursues him even here. Glass was invented by the ancient Egyptians, the use of glazed tiles for floors and walls in the Near East, porcelain in China, and the art of enameling on metal by Mediterranean artisans of the Bronze Age. Even his bathtub and toilet are but slightly modified copies of Roman originals. The only purely American contribution to the ensemble is the steam radiator.

In this bathroom the American washes with soap invented by the ancient Gauls. Next he cleans his teeth, a subversive European practice which did not invade America until the latter part of the eighteenth century. He then shaves, a masochistic rite first developed by the heathen priests of ancient Egypt and Sumer. The process is made less of a penance by the fact that his razor is of steel, an iron-carbon alloy discovered in either India or Turkestan. Lastly, he dries himself on a Turkish towel.

Returning to the bedroom, the unconscious victim of un-American practices removes his clothes from a chair, invented in the Near East, and proceeds to dress. He puts on close-fitting tailored garments whose form derives from the skin clothing of the ancient nomads of the Asiatic steppes and fastens them with buttons whose prototypes appeared in Europe at the close of the Stone Age. This costume is appropriate enough for outdoor exercise in a cold climate, but is quite unsuited to American summers, steam-heated houses, and Pullmans. Nevertheless, foreign ideas and habits hold the unfortunate man in thrall even when common sense tells him that the authentically American costume of gee string and moccasins would be far more comfortable. He puts on his feet stiff coverings made from hide prepared by a process invented in ancient Egypt and cut to a pattern which can be traced back to ancient Greece, and makes sure they are properly polished, also a Greek idea. Lastly, he ties about his neck a strip of bright-colored cloth which is a vestigial survival of the shoulder shawls worn by seventeenth-century Croats. He gives himself a final appraisal in the mirror, an old Mediterranean invention, and goes downstairs to breakfast.

Here a whole new series of foreign things confronts him. His food and drink are placed before him in pottery vessels, the popular name of which— china—is sufficient evidence of their origin. His fork is a medieval Italian invention and his spoon a copy of a Roman original. He will usually begin the meal with coffee, an Abyssinian plant first discovered by the Arabs. The American is quite likely to need it to dispel the morning-after effects of over-indulgence in fermented drinks, invented in the Near East; or distilled ones, invented by the alchemists of medieval Europe. Whereas the Arabs took their coffee straight, he will probably sweeten it with sugar, discovered in India; and dilute it with cream, both the domestication of cattle and the technique of milking having originated in Asia Minor.

If our patriot is old-fashioned enough to adhere to the so-called American breakfast, his coffee will be accompanied by an orange, domesticated in the Mediterranean region, a cantaloupe domesticated in Persia, or grapes, domesticated in Asia Minor. He will follow this with a bowl of cereal made from grain domesticated in the Near East and prepared by methods also invented there. From this he will go on to waffles, a Scandinavian invention, with plenty of butter, originally a Near-Eastern cosmetic. As a side dish he may have the egg of a bird domesticated in Southeastern Asia or strips of the flesh of an animal domesticated in the same region, which have been salted and smoked by a process invented in Northern Europe.

Breakfast over, he places upon his head a molded piece of felt, invented by the nomads of Eastern Asia, and, if it looks like rain, puts on outer shoes of rubber, discovered by the ancient Mexicans, and takes an umbrella, invented in India. He then sprints for his train—the train, not the sprinting, being an English invention. At the station he pauses for a moment to buy a newspaper, paying for it with coins invented in ancient Lydia. Once on board he settles back to inhale the fumes of a cigarette invented in Mexico, or a cigar invented in Brazil. Meanwhile, he reads the news of the day, imprinted in characters invented by the ancient Semites by a process invented in Germany upon a material invented in China. As he scans the latest editorial pointing out the dire results to our institutions of accepting foreign ideas, he will not fail to thank a Hebrew God in an Indo-European language that he is a one hundred percent (decimal system invented by the Greeks) American (from Americus Vespucci, Italian geographer).

7

Intergroup Relations: The Organizations

Americans of all ages, all conditions, and all dispositions constantly form associations. They have not only commercial and manufacturing companies, in which all take part, but associations of a thousand other kinds, religious, moral, serious, futile, general or restricted, enormous or diminutive. The Americans make associations to give entertainments, to found seminaries, to build inns, to construct churches, to diffuse books, to send missionaries to the antipodes; in this manner they found hospitals, prisons, and schools. If it is proposed to inculcate some truth or to foster some feeling by the encouragement of a great example, they form a society. Wherever at the head of some new undertaking you see the government in France, or a man of rank in England, in the United States you will be sure to find an association.

—Alexis de Tocqueville, *Democracy in America* (1945, vol. 2, p. 114)

Individuals, as individuals, generally count for little in the processes of modern nations. A major reason is that much individual behavior takes the form of role playing within organizational contexts. Individual attitudes and preferences are thus typically subordinated to the norms of groups that are organized to promote various objectives and interests.

Literally hundreds of organizations have ethnicity, nativism, nationality, or race as salient concerns. These organizations are so important in modern society that it would be a serious omission not to discuss them. They are not easy to classify because they vary in size, duration, organizational structure, and mission. One way to study them, however, is to identify their major functions and then briefly to discuss some representative organizations that perform those functions.

It should be borne in mind that the announced objectives of a particular organization may be a front for some other activity. Then, too, some organizations shift from one activity to another within a few months or years. And the same organization may have several functions at the same time. Generally, however, the important functions of the ethnic, racial, and nativistic organizations are value expression, adaptation and facilitation, reform, disjunction, revolution, conservation, and reaction.

Value Expression

A number of organizations have been formed to express and promote group-related values. These organizations are often primary, or face-to-face, groups, in which simply getting together is a major function. Such organizations may have as their announced aims the promotion and preservation of, for example, Norwegian (or German or Greek or Indian) literature, history, and music. Group traditions and customs typically are sustained through magazines and newsletters plus organizational meetings and festivals. At a typical festival—like the annual Grandfather Mountain (N.C.) Highland Games and Gathering of Scottish Clans—crafts are displayed, native songs and dances are performed, notable members of the group are honored, and friends and kin are united. In Delaware the Scottish-born or "born-Scottish" gather around New Castle—the port of entry for many Scottish immigrants—for the annual Scottish games. In 1973 approximately 10,000 came to share news, food, drink, and music. The agenda for the day included a piping and dance competition, a Highland Heptathlon (an athletic event), sheep-dog trials, a piped-band competition, and a massed band exhibition.

Among American Indians, a well known organization with value expression functions is the Native American church, commonly known as the "peyote church." So important is it that Hazel Hertzberg's study of modern Pan-Indian movements concludes, "It remains the most influential, most important, and largest Indian religious body, directly involving more Indians than any other Pan Indian group" (1971, p. 295).

The Native American church was incorporated in 1918. The ancestry of the organization, however, can be traced to pre-Columbian times, for the use of peyote (a spineless cactus that contains an hallucinogen now called "mescaline") in religious rituals is an ancient Mexican Indian practice. It spread to the United States in the 1870s, and the religion began to flourish at about the time of the great Indian messianic movement, the Ghost Dance.

Peyotists and Christians agreed on certain points—they both thought that alcohol was an evil in Indian life. Opponents of the peyote cult took the position, however, that the use of peyote was just as bad as drinking whiskey, and by 1890 an antipeyote drive was fully organized. Instead of destroying the religion, though, it served only to force it into a more stable organizational form. The first peyote churches to gain legal status were located in Oklahoma, but those in other western states soon followed (Nebraska, 1921; South Dakota, 1922; North Dakota, 1923; Colorado, 1946). The Canadian groups were incorporated in 1954.

The purpose of the Native American church, as stated in its charter, is to "foster and promote the religious belief of the several tribes of Indians in the State of Oklahoma, in the Christian religion with the practice of the Peyote Sacrament as commonly understood and used among the adherents of this religion . . ." (quoted in Hertzberg, 1971, p. 273).

Hertzberg (1971) has suggested several reasons for the growth of the cult, seven of which are relevant to this discussion. First, the old tribal religions were weakening, and Christianity seemed remote and difficult to understand; so a religion that combined Indian and Christian elements seemed a viable compromise between old and new. (In this sense the peyote church has adaptive functions.) Second, the group's identity as Pan-Indian, rather than as tribal, enabled members to express the idea of Indian brotherhood through religion. Third, through the peyote religion a number of Indians were "cured" of alcoholism. Fourth, the peyote religion was a social, as well as a religious, force that afforded its adherents an opportunity to meet together. Fifth, a flexible organizational structure enabled it to adjust to local conditions. Sixth, men were able to regain important and recognized social functions, which they had largely lost in their contacts with the white man. Seventh, the peyote church was an Indian religion. It was "something in which they could take pride, something which linked them with the Indian past but could function in the new and changed Indian present" (1971, p. 282).

Puerto Ricans in several large cities of the United States have formed organizations with value expressive-functions. An indivdual club is sometimes called a *club social de los hijos ausentes* ("social club of absent sons"). A specific club often will bear the name of some town or city in Puerto Rico. The term *club social* suggests that the organizations have expressive functions. "The main purpose," one informant told me, "is to get together." Nonmember Puerto Ricans sometimes attend social events. In order to be full-fledged members, however, individuals usually must be able to demonstrate that they or their families have had some connection with the Puerto Rican town after which the club is named. As these organizations grow in size, they tend to become more complex and have multiple purposes. Some Puerto Rican social clubs form credit unions, engage in political activities, and retain lawyers for their members.

American Blacks have long participated in organizations with expressive functions, to such a degree, in fact, that observers like Gunnar Myrdal have written that the enormous participation in "social clubs" is "pathological" (1962, pp., 952–955; first edition published in 1944). Myrdal wrote that participation drained off time and money that could be better spent in attaining business and political success and in breaking down caste barriers. Blacks were active in these organizations because "they were not allowed to be active in much of the other organized life of America." The only kind things that Myrdal could find to say about the social clubs were that they provide a training school in organizational and parliamentary skills and that they often provide death-benefit and sickness-insurance programs. (He noted, however, that the clubs have frequently failed to pay their claims, especially during the Depression.) Myrdal quoted Booker T. Washington, who had expressed the idea that the clubs (and secret societies in particular) could be means of creating capital and of teaching business techniques. He also acknowledged that they provide recreation and amusement; even the mutual-aid benevolent associations, Myrdal observed, tend to become recreational associations.

Myrdal characterized a typical social club as small (twelve to twenty-four members), intensely competitive with other clubs, short-lived, time-consuming, elaborately ritualistic, and heavily formalized (with a full slate of officers even if the organization had fewer than a dozen members). The agenda of a meeting (Myrdal, 1962, p. 953) usually includes business, while visitors wait in another room; card playing; eating; and a period of time devoted to what Myrdal described as "rather general unorganized conversation and hilarity." The clubs themselves range from decorous organizations composed of middle-aged women, in which formal dress was often required, to the "rather rough" younger groups of the upper lower class.

Sociologists have observed that middle- and upper-income Americans partici-pate more extensively in organizations of various kinds than do low-income Americans. This characterization apparently holds for American Blacks as well, except that even in the low-income strata Blacks are more likely to belong to organizations than are Whites of comparable income.[1] "Americans are joiners,"

---

[1] Recent studies have supported Myrdal's claim that the tendency of Blacks toward exaggerated affiliation and toward joining expressive, rather than instrumental associations is "pathological" (see, for example, Smith and Freedman, 1972, p. 164).

This advertisement (which appeared in **The New York Times** on January 21, 1973) shows that a single organization often has several functions—value expression, reaction, and conservation.

Myrdal wrote (1962, p. 952), and American Blacks in this respect are "exaggerated Americans."

Some organizations with value-expressive functions are secondary groups. For example, the Encyclopedia of Associations (Fisk, 1973) lists scores or organizations that have incorporated as fraternal benefit life-insurance societies. One illustration is the Sons of Scotland Benevolent Association, which was founded in 1876 for "Scotsmen and Scotswomen, their families, and descendents." The association's announced purpose is "to cultivate an appreciation of Scottish literature, history, music and poetry" (Fisk, 1973, p. 962).

Adaptation and Facilitation

Certain organizations attempt to help members of a given group meet the demands of the core society by providing services that facilitate group and individual activities. Adaptive and facilitative functions are especially prominent in the organizations of immigrant peoples, as has already been noted in connection with Puerto Rican social clubs.

The immigrant associations in the cities of West Africa, as well as those of Indians who came from the mountains to the cities of South America, are examples of primary groups with this function. Many of these groups begin as organizations in which the value-expressive function is central, but gradually this function is overshadowed by other activities.

How does a group with value-expressive functions develop into one with adaptive and facilitative functions? This problem has been investigated among the "locality groups" of Okinawans who immigrated to Hawaii (Kimura, 1968, pp. 331–338). When Okinawans first began arriving in 1900, other immigrants regarded them as an inferior out-group. In time, however, the Okinawans developed a cohesive social organization that enabled them to achieve a larger measure of social acceptance. The basis of their community life became the locality clubs, each of which bore the name of the geographical area in Okinawa from which the members had come. Locality clubs kept alive sentiments and memories of the old world—the value-expressive function—but they also provided mutual aid for members, gave scholarships and prizes to youths, and assisted in funeral arrangements for bereaved families.

In recent years many of these locality clubs have banded together to form a secondary group, the United Okinawan Association in Hawaii. Originally formed to help war-devastated Okinawa, it has gradually shifted its emphasis to projects involving education, health, and leadership training.

The minority-group practice of forming associations for mutual aid is of long standing. Historical records show that more than 100 mutual-aid societies for Blacks were in existence in the city of Philadelphia in 1849. According to one report almost half the city's non-White adults were members of "mutual beneficial societies." Funds were appropriated "to support the members in sickness, and to bury the dead" (Society of Friends, 1849, pp. 22, 23). One observer concluded that the funds thus spent "very considerably relieved the distress attendant on the sickness of the heads of families, and maintain a large portion of the people of colour, under privations, and in circumstances, which would otherwise throw them upon the public for relief" (1849, p. 23). This type of organization still exists in many Black communities of the United States—often in the form of burial societies—though they seem to be decreasing in number. One reason for the decline seems to lie in the fact that the government now provides similar services through social-security and welfare programs.

One of the best-known organizations with adaptive and facilitative functions is the National Urban League. Founded in 1910, it grew out of efforts to assist rural Blacks who had moved to northern cities to find jobs and housing. Staff and volunteer workers actually met migrant families at railroad stations and steamship docks and guided them to temporary shelters in the big cities. If it is admittedly difficult to find one's way in an unfamiliar large city when one is educated, well-off, and a member of the majority group, imagine the trauma that these early migrants must have experienced as strangers, illiterate and poor. Urban League workers helped them to find jobs, escorted them through unfamiliar city streets, and cared for their children.

The organization is now led by Vernon E. Jordan, Jr., who succeeded Whitney Young, Jr., as executive director in 1971. The membership of the organization in 1973 was approximately 50,000. The Urban League continues to emphasize equity in business, industry, and government; it seeks training for youth and adequate housing for the urban population. Today some of its early tasks have been taken over by government agencies, but many resources of the League are still directed toward facilitative activities—"smoothing out wrinkles in the adjustment process," as one member put it.

Urban League activities generally receive little public attention because many of them take place behind the scenes. Workers for the Urban League have functioned much as ombudsmen, negotiating with labor leaders and businessmen for jobs and with public officials for government services.

Reform

Some organizations attempt to change a system without overthrowing it. Whenever the circumstances appear to warrant it, they seek to change the laws by legislation or court review, administrative policies by executive order or strikes, and

COMMANDMENTS FOR THE VOLUNTEERS

I HEREBY PLEDGE MYSELF—MY PERSON AND
BODY—TO THE NONVIOLENT MOVEMENT.
THEREFORE I WILL KEEP THE FOLLOWING TEN
COMMANDMENTS:

1. *Meditate* daily on the teachings and life of Jesus.
2. *Remember* always that the nonviolent movement in Birmingham seeks justice and reconciliation—not victory.
3. *Walk* and *Talk* in the manner of love for God is love.
4. *Pray* daily to be used by God in order that all men might be free.
5. *SACRIFICE* personal wishes in order that all men might be free.
6. *OBSERVE* with both friend and foe the ordinary rules of courtesy.
7. *SEEK* to perform regular service for others and for the world.
8. *REFRAIN* from the violence of fist, tongue or heart.
9. *STRIVE* to be in good spiritual and bodily health.
10. *FOLLOW* the directions of the movement and of the captain on a demonstration.

I sign this pledge, having seriously considered what I do and with the determination and will to persevere.

NAME_____

(Please print neatly)

ADDRESS_____

PHONE_____

NEAREST RELATIVE_____

ADDRESS_____

Besides demonstrations, I could also help the Movement by: (Circle the proper items)

Run errands, Drive my car, Fix food for volunteers, Clerical work, Make phone calls, Answer phones, Mimeograph, Type, Print signs; Distribute leaflets;

The pledge form for volunteers used by Martin Luther King, Jr., during the Birmingham campaign, 1963.

beliefs and customs by propaganda, persuasion, or demonstrations. The strategies and specific objectives vary, but the general purpose remains the same—the system may survive, but change must occur.

Of the various organizations in the United States that have reform functions, the National Association for the Advancement of Colored People (N.A.A.C.P.) probably has been the most influential. The historian Herbert Aptheker has used the date of the founding of the N.A.A.C.P. as the point marking the "threshold of the modern period of American Negro history" (1951). The organization's origins were in the Niagara movement, which at its meeting in 1905 announced these objectives:

1. Freedom of speech and criticism
2. An unfettered and unsubsidized press
3. Manhood suffrage
4. The abolition of all caste distinctions based simply on race and color
5. The recognition of the principles of human brotherhood as a practical present creed
6. The recognition of the highest and best human training as the monopoly of no class or race
7. A belief in the dignity of labor
8. United effort to realize the ideals under wise and courageous leadership. (Niagara Movement, Constitution and By-Laws, 1905)

From the beginning, the N.A.A.C.P. showed a preference for litigation as a tactic for change. The organization also relied on the printed word. For almost a quarter of a century W. E. B. DuBois served as editor of the association's official publication, *The Crisis*. During the first four decades of its existence, the N.A.A.C.P. pressed for the legal rights of Blacks to equal educational opportunities, as well as for access to public accommodations and transportation. These early efforts should be interpreted in the context of the 1896 Supreme Court decision (Plessy *v.* Ferguson) which had upheld the constitutionality of "separate but equal" accommodations. The N.A.A.C.P.-sponsored suits insisted that the "equal" side of the formula be given more careful attention. The landmark decision came in 1954, when the Supreme Court ruled in Brown *v.* Board of Education and in Bolling *v.* Sharpe that segregation in the public schools is illegal at all levels. This event signified that a major institutional structure, the public-school system, can be altered. It also demonstrated that minority members have resources in the law and the courts (Berger, 1968, pp. 136–141).

The resources that organizations can tap in order to reform society are of several types. They have been delineated by the sociologist Joseph S. Himes (1970):

1. Economic power—the boycott, selective buying programs, strikes, and the like
2. Focused voting power—bloc voting, "single shotting"; canvassing within political parties and other organizations

3. Latent moral commitment—public display of abuses of fair play, publicity about inhumane treatment
4. Public opinion—power of the mass media, especially television
5. Due process—legal redress, power of the law and the courts
6. Fear—intimidation through massive demonstrations, confrontations, and threats; intentional and calculated violence.

When these elements of power are focused, they can have a decisive influence on the course of social affairs.

Some organizations press for reform though direct means like the sit-in and the boycott. The Gandhian National Congress party successfully used this approach against the British in India. More recently it has been used in the United States to achieve the goals of such organizations as the Congress on Racial Equality (C.O.R.E.) and the Southern Christian Leadership Conference (S.C.L.C.).

The Southern Christian Leadership Conference actually grew out of confrontations that resembled those fostered in the Gandhian program. Gandhi's doctrine of nonviolent resistance became a conscious model for the S.C.L.C. (Observe the nonviolent emphasis in the "Commandments for the Volunteers" used in the Birmingham campaign.) Formed under the leadership of Martin Luther King, Jr., in 1957, the organization during its formative years dealt primarily with segregated transportation facilities and voter registration.

King did not go as far as Gandhi in urging collective civil disobedience. At first he advocated the individual's right to break "unjust local laws" that conflicted with Federal laws. He eventually took the position that it was appropriate to challenge certain Federal policies and laws, especially those that had to do with the war in Vietnam.

The Urban League, previously mentioned for its adaptive and facilitative functions, is also involved in reform activities. A stated objective of the organization is "to eliminate from American life all forms of segregation and discrimination based on race or color, and to secure for Negro citizens and other economically disadvantaged groups, equal opportunity to develop their fullest potential and to share equitably the rewards and responsibilities for American citizenship" (Fisk, 1970, p. 759). Urban League strategists have usually preferred negotiation to confrontation, but the Urban League has helped to organize a number of strikes and demonstrations. Some observers feel that this activity was brought on by the organization's need to establish credibility with rank-and-file urban Blacks.

The Encyclopedia of Associations (Fisk, 1973) lists almost fifty civil-rights organizations, most of which have reform functions. Many do not formally limit their concerns to single minority groups. The Anti-Defamation League of B'nai B'rith is such an organization. It was founded in 1913, and its stated "ultimate purpose is to secure justice and fair treatment to all citizens alike and to put an end forever to unjust and unfair discrimination against, and ridicule of, any sect or body of citizens" (Schary, 1965, p. 66). Under its sponsorship a considerable number of pamphlets, monographs, and books have been prepared. A periodic survey of research in the area of intergroup relations is conducted by the League. Audiovisual supplies are made available to schools, churches, and civic clubs. The Anti-Defamation League probably is the best known source of scholarly material on intergroup relations in the United States. (Its address is 315 Lexington Avenue, New York, New York 10016.) The American Jewish Committee, through its Institute of Human Relations, provides somewhat similar services. (Its address is 165 East 56th Street, New York, New York 10022).

In actual practice, however, most of the civil-rights groups focus on the problems of single minority groups. Two examples are the National Association for Puerto Rican Civil Rights and the A. Philip Randolph Institute. The first concerns itself with legislation, labor, law enforcement, and housing, especially in New York City. It holds annual meetings, provides legal services, and in 1973 had an estimated 20,000 members. The second is named after the Black labor leader A. Philip Randolph. It was founded in 1964 to promote cooperation between Blacks and organized labor.

Disjunction

Throughout history various groups have espoused disjunction, or separation, from one political system in order to form another. Many of these groups have been nationalistic; that is, they have claimed that their groups ought to possess nations or territories of their own. They typically have asserted their right to rule themselves and to control their own social, economic, and political institutions.

In India long-standing differences between Muslims and Hindus eventually led to the formation of such organizations; the Muslim League became one of the most prominent. Its leader, Mohammed Ali Jinnah (1876–1948), took the position that Muslims could never expect fair treatment under the government planned by the Indian National Congress party of Mahatma Gandhi (1869–1948). In 1940 Jinnah demanded that a separate nation called Pakistan ("Land of the Pure") be established. When Great Britain offered independence to India in 1946, the leaders of the Indian National Congress and those of the Muslim League—still unable to settle their differences and in the wake of fierce riots between Hindus and Muslims—agreed that the subcontinent should be partitioned.

Important manifestations of separatism in the United States have occurred in the context of numerous organizations that have called upon American Blacks to return to Africa. One of the first was the American Colonization Society. That society—which included many prominent people of its times, men like Henry Clay, Francis Scott Key, and John Randolph—financed the return of slaves to Africa and encouraged the voluntary freeing of slaves. The African nation of Liberia was eventually established as a home for immigrants from the United States. Other similar ventures were undertaken on a smaller scale during the nineteenth century.

In the 1920s a Jamaican-born Black, Marcus Garvey (1887–1940), began to recruit American Blacks for his newly formed Universal Negro Improvement Association. He was successful in recruiting thousands of adherents for the association, which established all-Black businesses, purchased a steamship line, and assisted in the immigration of Blacks to Africa. A flamboyant and exciting speaker, Garvey talked of an uplifted race—not one equal to Whites but one that would be superior and independent. He actually induced only a few thousand immigrants to leave the United States and was himself eventually imprisoned for mail fraud, but he did succeed in raising the aspirations of a large segment of the Black population.

In 1928 the American Communist party, with the backing of Josef Stalin, introduced a separatist strategy known as the "Black Belt theory." The party at that time advocated that Blacks organize a separate republic in the Black Belt of the Deep South. Marxist strategists had seen a parallel between the conditions of Russian peasants, who had been the poorest, most backward people of Europe, and the conditions of the landless, illiterate Black masses of the United States. If a revolution could be sparked among the peasants of Russia, they reasoned, the same potential might exist in the United States (Young Socialist Alliance, 1970, p. 17).

In recent years the Lost-Found Nation of Islam in the West, as Black Muslims are officially known, has become a conspicuous advocate of Black nationalism. The organization's leader, Elijah Muhammad (formerly Elijah Poole), has demanded a portion of the United States—at least three or four states—for the settlement of American Blacks and for the eventual establishment of a Black republic (Essien-Udom, 1962, p. 285). Despite the similarity between this strategy and that of the Communist Black Belt theory, Black Muslim leaders have rebuffed efforts by the Communist party, primarily because Communists oppose private ownership and organized religion (Essien-Udom, 1962, p. 319).

The Black Muslims' perception of the "collective White man" as the devil is a prominent element of their organizational life. From this definition of the situation proceed rituals, politics, an interpretation of history, and a rigorous discipline that is imposed upon members.

The definition of the White man as evil provides a rationale for the Black Muslim practice of giving to each convert a new name. Muslim leaders are quick to point out that a Black person in the United States typically bears the name taken from some White person. A convert to the Nation of Islam makes formal application for a new name in a letter addressed to Elijah Muhammad:

> Dear Savior Allah, Our Deliverer:
> I have attended the teachings of Islam two or three times, as taught by one of your ministers. I believe in it. I bear witness that there is no god but Thee. And, that Muhammad is Thy Servant and Apostle. I desire to reclaim my Own. Please give me my Original name. My slave name is as follows: . (Essien-Udom, 1969, p. 221)

The behavior of boxing champion Muhammad Ali is more readily understandable in the light of this custom. When he first announced that he wished to be called Muhammad Ali instead of Cassius Clay, the public's reaction was bemused tolerance. But, for Ali, as for other Muslims, the use of one's "original name" is a matter of keeping the faith.

Black Muslim mythology incorporates antipathy for Whites, using it both as an explanation of present distress and as a key to a utopian future:

> The Original man, the first men to populate the earth, were non-white. They enjoyed a high level of culture and reached high peaks of achievement.
>
> A little over 6,000 years ago a black scientist named Yakub, after considerable work, produced a mutant, a new race, the white race.
>
> This new race was inferior mentally, physically, and morally to the black race. Their whiteness, the very mark of their difference from the black race, was an indication of their physical and moral depravity.
>
> Allah, in anger at Yakub's work, ordained that the white race should rule for a fixed amount of time and that the black man should suffer and by his suffering gain greater appreciation of his own spiritual worth by comparing himself to the whites.
>
> The time of white dominance is drawing near its end. It is foreordained that this race shall perish, and with its destruction the havoc, terror, and brutality which it has spread throughout the world shall disappear. (Howard, 1966, pp. 21, 22)

Antipathy for the "collective White man" manifests itself in institutionalized behavior like the Muslim drug-rehabilitation program, an activity that even critics admit is successful. A rehabilitation session has been described this way:

> The addict, writhing in pain, his nose and eyes running, is pouring sweat from head to foot. He's trying to knock his head against the wall, flailing his arms, trying to fight his attendants, he is vomiting, suffering diarrhea. "Don't hold nothing back! Let Whitey go, baby! You're going to stand tall, man! I can see you now in the Fruit of Islam!" (Haley, 1966, p. 261)

Socialization in the Muslim faith is arduous. It involves public commitment, regular attendance at temple meetings, and rigid observance of dietary and ethical rules. The "Thou shalt nots" include abstinence from pork, tobacco, alcohol, and narcotics. Gambling, domestic quarreling, discourtesy, lying, and stealing are proscribed. The rules are especially strict on the treatment of women, as is borne out by the words printed on a huge banner displayed on the platform of a Black Muslim convention: "We must protect our most valuable property, our women" (Howard, 1966, p. 17).

Malcolm X expressed the idea this way: "Beautiful black women! The honorable Elijah Muhammad teaches us that the black man is going around saying he wants respect; well, the black man never will get anybody's respect until he first learns to respect his own women!" (Haley, 1966, p. 221).

The size of the Black Muslim movement, when measured by the actual number of its members, belies the extent of its influence. Perhaps no more than 50,000 are active members. Atlanta, with its large population of Blacks, for example, had no more than 500 Black Muslims in 1973. "But," Charles Silberman has written, "they have captured the sympathy of an enormous segment of Northern urban Negroes, who are unwilling to embrace the Muslim's strict discipline and religious tenets but who are delighted to hear the anger they feel being expressed so clearly" (1964, p. 56).

The Lost-Found Nation of Islam in the West, like organizations discussed elsewhere in this chapter, has been troubled by bloody in-fighting, schism, and formation of rival groups. Its most recent cleavages can be traced to events surrounding the life and death of the Black Muslim leader Malcolm X (formerly Malcolm Little). Malcolm X, after his pilgrimage to Mecca, modified his attitude toward Whites and proclaimed that Elijah Muhammad was not morally fit to lead the organization. Malcolm X was assassinated later that year by several gunmen. Some of his followers became Sunni Muslims after his death. (Sunni Muslims are orthodox Muslims; they have four schools of law, named after Muslim teachers: Malikites, Hanafites, Shafiites, and Hanbalites.)

The Lost-Found Nation of Islam in the West can be viewed as a recent development in a long tradition of separatist organizations in the United States. In many ways Black Muslims appeal to the credulity of Blacks, as Malcolm X had begun to preach, before his assassination, but frustrated people tend to be credulous. A parallel can be found in Jamaica, where illiterate, poverty-stricken members of the Ras Tafari sect believe that the Atlantic Ocean will one day part and permit them to return to Africa. Parallels also can be found in Germany during the Great Depression of the 1930s, when Hitler was coming to power. Of those days, Stressmann has written, "They pray not only for their daily bread but also for their daily illusion" (quoted in J. A. C. Brown, 1967, p. 111).

Black Muslims ask for sacrifice, discipline, and self-denial. Frustrated people often find such appeals more persuasive than promises of ease and comfort.

The organization has been able to use antipathies against Whites to good advantage. Hatred of a common foe can unify a group and dissipate self-hatred. Sigmund Freud, in a perceptive comment on the dynamics of organizations that depend upon out-groups for their existence, wrote, "It is always possible to bind together a considerable number of people in love, so long as there are other people left over to receive the manifestations of their aggressiveness" (1962, p. 61).

American Blacks have not been alone in organizing groups that favor disjunction and separatism. Within the Chicano organizations, for example, partisan groups have announced separatist platforms. The activities of Reies Lopez Tijerina and the Alianza (the Federal Alliance of Land Grants) have received considerable attention during recent years. At issue are the millions of acres of land that were allegedly part of 1,700 land grants originally given by Spain and Mexico to colonizers who married Indian women. These original grantees were called *la raza* —"the (new) breed."

Tijerina was sentenced to prison in 1970 for his part in a skirmish between authorities and his followers at the Rio Ariba county courthouse (New Mexico), but interest in the land question has spread widely throughout the Chicano movement. The disputed territory, called Aztlan ("the Aztec nation"), includes all of Colorado and New Mexico, those sections of Arizona and California south of the thirty-fifth parallel, and parts of western Texas (Nabokov, 1970, pp. 464–466).

The process of organizational development has been essentially the same in other countries. For example, Ireland's internecine strife has been largely based in organization. It has affected other nations, including the United States, where funds and supplies have been contributed to the principal combatants—the Ulster Defence League (Protestant) and the Irish Republican Army (I.R.A.; Roman Catholic). The Irish Republican Army comprises several factions, some of which are both separatist and revolutionary, but all those classified as part of the I.R.A. apparently agree that Northern Ireland should pull away from British control. Some I.R.A. members, if not all, want the predominantly Protestant northern territory (Northern Ireland, or Ulster) to be united with the Roman Catholic-dominated south (the Republic of Ireland, or Éire—pronounced AIR uh).

The Irish Republican Army is one of several major separatist organizations that have arisen during the centuries-long struggle between British and Irish. Others have been called United Irishmen, the Fenian Brotherhood, the Irish Republican Brotherhood, the Invincibles, the Clan-na-Gael, and the Sinn Fein. Historically, some of these groups have been quite successful. After World War I a guerrilla war broke out in Ireland; it culminated in Great Britain's signing a treaty giving southern Ireland the status of a dominion and the name Irish Free State. The northern counties were excluded primarily because the Irish guerrillas had not been able to gain control of predominantly Protestant Ulster.

The Irish nationalist organizations illustrate one sequence of events that can take place when an alien group rules another by virtue of conquest. Opposition to this domination, David Annan (1967) has shown, initially takes the shape of a cultural organization with open membership. The aims of this organization gradually shift from cultural unity to demands for reform. If the demands are resisted, the organization may split into moderates and extremists or go underground. An underground group's aim is insurrection, and its organizational structure is usually military. The evolution of the Gaelic League into Sinn Fein is a useful example. The Irish attempt to counter the growing influence of English culture in Ireland during the early 1900s first began as an effort to revive the national language, Gaelic. At the same time, political efforts aimed at home rule were being made. When they failed, the original objective of preserving Irish culture (which had been eroding) was transformed into separatism, and the movement adopted a revolutionary ideology (Annan, 1967, p. 190).

Revolution

A revolution, in the classic sense of the word, is a development characterized by basic changes in social relationships during a comparatively brief span of time. Revolutionary groups, by this definition, are those committed to bringing about such radical changes.

Revolution and separatism are not mutually exclusive political objectives. An organization may pull away from an existing government in order to form a new one essentially like the old one, or it may be revolutionary in the sense that it intends to form a new government that will comprise social relations that have been profoundly altered.[2] We have seen that some of the Irish nationalist organizations had revolutionary objectives.

In contrast to separatism, reform is usually regarded as being at odds with revolutionary objectives, and revolutionaries often regard reformers as enemies. The reason is that reform programs, if they succeed, tend to make life more bearable under an existing regime. Revolutionaries know that people must entirely lose faith in a political system's ability to respond to their needs adequately if a revolution is to be successful.

How this loss of faith is to be attained is a debated issue. A statement of the Young Socialist Alliance illustrates the point; it urges its members to become involved in programs for community control:

> Many revolutionary nationalists feel that participation in such struggles whose demands are not consciously revolutionary but are for partial reforms such as more jobs in the construction trades . . . is wrong. Others reject the importance of such participation because they feel that only massive repression will revolutionize the Black community. Still others reject the need to organize the masses around partial demands because they feel that we already in a revolutionary period, and that the central task is organizing for armed struggle. . . . To rely on capitalist repression to revolutionize the community and to abstain from struggles over concrete issues leaves the community prey to the reformists. (Young Socialist Alliance, 1970, p. 27)

The Black Panther party is probably the best known Black revolutionary organization in the United States.

In 1970, at its national convention, the Black Panthers' minister of defense outlined the ultimate goal of the organization as a "stateless, communist world society free of oppression and full of human kindness" (Scott, 1970). He argued that neither separatism nor Black nationalism is a viable goal for Black people.

---

[2] That is what was the aim of the American Revolution and the reason, incidentally, that it is called a "revolution." The Americans wanted separation from England—disjunction —but they also abolished hereditary titles, the state church, and the monarchy.

Instead, the strategy advocated was one of "revolutionary intercommunalism" under which "oppressed communities" would cooperate to destroy capitalism. Black Panther leaders acknowledged that the organization had moved from nationalism to its present outlook during the years since its founding.

Groups like the Black Panthers seek to encompass each individual's total personality, in contrast to most civic organizations or business clubs, which generally require only partial involvement. Excerpts from the rules of the Black Panther party suggest the high level of personal commitment that is expected of the members:

> Every member of the BLACK PANTHER PARTY throughout this country of racist America must abide by these rules as functional members of this party. CENTRAL COMMITTEE members, CENTRAL STAFFS, and LOCAL STAFFS, including all captains subordinate to either national, state, and local leadership of the BLACK PANTHER PARTY will enforce these rules. Length of suspension or other disciplinary action necessary for violation of these rules will depend on national decisions by national, state or state area, and local committees and staffs where said rule or rules of the BLACK PANTHER PARTY WERE VIOLATED.
> Every member of the party must know these [verbatim] by heart. And apply them daily. Each member must report any violation of these rules to their leadership or they are counter-revolutionary and are also subjected to suspension by the BLACK PANTHER PARTY. (1970, p. 31)

An organization that seeks total commitment from its members is especially likely to experience intense and often violent internal conflicts. The reason, as Lewis Coser (1956, pp. 67–69) has shown, is the nature of the interaction among the members. Organizations that demand only partial involvement of their members, like a chamber of commerce, tend to avoid violent episodes because the members keep their personalities in reserve. The more group members participate as whole persons, the more likely it is that the quarrels that break out will become personal and expand to other issues. In groups that have dangerous objectives, internal division and quarreling are even more likely. The less-involved member is seen not only as a deviant but also as a threat to the existence of the group. These general principles hold for several types of organizations discussed in this chapter. Organizations with separatist, revolutionary, and reactionary functions are continually experiencing schisms.

The Black Panthers have been especially prone to internal divisions. In 1970 the organization included the most celebrated of the ghetto militants, and it had the support and patronage of wealthy and distinguished persons in the White community. Within a year, however, disintegration had begun, in the classic tradition—attacks from without and warring within. Eventually a split in leadership occurred, between Huey Newton and Eldridge Cleaver. The prevailing emphasis of the Panthers shifted from violence and disruptive strategies to community organization and political activity (Panthers ran for mayor and the city council of Oakland, California, in 1973). This development highlights the fact that the tendency of value-expressive or reform organizations to become revolutionary is not irreversible. At certain times revolutionaries and revolutionary organizations moderate their objectives and become more reformist. Newton has commented on this point:

> A reformist and revolutionist might do the same thing at a particular time in history, but the difference is whether the action is open-ended or cul-de-sac. The reformer is an opportunist, who will make it better for now, but will also build an obstacle against future development. The revolutionist may appear the same, but he won't do anything to put up blocks or obstacles to future levels of development. I have to be very careful working with the liberals and the progressives, because they will lead me into the cul-de-sac of friendship. And the white radicals will lead me into alienation, where I can't be of help in raising the consciousness of the community. (Quoted in Rogers, 1973, p. 158)

Conservation and Reaction

Organizations are formed at various times with the intent of preserving society from trends perceived by group members as dangerous. Some of these groups resort to extralegal force in order to prevent change. Others do not have to resort to illegal stratagems because they have access to resources that enable them to operate within the law. Indeed, such organizations may advocate programs of law, order, and patriotism.

The Citizens' Councils of America is such an organization. Known in the South as "the White Citizen's Councils," the parent organization was founded in 1954 at Jackson, Mississippi. A decade ago, the Councils had an estimated 750,000 members. Today, the number of active members probably has dwindled to a fraction of this unofficial estimate (Fisk, 1973, p. 918). Members of local and state councils are supposedly committed to nonviolence and to the principles of states' rights and "racial integrity." Organizational goals include efforts to "prevent race-mixing or forced integration; avoid racial violence; maintain and restore legal segregation; defend states' rights against federal usurpation; reverse the Supreme Court's 'Black Monday' decision of May 17, 1954" (Fisk, 1973, p. 918). Activities involve providing speakers for schools, churches, and civic groups; working with the mass media; and conducting training sessions for leaders. The Councils maintain a library of approximately 1,500 volumes on race differences, history, anthropology, intelligence testing, political science, and subversion. They publish a monthly periodical, *The Citizen*.

The National States Rights Party (N.S.R.P.) provides a model for an organi-

---

AMERICA NEEDS YOU

The National States Rights Party is a patriotic political Party.
We are loyal White Americans who are working to win our goals in
a 100% legal and political way.

Our Party stands for:

. JESUS CHRIST
.· Upholding U. S. Constitution
. America First
. Freedom of Speech and Press
. NO world government
. Abolition of United Nations
. No More Foreign Give-aways
. Large Old Age Pensions

. WHITE SUPREMACY
. A Free White America
. The White Race and its Pre-
    servation
. Expulsion of All Communists
. Only White Christian Immi-
    gration
. Free Enterprise and High Wages

       Racial Separation and for giving all Africans in
       America a rich Country of their own in Africa.

HIRE WHITES ONLY

N.S.R.P. calls upon all Whites to protect themselves by "firing all negroes"
and hiring loyal Whites only, except in few cases where unconstitutional
laws actually force Whites with large number of employees to hire negroes.
Ostracize all Jews, communists, negroes and negro-lovers--have nothing to do
with them. They are our enemies. America belongs to us Whites and we must
stop all race-mixing.

Advertisement by the National States Rights Party, 1970.

zation with reactionary objectives. Its official publication, *Thunderbolt*, unabashedly supports White supremacy and anti-Semitism. Claiming to represent the White man's point of view *Thunderbolt* publishes "the news suppressed by the Daily Press." The organization's national headquarters is in Savannah, Georgia; its national chairman is J. B. Stoner. It claims to be "the largest White Racist political party in America," and circulation of its publication is highest in Alabama, California, Florida, Georgia, Ohio, Mississippi, and Illinois (*Thunderbolt*, February 1970, p. 9). Like the Citizens' Councils of America, the National States Rights Party insists that its activities are strictly legal.

The Ku Klux Klan, however, is a reactionary organization with a long tradition of extralegal activities. Organized in the aftermath of the Civil War, the Klan opposed Reconstruction and promoted White supremacy. Although it was officially disbanded in 1869, local units became a stealthy force in keeping Blacks away from the polls and in enforcing local mores.

In 1915 the Klan once again burst into national view. This time the original platform of White supremacy included some additional items: nativism, anti-Catholicism, antiunionism, and anti-Semitism. At the peak of its growth in the 1920s and 1930s, the Klan boasted 3 million members.

A highway billboard in North Carolina, 1970.

That large membership has gradually dwindled to an estimated 40,000 (1965), but attempts at reviving the Klan persist. The "new" Klansman emphasizes his stance as an anticommunist. His vocabulary includes ideas and rhetoric from the civil-rights movement: "nonviolence," "massive rallies," "economic boycotts," and "voter-registration drives" (Long, 1964, p. 8). The Klan's revival has been stymied by the imprisonment of its leaders, by internal divisions,[3] and by the unfavorable image that it projects.

During 1974, when court-ordered school busing in Boston resulted in an outbreak of violence, the Knights of the Ku Klux Klan reportedly sent organizers to the area. The Klan, in fact, is reported to have taken credit for hassling Senator Edward M. Kennedy when he tried to address an antibusing crowd (AP, 1974).

The sociologist James Vander Zanden (1960) thinks that the Klan appeals to the status needs of its adherents. Klansmen are usually recruited from the ranks of laborers, mechanics, and industrial workers. Typically a Klan leader is the owner of a small gas station or a general store, a deputy sheriff, or a traveling salesman. Although members usually do not have prestigious occupations, they tend to identify with the middle class. As a result, Vander Zanden reasons, the individual Klansman may "need" to prove that he is a person of worth. The approved path to a satisfactory self-image is through making a distinction between one's self and the Blacks, through organized conformity to the caste system, and through "one-hundred-percent Americanism" (1960, pp. 456–462).

[3] Today there is no single, united group under the name Ku Klux Klan. Five main Klans have been reported: The United Klans of America, Inc. (Tuscaloosa, Ala.); The White Knights of the Ku Klux Klan (Miss.); The United Florida Ku Klux Klan; The Original Ku Klux Klan of the Confederacy; and National Knights of the Ku Klux Klan (Ga.).

Organizations with conservative or reactionary objectives pass through a development similar in certain respects to that of revolutionary or separatist organizations. The Mafia is a case in point. Those who know of this organization via the movie *The Godfather* or the novel on which it is based may not be aware of the group's evolution. In its earliest form it was a conservative group in Sicily (Annan, 1967, pp. 242–262). In the eleventh century, when the Normans conquered the island, many dispossessed Sicilians ran to mafias ("places of refuge") in the hills, to avoid becoming serfs. Later, when the Spanish Inquisitors came in the fifteenth century, the outlaw families who lived in the hill country formed a resistance movement. Through the years they came to be known as champions of the oppressed. To this day, according to some sources (Annan, 1967), Sicilians refer to the Mafia as the "Honored Society." The Mafia, by means of a tightly knit organization worked out through the centuries, has hung on tenaciously, even though civil authorities have attempted to abolish it.

Overview

Members of dominant groups may consider it curious or even froward that minorities should want to organize into groups, unless they can cast themselves in the role of outsiders. Then the reasons become more apparent. For example, whenever an American corporation transfers one of its families overseas, the family members may have serious adjustment problems. The problems associated with learning to respond to strange cues in a new country may be intensely stressful. Meeting another American, eating familiar foods, or simply being able to speak English can be sheer pleasure. Without these supports, culture shock is often severe. No wonder, then, that Americans overseas keep up a round of parties, send their children to American schools when they can, establish English-speaking churches, and support various organizations from bridge clubs to country clubs.

In the same way, immigrants to our own country band together when their resources, values, and numbers permit. The reasons are similar—to socialize, preserve the group heritage, to educate the young, to facilitate the advancement of group members in the core society, to protect the interests of the group, to withstand oppression.

The different purposes for which individuals of similar background organize are the basis of the classification used in this chapter. The characteristics of the organizations thus formed depend on such factors as the norms and organizations of the host society, economic conditions, and the size and composition of the memberships themselves. Persons who originally come together only for fellowship may emerge as reformers in the face of discrimination, as reactionaries in the face of change, as revolutionaries in the face of persecution or unfulfilled rising expectations.

For Further Reading

Many of the items among the references cited may be considered as recommended reading as well.

Coser, Lewis. *The Functions of Social Conflict.* New York: Free Press, 1956.

Fisk, Margaret (ed.) *Encyclopedia of Associations.* Detroit: Gale Research, 1973

Goldman, Peter. *The Death and Life of Malcolm X.* New York: Harper & Row, 1973.

Hoffer, Eric. *The True Behavior.* New York: Harper & Row, 1951. (Perennial Library Edition, 1966).

MacKenzie, Norman. *Secret Societies.* New York: Holt, Rinehart and Winston, 1967.

March, James G. (ed.). *Handbook of Organizations.* Chicago: Rand McNally, 1965.

March, James G., and Herbert A. Simon (with the collaboration of Harold Guetzkow). *Organizations.* New York: Wiley, 1958.

Parris, Guichard, and Lester Brooks. *Blacks in the City: A History of the National Urban League.* Boston: Little, Brown, 1971.

Rose, Arnold. *The Power Structure: Political Process in American Society.* New York: Oxford University Press, 1967.

Sills, David. "Voluntary Associations: Sociological Aspects," *International Encyclopedia of the Social Sciences,* vol. 16. New York: Macmillan, 1968. Pp. 362–379.

Smith, Constance, and Anne Freedman. *Voluntary Associations: Perspectives on the Literature.* Cambridge, Mass.: Harvard University Press, 1972.

BIGOTRY MONEY GETS TIGHT

THE ATLANTA **CONSTITUTION**

A particular organization's impact upon a society often varies considerably through time. A number of organizations that once had awesome power are so feeble today that most of their resources are spent simply surviving. Only pride of group and a sense of duty keep these groups intact. Some have disbanded.

This characteristic of group life is true of organizations generally, not only of minority or nativistic ones. A local chapter of the American Association of University Professors, for example, will become a force to be reckoned with when some issue develops to threaten academic freedom. At other times it may have difficulty attracting a handful of members to a meeting.

The following article tells how some of the minority and nativistic (and reactionary) organizations are faring in the 1970s. Obviously, some of them—Black and White—are not doing very well. Why? Because the problems that they formerly dealt with are no longer considered critical by many potential supporters. Then, too, some of the organizations lack effective leaders. Others have been discredited. Finally, some of the organizations have been torn apart by in-fighting and schism.

It's tough being an organized bigot these days.

White-baiters on the left and black-haters on the right find memberships shrinking, public support withering and money growing tight.

The KKK in Atlanta is dying. SNCC is dead. Similar groups are mounting last-minute, sometimes half-hearted fights for life.

Even organizations committed to inter-racial cooperation—the Southern Christian Leadership Conference (SCLC) is one—face similar fates.

Purveyors of either harmony or hate find the market has grown bearish in metro Atlanta.

Bucking the trend are black separatist groups that have shown an increase in strength, partly because of their recruitment efforts among the young. At the same time, however, such groups are encountering increasing intolerance from the police and members of their own race.

This is the mixed picture that emerges as the race struggle of the '60s shifts into the "post-movement" era.

Old-line Negro organizations that fed off the fight against "official" segregation, in voting registration for example, have been defeated by their own victories.

A decade of civil rights progress has taken the wind out of their sails.

In turn, their decline has brought confusion to their white enemies, who are left without the highly visible targets—street marchers, freedom riders and counter sitters—that once sustained their fight.

Gaining new vitality in the shift are black groups fighting the "person-to-person" bias untouched by law.

Economic in thrust, they seek an end to undercover discrimination by attacking production and service processes or pushing for a black pullout from a white-dominated business world.

Hardest hit in the "post-movement" shuffle have been the apostles of hate on the white right like the Ku Klux Klan.

A klan membership drive last year failed to draw the young blood desperately needed by Atlanta's "white knights."

According to informants, the cross-burnings and night rides of the last 100 years have given way to klan reunions in Tucker, where a few old faithful gather to bemoan black advances and talk about the good old days.

James R. Venable of Stone Mountain, imperial wizard of the National Knights of the KKK, quietly plies his trade in his Decatur law office and resists interviews.

The former Georgia Grand Dragon of the United Klans of America, Calvin Craig, says he has rejected offers to reassume leadership of the klan.

Busy putting together a new political action group, he dreams of a klan museum.

Meetings of the rabidly antiintegrationist White Citizens Council in the metro area have failed to draw more than about 25 persons each during the last few years.

No gatherings have been reported in the last six months, giving rise to speculation that the group has disbanded.

Membership in the National States Rights party, headquartered in Marietta, continues "small," according to inside reports, but the actual number is kept secret by party leaders J. B. Stoner and Edward Fields.

Meetings attract 50 to 75 persons. The circulation of the *Thunderbolt*, the party's virulently antiblack newspaper, is not divulged.

Members of other white hate groups may be drifting into the NSRP, drawn by Stoner's relatively successful forays into the political arena, experts in area race relations suggest.

And the group may serve as a magnet if the white racism now dormant is ever revived, they add.

For now, however, few white Atlantans are touched by the activities of white racist groups.

The opposite is true of the black community, where militant separatists like the black Muslims wage intense recruitment campaigns in black communities and on downtown streets.

But officials believe the Muslims, despite their avowed hatred of whites and sometimes-violent confrontations with police, prefer self-help to race war.

And though their evangelism irks many blacks, the followers of Elijah Muhammed have gained considerable respect for building a separate system of black capitalism in the form of cafes, meat markets, bakeries and grocery stores.

Another openly anti-white group, the Black Panther party, has enjoyed less success, despite attempts at similar self-help programs.

It's work here is conducted largely by one man: Ron Carter, whom police call the city's "only known active Panther."

Other Panthers, however, may be leading less active lives in Atlanta, and members of the party's "combat" unit, the Black Liberation Army, are known to stage occasional sorties into the metro area.

Still, police raids and internal friction have apparently taken a heavy toll. The party, in the view of one high-ranking police official, is "virtually non-existent here."

Other "get-tough" black groups with names like Black Citizens Against Police Oppression occasionally spring up, stage protests, then die.

An official of the Atlanta Police Department's civil disturbances division says: "A persistent problem with militant groups is the continual struggle for power among the radicals themselves."

The fact that so many of the ad hoc groups are antipolice in origin suggests that many militant organizations, though regarded as generally racist, are only responding to particular situations.

Among the more moderate black groups, the most viable and most visible is the SCLC chapter led by Hosea Williams.

It appears to enjoy widespread support among poor blacks for its ventures into labor relations, an area which many Negroes believe traditional civil rights organizations have wrongly ignored.

(The Rev. Joe Boone's Metropolitan Atlanta Summit Leadership Conference has also moved into the economic area, which is fast shaping up as the next "civil rights" battle front.)

In contrast, the SCLC parent group has been shattered by money shortages, staff disputes and the Rev. Ralph David Abernathy as president.

Some say the SCLC deserves to die, claiming it is just a sentimental holdover from a bygone era. The NAACP here also is in trouble. Local NAACP officials have been excommunicated for taking part in the school settlement plan.

If the NAACP and SCLC indeed are unable to survive in an evolving world, what will take their place? The answer holds a clue to the future of race relations in Atlanta.

8

Intergroup Relations: The Individual

Culture always walks on two legs.

—Eugene Fischer (Quoted in Kluckhohn, 1962, p. 46)

*Neither the life of an individual nor the
history of a society can be understood
without understanding both.*

—C. Wright Mills (1961, p. 3)

Societal influences always encompass individual behavior. Individuals in every
society think of themselves in terms of the roles they play, define themselves as
members of groups—families, nations, religions, social classes, and clubs—
and adopt attitudes and beliefs congruent with their reference groups. Yet no
matter how encompassing group influences may be, it is still the individual who
hates, loves, projects, discriminates, and displaces aggression. In order to consider
this aspect of intergroup relations, the social-psychological perspective is used, and
the individual actor becomes the unit of study.[1]

[1] Parts of this chapter, particularly the material on prejudice, are based upon Howard
J. Ehrlich's excellent review (1973) of social-psychological studies.

Self-Concept and Group Identification

Human personality clearly is more than a combination of relatively fixed traits. Instead, it can be viewed as a flow of behavior—a series of events—arising from the continuous interaction of the individual with other actors in various situations. (Simpson and Yinger, 1965:52) This flow of behavior, to use an idea of Erik H. Erikson, has a certain sameness about it both in its essential quality (self-sameness) and in the sharing of this quality with others. It is this persistent sameness that constitutes a person's identity.

We come to know ourselves primarily through the reactions of other people to us. Our developing perceptions of their reactions are incorporated into our conceptions of ourselves. Their reactions are communicated through symbols—words, gestures, facial expressions, etc. Charles Horton Cooley formulated the concept of the "looking-glass self" to interpret this aspect of personality development. Those with whom we interact are a kind of mirror that enables us to form a conception of what we are like. Obviously some people are more important to us than others. The important persons, the individuals and groups of which we are aware, are *reference others*. We also internalize the reactions of a larger audience, sometimes called (by George H. Mead, for example) the "generalized other." Such interplay between the self and society means that the individual personality is not quite so individual after all. We think of ourselves in terms of others who are important to us.

The process of identifying with a group and thinking of oneself in terms of a group begins early in childhood. This development seems to parallel the development of the capacity to make gender identifications. Children begin to use gender categories (boy-girl, man-woman, mother-father) at about age three years, and most children are able to identify their own genders by this age.

Studies of American youngsters suggest that children as young as age three or four years are able to make distinctions among ethnic groups. Black youngsters, for example, at age four years are aware of their group and also often know the relevant words and phrases used to describe members of other groups. Studies of Jewish children reveal similar findings. Until age eight or nine years, however, group labels may be used by youngsters in an unskillful manner without any well-developed idea of group categories. Such use by youngsters may be reinforced by the inadvertent discovery that the words have shock value.

The individual's developing sense of identity with a group and the ability to distinguish among groups further parallel the development of gender identity. Even though children learn to make group and gender distinctions by age three or four years, they often perceive these categories as varying. A female playing a "male" role may be identified as a male. Similarly, children sometimes perceive ethnic identity as varying. One study (Radke, Trager, and Davis, 1949) reports children making the following statements:

FIGURE 8 Identifying with a group and evaluating one's self by means of this group identity apparently begins early in childhood. Various studies indicate that children as young as age 3 or 4 are able to make distinctions among ethnic groups. (Photo by Michael A. Woodlon, courtesy of the U.S. Commission on Civil Rights.)

"Little boys when they get dirty get into a colored boy, and when they get clean get into a white boy."

"He got dirt on his face and his momma didn't wash him."

Researchers have found that by age six or seven years the majority of children seem to be certain about categories, even though changes in appearance or tasks occur.

The categories that are used to designate particular groups serve to evaluate them as well. This aspect of categorical learning is discussed more fully later in this chapter in the section on prejudice. In terms of our interests here, the evaluative aspects of categorical learning also affect the individual's self-concept. An individual who finds that identification relationships provide at least a partial answer to the question "Who am I?" still may be troubled by the question "How am I regarded?" It can be argued with some logical justification that an individual's self-regard is closely associated with the perceived status of the actor's membership groups or reference groups.

Do research findings bear out this line of reasoning? The answer is "usually." Various techniques have been used: playmate selection, games, doll tests, and picture tests.

In a study of approximately 400 children, 60 percent of the Blacks but only 10 percent of the Whites preferred to play with those of the *other* group. In another study of Black children between the ages of three and seven years, the researchers reported that Black children perceived children of their own group to be aggressive and bad more often than White subjects saw White children as having these characteristics. In addition, both Black and White subjects most frequently picked White children as "winners in a game" (Morland, 1962, pp. 271–280; Stephenson and Stephenson, 1958, pp. 300–410).

In a classic study, Kenneth B. Clark and M. P. Clark (1947, pp. 169–178) used Black and White dolls and asked their subjects to "give me the doll that looks like you." They reported that 66 percent of the Black children chose a Black doll and that the remainder chose a White doll. One interpretation of their findings is that members of a group accorded low status by surrounding groups may psychologically reject membership in their own group.

Two recent studies similar to the Clark doll study report considerable amounts of negative self-evaluation among minority members. In a 1970 study conducted with seventy-four five-year-old boys (sixty-five Blacks and nine Whites) in a Head Start program in southeast Alabama (Mundy and Williams, 1970), four questions were asked:

1. Which one looks like a Black child?
2. Which one looks like a White child?
3. Which one looks like you?
4. Which one would you like to be?

The children were tested in pairs by two experimenters, one Black and the other White; the same questions were asked by both experimenters. The children were alternated so that *each child received the same questions twice*. This careful procedure was used in order to measure whether or not part of the variance was produced by interviewer characteristics (such as whether the interviewer was Black or White).

Questions 1 and 2 received 100 percent appropriate responses from all subjects. This response pattern makes improbable an interpretation that the Black doll did not resemble Blacks or that the White doll did not resemble Whites. All White subjects responded appropriately to both experimenters on questions 3 and 4. The Black children did not respond uniformly to these two questions. On question 3, 86.1 percent chose the Black doll and 4.6 percent chose the White doll for both experimenters, and 9.2 percent reversed their responses. On question 4, 56.9 percent chose the Black doll and 26.1 percent chose the White doll for both the experimenters, and 16.9 percent reversed their responses for the two experimenters. The responses to items 3 and 4 do show an interviewer effect, but they also indicate substantial amounts of negative evaluation on the part of Black children.

The second study was conducted with eighty-five children (thirty Mexican-American, twenty-five Black, thirty Anglo) who attended an unsegregated pre-kindergarten program in San Jose, California (Darrett and Davey, 1970, pp. 19, 20). The study population comprised forty-seven girls and thirty-eight boys, whose mean age was four years, seven months.

Eighty percent of the Mexican Americans chose the Anglo doll as looking like themselves, 83.3 percent of the Anglos chose it, and 48 percent of the Blacks chose their own group doll. The frequency and proportion of subjects who chose the Anglo or Black doll as a playmate are shown in Table 4.

TABLE 4   PROPORTION AND FREQUENCY OF CHILDREN'S SELECTION OF THE DOLL THEY PREFERRED FOR A PLAYMATE, BY GROUP.

Group	Black Doll		Anglo Doll		No Preference	
	Percent	No.	Percent	No.	Percent	No.
Blacks	48.0	12	52.0	13		
Anglos	16.7	5	83.3	25		
Mexican-Americans	16.7	5	80.0	24	3.3	1

SOURCE: Darrett and Davey, 1970, pp. 19, 20.

A number of studies show that the tendency of Black children to identify with Whites and to reject their own group decreases as they grow older. This change probably occurs because, as children grow older, they come to terms with the reality that their color and the place it assigns them in society probably cannot be escaped.

Each of the studies just described reveals that minority youngsters may identify with the dominant group and perhaps also have negative self-esteem. A few recent studies, however, indicate that all minority members do not have negative self-concepts, nor do they always esteem members of the dominant group more highly than themselves. A study of eighteen Black youths in a freedom school in Harlem (D. W. Johnson, 1966, pp. 266–272) revealed that Blacks rated Black equal to White on a series of concepts relevant to attitudes toward the respective groups. In a study in Lincoln, Nebraska (Hraba and Grant, 1970), the researchers found that Black youngsters in all age categories preferred Black dolls to White ones and that this preference increased with age. The researchers interpreted the difference between their own findings and those of Clark and Clark to be perhaps attributable to the impact of a two-year Black-pride campaign in the city. In both the Lincoln, Nebraska, and the Harlem studies, the positive impact of the civil rights (or Black pride) movement appeared to offset the tendency of the subjects to have negative valuations of their group and, by implication, negative valuations of themselves.

The Harlem study (D. W. Johnson, 1966) and the Lincoln, Nebraska, study (Hraba and Grant, 1970) do not disprove the general principle that self-concept is related to the perceived status of a person's identification groups. It suggests, rather, that the impact of this process varies according to the individual's background and subgroup membership. What has been interpreted as rejection of self may actually be rejection of one's status. The two mechanisms apparently are related in complex fashion. These studies further suggest that group evaluations (and, by implication, self-evaluations) have a dynamic quality that varies with changing social contexts.

Personality Dynamics and Intergroup Relations

Social psychology, as a field, has been greatly influenced by Sigmund Freud. Even contemporary social psychologists who reject elements of Freud's original theoretical formulations make frequent references to the psychic mechanisms that he described. Freud's work blasted the notion that thinking is simply an obvious and rational way of discovering reality. His studies led him to believe that individuals conceal certain ideas and motives even from themselves. He viewed thinking as a complex matter of making peace among three competing forces: the *id,* external reality, and the *superego* (La Barre, 1968, p. 66).

Freud called the conscious, executive part of the personality the "ego." The ego responds, first of all, to the demands of the id, which consists of everything that is inherited, including the instincts. Freud regarded the sexual drive as the fundamental biological instinct. Whenever id needs are repressed, *neurosis* occurs. The ego is also called upon to adapt to environmental reality. If it loses its adaptive relation to the external world, *psychosis* occurs. In addition, the psyche must adapt to the moral demands of a specific society. Moral demands precipitate in the mind as learned conscience, or superego. If moral demands are utterly rejected and not incorporated into the personality, *psychopathic* behavior occurs (LaBarre, 1968, p. 66). In everyday life the ego makes use of a number of defensive and adaptive strategies like *displacement* and *projection.* These strategies commonly figure in intergroup situations.

Displacement and Scapegoating

It is normal to be blocked at one time or another from attaining various goals toward which we have been impelled by our drives and by our culture. An individual may attempt to handle the frustration associated with such experiences either by storing up hostility within, by striking out at its source, or, if the cause of the frustration is unknown or too powerful to strike at, by directing hostility toward a substitute target.[2]

The latter alternative—directing hostility toward a substitute target that cannot be realistically considered the cause of the frustration—is called *displacement*. The target itself is sometimes called the "scapegoat," a concept derived from an ancient religious ceremony in which the sins of the community were ritually transferred to a sacrificial animal[3] (*Leviticus*, 16:5).

Displacement may involve individuals or entire groups. The Japanese persecution of Koreans toward the end of World War II and Nazi persecution of Jews in Europe appear to have been instances of displaced aggression in the face of frustration. The German propaganda ministry, it seemed, was especially likely to intensify anti-Semitic activity just after a military defeat. This general principle may also account for some of the aggression against minorities that has occurred closer to home, like lynching in the United States. For several years a study of lynching was conducted at Tuskegee Institute. It was observed that the number of lynchings tended to increase whenever the price of cotton declined. This variation could, of course, be attributable to chance, or it may be a spurious correlation. One plausible explanation of the phenomenon, however, is that the general level of frustration was closely tied to the price of cotton, particularly in the South, where cotton was king. A sharp drop in prices meant widespread unhappiness, and lynching appears to have been one outlet for pent-up frustration.

No criteria presently available can be used to predict unerringly who will be chosen as targets for displacement. (See Allport, 1958, pp. 330–333; Berry, 1965, pp. 308–309.) Members of a group are likely to be chosen as scapegoats, however, if they are easily recognizable as such, if the group has been singled out for ill will in the past, if it is concentrated geographically, and if its members are numerically or politically weak. A group will often be singled out for scapegoating if it is perceived as a "safegoat," that is, not strong enough to destroy the attacker. The Jewish population of Germany before World War II met all these criteria. The Jews had long borne the stigma of Christ killers. Their customs and their surnames made them noticeable; when these features were not sufficient, visibility was manufactured through signs, insignias, and so on. They were an urban people and, in Europe, they had long lived in ghettos. Finally, they were not numerically or politically powerful. We do not suggest that German Jews had

----

[2] In the original statement of the frustration-aggression hypothesis (Dollard *et al.*, 1939), it was claimed that aggressive behavior *always* presupposes the existence of frustration and that the existence of frustration always leads to some form of aggression. This generalization—especially the "always"—has been challenged in subsequent writings by scholars who insist that frustration does not always lead to aggression and that aggression is not always the dominant response to frustration (Ehrlich, 1973, p. 151).

[3] Scapegoating is a specific type of displacement.

no political or economic influence; but, in the aggregate, they were "safe." Finally, "The Jews were not selected indiscriminately," J. A. C. Brown has written, "but because they represented a traditionally and culturally acceptable scapegoat in central and eastern Europe generally" (1967, p. 70).

Displacement is often tied to status needs. The target of displaced aggression frequently is an individual who is low on the "pecking order." The expression "pecking order" is apt, for many species of birds are known to establish ranking systems in which weaker birds, whenever attacked by stronger ones, attack still weaker birds and so on down the line to the lowly birds who are pecked by all.

In human groups, individuals who fail by prominent standards in their society may find displacement one way of enhancing their own self-esteem. A person can live with a string of failures, it appears, as long as someone else is perceived to have lower status. This social-psychological dynamic could account for the finding from a number of studies indicating a great deal of open antipathy at the bottom rungs of the social ladder.[4] It is particularly apparent in the fighting among various minorities in urban slums. A plausible explanation is that some individuals satisfy their needs for achievement by dominating others, no matter what their status may be. Evidence from small-group studies suggests that weakness by itself is not, however, sufficient grounds for being singled out as a scapegoat. The very weakest person may not be the target of displaced hostility. It is when weakness is associated with some characteristic particularly disliked by the attacker that a person is likely to be chosen as a scapegoat (Harding, 1969, p. 35).

Projection

When individuals attribute to others the characteristics that they do not recognize in themselves, their attribution is called *projection*. It is "like the hysteric old maid who looks constantly and with delicious fearfulness for the burglar under the bed she unconsciously wishes were in bed with her. The lustful burglar has the wicked wish, not she!" (LaBarre, 1968, p. 67). An individual whose thoughts dwell

---

[4] This observation in no way suggests that members of the upper classes are without prejudice or that they abstain from discrimination. True, on questionnaires, individuals in the upper-income levels tend to show less prejudice than do lower-income people. This test variation can be explained partly by the fact that upper-income people typically have had more formal education and more varied experiences than have lower-income people. To some extent, upper-income people may be "test wise," in the sense that they have been exposed to college teachers and testing experiences and have learned how to be subtle and adroit. In short, they know that it is not usually advantageous to appear highly prejudiced. This is a partial explanation. What seems likely is that individuals of both strata are prejudiced and that they manifest their prejudice in different ways and in terms of particular situations. Such behavior, as Loewen correctly observes, tends not to be "a constant or even a varying characteristic of the individual, but a response to be comprehended only with knowledge of its intended audience and situation—a structural act" (1971, p. 105).

upon the immoral or unseemly behavior of others can experience vicarious pleasure at such behavior yet at the same time be able to feel innocent and even indignant about it. Individuals or groups singled out for projection (and displacement) are likely to be those with strongly disliked characteristics. Available evidence suggests "the differences most disliked by the prejudiced individual are those he unconsciously recognizes and rejects as potential characteristics in himself" (Harding, 1969, p. 35).

The Prejudiced Personality

Considerable research interest has been directed toward testing the hypothesis that prejudice is the central dimension of a particular personality type. The classic work on this topic, *The Authoritarian Personality* (Adorno *et al.*, 1950), was an attempt to delineate the personality characteristics of highly prejudiced individuals. The study population included college students and selected noncollege-educated adults; the central part of the study consisted of intensive clinical interviews with forty-five anti-Semitic individuals and thirty-five people who showed little anti-Semitism. High correlations were obtained among respondents' scores on an anti-Semitism scale (A scale), an ethnocentrism scale (E scale), and a fascism (F) scale.

The authors reported that the highly prejudiced individuals came from families in which parents demanded strict obedience and in which relatively little affection was shown. Little opportunity for spontaneous development of the self was permitted. Children from such families developed submissive behavior patterns and repressed hostility that could not be openly directed toward parents. In a world that they came to view as threatening, they found safety in rigidly conforming to conventional patterns of behavior.

Viewed as a personality type, the authoritarian personality is prone to projection and displacement of hostility. He is basically insecure and views life as capricious and threatening. His prejudices apparently help him to support his self-image. He generally places a high value on power and toughness, admires strong leaders, and despises weak groups.

As social-science research, Adorno's study has generated an enormous amount of comment. Its strong points are the use of multiple measurement techniques and a careful attempt to measure different levels of personality. The study did not, however, adequately control for educational attainment and organizational membership, and the sampling procedures were not given careful attention. Also the sample size was rather small. It is thus not known how widely the findings of the study can be generalized. In follow-up studies in which the level of education has been controlled, the correlations have remained significantly high. The question whether or not authoritarian child-rearing practices produce children with low frustration tolerance, repressed hostility, and other personality factors that later generate hostile attitudes has not yet been fully answered (Harding, 1969, p. 39).

Some critics think that the Adorno study equates authoritarian tendencies with a right-wing political philosophy. It leaves unanswered the question whether or not there are "left wing" individuals with the same characteristics. Studies by Milton Rokeach indicate that the authoritarianism studied by Adorno and others is perhaps a variety of a personality syndrome that Rokeach identifies as *dogmatism*—a relatively closed mental set organized around a central cluster of beliefs (1956, p. 3). According to Rokeach and his students, this closed cognitive organization provides a basis for intolerant behavior.

By means of a "dogmatism scale" Rokeach has attempted to measure bigotry in such a way that bigots of the left, center, and right obtain approximately the same scores on a test. In a set of studies designed to test the centrality of belief systems, Rokeach has reported that, when an individual is confronted with a choice between a person of a different ethnic group who agrees with him on a belief of fundamental importance and a person of his own group who disagrees with him on the same belief, most individuals will overlook group affiliation and will prefer those whose beliefs are congruent with their own (1960, chap. 7). Clinical confirmation of the relation between dogmatism and prejudice can be found in Rokeach and Fruchter (1956)—a correlation of .52—and in Rokeach (1956), where correlations (r) ranging from .30 to .53 between scores on various ten-item measures of ethnocentrism and several forms of a dogmatism scale are reported (see Ehrlich, 1973, pp. 143–146). The further claim by Rokeach and his associates that ethnic attitudes can be accounted for *entirely* by belief congruence has not gained wide acceptance by social scientists (Harding, 1969, p. 37).

Prejudice and Stereotyping

Social psychologists commonly use the concept of stereotype as a rubric for discussing the *cognitive* dimensions of prejudice. In this context, stereotypes are beliefs about particular groups of people, especially those beliefs that exaggerate qualities presumed to characterize the groups. The original usage of the word— for a printing plate on which are formed fixed representations—is consistent with the way that it is used in intergroup studies. Stereotypes tend to ignore the possibility of individual variation (see Lippmen, 1922, pp. 79, 96). In social usage, ethnic stereotypes are generalizations that function in a manner congruent with the second-order abstractions discussed in Chapter 1 of this book: Every person is, in certain respects, like *some* other people. The ethnic stereotype ignores the differences *within* the category.

Although stereotypes need not be negative, most of the research conducted on the topic has involved negative stereotypes. The reason for this research interest may derive from the bias of social scientists toward viewing prejudice as an aberration and a corresponding attitude that generally favors ameliorating social problems. It may also be that there are simply more negative stereotypes than positive ones or, at least, that negative stereotypes are more conspicuous and more readily studied than are positive ones. In support of the latter view, some researchers find that individuals are likely to differentiate more precisely among negative, threatening figures in the social environment than among nonthreatening figures. Such behavior certainly has functional importance, inasmuch as we are thus able to isolate and identify potentially dangerous individuals (Irwin, Tripodi, and Bieri, 1967, vol. 5, pp. 444–449). This "vigilance hypothesis" is consistent with other research findings that, when negative and positive information about an individual are presented in equal amounts, negative inputs dominate. Research also suggests that it is more difficult to change a disliked person into a liked person than it is to change a liked person into a disliked person (Ehrlich, 1973, p. 54).

How does one learn prejudice? It can be argued that this question is not appropriate because prejudice *follows* action. Indeed, in some situations, discriminatory behavior does come first; then follow prejudices, which function to support and rationalize overt behavior. Groups often develop belief and disbelief systems to "explain" discriminatory behavior after the fact. On the other hand, children who are born into systems in which discrimination occurs learn the reigning prejudices long before they experience any personal need for them. So prejudice may either precede or follow discrimination.

The nature of language facilitates the learning of prejudice. The English language, for example, includes words that reflect built-in evaluations based upon color. Some of these evaluations are subtle and implied. The word, "black," for example, often has negative connotations, as in the following expressions: blackmail, black list, black market, black mark, black magic, black-hearted, blackguard, black lies, and so on. (One of the few positive connotations of blackness is the phrase "in the black," as opposed to "in the red.") One reason that the phrase "Black power" is frightening to Whites, James Farmer has stated, is the negative connotation usually associated with blackness. Some usages are less subtle. The word "colored" for instance can imply sweaty, run-down, unkempt, or shiftless. Language usage, however, can be manipulated. Black Muslims have had considerable success teaching adherents that *White* is sickly, wicked, sinister, and weak. Some words have historically derived usages that are very explicit. In New Mexico it is a social blunder to refer to older Spanish-speaking families as Mexican, even though it is quite proper to do so in Texas. The preferred term is Spanish-American. The less prestigious term Mexican is reserved for recent immigrants from Mexico. In much the same way, the use of the words "nigger," Negro, "colored man," Black, and Afro-American convey varying evaluations of the people categorized, as well as the kind of behavior considered appropriate for them.

It was mentioned earlier that children begin to make group distinctions at about age four years. This cognitive ability develops gradually, although there is evidence that awareness of other groups develops earliest among children who live in areas where group definition is a matter of heightened social concern. Research that attempts to pinpoint the age at which negative stereotypes begin to stabilize show consistency in cross-sectional studies of second- to tenth-grade school children, and of fifth- to eight-graders. Young children, according to W. E. Lambert and O. Klineberg (1967), tend to base their categorical judgments on physical features, clothing, language, and customs. By age ten years, however, the criteria have shifted to personality characteristics and differences in beliefs. When researchers have asked adults the age at which they first began to develop negative attitudes toward specific groups, the median response has ranged from twelve to sixteen years old (Ehrlich, 1973, p. 121). These data, however, leave something to be desired. Conceivably, children reared in isolated, homogeneous areas would have little occasion to believe anything good or bad about certain groups, except insofar as they were exposed to information through the mass media or the schools. The formation of negative attitudes toward such groups would probably occur much later than it would among persons reared in situations characterized by regular or tense interaction with the groups in question. The age at which a person begins to form stereotypes about a particular group will thus depend upon the period of the individual's life during which the group becomes salient to him, either in terms of information available or through personal contact. If the initial encounter is unpleasant and if it occurs fairly early in childhood, some findings indicate that these experiences can come to be anchors for coding and evaluation of future experience.

From whom do individuals learn stereotypes? In one study six-year-olds were asked where they had learned about ethnic differences. They responded, first, from their parents and, second, from movies and television. From about age ten years, the reported sources shifted to impersonal ones—television, movies, books, magazines, and textbooks (Lambert and Klineberg, 1967). This pattern is not an unexpected one. In American society, the family appears to have greater importance in disseminating ideas during the preschool and elementary-school years than it does during adolescence. There is variation, however, within the family. Similarity of the stereotypes of parents is greater than that of the stereotypes of parents and children, and siblings' stereotypes display higher correlations with each other than with those of the parents. The correlations do not appear to result from similarities in age, nor do cross-sex or same-sex combinations affect the correlations. Social class, however, does affect the strength of the correlations. Stereotypes of parent-child pairs from lower-status occupations tend to correlate higher than do such pairs from higher-status occupations. One plausible explanation is that members of high-status families are exposed to greater diversity of ideas and information than are those of low-status families (Ehrlich 1973, p. 112).

Prejudice and Affect

The affective dimension of prejudice is a neglected area of social psychology. Present knowledge has been drawn from three sources: evaluation of the emotional content of particular statements, beliefs or disbeliefs, words, and phrases; evaluation of the tenacity with which certain beliefs or disbeliefs are maintained, even in the face of opposition; and measurement of physiological responses to various stimuli.

Although a few studies have dealt with the language of affect, Ehrlich's review (1973) of the social-psychological literature includes only one study that attempted to measure the affective dimension of ethnic attitudes. Several studies, however, have sought to measure affect by means of physiological responses. Most of these involve the galvanic skin response. (The galvanic skin response, or G.S.R., is a measure of electrodermal reactivity. A fall in skin resistance to the flow of electrons is associated with secretions of the sweat glands, which are under the control of the sympathetic nervous system.)

Most of these studies show some association between physiological variables and ethnic attitudes, but not enough evidence is available to establish a firm link between prejudice and emotion. The following research finding, however, suggests such a link: Those who manifested high prejudice toward Blacks (as measured by an attitude scale) displayed greater G.S.R.s when exposed to photographs of Blacks (or to photographs of Blacks interacting with Whites) than did those with low prejudice scores (Vidulich and Krevanick, 1966).

Prejudice and Behavior

Not all statements of belief or disbelief about ethnic groups imply action. For example, the statement, "Blacks have natural rhythmic ability" does not necessarily imply any behavorial intention, whereas the statement "I would not live next door to a Japanese" is explicit. The first statement reflects a stereotype, but it does not articulate the idea of *social distance*—the concept most frequently used when researchers study the behavioral or conative (action) aspects of prejudice.[5]

Social distance as a concept was introduced by Robert Park in 1924 and made operational by E. S. Bogardus in the following year. As originally conceived, social distance is the degree of intimacy that generally characterizes personal and social relations between peoples. During subsequent years four specific types of

[5] At least one researcher (Mann, 1959) thinks that social-distance scales measure the affective component of prejudice.

TABLE 5   SOCIAL-DISTANCE RANKS OF AMERICANS, 1926–1966

Target Group	1926	1946	1956	1966
English	1.0	3.0	3.0	2.0
Americans (U.S., white)	2.0	1.0	1.0	1.0
Canadians	3.5	2.0	2.0	3.0
Scots	3.5	5.0	7.0	9.0
Irish	5.0	4.0	5.0	5.0
French	6.0	6.0	4.0	4.0
Germans	7.0	10.0	8.0	10.5
Swedish	8.0	9.0	6.0	6.0
Hollanders	9.0	8.0	9.0	10.5
Norwegians	10.0	7.0	10.0	7.0
Spanish	11.0	15.0	14.0	14.0
Finns	12.0	11.0	11.0	12.0
Russians	13.0	13.0	22.0	22.0
Italians	14.0	16.0	12.0	8.0
Poles	15.0	14.0	13.0	16.0
Armenians	16.0	17.5	18.0	19.0
Czechs	17.0	12.0	17.0	17.0
Indians (Amer.)	18.0	20.0	19.0	18.0
Jews	19.0	19.0	16.0	15.0
Greeks	20.0	17.5	15.0	13.0
Mexicans	21.0	23.5	26.0	26.5
Japanese	22.0	28.0	24.0	23.0
Filipinos	23.0	22.0	20.0	20.0
Negroes	24.0	27.0	25.0	26.5
Turks	25.0	23.5	21.0	24.0
Chinese	26.0	21.0	23.0	21.0
Koreans	27.0	25.0	28.0	25.0
Indians (India)	28.0	26.0	27.0	28.0

SOURCE: Adapted from Bogardus by Ehrlich, 1973, p. 74.

phenomena have been studied under the rubric of "social distance" (Ehrlich, 1973, p. 62):

1. *Manifest norms* of behavior—*inferences* about social distance derived from actual behavior (like intermarriage, open housing, admission policies to clubs, schools, and the like); the behavior itself is usually discussed under the rubric of "discrimination"
2. *Idealized norms* of behavior (values)—indicators of preferences for certain types of behavior
3. *Social norms* of behavior (social distance)—indicators of the legitimacy and

social acceptability of varying degrees of intimacy between members of respective groups

4. *Personal norms* of behavior (personal distance)—indicators of an individual's intention to personally engage in behaviors of varying degrees of intimacy with persons of target groups.

The conceptual distinction between personal distance and social distance is somewhat congruent with the now well-known distinction between *individual* racism and *institutional* racism (Knowles and Prewit, 1969). Individuals, as individuals, are not usually permitted great latitude in deciding the degree of distance to be maintained among members of various groups. Usually a consensus on the distances that are proper develops. Gradually, these distances become crystallized into customs, mores, and laws. This process is not necessarily spontaneous or random. Instead, the process often involves manipulations by élites and other interest groups, a phenomenon to be discussed in Chapter 9.

Long-term interest in social distance has permitted some trend analysis. Available studies show that the various targets of social distance in the United States have remained in essentially the same order during the forty years reported (see Table 5). Some fluctuation has occurred, the most apparent being in the respective ranks of Japanese, Germans, and Italians immediately following World War II. The category Russians also shows wide fluctuation. Overall, the social-distance means have decreased slightly (from 2.14 in 1926 to 1.92 in 1966), and the spread of scores has decreased sharply (from 2.85 in 1926 to 1.56 in 1966).

In certain experiments investigators have manipulated various attributes of target groups to see what effect they have upon social-distance ratings. In one of these studies, H. C. Triandis and L. M. Triandis (1960) measured social distance, using sixteen constructs that consisted of combinations of ethnicity, occupation, religion, and nationality. One of the constructs, for example, was formulated "a Portuguese Negro physician of the same religion as you" and another, "a white Swedish truck driver of a different religion." The results were subjected to factor analysis and yielded the following results: Approximately 77 percent of the variation in the social-distance scores was accounted for by ethnicity, 17 percent by occupation, 5 percent by religion, and 1 percent by nationality.[6] In other studies, religious belief has been observed to be more important than either race or sex

[6] It is interesting that W. Lloyd Warner and Leo Srole (1945, pp. 290–292) reached similar conclusions about the effect of these variables vis à vis the predicted rate of assimilation of various groups into Ameican society. Their procedures were quite different from those described here, and the level of analysis was of a different order, but the findings are congruent. Representative categories (and predicted time for assimilation) from their study are "Light Caucasoid—English-speaking Protestants (very short); Light Caucasoid—Protestants not speaking English (short); Light Caucasoid—English-speaking non-Christians (short to moderate); Dark Caucasoids—*e.g.,* Protestant Armenians (moderate); Mongoloids —*e.g.,* American Chinese and Japanese (slow); Negroids—*e.g.,* Most American Negroes (very slow)."

in determining social distance (Rokeach, Smith, and Evans, 1960; Smith, Williams, and Willis, 1967).

Most studies have shown high correlations among the three components of prejudice—the cognitive, affective, and conative. These correlations may partly result from the measurement techniques employed, however.[7] It has been argued that the correlations would be lower if researchers were to score the several components by different methods, rather than by the paper-and-pencil self-rating methods usually used. Indeed, one researcher found that correlations of self-ratings with observer ratings (of actual behavior) were negative for White participants, even though they remained positive for Black participants (Mann, 1959).

Prejudice, Intelligence, and Other Cognitive Variables

Several studies have revealed that those who score high in prejudice tend also to score low on formal tests of intelligence and to manifest relatively closed cognitive structures. The magnitude of the correlations, however, is usually not great. At least two studies have reported contrary evidence: E. B. Bolton (1935) reported no statistically significant correlations. B. Kutner (1958) found that his high- and low-prejudiced children were not differentiated by scores on the Pinter-Durost Intelligence Test. Kutner's study—which was based on a sample of sixty seven-year-olds in an upper-middle-class Boston suburb—did reveal other mental functions associated with prejudice. He characterized the two groups as follows:

PREJUDICED CHILD	UNPREJUDICED CHILD
1. Rigidity	1. Flexibility
2. Overgeneralization	2. Realistic generalization
3. Categorizing and dichotomizing	3. Individualizing
4. Concretization	4. Abstraction
5. Simplification	5. Retention of complexity
6. Furcation	6. Retention of totality
7. Dogmatism (omniscience)	7. Lack of dogmatism
8. Intolerance of ambiguity	8. Tolerance of ambiguity

(Kutner, 1958, p. 42)

Nine years later thirty-three individuals from the original study group were retested by Kutner and Gordon (1964). As in the earlier study, the less prejudiced individuals showed generally greater cognitive ability than did the more prejudiced individuals (1964, p. 74). Also, the mean I.Q. (based on scores on the Pintner-Steward Intelligence Test) for the less prejudiced category was 119.3, whereas that

---

[7] See McGuire (1969) and Ehrlich (1973, pp. 101–108) for further discussion of the interconnections of the components of prejudice.

for the more prejudiced category was 110.9. This difference is significant at the .05 level. Noting that the difference was not statistically significant for the original sample (which was larger), the researchers explained, "The fact that no such difference emerged from the original sample is doubtless due to sampling variation" (Kutner and Gordon, 1964, p. 70). The researchers found a "hard core" of more prejudiced subjects (reportedly so at age seven years who were found to be so nine years later. Another "hard core" of less prejudiced subjects still retained their tolerant views at age sixteen years and were "manifestly superior in cognitive ability over the nine year interval." The researchers concluded, "A portion of the general intellectual make up—the capacity to reason logically—is impaired among those showing a high degree of social bigotry" (1964, p. 71).

It would be convenient to be able to attribute all ethnic prejudice to cognitive impairment. Prejudice then could be thought of as an aberration of normal mental processes. The evidence cited here does seem to lend some support to this view. The relationship between prejudice and intelligence, at least insofar as intelligence is measured by standardized tests, may be a society-specific phenomenon, however. In the United States an individual who scores high on an intelligence test tends also to have had more extensive educational experiences than does the low scorer. The high scorer, as a result of reading and an enriched environment, is also more likely to have been exposed to the well-developed norms of tolerance that have characterized the intellectual mainstream of our society in recent years. It can be argued further that the high scorer on the "intelligence" items will tend to be "test-wise" on the "prejudice" items and will choose those responses calculated to make him appear tolerant, democratic, and fair-minded.

At any rate, available evidence from psychological tests and from historical data indicates that the relationship between level of intelligence and prejudice is not clear. Leaders of the Third Reich, for instance, seem to have been above average in intelligence, yet they administered racist policies so brutal that they shocked the world. Other examples of groups who, by most accounts, were bright but ruthless can be cited. These data do not rule out the possibility of any relationship between intelligence and prejudice, but they should serve as a caution against the belief that high intelligence by itself is a guarantee against prejudice.

Prejudice and Reference Groups

One of the early studies on the importance of reference-group behavior revealed that reference-other expectations appreciably influenced the subjects' affect toward minorities. Specifically, when White respondents were asked how they would feel about dancing with a Black person, their responses indicated that their social-distance feelings reflected the reactions of parents and friends "just as much as or more than" they reflected the experience of fairly close contacts with Blacks. The researchers make the following observation: "The field interviews emphasized how very much individuals tend to see their own behavior through the eyes of the significant other persons with whom they associate" (Williams, 1964, pp. 35).

In another study, researchers asked college students if they would be willing to be photographed with a Black of the opposite sex. Each respondent was then given a photograph-release agreement, which listed seven ways that the photograph might be used. The respondent was instructed to sign any or none of them. The provisions of the releases ranged from showing the photograph only to professional sociologists to using it as part of a nationwide campaign advocating desegregation. By means of an earlier study, the researchers had already obtained a social-distance measure toward Blacks for each respondent. Following the subject's response to the release statement, he was asked: "Was there any particular person or group of people . . . who came to mind when you decided to sign (or refused to sign) this document? That is, are these people whom you felt would approve or disapprove?" (DeFleur and Westie, 1958).

The researchers found that approximately 30 percent of those studied displayed "discrepant behavior." The discrepancy between the respondent's social-distance score and willingness to be associated with specific kinds of intergroup activities was interpreted by researchers as attributable to reference-other behavior.

The impact of reference-others who might disapprove of certain kinds of behavior may help to explain the long-observed phenomenon that a person's verbal report of his attitudes often has a low correlation with actual behavior toward the object of the attitude. Research techniques widely used in the social sciences probably increase the likelihood of obtaining such low correlations between test responses and actual behavior. Typically, participants in research are told that their responses will remain anonymous. Thus assured of secrecy, participants may really be telling only their *wishes*—what in their own hearts they would like to do if they were in some ideal situation. Little wonder then that the test responses are not very good predictors of behavior. If, instead, participants were told beforehand that their responses would be made available to certain groups (as DeFleur and Westie did with the photograph releases), there would possibly be fewer participants in some studies, but the correlations between test responses and actual behavior probably would be higher.

Types of Minority Responses

Certain types of behavior are predictable whenever individuals occupy subordinate positions, just as certain types of behavior are predictable when they occupy dominant positions. Whenever individuals feel that they are being discriminated against because of their affiliations with a particular group, they are likely to adopt modes of behavior that have come to be known in the social sciences as "minority responses" or "minority behavior."[8] These modes of behavior are not limited to members of ethnic groups and certainly not to any one ethnic group. Furthermore, they are not restricted to peoples that occupy unprivileged positions in society. Such responses may be found among superordinate groups as well. In all likelihood, a White Protestant who happened to find himself confronted by a threatening crowd in Harlem or in Chinatown would bluff, clown, or retreat rapidly!

There is thus risk in calling these responses "*minority* responses," inasmuch as the uncritical use of such classifications can amount to stereotyping. At one level of analysis minority responses are alternative forms of adaptive behavior to which all humans, minority and majority, resort: attack, approach, cessation of response, and retreat. For example, a White, middle-class high-school student who fails to make the football team may criticize the coach for unfairness, may intensify his efforts at his studies, or may become gloomy and brooding. What is of interest to social scientists studying intergroup relations is the characteristics that these responses have when made by those with a minority perspective.

Minority responses cover a wide range of behavior. Even within the same group there is often great variation in the ways in which given individuals cope with similar problems. To complicate the matter further, an individual member of a particular group may engage in one, several, or none of these types of responses. It should be borne in mind that they are *types* of responses—hypothetical constructs emphasizing certain characteristics and ignoring others. The basic motivation for each minority response is, however, the same: Individuals believe that they are being treated differently because they are associated with a particular group. In the following discussion we shall outline the more common types.

Distrust and Suspicion

Some minority members carry a feeling of suspicion into any situation in which outsiders must be dealt with. They may not have known discrimination themselves, but the experiences of friends and kin or the group tradition may have conditioned them to disbelieve what outsiders say and do. If minority members have been "burned" in earlier experiences, they are all the more likely to be distrustful. Such experiences seem to serve as anchors for coding and evaluating subsequent contacts with members of other groups. The minority member thus concludes from these unpleasant experiences that all outsiders are potentially dangerous.

---

[8] Gordon W. Allport called these modes of behavior "traits due to victimization." I prefer not to call them "traits" but have incorporated relevant material from Allport's list (1958, pp. 139–156) into this section. The word "trait" sometimes conveys the idea of a relatively permanent quality of an individual's personality. That connotation is not intended in this discussion. "Minority behavior," as used here, refers to dynamic phenomena. A "minority response" is adaptive behavior that may vary from one situation to another.

This type of minority response, which is entirely predictable, can be galling to individual members of dominant groups who may think of themselves as unprejudiced and tolerant. To have to prove the genuineness of their attitudes seems insulting. It is not uncommon for distrust and suspicion on the part of minority members to trigger a "They can go to Hell!" response on the part of such a member of the dominant group. A predictable minority response thus produces an equally predictable dominant-group response.

Obsessive Concern

Members of dominant groups are generally aware that minority members sometimes feel uncomfortable about their status. But they are not as likely to recognize the depths of those feelings or that some minority members feel a continuous sense of outrage or apprehension. They tend to be surprised when some word or action not intended to be annoying results in an explosion of anger. James Baldwin, in *Notes of a Native Son*, has likened such an obsession to a "dread, chronic disease. One who has it can never be carefree again, for the fever can break out at any moment." He adds, "There is not a Negro alive who does not have this rage in his blood. . . ."

Baldwin attributes this obsession to the minority member's belief that he will always be dealt with as a member of his group and not as an individual. Because he "knows" that he will be evaluated regularly on that basis alone, "race" tends to be read into every unpleasant experience. In many instances, of course, such an interpretation is more than justified. Sometimes, however, the obsession serves as a defense mechanism protecting the individual from bearing personal responsibility for failure. It also can have a function not greatly dissimilar to a "game" that Eric Berne named Wooden Leg. Wooden Leg, as the following quotation indicates, is based on the individual's personal presumption that there is no point in trying. Such behavior tends to stimulate another response called I'm Only Trying To Help You.

> The thesis of "Wooden Leg" is, "What do you expect of a man with a wooden leg?" Put that way, of course, no one would expect anything of a man with a wooden leg except that he should steer his own wheel chair. On the other hand, during World War II there was a man with a wooden leg who used to give demonstrations of jitterbug dancing, and very competent jitterbug dancing, at Army Hospital amputation centers. There are blind men who practice law and hold political offices (one such is currently mayor of the writer's home town), deaf men who practice psychiatry and handless men who can use a typewriter.
>
> As long as someone with a real, exaggerated or even imaginary disability is content with his lot, perhaps no one should interfere. But the moment he presents himself for psychiatric treatment, the question arises if he is using his life

to his own best advantage, and if he can rise above his disability. In this country the therapist will be working in opposition to a large mass of educated public opinion. Even the close relatives of the patient who complained most loudly about the inconveniences caused by his infirmity, may eventually turn on the therapist if the patient makes definitive progress. . . . All the people who were playing "I'm Only Trying To Help You" are threatened by the impending disruption of the game if the patient shows signs of striking out on his own, and sometimes they use almost incredible measures to terminate the treatment. (1967, p. 160)

Overt Aggression

Perhaps the least complicated response to the frustrations of minority status is aggression. The response may be verbal or physical, and it can come without any warning. An army officer once told the author about an incident that occurred when a military policeman was questioning a young Black man about a disturbance: "The MP made the mistake of calling the recruit, 'Boy.' The young man's reaction was so violent, he almost tore up the patrol car!"

It is not uncommon for minority members to bully or intimidate majority-group members, especially when the latter venture into minority territory or are otherwise vulnerable. In its more subtle forms, minority hostility may take the form of bluffing. The purpose is often to create the impression that members of the group are tough and dangerous. During a recent riot at a state prison where Blacks greatly outnumbered Whites, the *Whites* painted a huge sign: "White Power." In this instance, Whites constituted the numerical minority, but they apparently felt that they could protect their interests if they convinced the Blacks that reprisals would be serious.

Feelings of Superiority

Instead of feeling inferior to the dominant group, some minority individuals feel infinitely superior to it. A Chinese-American who had grown up in the Mississippi Delta once told the author: "Years ago when the Chinese were day-laborers building railroads across America, even the poorest Chinese took a condescending view toward the White men around him. The Chinese were convinced they were members of an ancient and advanced civilization, and their White bosses were practically uncivilized."

During the past few decades, a number of studies have reported that inferiority feelings are common among American Indian groups. But such feelings were not always present. Booker T. Washington, who worked with Indian students at Hampton Institute in the 1880s, wrote that Indians generally felt superior to other groups:

On going to Hampton, I took up my residence in a building with about seventy-five Indian youths. I was the only person in the building who was not a member of their race. At first, I had a good deal of doubt about my ability to succeed. I knew that the average Indian felt himself above the white man, and, of course, he felt himself far above the Negro, largely on account of the fact of the Negro having submitted to slavery—a thing which the Indian would never do. (1937, pp. 97, 98)

Today American college students probably would be surprised to know how they are perceived by some international students on their campuses. International students are often too diplomatic and discreet to reveal their true feelings to outsiders, but in privacy they often compare Americans unfavorably with their own people.

Strengthening In-Group Ties

Some minority members who have been rejected by the dominant group (and some who have not) intensify their efforts to be accepted by their own people. One reason for this reaction is that a person who lacks a sense of community with others must absorb the shock of discrimination alone.

Kurt Lewin, in his famous essay "Self-Hatred among Jews" argued that group morale and cohesion increased whenever external forces of rejection and persecution were strong (1948). Conversely, during those periods when pressures on the Jews were relaxed and boundaries lowered, group solidarity became fragmented. The result for the individual under those circumstances was that he stood unprotected against rebuffs and rejection.

The emphasis on Black solidarity that gained momentum in the 1960s illustrates the strengthening of in-group ties on a massive scale. One of its most noticeable effects in recent years has been the almost stylized response of Blacks to other Blacks as "brothers" and "sisters." Similar behavior has been characteristic of successful mass movements in the past. The promise of fellowship to otherwise detached individuals can be appealing. Such a benefit to the individual is not without its price, however. Although the individual gains in terms of fellowship, protection, and sustenance, there is a loss in terms of autonomy. Personal identity tends to be submerged in group identity, and personal freedoms are given up for corporate goals.

Intensified Striving

To some people, a perceived handicap is a stimulus to redoubled efforts. The feeling that the "eyes of all people are upon us"—to use a theme from early Puritan sermons—is really rather common among minorities. It comes through to the individual as a motive for making an extra effort. Parents use it as a technique for prodding their children to achieve. The extra effort may even take on mystical meaning, becoming proof that a person from a given group can succeed. Émile Durkheim believed that it occurs frequently enough to justify its being called a "law."

> It is a general law that religious minorities, in order to protect themselves better against the hate to which they are exposed or merely through a sort of emulation, try to surpass in knowledge the populations surrounding them. Thus Protestants themselves show more desire for knowledge when they are a minority of the general population. The Jew, therefore, seeks to learn, not in order to replace his collective prejudices by reflective thought, but merely to be better armed for the struggle. (Durkheim, 1951, pp. 167–168)

Focused Behavior on Other Out-Groups

Some individuals who are discriminated against will try to inflict upon others a measure of what they have received. It was mentioned earlier that individuals who are deprived of power and status themselves sometimes find an outlet for their frustration by victimizing those with less power and status than they (through displacement). Sometimes a minority member will decide that the way to be accepted in the core society is to take on its prejudices conspicuously. It was commonly observed in the Jim Crow South that newcomers from other regions frequently would be more careful about observing traditional "racial etiquette" than were long-term residents. It seemed to be the newcomer's way of joining the club. (There is a parallel between this kind of behavior and that of a new convert to a religion. The convert frequently is more zealous about the rules than are the older members.)

Some minority members feel a consciousness of kind with other subordinate peoples. Anger is felt because of their grievances, and vicarious pleasure is experienced whenever the other minority group scores a victory. James W. Leowen, in his excellent discussion of the Chinese in Mississippi has written:

> Chinese merchants report little difficulty in getting along with other ethnic groups. "The Jews are the best friends we ever had," according to a Greenville grocer; while in Vicksburg a Lebanese banker was the first to express willingness to loan money for a Chinese merchant to buy a home in an exclusive white suburb. And in Shaw, a Chinese merchant told me: "The Italians accept Chinese better than the old-line families do. I *know* that." Nor was this an isolated opinion; most Chinese whom I asked agreed with it. (1971, p. 114)

It is difficult to predict whether or not minority members will be prejudiced toward other out-groups or will side with them. It seems safe to generalize that hostility is likely between two minority groups competing for scarce goods and services. If a minority group's relationship with the dominant group is precarious, the vulnerable minority may side with the dominant group against the third group out of expediency. It does not follow, however, that minority members who feel secure will necessarily support members of other minority groups.[9]

Identification with the Dominant Group

The publicans of Palestine during the first century A.D. represent an old pattern of identification with a dominant group. A publican was an individual who contracted to collect taxes for the Roman government. Some of the publicans were Jews who had accepted the responsibility of collecting taxes from their fellow countrymen. Although they were rewarded handsomely by the Romans, they were despised by their own people. Usually they were expelled from the synagogues and denied access to the religious and social life of the community.

Conspicuously identifying with the dominant group was unpopular then, as it is now. Uncle Tom, Oreo, and Uncle Tomahawk are typical labels reserved for minority members who are accused of similar behavior today.

Minority members may try to identify simultaneously with the dominant group and with their own, or they may attempt to reject their group of origin. Motives vary when this behavior occurs. Some individuals may become ashamed of their origins, especially if travel, wealth, or a new environment has provided them with other role models. One's own people then come to be viewed as the proverbial "poor relatives." A Gypsy may no longer want to be a Gypsy. An Indian may reject the reservation and "Indianness." A "hillbilly" in the city may come to scorn grits, collards, and turnip greens. The essence of the marginal situation, as Stonequist has described it, is "a contrast, tension or conflict of social groups divergent in race or possessing distinct culture in which members of one group are seeking to adjust themselves to the group believed to possess greater prestige and power" (1937, p. 121).

The person who identifies with the dominant group may decide to "pass." Ethnic passers may change their names or occupations if they are give-aways; a racial passer may claim descent from a less stigmatized group. A Black who passes may say that his ancestors are Indian or Spanish. Italians or Armenians may change their names. Obviously, passing is a real option only for those individuals whose original identity is not conspicuous (Blacks whose physical features are similar to those of Whites, and the like). Passing often proves to be psychically stressful for two reasons: It is usually necessary to cut ties with family and old friends, at least, publicly, and it is necessary to be constantly on guard against disclosure.

---

[9] Students who wish to explore this subject further may find discussions of game theory (Messick, 1968, part 3) and triadic theory (Caplow, 1968) useful in formulating hypotheses about the various coalitions possible to minorities vis à vis dominant groups.

Clowning

Research with small groups has shown that a low-status member may resort to clowning as a defensive strategy. Making fun of oneself or one's group may smooth irritated feelings in tense situations. If the situation is threatening, clowning can divert aggression to other objects. Clowns, however, may not inwardly accept the valuations they outwardly place upon themselves but may instead deliberately play the role out of desperation. Clowning also can mask envy, contempt, and anger. Its aim may be to "put down" the opponent by slyly mocking him.

Cunning and Slyness

Cunning and slyness are responses similar to what Erving Goffman calls "role distance." An individual plays a particular role "tongue in cheek" without really meaning it and with an ulterior motive. In such instances the thoughts that the individuals truly relish are quite contrary to the fiction that their roles project.

Jean-Paul Clébert writes of the Gypsies in Europe, "They systematically tell lies, thereby providing evidence of the normal, self-defense reflex on the part of a minority that has so long been exposed to the most exorbitant demands" (1969, p. 17). Although Clébert's characterization of Gypsies is obviously stereotypical, it does underscore the fact that deception is a "normal" defense of this subordinate people. Nor is this response limited to minorities. Many individuals consider it proper to cheat, deceive, or steal from members of out-groups. Such behavior is considered wrong only if it is directed toward one's own people.

Cunning and slyness also can be classified as "innovation" in the sense that Robert K. Merton uses the word (1964) in his well-known typology of modes of adaptation. Merton's typology is based on the idea that particular responses occur with varying frequency among different subgroups of a society, primarily because members of certain groups are differentially subject to cultural stimulation, as well as to social constraints. Innovation, as a mode of behavior, involves acceptance of culturally approved goals by individuals who use illegitimate means to attain those goals. This response arises partly because individuals in certain strata of society internalize the cultural emphasis upon pecuniary success but lack equitable access to legitimate means for becoming successful (Merton, 1964, pp. 144, 145).

Avoidance, Withdrawal, Retreat

Minority members sometimes deliberately avoid or retreat from situations in which it is likely that unpleasantness or failure will occur. Before implementation of the Civil Rights Act in the 1960s, the Haliwa Indians of North Carolina would not attend a theater in the nearby town because they were unwilling to be assigned to the "colored" section. Instead, they would drive forty-five miles to a drive-in theater or would not attend at all (Dane and Griessman, 1972, pp. 694–710). If physical retreat is impossible, minority members may retreat psychologically. Such psychological responses include the behavior of those who remain in touch with reality but impassively "tune out" dissonant influences.

Contrary to popular belief, there is almost no historical evidence to support the view that oppressed peoples *inevitably* rise up against their masters and over-throw them. In fact, the preponderance of evidence is to the contrary. Minority members often yield without protest and become quietly passive. They defer their victories until they are able to lay their burdens "down by the Riverside." Or their responses may be even less hopeful than that. They may become fatalistic and submit to divine will or to the "luck of the draw."

Three decades of research on the attitudes of American Indians verify the existence of this type of minority response. Withdrawal and retreat are frequently reported responses. The terms that researchers use in these studies are *alienation, hopelessness, powerlessness, rejection, estrangement,* and *frustration* (Berry, 1968, pp. 92–98). In the San Francisco area, the common attitudes of Indians toward the White community are reportedly suspicion and fear of rejection. In Michigan, Ralph West—himself an Indian—writes, "even long residence in Detroit fails to dispel the sense of inferiority" (1950). That this type of response characterizes large numbers of individual Indians in no way contradicts the fact that a substantial number of American Indians have become militant within recent years. Both types of behavior are adaptive responses.

Avoidance, withdrawal, and retreat are often apparent in the classroom and in the work setting. Youngsters who are constantly corrected for speaking non-standard dialects of English may react defensively and quit talking. Ironically, they may then be labeled "nonverbal."

By the time that minority youngsters are old enough to hold jobs, their cumulative experience of rejection and failure may have become an established pattern. They may already bear the "mark of a loser." Elliot Liebow (1967), in his study of low-income Black men in Washington, relates how their low self-esteem and fear of being tested again and failing affected their performance at work: "Richard refuses such a job, Leroy leaves one and another man, given more responsibility and more pay, knows he will fail and proceeds to do so, proving he was right about himself all along. The self-fulling prophecy is everywhere at work" (1967, p. 56).

Pathological Reactions

The minority experience can be so stressful that an individual will lose the ability to cope with reality. How often does this experience occur? Frequently, available information suggests. One state's admissions to mental-health facilities (North Carolina, 1961–1968, diagnosed illness, by race) showed lower total admission rates for Blacks than for Whites, but Blacks were numerically overrepresented for paranoid schizophrenia and other psychotic reactions. Whites had higher rates of drug and alcohol abuse. These rates may well reflect differential access to resources or varying levels of toleration in the home communities.

Nationwide, admission rates to state and county mental hospitals tell a different story. As can be seen in Table 6 the non-White rate of admission is about one and a half times that of the White rate within each sex group. This phenomenon has been long recognized. Higher admission rates to state mental hospitals for non-Whites have been noted in studies that date back to the 1920s.

TABLE 6 AGE-ADJUSTED[1] ADMISSION RATES TO STATE AND COUNTY INPATIENT SERVICES, BY SEX AND COLOR, U. S., 1969, PER 100,000 POPULATION.

Color	Both Sexes	Males	Females
White and Non-White,			
Total	249.7	310.0	195.4
White	233.5	292.5	179.9
Non-White	373.1	452.3	305.6

SOURCE: U.S. Department of Health, Education and Welfare, Public Health Service, "Statistical Notes 26–50," September 1971, p. 2, Note 41.

[1] Adjusted to the U.S. population, March 1969.

Care should be used in interpreting these statistics. They should not be regarded as measures of the incidence of mental illness, primarily because the relationship between admission rates to mental-health facilities and the true incidence in the population is not known (U.S. Department of Health, Education and Welfare, Public Health Service, 1971, p. 2).

These statistics are not controlled for social class, marital status, or geographical location, all of which are known to be related to the rate of admission to mental hospitals. Studies have consistently shown an inverse relationship between income status and mental illness. Individuals in lower socioeconomic categories are more likely to be referred to treatment facilities by the courts, more likely to be diagnosed as psychotic than as neurotic, and more likely to be treated in public facilities than in private hospitals. Mental illness thus does appear to be associated with certain minority situations but not necessarily any one group (see the discussion of spurious correlations in Chapter 2).

Overview

"Just as the bed of a stream shapes the direction and tempo of the flow of water," Gordon Allport once wrote, "so does the group determine the current of an individual's life" (Lewin, 1948, p. viii). The interdependence between the individual and the group is the basis of the social-psychological perspective. Within this perspective, some basic questions involve self-concept and group identification, personality dynamics, prejudice, and types of minority responses.

The process of identifying with groups and thinking of oneself in terms of a group begins early in childhood. Youngsters typically can make distinctions among group categories by age three or four years. Identification relationships help to provide the individual with an answer to the question "Who am I?"

The corollary question "How am I regarded?" is partially answered in terms of the perceived status of the groups with which the individual identifies. The impact of this process seems to vary with the individual's background and subgroup memberships.

A number of defensive and adaptive strategies, like displacement and projection, occur within the context of intergroup relations. Displacement involves directing hostility toward substitute targets that cannot be realistically considered the causes of frustration. The target of displacement may be individuals or entire groups. Projection is a psychological process in which individuals attribute to others characteristics that they do not recognize in themselves.

Prejudice may be thought of as having three dimensions—cognitive, affective, and conative (action). When social psychologists study the cognitive dimensions of prejudice, they typically use the rubric "stereotype." Stereotypes are beliefs or disbeliefs about particular peoples, especially those that emphasize characteristics presumed to be typical of the groups. Research indicates that stereotype formation may begin as early as age four years. Youngsters have ranked the sources of stereotypes: first, parents and, second, movies and television. At about age ten years the ranking of reported sources shifts to impersonal ones—television, movies, books, and the like.

Stereotypes as beliefs or disbeliefs can be studied in terms of direction, intensity, salience, or centrality.

Some scholars have claimed that there is a personality type of which prejudice is a central dimension. This personality type—called the "authoritarian personality" by Adorno and his colleagues—is prone to displacement and projection. Such a person is basically insecure, views life as capricious and threatening, admires strong leaders, and despises weak groups.

Some researchers have criticized Adorno's approach because it tends to equate authoritarian tendencies with right-wing political philosophy and ignores similar behavior on the left and in the middle. Rokeach has suggested that the underlying phenomenon being studied is *dogmatism*—a relatively closed mental set organized around a central cluster of beliefs.

Social distance, with its various conceptual refinements, is the rubric most often used by researchers who study the conative (action) dimension of prejudice. Research since the concept was introduced by Robert Park (1924) and made operational by E. S. Bogardus (1925) shows a high degree of stability in the rankings of various target populations in the United States.

Some studies of the relationship between cognitive skills and ethnic prejudice show that highly prejudiced individuals tend to have less well-developed cognitive skills than do relatively unprejudiced individuals. The relationship between intelligence and prejudice is, however, a complex one and, at this stage of research, poorly defined.

The adaptive responses mentioned in this chapter constitute a range of behavior frequently found among people with a minority perspective: neurotic obsessions, denial of membership, clowning, strengthening in-group ties, psychotic reactions, cunning and slyness, bluffing, bullying, feelings of superiority, and overt aggression. In fact, each of these responses is often found within the same group. It should be remembered that they are types of reactions, not stereotypes, fixed and unvarying characterizations about a group. As types, they emphasize certain characteristics and ignore others.

It should not be inferred that the minority life style is necessarily neurotic, psychotic, or devious. Unfortunately, some of the literature on minorities has emphasized the pathos and despair associated with the minority situation and has implied that realistic and psychologically mature adaptive strategies are not present. Nothing could be farther from the truth. Minority peoples—sometimes, bitterly, sometimes good-naturedly—cope with their respective realities as do members of the superordinate groups: by attacking, approaching, ceasing the response, or retreating. Social scientists are interested in the ways in which a minority perspective affects behavior, whether the actor is actually a member of a subordinate or a superordinate group.

For Further Reading

Many of the items among the references cited may be considered as recommended reading as well.

Allport, Gordon, *The Nature of Prejudice*. Addison-Wesley, 1954, also published as a Doubleday Anchor Book, 1958. See especially Chapter 25, "The Prejudiced Personality"; Chapter 27, "The Tolerant Personality"; and Chapter 9, "Traits Due to Victimization."

Banks, James A., and Jean D. Grambs (eds.). *Black Self-Concept: Implications for Education and Social Science*. New York: McGraw-Hill, 1972.

Billingsley, Andrew. *Black Families in White America.* Englewood Cliffs, N.J.: Prentice-Hall, 1968.

Coles, Robert. *Children of Crisis: The South Goes North.* New York: Little, Brown, 1971.

Ehrlich, Howard J. *The Social Psychology of Prejudice: A Systematic Theoretical Review and Propositional Inventory of the American Social Psychological Study of Prejudice.* New York: Wiley, 1973.

Heiss, Jerald, and Susan Owens. "Self-Evaluations of Blacks and Whites," *American Journal of Sociology,* 78 (September 1972), 360–370.

Porter, Judith D. R. *Black Child, White Child: The Development of Racial Attitudes.* Cambridge, Mass.: Harvard University Press, 1971.

Rohrer, John H., and Munro S. Edmonson (eds.) *The Eight Generation Grows Up: Cultures and Personalities of New Orleans Negroes.* New York: Harper & Row, 1964.

Rokeach, Milton. *The Open and Closed Mind.* New York: Basic Books, 1960.

Wagner, Nathaniel N., and Marsha J. Haug. *Chicanos: Social and Psychological Perspectives.* St. Louis: Mosby.

Yancy, William L., Leo Rigsby, and John D. McCarthy. "Social Position and Self-Evaluation: The Relative Importance of Race," *American Journal of Sociology,* 78 (September 1972), 338–359.

THE SHOCK OF BLACK RECOGNITION
JAMES FARMER AND RALPH BUNCHE

"Who am I?" is one of the basic questions that some individuals are forced to contemplate more often than others. It probably is answered several different ways during even the most uneventful life. The fact that this experience can be traumatic for some minority persons is documented in the following accounts.

The earliest memory of my life is of an incident which occurred when I was three-and-a-half years old in Holly Springs, Mississippi. My father was registrar and professor of religion and philosophy at Rust College, a Negro Methodist institution there.

One hot summer day, my mother and I walked from the college campus to the town square, a distance of maybe half a mile. I remember it as clearly as though it were a few weeks ago. I held her finger tightly as we kicked up the red dust on the unpaved streets leading to the downtown area. When we reached the square she did her shopping and we headed for home. Like any other three-and-a-half-year-old on a hot day, I got thirsty.

"Mother," I said, "I want a Coke." She was just as insistent that we could not get a Coke now. "Do as I tell you," she said, "wait 'til we get home; you can have a Coke with plenty of ice."

"There's a little boy going into a store!" I exclaimed as I spied another child who was a little bigger than I. "I bet he's going to get a Coke." So I pulled my mother by the finger until we stood in front of what I recall as a drugstore looking through the closed screen doors. Surely enough, the other lad had climbed upon a stool at the counter and was already sipping a soft drink.

"But I told you you can't get a Coke in there," she said. "Why can't I?" I asked again. Her answer was the same, "You just can't." I then inquired with complete puzzlement, "Well, why can he?" Her quiet answer thundered in my ears. "He's white."

We walked home in silence under the pitiless glare of the Mississippi sun. Once we were home she threw herself across the bed and wept. I walked out on the front porch and sat on the steps alone with my three-and-a-half-year-old thoughts.

—James Farmer

One of my earliest recollections of a racial experience came when I was about six or seven years old. My father was an itinerant barber and had gone from Detroit to work in a shop in Knoxville, Tennessee, with the thought that the milder climate there would be helpful to my mother's failing health. My father had gone ahead and my mother and I were traveling together in a coach. Somewhere along the way, obviously below the Mason-Dixon line, at a station stop the conductor informed my mother that we must move back to a coach for "colored" passengers, that is, the Jim Crow's coach. My mother indignantly refused to move and quite an argument ensued between her and the conductor, who finally gave up and left us alone. My mother later explained to me what had happened and why, and particularly why she could not move and maintain any dignity and self-respect. She told me that we were lucky not to have been arrested. I was shaken by the experience because I feared for my mother's safety and my own, since the conductor got red in the face with anger and shouted at us.

—Ralph Bunche

THE LUMBEE INDIAN IN THE CITY
JOHN GREGORY PECK

Along the swamps and bottomlands of North Carolina's Lumbee River resides a nonreservation people who have come to be known as Lumbee Indians. In earlier years they were called Croatan Indians or Cherokee Indians of Eastern North Carolina, and in recent years a subgroup has chosen the name Eastern Band of the Tuscaroras. During World War II, many of the younger people began to migrate to an enclave in Baltimore, Maryland. The migration pattern, however, has tended to be circular; many people eventually return to Robeson County or to one of the adjoining counties in North and South Carolina.

This selection describes the adjustment process of an immigrant from rural to urban life, as that process is perceived by a young Lumbee male. It is based upon participant observation[1] by the author in Baltimore, Maryland and in North Carolina during 1968 and 1969.

---

[1] The information that follows is a composite—the incidents and feelings were drawn from many hours of interviewing and "just talking" with the young men on East Baltimore Street. When the author began his field work in the summer of 1968 as a stranger in the community, most of the Indians in the bars and restaurants would not even look at him, would not even acknowledge his presence. The only way he knew that *they* knew he was a stranger who did not "fit" was that the proprietors of the establishments stopped paying off on the pinball machines when he was around—and the Indians did not ask any questions or kick up any rumpus. By the end of the summer, he was being approached by newcomers on the street and a few Indians who had moved off and were back for an evening's fun as if he were Indian too. If learning a culture is learning the rules and recipes, then he learned them well enough to fit in with at least *some* members.

If you are a young Lumbee, when you come to Baltimore you usually have little if any money, but you have other currency. You can always find someone you know, or someone who knows one of your friends. You have only to look in the Moonlight Cafe to see who's playing the pinball machine, or Volcano's back room, or wander into Sid's Ranchhouse to watch the pool players, and in a little while or an afternoon someone who is familiar will come along. They won't be surprised to see you. They'll kid you a bit and ask what kind of trouble you got into back home that sent you up to Baltimore, and they'll buy you a drink and help you get settled, help you feel at home. Somebody feeds you, somebody puts you up with a place to sleep. You drift around, beginning to find out what's happening, to get the feel of the city.

Nobody pushes you to find a job right away; to get out on your own. You've got a lot to learn: like where the jobs are and what they pay; like who's around and where the boundaries are. This may take a week or a month, or you may never learn it and become one of the old men sitting in the doorways on Broadway, drinking your port out of a paper sack. Or you may be just passing through, deciding to go on to other places or to go back home. There's no pressure, except the pressure of your own need for independence, your own pride.

You find that the best jobs for Indians are in the building trades—the nonunion piecework jobs of roofing, or hanging sheetrock, or laying floor by the foot, where you can make eighty dollars in a day if you hustle. And you find that there are good jobs in the steel plants out at Sparrows Point, where you can make almost $200 a week with Saturdays and overtime. Or you find out about the plant where most of the women work, where they make plastic jewelry and handbags and things and where they have a union and the money looks mighty good.

And you find out that most of the young men your age work two, three, maybe four days a week and spend the rest of the time around Sid's and the Volcano and the Moonlight or messing with the girls. And it seems like someone's always having trouble with the law, having papers drawn down on him, being arrested, or going to court. Somebody's always messed up for some reason, from a cutting, from an accident, or from a hangover the last weekend.

Later you'll find out that many Indians move on—to the suburbs of Towson, Patterson Park, and the Point or farther into the county. Even more drift on back home to settle down. Among those who stay most will move off the street by the time they reach their thirties and will quit their drinking, fighting, and chasing around and will settle down to raise their families. They may move only a block, but in the city a block can be a world away.

You find that being Indian is different in Baltimore than it is in Robeson County. You find that girls are easier to get: not just Indian girls but Polish girls and hillbilly girls and just girls that hang around the neighborhood. And you find out what a lesbian is and that a dyke can be just as tough and twice as mean as any Indian that you ever knew. You find out that every store sells wine and that every bar sells whiskey and few people ask how old you are: but just what color your money is. And most of all you fill yourself with the excitement and exhilaration of crowds, noise, lights, music, whiskey, and people, and a clock that has nowhere to go and nothing to do.

You find out that all the red-brown painted buildings belong to Hiken and that he's a good landlord, with two maintenance men living in the neighborhood; he comes and fixes up anything that's wrong and cleans and sometimes paints his apartments between tenants. And maybe he hollers a bit if a window or a door gets broken or kicked in, but he fixes it, and he's not quick to have you thrown out if you miss your rent payment. Hiken grew up in the neighborhood when it was still fashionable and Jewish, and he still runs the store that rents dress suits on the corner, which his father started when he was a kid, even though he now lives out in the suburbs. You find out that some of the other landlords aren't so nice and that some of the three-story buildings they rent have as many as five apartments in them, that rent from twelve dollars to thirty dollars a week. And you learn that in many buildings on Baltimore Street no one locks the door, because someone will just break in anyway; so you don't accumulate much of value that you leave around.

You find out that the best place to find people in the mornings is at the Moonlight Cafe and if you get there early, you might even get a chance to work on one of the building jobs, hanging sheetrock or roofing, if someone doesn't show up for the crew that morning. By noon there will be lots of activity up and down the street, with the kids running around and people going to and from the stores and homes and bars, and you will become aware of the large number of "day people" who inhabit the neighborhood: the "day people" in their suits and white shirt sleeves and social-worker dresses; the process-servers, lawyers, and salesmen, the Greek shopkeepers and deliverymen in their uniforms and the hippy poverty workers. The strangers who ask question are to be avoided, to be put off, because not much good can come from them.

Evenings—evenings are the best, when the cars parked along the streets belong to the people who live there. Evenings are when you make the perpetual three-block tour from the Moonlight to Sid's to the Volcano to the Moonlight, when you sit on your white marble steps or stand in quiet conversation groups along the street, watching the parade of people. Evening is when people catch up on the gossip; and gossip is Indian-centered, Indian-made.

Life is good in the city for the Indian. There are plenty of jobs, when you want to work, and you're always free to quit and find a new one if the boss is slow to pay or if he doesn't like it when you go back home for a few days. The corner store sells fresh North Carolina pork pudding, and the Church of God down the street has a barbecue every Friday, with all the back-home foods. Someone is always going back home or coming up to Baltimore, and you never lose touch with things. Life is good in the city, especially if you're young and know you don't have to be there forever.

Some things are different in the city, though: the law, for instance. Down home, if there were papers out on you, you knew ahead of time. And if there was real trouble, they would let your daddy know about it, or your grandfather, and maybe he could take care of it. Down home they respected a man who worked hard in his fields, paid his debts, and kept a good family name. In the city it's different. If there's trouble—a shooting, cutting, or just a fight, even, the police show up (they never come until its over) and grab anybody, anybody who's standing around. And they push you around and curse you. They don't care who you are.

Or the judges. In the city they'll issue papers to anyone who comes in and makes a charge. Now, down home these people *know* when it's just meanness. They don't need a court to tell just foolishness from real hurt. And the judge down home never calls an Indian an "animal"—he was Indian himself. No, the law is different in the city, and it's a *bad* difference.

The prisons are different too. Down home there is an Indian prison— Indian guards, Indian inmates, even Captain Brooks, who runs it. It's in the country, where there are trees; when the wind blows, it blows the corn in the fields. There are no walls: only a fence, and anyone who drives by can blow his horn, at you, and you never lose track of what's going on with your people. And if you're in for a long time, you can get out on work-release to see that your family's taken care of; and you can keep busy. But in the city it's brick walls and never any sunlight, never any fresh air, never anything green, and never anything to do. Some people say that they would rather do a year down home than four weeks in a Maryland jail.

There are some good things about the city, though. You can get anything you want in the city, if you look. You can get a new car with nothing down, a watch from the guy with the funny hat that sells jewelry from bar to bar, or a used radio from the kids that peddle hot merchandise. You can get a girl—any kind or shape of girl—for an hour, an afternoon, or a month, and she'll treat you right, work for you, take care of you. You can get a buddy to drink, play cards, or just drive around with; all you have to do is walk down to the corner. And you can get a drink, in the morning or the middle of the night. You can get a drink on Sunday. No one, says no.

And people in the city treat you right. If you're an Indian, then you're an Indian. Lumbee, Cherokee, Seminole, Creek—it doesn't matter. You can go any-where, and do anything, and be with anybody; and nobody cares, and you find that the girls like your brown eyes and brown skin, hard muscles, and easy-come, easy-go attitude. Somehow it's easier to feel like a man in the city.

Some things aren't important in the city. For one thing, the kind of house you live in: it doesn't matter that some people may consider your neighborhood a slum. The important thing is that you live close to where things are happening, close to your friends, close to the action on East Baltimore Street. For now it's a place to flop, a roof over your head, and when you finally settle down and start to *live* somewhere (not *stay* for awhile, as you do in Baltimore) it will be a home in the country, like down home in Robeson County. And it will be a brick home. Somehow, even though you're in Baltimore, the city isn't where your territorial investment belongs.

Another thing about the city—people behave differently. You don't have to live by the same rules you lived by back home. If you shack up with a girl for a while, it's no big thing, and nobody gets after you, like your mother or her people. If she has a kid—yours or someone else's from before—why that's no problem either. Blue eyes, brown eyes: kids are kids and you love 'em and holler at 'em, and beat 'em when they need it, and do for them as best you can. They come as part of the deal, and you accept it. Legal things, like marriage, divorce, birth certificates, residence and all that, are run by different rules in the city—the law does not see a person—a Lowery, a Dial, or an Oxendine—and you avoid it as much as you can.

The city is a thing to be used, but not a thing that uses you. It's a place where you have the final control, the real control, of staying or not staying. You come to it to take the things it has—the better jobs and money, the excitement, and freedom, and freedom from responsibility—but you are *in* it not *of* it. You really "belong" down in Robeson County, and that's where you expect to return, so your investment in the turf in Baltimore is minimal. The idea of "community" or "community participation in development" is irrelevant to you. You may have been in the city for two weeks, two months, or half a dozen years; your kids may be in school, and you may be a registered voter, but you expect to go somewhere else, and this isn't your "community."

Part of the city sticks to you, too: It's more than the smog, the grime, the pushing around, and the easy-come—easy-go money. You get used to things; like four-channel television. Or your kids speaking with a different kind of accent. You get used to the variety of material and technological products available in the city, and you learn how to use them and how to acquire them. From your East Baltimore Street base you learn how to manipulate a personnel man at the steel mill, an urban transportation system, a dozen strangers every day, and the competitive buying, selling, and getting ahead that is the urban environment. What's sticking to you are the bits and pieces of what sociologists call "social mobility," and you feel you have a competitive edge because the people you're competing against, the other migrants to the city, are the Mountain people and the Blacks, and you're an Indian. And, living in the ghetto, you know *you're* not going to *stay* there.

For many of the Lumbee, then, the ghetto is a training, rather than a terminal, situation; it is a transitional acculturation point through which a series of people pass. Some of the Indians go on to enter the blue-collar and middle-class communities of the city. Many return home to North Carolina or go on to other areas. Some become locked into the patterns of the ghetto, but they will not form a "community."

For the Lumbee and many people like them, the urban enclave may well serve as a necessary acculturating mechanism, a socializing and learning experience through which they pass. To destroy it, to "eradicate the slums," may destroy one of our most valuable training devices for the urbanization of rural people. Equally dangerous may be the policy of attempting to "stabilize" these enclaves in order to create "communities," for this policy tends only to fix the people in place.

The East Baltimore Street enclave, then, can be viewed as providing a buffer area for the newly arrived Indian. Only minimal changes are required in his attitudes and values for him to operate within the Indian enclave. The enclave provides a sanctuary within which he can retreat and a framework by which he can rationalize or discount any failures that he may experience in coping with the larger urban environment. There is a group of Indians who are available to teach him the skills of the city at his own speed and in his own cultural framework. He always has the option of returning home to North Carolina without shame or loss of face.

The Baltimore Indian ghetto is more than a collection of substandard houses, neighborhood bars, and crowded schools. It is an "urban station," a place where the migrant can stop on his way to somewhere else. While he is there, he sees the sights, meets a few of the inhabitants, gets a feel for the local scene. Its essential function is educational for the Indian migrant, and the ghetto provides both the teachers and the curriculum in his urban socialization process.

MANCHILD IN THE PROMISED LAND
CLAUDE BROWN

The movement of Blacks out of the rural South into northern and western cities is one of the most important events of American history. Seldom before has a migration involved so many, so quickly, so thoroughly. In the selection that follows Claude Brown eloquently describes how demography and human biography have merged, and tells what has been the effect.

I want to talk about the first Northern urban generation of Negroes. I want to talk about the experiences of a misplaced generation, of a misplaced people in an extremely complex, confused society. This is a story of their searching, their dreams, their sorrows, their small and futile rebellions, and their endless battle to establish their own place in America's greatest metropolis—and in America itself.

The characters are sons and daughters of former Southern sharecroppers. These were the poorest people of the South, who poured into New York City during the decade following the Great Depression. These migrants were told that unlimited opportunities for prosperity existed in New York and that there was no "color problem" there. They were told that Negroes lived in houses with bathrooms, electricity, running water, and indoor toilets. To them, this was the "promised land" that Mammy had been singing about in the cotton fields for many years.

Going to New York was good-bye to the cotton fields, good-bye to "Massa Charlie," good-bye to the chain gang, and, most of all, good-bye to those sunup-to-sundown working hours. One no longer had to wait to get to heaven to lay his burden down; burdens could be laid down in New York.

So, they came, from all parts of the South, like all the black chillun o' God following the sound of Gabriel's horn on that long-overdue Judgment Day. The Georgians came as soon as they were able to pick train fare off the peach trees. They came from South Carolina where the cotton stalks were bare. The North Carolinians came with tobacco tar beneath their fingernails.

They felt as the Pilgrims must have felt when they were coming to America. But these descendants of Ham must have been twice as happy as the Pilgrims, because they had been catching twice the hell. Even while planning the trip, they sang spirituals as "Jesus Take My Hand" and "I'm On My Way" and chanted, "Hallelujah, I'm on my way to the promised land!"

It seems that Cousin Willie, in his lying haste, had neglected to tell the folks down home about one of the most important aspects of the promised land: it was a slum ghetto. There was a tremendous difference in the way life was lived up North. There were too many people full of hate and bitterness crowded into a dirty, stinky, uncared-for closet-size section of a great city.

Before the soreness of the cotton fields had left Mama's back, her knees were getting sore from scrubbing "Goldberg's" floor. Nevertheless, she was better off; she had gone from the fire into the frying pan.

The children of these disillusioned colored pioneers inherited the total lot of their parents—the disappointments, the anger. To add to their misery, they had little hope of deliverance. For where does one run to when he's already in the promised land?

PRISONERS OF CASTE SEGREGATION

W. E. BURGHARDT DUBOIS

A minority individual may try to cope with his or her situation by trying first one response, then another. Some individuals who begin by fighting back will later turn to cunning and slyness and will finally identify with the dominant group. Others begin as conformists who identify with the dominant group but, after being rejected, turn to their own people. Such sequences of response can be discerned in the writings of many minority members. W. E. B. DuBois's tale of the prisoners of caste segregation is a classic statement.

It is difficult to let others see the full psychological meaning of caste segregation. It is as though one, looking out from a dark cave in a side of an impending mountain, sees the world passing and speaks to it; speaks courteously and persuasively showing them how these entombed souls are hindered in their natural movement, expression, and development; and how their loosening from prison would be a matter not simply of courtesy, sympathy and help to them, but aid to all the world. One talks on evenly and logically in this way but notices that the passing do not hear; that some thick sheet of invisible but horribly tangible plate glass is between them and the world. They get excited; they talk louder; they gesticulate. Some of the passing world stops in curiosity; these gesticulations seem so pointless; they laugh and pass on. They still either do not hear at all, or hear but dimly, and even what they hear, they do not understand. Then the people within may become hysterical. They may scream and hurl themselves against the barriers, hardly realizing in their bewilderment that they are screaming in a vacuum unheard and that their antics may actually seem funny to those outside looking in. They may even, here and there, break through in blood and disfigurement and find themselves faced by a horrified implacable, and quite overwhelming mob of people frightened for their own very existence.

It is hard under such circumstances to be philosophical and calm, and to think through a method of approach and accommodation between castes. The entombed find themselves not simply trying to make the outer world understand their essential and common humanity but even more, as they become inured to their experience, they have to keep reminding themselves that the great and oppressing world is also real and human and in its essence honest. All my life I have had continually to haul my soul back and say, "All White folk are not scoundrels nor murderers. They are, even as I am, painfully human."

9

Social Control
and
Intergroup
Relations

The strongest man is never strong
enough to be master all the time, unless
he transforms force into right and
obedience into duty.

—Jean Jacques Rousseau,
The Social Contract (1972: p. 52)

Social control, in its broadest sense, involves the processes, planned and unplanned, by which individuals are taught, persuaded, or compelled to conform to the norms of a society (Roucek, 1956, p. 3). When the concept is applied to intergroup arrangements, it describes the ways in which minorities are brought to conform to the norms of the core society. The concept also refers to the ways in which a dominant group uses its power. Members of a minority, as well as those of the majority, are taught, persuaded, or compelled to conform to the respective norms associated with superordinant—subordinant relationships. Power, after all, cannot be overused or underused, or the dominance of a group and the established system may be threatened.

    In this chapter we pay particular attention to the maneuvers and devices that are used to keep minorities in check. They go under various names: "apartheid," "separate development," "law and order," "Africa for Africans," "Jamaica for Jamaicans," and so on. At times their advocates have had the temerity to call them policies of "supremacy," but called by any name, they are essentially strategies of social control.

Force and the Threat of Force

All societies are maintained at some level by force or by the threat of force. This fact of social life is as true of industrialized nations as of primitive tribes. The use of force in a society may be legal, that is, carried out under the aegis of the government, or force may be exercised in extralegal ways like vigilantism.

Extragovernmental Use of Force

Many societies have a tradition of using private direct action to maintain order. In the United States such a tradition has merged with a long history of nativism and racism. The coupling of these traditions has often resulted in vigilante violence expressed in racist forms (Skolnick, 1969, pp. 211–217).

Certain characteristics of the American frontier provided a rationale for vigilantism. Much of the frontier was undeveloped. In rural areas lawmen were few and often untrained, and courts were far away. The emerging towns were not much better. In order to survive, a person had to learn to fend for himself. In this context, private groups were formed to enforce laws, apprehend alleged violators, try them, and punish them. The supposed aim of private law-enforcement ventures was generally the maintenance of order. Some organizations, like the San Francisco Vigilance Committee of 1851 and the Great Committee of 1856, were composed for the most part of respectable citizens who sought neither legislative change nor reform but only the punishment of criminals and undesirables. In practice, foreigners and minority groups, especially Mexicans and Orientals, bore the brunt of vigilante justice. A similar pattern characterized the development of the Ku Klux Klan in the South. The Klan, which emerged in the aftermath of the Civil War, used extralegal measures to punish individuals, usually Blacks, who violated local mores.

Extralegal behavior takes on a quasi-legal status when it is continued over a long period of time or occurs during a time of public excitement. The memoirs of an Atlanta police chief, Herbert Jenkins, tell how this societal character evolved during the 1930s. Klan membership was on the rise at the time, and many policemen joined the Ku Klux Klan ranks. Membership meant acceptance in the "ingroup." So important was its impact, Jenkins recalls, that for many, Klan allegience was more important than the policeman's oath to society (Jenkins, 1970, p. 4).

The *pogrom* is another extralegal strategy that has been employed against minorities particularly in eastern Europe and Russia. The word itself is Russian and means "riot." A pogrom is an attack by some segment of the population upon a minority while the authorities look the other way. By means of pogroms the tsarist regime sought to divert upon the Jews the frustrations of the masses. Severe pogroms occurred in 1881–1882 and between 1903 and 1921.

Governmental Use of Force

The concept of the state implies sovereignty over a geographical area within which the government has the exclusive right to use force. An individual or group must conform to the prescribed order or risk punishment.

Sanctions include fines, imprisonment, banishment, segregation, torture, and execution. All have been applied to various minorities at one time or another. The Soviet Union during the Stalin era banished six ethnic groups—the Ingush, the Chechens, the Crimea Tartars, the Kalmyks, the Karachai, and the Balkans— to remote regions because of their alleged collaboration with the Nazis. The history of the United States includes the fining and imprisoning of civil-rights leaders (notably during the 1950s and 1960s), the Cherokee Trail of Tears, and the relocation of Japanese-Americans during World War II. In the Union of South Africa, a part of the eastern seaboard called the [Transkei] has been converted into special territory for Bantus. These examples are but a few of the numerous instances in which minority peoples have been dealt with by force within the context of official authority.

Whenever the state and its religious institutions become aligned, the use of force becomes doubly legitimated: In medieval Europe the interests of church and state coincided in the Holy Crusades against infidels. Jews were required to wear a badge of identity and were excluded from various professions and occupations.

With or without religious sanctions, dominant groups frequently engage in direct and unabashed measures to keep minorities in check. Indians in many parts of Latin America and people of color in the Union of South Africa are thus treated as peoples apart. The question of their inherent equality is not an issue that vexes the national conscience, at least not until recently. In such settings few minority members receive formal education beyond rudimentary levels. A group may be assigned to a geographical area where it can be readily observed. The Jewish ghetto in Europe, as we have seen, gradually came to have this kind of social-control function, as did the Indian reservations in the United States and the Transkei in the Union of South Africa.

When moderate measures fail, retribution is sometimes swift and final. There is no way to know just how many minority communities have been wiped out throughout history. Indian tribes in the Caribbean, African slaves in parts of South America, and aboriginal peoples of Tasmania are three known instances. In one of the bloody, little-known wars of this century, thousands of Nilotic Blacks have been slain in the Sudan by dominant Arab groups.

The word "genocide" is applied to the intentional extermination of an entire people. Its Greek roots are *genos* ("kind or people") and *cide* ("killing"). The term was first widely used to describe the attempted extermination of the Jewish people by Nazi Germany.

Two centuries ago, when American colonists were fighting Indians, an ethic based upon warfare prevailed. If a battle thoroughly wiped out Indians, it was an occasion for celebration, not soul searching. Witness, for instance, the following announcement of bounties for Indian scalps:

> Given at the Council Chamber in Boston this third day of November 1755 in the twenty-ninth year of the Reign of our Sovereign Lord George the Second by the Grace of God of Great Britain, France, and Ireland, King Defender of the Faith.
>
> By His Honour's command
> J. Willard, Secry.
> God Save the King
>
> Whereas the tribe of Penobscot Indians have repeatedly in a perfidious manner acted contrary to their solemn submission unto his Majesty long since made and frequently renewed.
>
> I have, therefore, at the desire of the House of Representatives . . . thought fit to issue this Proclamation and to declare the Penobscot Tribe of Indians to be enemies, rebels and traitors to his Majesty. . . . And I do hereby require his Majesty's subjects of the Province to embrace all opportunities of pursuing, captivating, killing and destroying all and every of the aforesaid Indians.
>
> And whereas the General Court of this Province have voted that a bounty . . . be granted and allowed to be paid out of the Province Treasury . . . the premiums of bounty following viz:
>
> For the capture of every male Penobscot Indian above the age of twelve and brought to Boston, Fifty Pounds.
>
> For every scalp of a male Indian above the age aforesaid, brought in as evidence of their being killed as aforesaid, Forty Pounds. . . .
>
> For every scalp of such female Indian or male Indian under the age of twelve years that shall be killed and brought in as evidence of their being killed as aforesaid, Twenty Pounds. (Paine, 1897, p. 465)

The reader will note the grim economics of the offer—scalps of women and children would be purchased at half price. Perhaps women and children were less threatening, more plentiful or easier to kill!

The resort to force in order to control a minority is direct and often effective, but it has its limitations. Individuals and groups that comply only under threat of violence are potentially dangerous and require ever-watchful keepers. When those who have been controlled reach the point at which they are willing to say "Go ahead kill us" and mean it, that is the day the power relationship ceases to exist (Dabaghian, 1970, p. 262).

Economic and political considerations figure in the decision. The dominant group may thus calculate: How much is the group worth alive? How many can be punished as an example to others? What are the alternatives that will allow the group to be spared and still controlled? (Dabaghian, 1970, p. 262).

In modern nations, law-enforcement officers are usually authorized to use force only within the limits set by laws, codes, and regulatory procedures. The following rule from the *Texas Law Enforcement Officers' Handbook* is one such regulation:

> A peace officer in making an arrest has the right only to use that amount of force reasonably necessary to effect the arrest and to detain the prisoner. . . . All peace officers should remember that generally the sole purpose of an arrest is to bring the alleged culprit before a court of law and not for the purpose of giving any peace officer the opportunity of wreaking the public's or his personal vengeance upon the prisoner. (U.S. Commission on Civil Rights, 1970, p. 2)

Minority groups complain that this regulation describes the ideal, not the actual. Spanish-speaking people in the Southwest, for instance, complain of excessive use of force against them, particularly in the small towns. This discrepant behavior arises partly from their lack of power, their inability to punish government officials who violate the code, and their underrepresentation in law-enforcement ranks. In 1970, for instance, 28 of the 1,740 uniformed and plain-clothes officers of the Texas Department of Public Safety were Mexican-Americans—1.6 percent of the force (U.S. Commission on Civil Rights, 1970, p. 82). At the time of the survey, people of Spanish descent constituted about 14 percent of the population. Nationwide, according to a 1970 survey (Race Relations Information Center, 1970), about 98 of every 100 uniformed state troopers were Caucasian. Ten states had no Blacks, and an additional ten had only one each. California, at the time of the survey, had the highest number (eighty) of non-White troopers.

FEW NEGROES HOLDING STATE TROOPER JOBS

NASHVILLE, Tenn. (AP) A preliminary survey of the racial composition of the nation's 40,000 state policemen indicates there are no more than 250 Negroes employed in that branch of law enforcement.

The survey was made by the Race Relations Information Center in Nashville.

The center reports that 98 or 99 of every 100 uniformed troopers in the nation are Caucasian, with the remainder Negro or of some other minority group.

Ten states—Alabama, Idaho, Iowa, Massachusetts, Mississippi, Nebraska, North Dakota, South Dakota, Vermont and Wyoming—have no Negro state policemen, the center said.[1]

California, with 80 Negroes and 174 from other minorities, has the highest number of nonwhite policemen, according to the center.

[1] Editor's note: Several of these states—some under court order—had by 1975 employed Black state troopers.

The center says New York, with a state police force of 3,275 men, has eight Negro troopers, and Oklahoma, with a force of 485 men, has an estimated 100 Indian troopers.

Ten states, according to the center, have one Negro officer each: Delaware, Florida, Georgia, Minnesota, Oregon, Rhode Island, Utah, Virginia, West Virginia and Wisconsin.

Tennessee, with 628 highway patrolmen, has seven Negroes on the force, the center said. (Race Relations Information Center, December 10, 1970)

The Law and Social Control

If distinctions based on race or ethnicity are considered important in a particular society, then it is likely that its laws will have something to say on the subject. The reason is that all the *institutions* (marriage, inheritance, suffrage, and so on) and all the *relationships* (husband-wife, buyer-seller, parent-child, employer-employee, and so on) that a society considers important will be defined and analyzed in a fully developed legal code. In the United States "racial" distinctions have been important; accordingly, a mass of legal documents have defined what "race" is, who belongs to a race, and what activities are possible for its members.

Laws are generally a conservative element in society, in that they help to make interaction predictable. They have the effect of crystallizing behavior patterns that have already become customary by defining the limits of deviation and setting the penalties for infractions. Laws protect various strata from one another, typically favoring "haves" instead of "have nots."

Legal codes comprise many underlying principles, some of which may be contradictory. For instance, the same legal code that acknowledges the rights of the poor—widows, orphans, and the destitute—may also permit a system of money lending that has the effect of keeping them poor. One legal tradition holds that an individual proprietor has the freedom to run a business just about as he or she pleases, as long as nothing illegal occurs. Another tradition holds that any citizen has the right to purchase services and goods from a publicly licensed business. In former years, legislatures and courts favored the first tradition and permitted motels and restaurants to exclude Blacks and other minorities. The law thus upheld one set of values over another.

The work of legislative bodies and the courts is seldom uniformly enforced. Enforcement agencies may resist administering the law or carrying out court decrees, especially if there is widespread agitation about some social value.

In a historic conflict a president of the United States refused to administer a U.S. Supreme Court decision. The legislature of Georgia, it seems, had passed resolutions in 1827 declaring that the Cherokee lands belonged to Georgia absolutely and that the Indians were only "tenants at her will." Until that time the Cherokees, by treaty with the Federal government, had ruled their own territory as a "nation" under the protection of the United States. In 1832 the Supreme Court ruled that Georgia's Cherokee Indian statutes were "repugnant to the constitution, laws and treaties of the United States." The State of Georgia, however, scoffed at Chief Justice John Marshall's opinion and flouted the mandate of the Supreme Court. President Andrew Jackson defied the Chief Justice. "John Marshall has made his decision," President Jackson reportedly remarked, "now let him enforce it!" The Supreme Court found itself powerless. "The judgment in Worchester vs. Georgia came to nothing; the mandate was never obeyed, never heeded" (Beveridge, 1919, pp. 540–551).

The application of sanctions is often intended to have exemplary impact; that is, the punishment of one offender is intended to deter other would-be offenders. This intention underlies both legal and extralegal applications of sanctions. For instance, night-riding Klansmen have been known to boast that one flogging or house burning would keep "all the colored people in the county in their place." When the application of force occurs within a legal context, its exemplary, or deterrent, function is sometimes explicitly stated in the law itself. Witness, for example, the 1712 Slave Code of South Carolina:

> And it is further enacted by the authority aforesaid, that if any negroes or other slaves shall make mutiny or insurrection, or rise in rebellion against the authority and government of this Province . . . the offenders shall be tried by two justices of the peace and three freeholders . . . who are hereby empowered and required to try the said slaves so offending, and inflict death, or any other punishment, upon the offenders, and forthwith by their warrant cause execution to be done, by the common or any other executioner, in such manner as they shall think fitting. . . . Provided, nevertheless, that then and as often as any of the aforementioned crimes shall be committed by more than one negro, that shall deserve death, that they and in all such cases, if the Governor and council of this Province shall think fitting, and accordingly shall order, *that only one or more of the said criminals should suffer death as exemplary*, and the rest to be returned to the owners, that they, the owners of the negroes so offending, shall bear proportionately the loss of the said negro or negroes so put to death. . . . (Cooper and McCord, 1836, vol. 7, pp. 352–357; italics added)

Law is an effective means of controlling behavior because it provides a way of uniting those who obey against those who disobey. The law accomplishes this end, in part, by telling members of the dominant group not only how they *may* treat members of an out-group but also how they *must* treat them. The historian Winthrop B. Jordan has correctly observed that the colonial slave codes, which seem to have been intended only to discipline slaves, were aimed, paradoxically, at disciplining Whites. These laws told the Whites what they had to do. "The maintenance of slavery depended on mass consent among the white population, on widespread agreement that every master should, indeed had to maintain effective control" (Jordan, 1969, p. 109).

Political Maneuvers

In the United States democratic principles are officially acknowledged, yet, as Gunnar Myrdal and others have shown, the nation includes high-status groups that seek to limit the political power of minorities. This situation has resulted in political strategies that, on one hand, maintain the appearance that democratic principles are being followed yet, on the other, perpetuate the power and privilege of dominant groups. These strategies have taken several forms (See U.S. Commission on Civil Rights, 1968).

1. *Refusal to register minority group members as voters* has been accomplished by outright threat of violence, by laws that exclude certain groups, by poll taxes and literacy tests. Voter-registration records compiled before passage of the Voting Rights Act of 1965 show that relatively few non-Whites were registered to vote. In Georgia, for instance, 27.4 of the non-Whites of voting age were registered, whereas 62.6 percent of the Whites were registered. Registration for the same state was 52.6 percent of non-Whites and 80.3 percent of Whites after passage of the act (U.S. Commission on Civil Rights, 1968, p. 13).

2. *Diluting the minority vote* is known in its classic form as "gerrymandering." Gerrymandering is dividing a political area in such a way as to give an unfair advantage to one group or party. Whenever a minority is concentrated in a particular district, its vote can be effectively diluted by consolidating that district with one in which the dominant group outnumbers the minority. Until curbed by the U.S. Supreme Court in 1971, many cities were diluting the minority vote of the downtown areas by expanding their boundaries to take in suburbs.

3. *Preventing members of the minority group from becoming candidates for office* involves abolishing elected offices, extending the terms of incumbent majority-group officials, substituting appointment for election, increasing filing fees, and otherwise raising requirements for getting on the ballot.

4. *Discrimination against the minority group's full participation in selection of candidates* includes exclusion from precinct meetings where party officials are chosen, omission of the names of registered persons from the voter list, failure to provide sufficient voting facilities in areas with heavy minority-group registrations, harrassment of voters by election officials, refusal to assist inexperienced or poorly educated voters, exclusion and interference with minority group "poll watchers" (in many states each candidate, or his representative, has the right to observe the voting in each polling place), vote

fraud (discrepancies between the count of the poll watchers and the official tallies by election officials), and threat of reprisals.

5. *Denial of legal privilege* frequently is masked by legal fictions to which a society may resort in order to reconcile outright denial of legal privileges with democratic principles. For example, the Chinese in California could not testify against Whites in court until the Revised Code was passed in 1873. The legal basis for this discrimination was the legal fiction that Chinese were American Indians. As Indians at the time were denied certain political privileges, the Chinese could be lumped in the same category and similarly excluded (Coolidge, 1907, p. 77).

Control of Numbers

Some groups maintain their dominant positions by controlling the size of the minority groups, restricting the rate of immigration so that the prevailing population ratio is not disturbed.

In the United States, only qualitative limitations restricted the flow of immigrants until 1920.[2] The 1921 Act placed the first numerical ceiling upon immigration. Each country's quota was to be 3 percent of the number of people born in that country who were residing in the United States, as reported in the 1910 Census of Population. In 1924 a new formula was enacted for computing quotas. It allowed immigration of 2 percent of the number of people born in each country who were residing in the United States, as reported in the 1890 Census of Population. This act also established minimum quotas of 100 for each group. In 1952 the Immigration and Nationality Act set the national origins formula at one sixth of 1 percent of the population in the 1920 Census. The act of 1965 continued the quotas established under the 1952 act but established a new preference system. According to the 1965 formula, at the end of each year the numbers allocated to a given country that were not used were transferred to an immigration pool and were made available to preferred immigrants who could not obtain visas because the quotas for their country were exhausted.

In 1968 a limit of 17,000 was set for immigrants from countries outside of the Western Hemisphere, with a 20,000 maximum for natives of any one country. Individual selection is made on the basis of preferences that favor family reunification and immigration of people with skills and talents that are needed in the nation (U.S. Bureau of the Census, 1970). The United States occasionally has enacted special quotas for refugees from certain countries and for victims of nat-

[2] The Japanese Exclusion Act and the famous Gentlemen's Agreement with Japan represent major exceptions to this general immigration policy. The information on immigration policy presented on this page is abstracted (U.S. Bureau of the Census, 1970, p. 89).

ural calamities. The practice of recruiting people with highly prized skills from other nations, allowable under present immigration policies, has been called the "brain drain." The "brain drain," understandably, has caused resentment toward the United States, particularly in developing nations where the loss of even a few scientists, doctors, or scholars is severely felt.

The assumptions that underlie selective immigration policies are, in some instances, rather obvious. First, before 1920 the United States was an expanding industrial nation that needed a continuous supply of cheap labor. The flow of immigrants was encouraged in order to meet that need, and all but the most undesirable were welcomed. Second, the fact that national quotas have been based upon an ethnic ratio as it existed at some earlier time indicates a preference for keeping things essentially as they are. Third, the policies limiting immigration from outside the hemisphere indicates a preference for Occidental, rather than Oriental, people. (These policies also imply a view of the assimilability of Oriental people.)

Restricting the flow of immigrants has had unanticipated consequences. For example, the young Chinese men who were brought to the United States as laborers usually were not permitted to bring along their wives. These men, once they had reached the United States, often found themselves isolated because of their poor English, their lack of specialized skills, and local discrimination.

> The long womanless condition of the Chinese in America is one of the most profound and least discussed factors affecting Chinese communities and acculturation. With the vast Pacific Ocean separating him from domestic joys and companionship, the Chinese sojourner relied on the tong-controlled brothels for sex, attended the gambling and opium dens for recreation and respite from the day's toil, and paid homage and allegiance to his clansmen, Landsmanner, and fraternal brothers to secure mutual aid, protection and a job. Unable to procreate and rear children in America, the homeless sojourner watched helplessly as his estranged Chinaborn sons followed in his footsteps and fell into the established Chinatown way of life. (Lyman, 1968, p. 330)

Switzerland, widely praised for achieving a harmonious pluralistic balance among several ethnic groups, has tightly controlled its immigration policies. The effect has been the creation of what is, in effect, a high-priced neighborhood in Europe. Poverty has been controlled in the country partly because individuals without livelihoods, regardless of descent, are not allowed to become permanent citizens.

Great Britain has been engaged in recent years in an ever more intense debate over its immigration policies. Until 1962 immigration from Commonwealth nations was not restricted, but when Blacks from the Caribbean, as well as Pakistanis and Indians from East Africa began to arrive in unprecedented numbers, tensions mounted. Many of the ugly features of racism have appeared, poorer sections of the cities have felt the major impact of immigration, and politicians

The only Smethwick candidate who has always called for the strictest control of immigration is

PETER GRIFFITHS

remember this when you cast your VOTE

FIGURE 9   British Election Campaign Advertisement, Conservative candidate, 1964 General Election.

predictably have taken up the racial theme in order to be elected. Parliament, in 1971, began consideration of a bill to restrict the immigration of non-Whites. Australia has had an immigration policy that militates against Orientals and other non-Whites ever since the Chinese Immigration Restriction Act of 1878. About 10,000 non-Whites (1973 estimate) are admitted each year, but they must have desired job skills or have relatives or close friends who are Australian citizens. A key criterion is the likelihood that the immigrant will "blend into Australian society." The nation's policy of subsidizing the transportation of Whites from Europe and the United States has attracted a number of immigrants, many of whom have come from southern European countries. This emphasis has created new problems because some of the immigrant groups, particularly Italians, have become objects of ethnic discrimination in their adopted lands.

A minority's size also can be regulated by lowering its birth rate. Several methods have been used historically—segregation of males from females, castration, abortion, and infanticide. A biblical reference alludes to infanticide in the well-known story of the birth of Moses:

> And the king of Egypt spake to the Hebrew midwives . . . When ye do the office of midwife to the Hebrew women, and see them upon the stools; if it be a son, then ye shall kill him: but if it be a daughter, then she shall live. And Pharaoh charged all his people, saying, "Every son that is born ye shall cast into the river, and every daughter ye shall save alive" (*Exodus* 1:15, 16, 22).

Closer to home, the Federal government in recent years has funded family-planning programs that distribute contraceptives and sterilize certain clients, presumably on a voluntary basis. These programs appear to be motivated by both humanitarian and economic considerations (prevention of sickle-cell anemia and reduction of welfare costs). A number of individuals have been quite critical of these activities, however, and have branded them—especially sterilization—"genocide."

Keeping Members of the Dominant Group in Line

A dominant group must see to it that its own members observe the boundaries. Members who ignore them may be dealt with severely. During the civil-rights conflicts of the 1960s Whites who were classified as "nigger lovers" were subjected to ridicule and violence, and several were killed. "If the niggers in Mississippi gets out of line," an elderly White native of McComb said during the height of the civil-rights tension, "we'll kill 'em. But let me tell you who we'll kill first. We'll kill the White man who leads 'em." Later events in Philadelphia, Mississippi, and elsewhere bore out the seriousness of his threat.

The motivation behind this behavior is determination that those individuals will not threaten the existing system of relationships. They violate, perhaps even defy, the rules that others are trying to enforce. In certain respects, those who are regarded as traitors to their people are dealt with in much the same way as "rate busters" in factories are treated. In a White-dominated society, a White who refuses to dominate is a curiosity at best and at worst a threat.

It was mentioned earlier that laws can have the effect of binding together members of a ruling group by requiring them to impose sanctions on deviants. This statement squares with a general principle of social control: that divisiveness within ruling groups must be kept in bounds.

The Use of Intermediaries

Georg Simmel has observed that relations among groups, once they cease to be based upon absolute coercion, become social *inter*actions. He meant that each party begins to take into account the needs, wishes, and attitudes of the other. In order to do so, dominant groups often seek to identify key individuals in the subordinate group who can provide them with information about the group. These key individuals, known variously as *intelligentsia*, Uncle Toms, or by no name at all, are used by the dominant group as intermediaries to provide information, make arrangements, and so on.

The role of the intermediary is dependent upon the structure and discipline of the interacting groups, as well as on his own prestige. Some minorities are tightly structured and have key individuals who are able to negotiate with the dominant group. If the leader makes a commitment, the minority group will honor it. The arrangements, or "deals," that intermediaries are called upon to make vary—"delivering" a bloc of votes at election time, "cooling" tensions during a period of disturbance, keeping various members of the minority community in line, and so on. James W. Loewen, in his book *The Mississippi Chinese* (1971) reports that Chinese in certain Mississippi Delta towns were able to have their children admitted to White schools and to gain other perquisites of White status by agreeing to maintain social distance between themselves and Blacks. Chinese leaders persuaded Chinese males to end relationships with Black females and to throw out their Chinese-Black kin. They ostracized stubborn individuals or forced them to leave the community. Furthermore, they performed the social function of certifying that all Chinese children admitted to the school system were not of mixed descent (1971, p. 176).

Intermediaries can help to stabilize intergroup relations. Relations among groups can be precarious and tense if the members of each do not know what the others are thinking or if their leaders are not strong enough to make commitments that will be honored. It is important to note that, for such relationships to occur, key individuals usually must be present in both groups. The minority com-

"Take ... good ... care ... of ... yourself, ... you ...
belong ... to ... me-e-e. ..."

FIGURE 10   Reproduced by special permission of **Playboy** magazine; copyright © 1969 by HMH Publishing Co., Inc.

munity will identify individuals of the dominant group whom they believe to be trustworthy and strong. In the same way, the dominant group will identify those it believes to be dependable as sources of information or with whom it can reach agreements.

Socialization

It is easy enough to think of social control as external to the individual—police, legislatures, reservations, even physical structures like walls, gates, "No Trespassing" signs, and prisons. But social control is not truly effective if its mechanisms are merely parts of the external environment. Ways must be found to instill the norms into the individual's consciousness. The ultimate instrument of social control is norms that are so much a part of the individual that they are habitually followed or are felt to be proper and right.

The concept of socialization, as it is used in the social sciences, implies a social-control function. Socialization has to do with the ways that individuals learn the norms of society, beginning at birth and continuing through life. Émile Durkheim, for example, wrote at great length on the coercive influence of social phenomena on the individual. Social facts, by Durkheim's definition, are "ways of acting, thinking, and feeling, external to the individuals, which are endowed with a power of coercion, by reason of which they control him. These collective manifestations are revealed as soon as I try to resist them" (1966, pp. 4, 5).

Throughout life the individual is conditioned by information that is either withheld or provided. The language that the child learns shapes his or her experience by means of the concepts and categories that it contains or lacks. During the years of formal education, the school both binds and frees its pupils; it opens new areas of knowledge, thus freeing them, but it also binds them by rewarding them for learning certain things and punishing them if they do not. Throughout the experience, rewards and punishments will be dispensed according to what is learned, how much is learned, how information is articulated, and how well the pupil behaves.

Schools sometimes ask for creativity, but they do not want too much. The truth is that society cannot stand too much creativity. If every individual were greatly creative and hence unpredictable, the orderly interactions upon which societies depend would break down. So schools, as little societies, begin to teach youngsters how much creativity will be tolerated.

Religious organizations have similar social-control functions. They communicate information, withhold information, reward certain ideas, and punish others. Religious organizations also attempt to inculcate common perspectives in their adherents. By means of religious teachings, subordinate people can learn to obey their masters without revolting and to wait patiently for heavenly rewards. At the same time masters can learn that their power and accumulated wealth are trusts given them by God.

The practice of using special catechisms to indoctrinate slaves in the nineteenth-century United States is evidence of the religious social-control function (*Southern Episcopalian*, April 1854):

Q. Who keeps the snakes and all bad things from hurting you?
A. God does.
Q. Who gave you a master and a mistress?
A. God gave them to me.
Q. Who says that you must obey them?

A. God says that I must.
Q. What book tells you these things?
A. The Bible.
Q. How does God do all his work?
A. He always does it right.
Q. Does God love to work?
A. Yes, God is always at work.
Q. Do the angels work?
A. Yes, they do what God tells them.
Q. Do they love to work?
A. Yes, they love to please God.
Q. What does God say about your work?
A. He that will not work shall not eat.
Q. Did Adam and Eve have to work?
A. Yes, they had to keep the garden.
Q. Was it hard to keep that garden?
A. No, it was very easy.
Q. What makes the crops so hard to grow now?
A. Sin makes it.
Q. What makes you lazy?
A. My wicked heart.
Q. How do you know your heart is wicked?
A. I feel it every day.
Q. Who teaches you so many wicked things?
A. The Devil.
Q. Must you let the Devil teach you?
A. No, I must not.

On balance, it should be noted that the Christian view of brotherhood proved to be an idea that eventually upset the accepted pattern of master and slave. Some masters from the beginning, in fact, had feared that this upset would occur and opposed the preaching of the Gospel among their slaves. It seems that churches, like schools, can be used to control populations, but the results are not always what the masters intend.

The teaching profession, as we have seen, is entrusted with bringing the young into accord with the expectations associated with membership in the society. The clergy has the function of investing these expectations with meaning and worth. The legal profession helps to resolve conflicts that arise when societal expectations and actual behavior do not properly correspond. The fact that the professions have social-control functions does not mean that teachers, clergymen, and lawyers uniformly conspire to keep low-status people in their places. In many instances quite the opposite is true. Some teachers produce students who refuse to play traditionally accepted roles, some clergymen challenge the assumptions of the system, and some lawyers counsel clients on ways to beat the system. But there are countless instances in which teachers, clergymen, and lawyers have uniformly supported systems that discriminated against minorities.

The motivation for such behavior is not difficult to discover. A small-town southern lawyer who chooses to defend a Black against a White runs the risk of losing all his White clients. The same has been true of West Coast lawyers who defended Orientals. Until recently in some states, a school teacher who taught "race mixing" could expect trouble, tenure laws or no. Scores of White pastors lost their churches during the 1950s and 1960s because their ideas on intergroup relations were too "liberal" for their congregations. It seems clear that high-status clients will not long support professionals who threaten arrangements that bring those clients wealth and power.

Etiquette

The word "etiquette," according to tradition, originally meant "Keep off the grass!" In the days of Louis XIV, it seems, visitors to the palace at Versailles were kept from trampling on the flowers and shrubs by means of small posts, or "etiquettes," which had been erected for the purpose. The king decreed that no one was to go beyond the bounds of the "etiquettes." This etymology of the word is remarkably close to its present English meaning—a system of boundaries and social distances.

A system of etiquette can be thought of as a kind of road map indicating the degree of intimacy that exists between social positions (social distance). A well-developed code of etiquette also shows heavily traveled and safe modes of behavior, as well as those modes of behavior that are undergoing change and are potentially hazardous. Persons who have been socialized in a stable society carry the etiquette with them as a kind of mental image.

In traditional societies, social distances between individuals are carefully regulated by custom. Although such custom curtails individual freedom, it also enables different individuals and peoples to live in close geographical proximity with a minimum of overt difficulty. In one of the few sociological studies ever done on the etiquette of intergroup relations, Bertram M. Doyle made this observation on the etiquette of slavery:

> . . . Where a Code was observed, relations moved smoothly. If there were no forms established—as in the instance between free Negroes and white persons —confusion resulted. . . .
> Though the characters in this vast drama changed with the passing of time, the human nature of the participants did not change. Moreover, the code of relations which bound the cast together—and under which they were enabled to carry out a corporate existence—became crystallized by experience and fortified by habit. (1971, pp. 101, 102)

In the course of time, a system of etiquette grows up around any transactions that regularly occur between peoples, and it eventually comes to govern the situation. I recall one of my first experiences with this phenomenon. During the 1950s I worked weekends as cashier at a supermarket in a small city in South

FIGURE 11   Physician's Office in Alabama, 1965. (Courtesy of William F. Hodgkins).

Carolina. The first of the month was check-cashing time. One Saturday, after I had cashed the check of a Black school teacher, the store manager called me aside to tell me that I had annoyed a customer. "How?" I asked. "Do you recall cashing a check for a colored man?" "Yes," I responded. "Well, you called him 'Mr.,' and one of our white customers complained." In this situation, I was not an outsider blundering in an unfamiliar situation, for I had grown up in the area. Instead, I was a youngster being instructed in local etiquette.

Today many of the old forms of etiquette have disappeared, except in small towns and rural areas. In metropolitan areas, especially, new codes of etiquette are evolving to fit the interaction patterns that resulted from changes that occurred in the 1950s and 1960s. In sociological parlance, the United States at present seems to be in a period of accommodation.[2] If relatively few changes occur during

---

[2] Accommodation, according to George A. and Achilles G. Theodorson, is "a process of social adjustment in which groups in conflict with each other agree to terminate or prevent further conflict by temporarily or permanently establishing peaceful interaction. This type of social interaction allows antagonistic groups to maintain their separate identities and attitudes, with the exception of those attitudes that would lead to disruptive conflict" (1969, p. 3).

this decade, habits will eventually crystallize into obligatory behavior, and a new code of etiquette will evolve.

A code of etiquette, once learned, enables individuals to interact in delicate situations with a minimum of stress. For example, an individual who learns how to greet a person of a particular status can greet a total stranger of the same status without difficulty. He or she knows the etiquette. Similarly, in intergroup relations individuals from different groups can interact with one another with minimum embarrassment or uncertainty if there is a code of etiquette and if the actors know and accept it.

An Assortment of Other Stratagems

It would be impossible to present a complete list of all the strategems that dominant groups have used in dealing with subordinate peoples, because of the many local variations that occur. Powerful groups, it appears, can be very imaginative in their use of resources. What is offered here is a brief illustrative listing.

"Divide and rule" is an ancient adage that expresses a tactic used by countless dominant groups. Roman generals employed the principle in their dealings with barbarians. Roman armies were filled with mercenaries who had been recruited from non-Roman groups. American colonists took advantage of tribal jealousies and animosities in dealing with the Indians. The records of many of the early Indian wars show Indians fighting Indians. Settlers wrote in their diaries and letters that they would be destroyed unless they could keep the Indians divided. The principle of exploiting internal divisions also was embodied in the African slave trade. Plantation owners purposely avoided purchasing large numbers of slaves from the same tribe because they were afraid that individuals who spoke the same language and shared the same traditions would unite and revolt.

It should be pointed out that this strategy is a two-edged sword—dominant groups are vulnerable, as well as subordinate peoples. As we shall see in Chapter 11 it can be used as a tactic for altering intergroup relations.

Inasmuch as discrimination against a group is a function of the group's visibility, a whole range of activities has centered around identifying individuals as members of out-groups. Photographs or questions about religious preferences have been required on application forms for employment, club membership, or school admission. Members of minorities have been required to wear distinctive clothing or to submit to tattooing or branding in order that they might be readily identified.

A system of requiring a sponsor before an individual can obtain membership in an organization is a powerful mechanism of social control. The professions and many other occupational categories, labor unions, and most clubs and fraternities use some system of recommendation or sponsorship. The fact that it is used legitimately by many groups makes it all the more effective when it is used to discriminate against an out-group.

One common strategy of social control is to restrict essential information to members of the in-group. An employer may avoid using classified advertisements to carry news about better job openings. One utility-company official explained that his organization sought only manual laborers and helpers through ads, never linemen. When the Federal government toughened its stand on discrimination in housing, many landlords began to advertise vacant units by word of mouth, rather than by newspaper ads. (If housing is scarce, this strategem can be very effective.)

Members of a minority may be denied essential services or needed resources. For example American Blacks have not done well in agriculture. The number of Black farm operators has never been great, but during the past two decades it has declined precipitously. There are several reasons: Blacks have been unable to purchase large quantities of fertile land; they have not been able to obtain capital for seed, fertilizer, and equipment; they often have lacked information about advanced agricultural techniques; and in recent years Blacks have not obtained substantial acreage allotments for several cash crops. The first three factors require little elaboration, but the fourth—obtaining acreage allotments—deserves a brief comment. Allotments of acreage to grow certain agricultural commodities are regulated by the Agricultural Stabilization and Conservation Service (A.S.C.S.) through community and county committees. The A.S.C.S. has a legitimate objective: the prevention of overproduction of farm products. By regulating the number of acres that can be planted, it can stabilize the market and assure farmers of a basic income. The local committees that make the decisions about acreage are composed of elected members, who tend to be White owners of large farms. Although the number of minority members of community committees has increased in recent years, the county committees—the ones with real power—were still practically all White in 1970 (see Table 7).

The basis of some strategies of social control is subterfuge or harrassment. Restaurant owners, when required to comply with antidiscrimination laws, have been known to offer inferior food to minority individuals or to serve them in a desultory manner. Or they have resorted to the legal fiction of calling their restaurants "private clubs." In some areas skating rinks, swimming pools, bars, and pool rooms—once open to the public—are now known as private clubs. Minority members who have tried to buy or rent houses in previously segregated communities have sometimes faced harrassment of various kinds—threatening phone calls, picketing, insults, violence—or ostracism.

Not much imagination is required to see how these strategies can be used against members of out-groups. Changing societal conditions, of course, bring new approaches. An alteration in the economy or in the legal code may cause abandonment of today's strategems, which may be viewed a few years later as relics of an unenlightened age, like White and Colored restrooms and water fountains.

TABLE 7   COMMITTEE COMPOSITION OF AGRICULTURAL STABILIZA-
TION AND CONSERVATION SERVICE (ASCS), 1970*

| | Committeemen | | | |
Ethnic Group	County		Community	
	No.	Pct.	No.	Pct.
Negro	2	1	144	1
American Indian	8	1	63	1
Oriental	0	0	2	1
Spanish surname	41	2	139	1
White	1,620	97	10,016	97
Total	1,671	100	10,364	100

SOURCE: U.S. Department of Agriculture; correspondence in the possession of the author, March 1973.

* ASCS programs are administered through State, county, and community committees. State committee members are appointed by the Secretary of Agriculture. Community committeemen are elected by farmers who are eligible to participate in ASCS programs. County committeemen are elected by the chairmen of community committees.

[1] Less than 1 percent.

Obviously, not all social controls are equally effective. Some tactics prove to be useless and are eventually abandoned. Some boomerang and actually injure members of the dominant group. An example is the anti-Japanese land law (1913), which prohibited those ineligible for citizenship—primarily foreign-born Japanese—from owning or leasing agricultural land in California. The law proved a hardship for many White landowners who wanted to rent to Japanese tenants, so it had to be amended to permit leasing (Peterson, 1971, p. 52). It seems clear that the struggle for status is a dynamic and continuing process. A dominant group will try first one and then another tactic in order to stay in power. A subordinate group will respond as best it can in order to make the most of the situation. Rarely, if ever, is either the majority or minority entirely passive.

Overview

Social control, as applied in intergroup relations, includes the processes that bring about conformity to the norms of the core society. Put more starkly, keeping individuals and groups in line is what social control is all about.

Force or the threat of force is implied in any continuing society. Such force may have the sanction of government, or it may be extralegal, as in the example of pogroms or lynchings. In nations with well-developed legal codes, law-enforce-

ment officers are not permitted to wreak personal or public vengeance upon prisoners. Their task is to bring alleged culprits to courts of law. Historical examples
indicate that even in courts of law, however, minorities may not do well, often
because of inherent contradictions in legal traditions.

Dominant groups can resort to a number of political maneuvers in order to
stay in power—gerrymandering, denial of legal privilege, poll taxes, and the like.
They also may control the number of immigrants coming into the territory so as
not to lose the numerical balance of power. Many modern nations, including the
United States, have a tradition of excluding people from certain countries or
groups. Some of the assumptions that underlie selective immigration policies are
rather obvious. An influx of workers in certain occupational categories would cause
unemployment or serious competition with local people for jobs. Then, too, certain
people are sometimes perceived to be less assimilable than others.

A dominant group must see to it that its own members observe the norms.
Power, after all, cannot be overused or underused, or else the dominance of the
group, as well as the established system, may be threatened.

The effectiveness of a strategem for social control obviously depends upon
the specifics of a given situation. A tactic that might work with an illiterate group
would fall flat when tried with an educated group. Tactics that were effective a
generation ago are often ineffective today. Some tactics, however, like systems of
sponsorship, "divide and rule" strategems, and restricting vital information have
been used repeatedly and often with much success.

The obvious mechanisms of social control are those that are external to the
individual—police, legislatures, courts, even physical structures like walls and
prisons. Social control also depends upon *internal* mechanisms in order to be truly
effective. The individual is within society, but society is also within the individual.
Individuals are socialized in such a way that they carry a kind of rule book (a
code of etiquette) and an enforcer (conscience and the like) with them. Whenever it occurs, socialization has the effect, in Rousseau's words, of transforming
"force into right and obedience into duty."

For Further Reading

Many of the items among the references cited may be considered as recommended
reading as well.

Doyle, Bertram W. *The Etiquette of Race Relations in the South.* Chicago: University
of Chicago Press, 1937.

Durkheim, Émile. *The Rules of Sociological Method.* New York: Free Press, 1966
(originally published, 1938).

Knowles, Louis L., and Kenneth Prewitt (eds.). *Institutional Racism in America.*
Englewood Cliffs, N.J.: Prentice-Hall, 1969.

Lyman, Stanford, and Marvin B. Scott. "Territoriality: A Neglected Sociological Dimension," *Social Problems*, 15 (1967), 236–249.

Marx, Gary T. *Racial Conflict: Tension and Change in American Society.* Boston: Little, Brown, 1971.

Pitts, Jesse R. "Social Control." In David L. Sills (ed.), *International Encyclopedia of the Social Sciences*, vol. 14. New York: Macmillan, 1968. Pp. 381–396.

Roucek, Joseph S. *Social Control.* Princeton: Van Nostrand, 1956.

Skolnick, Jerome H. *The Politics of Protest.* New York: Simon & Schuster, 1969. (Jerome Skolnick was director of the Task Force on Violent Aspects of Protest and Confrontation of the National Commission on the Causes and Prevention of Violence.)

Sumner, William Graham. *Folkways.* New York: Dover, 1906.

U.S. Commission on Civil Rights. *Political Participation.* Washington, D.C.: Government Printing Office, 1968.

White, Leslie A. *The Science of Culture: A Study of Man and Civilization.* New York: Grove, 1949.

RHODESIA'S GOOD, WHITE LIFE

Rhodesia is one of the places in the world where a numerical minority is the ruling group. In Rhodesia, White supremacy is explicit and legal. Such an arrangement was much more common during the days of colonial expansion than it is today. The effects of the arrangement are described in the following **Newsweek** release:

Back in colonial times, the more aristocratic white settlers of Kenya and the Cape used to dismiss Rhodesia as "the sergeants' mess of Central Africa." Another popular saying had it that "Kenya is for officers, Rhodesia for other ranks." Even yet, many of the descendants of the younger sons and enterprising provincial lads who first opened up the California-size chunk of bush country around the turn of the century resent that slur. But not too much. For thanks to Rhodesia's white supremacist rule, the nation's 250,000 whites can console themselves with the thought that, for the time being at least, they are among the most pampered "non-coms" in the world.

To its white inhabitants, Rhodesia still offers the good life on a grand scale. For the wealthy, that means a spacious home on several acres of landscaped grounds ablaze with flowers, a couple of cars, a swimming pool and several servants. Even for middle-income whites, the living is relatively easy. For in Rhodesia, the good life still comes very cheap. Food is inexpensive, a five-room house in the capital rents for about $90 a month, and there is a seemingly endless supply of African servants, all willing to work a six-day week for the going rate of $4 to $7. Indeed, of 35 major cities around the world studied recently by London's Financial Times, only three—Dublin, Belgrade and Moscow—were cheaper to live in than Salisbury.

To make things even merrier, wages for Rhodesian whites are high. The average white worker earns nearly $4,500 a year, or at least ten times more than his black counterpart. And few whites have to worry about unemployment. According to the latest figures, only 451 whites were out of work in the entire country. By comparison, estimates place black unemployment at well over the 100,000 mark—and that does not include the many thousands who are underemyloyed on farms in the tribal trust lands. But no one really knows the extent of black unemployment; characteristically, the government has never really bothered to study the subject.

Citadel: The good life, in short, is not only cheap; it is totally one-sided. The civil service is a white citadel; no African has yet been employed at an administrative level and, except for a handful of veterinarians and doctors, most blacks working for the government hold down low-level jobs as messengers, lab assistants or the like. Similarly, "whites only" trade unions and professional associations remain determined to keep blacks out of high-paying jobs. And even before a young African enters the job market, he faces devastating discrimination. In the last year, the Rhodesian Government spent as much on white school children—$25 million—as it did on blacks, who are twenty times as numerous. And although Salisbury recently put a ceiling on the money spent to educate Africans, no limit was set on expenditures for white children.

Over the years, such discrimination has only served to reinforce the white Rhodesian's conviction that he is a special case, the standard bearer of white civilization in a sea of black backwardness. Many white Rhodesians take a paternal attitude toward the blacks. White women run schools for black children, and white land-owners consider the welfare of their black workers to be their personal responsibility. But as Lord Malvern, a former Rhodesian Prime Minister, once put it, this relationship is "a partnership between the rider and the horse." And a good many recent immigrants and lower-class whites do not even indulge in paternalism. To them, the African is a "munt" (a derogatory usuage of the African *muntu,* meaning "person"). In Salisbury bars, the whites have recently been playing what they call "the munt game," involving exchanges such as: "What is an African politician? An embezzlemunt." "What is Bishop Muzorewa? A detri-munt." "What is a light-skinned African? An improve-munt." And although the laughter that greets these jokes is for the most part good-humored, it reveals a profound lack of sensitivity—especially since the hilarity frequently takes place within the earshot of black servants.

It all seems strangely out of date. "In some respects," reports NEWSWEEK's Peter Webb, "Rhodesia reflects the values and culture of an English garden suburb before World War II—a Surrey with a lunatic fringe on top. On Saturday nights at Meikle's Hotel, the candlelit tables are packed with couples dining on smoked salmon and roast venison and dancing to Jack Dent and his trio playing such favorites as 'Bye, Bye, Blackbird' and 'My Blue Heaven.' The nightclubs feature the worst strippers in the world, and the comedians' jokes reach back to antiquity. All in all, you get the feeling that the mass of white Rhodesians, kindly, hospitable people in the main, live in a dreamworld of their own making—a dreamworld they're determined to preserve as long as possible."

It is precisely this anachronistic life-style that lures many whites to Rhodesia. Brigadier Andrew Dunlop, a former British Army officer who served with the Argyll and Sutherland Highlanders in World War II, says he decided to settle in Rhodesia "when I saw the way Churchill was thrown out by returned heroes' votes. I decided to come to Rhodesia, where there was still a British tradition." Even the most recent immigrants obviously relish the thought of stepping back into an earlier time—and into a racially superior role. Asked how long it takes most new arrivals to adjust themselves to their privileged new existence, one Rhodesian sociologist replies: "Oh, about half an hour."

THEY DID NOT KNOW
IT WAS ILLEGAL
TO KILL INDIANS

Ibague, Colombia—Nine men who were acquitted of killing 16 Indians during a Christmas party face a second trial, according to a release from United Press International.

During the trial, the men gave as their defense that they "did not know it was illegal to kill Indians." The murders occurred in 1967 on a cattle ranch near the Venezuelan border.

The Indians, including several women and children, were invited to a Christmas party and were later slain. They were not tried until 1972. The second trial is scheduled to begin August 28, 1973.

10

Intergroup
Conflict
and Collective
Behavior

Toward the end of the 1960s, when the coming of summer usually signaled the renewed outbreak of urban riots, it was widely held that this kind of collective behavior was unique to the United States. Some believed it to be a symptom of modern times and a bad one—a departure from the calm of earlier days. An interpretation popular in some quarters attributed practically all the disturbance to race. These deficient interpretations grew out of lack of a sense of history and misunderstanding of certain sociological principles.

Collective behavior involving riots, conflict, and violence has not been limited to the United States. Contrary to rhetoric, it is not at all clear that the United States is the most violent nation that has ever existed. Several other peoples and political entities deserve consideration for this distinction, including the Huns, the Turks, the Goths, the Mongols, Nazi Germany, the Roman empire, and the Aztec, Zulu, and Inca empires, to mention just a few.

Violent collective behavior certainly is not unique to modern times. Riots occurred in ancient Egypt and in the Greek city states. Thucydides' account of the disturbances that culminated in the Corcyraean Revolution became a famous passage in antiquity:

> Later on, one may say, the whole Hellenic world was convulsed. . . . Revolution thus ran its course from city to city, and the places which it arrived at last, from having heard what had been done before, carried to a still greater excess the refinement of their inventions. . . . Words had to change their ordinary meaning and to take that which was now given them. Reckless audacity came to be considered the courage of loyal ally; prudent hesitation, specious cowardice; moderation was held to be a cloak for unmanliness; ability to see all sides of a question, inaptness to act on any. . . . The cause of all these evils was the lust for power arising from greed and ambition; and from these passions proceeded the violence of parties once engaged in contention. (Finley, 1951, pp. 189–190)

Throughout the days of the Roman empire riots were a rather common occurrence. During the eleventh and twelfth centuries the emerging cities of medieval Europe were the scene of repeated outbreaks of street fights and riots. In fact, riots seem to be a conspicuous feature in the history of all modern nations. For this reason and because a riot epitomizes collective behavior, particular attention is given to the subject in the discussion that follows.

Collective Behavior

Definitions

All group behavior is "collective," in one sense of the word. The concept "collective behavior" as it is used in social science, however, refers to groups that are characterized by the spontaneous development of norms or relations—crowds, publics, social movements, lynchings, and riots. Collective behavior, in this sense, is nontraditional behavior. A *riot*, as a form of collective behavior, is a temporary, violent outbreak of civil disorder that falls short of an attempt to overthrow the government. As a legal concept, a riot is a criminal offense against public order by a group (legally defined as three or more people) and the use of violence, however slight. Common law distinguishes among three offenses that involve group breaches of the peace (in ascending order of seriousness): *unlawful assembly, rout,* and *riot.* An assembly is legally defined as unlawful if the participants share a common illegal purpose. *Rout* is an unlawful assembly that has taken some step, short of actual violence, to implement its purpose. Rout becomes riot when violence occurs.

It is inaccurate to describe the disturbances of the 1960s, like those in Watts, Newark, and Detroit, as "race riots." Although most of the riots in these places involved minorities, few of the clashes were between ethnic or racial groups as such. The participants themselves used terms like "rebellion," "insurrection," and "protest" to describe the outbursts.

The less obvious but more basic conflict in those disturbances was between minorities and representatives of the established political order. In many instances, the fact that most of the rioters were Blacks and law-enforcement personnel predominantly White obscured the fundamental conflict between the establishment and those who were unhappy with it. Arthur I. Waskow's description of the 1964 riots makes this point clear:

> By Monday, when the [Rochester] riot ended, 750 people had been arrested on charges of looting, riot, and unlawful possession of firearms. About three-fourths of them were Negroes, the rest white youths who had begun to move into the rioting on Saturday and even more on Sunday night. . . .
>
> The last of the rash of late-summer riots occurred in Philadelphia, and again *it was much more a clash between Negroes and policemen than between two civilian populations.* (Waskow, 1967, pp. 258–259; italics added)

The fact also that several of the disorders, like the Chicago riot of 1966, involved minority groups other than Blacks supports this view. This interpretation does not suggest that group antipathies were irrelevant in the disturbances. Relations between minority and dominant groups did figure in each situation. But the disturbances did not take the form of clashes between aggregates defined along the lines of ethnicity alone.

Scope

Historically, minority antagonisms have been by no means the principal occasion for inciting riots. Political, economic, religious, and other dissatisfactions have been far more important. The riots of eleventh- and twelfth-century Europe, for example, arose out of a confrontation between the emerging middle class and the representatives of high feudalism. The historian Henri Pirenne has observed: "During the initial period the middle class and the bishops lived in a state of permanent hostility and, as it were, on the point of open war. Force alone was able to prevail between such adversaries, equally convinced of their rights" (1956, p. 128). It is clear that religious controversies, labor disputes, royalism, socialism, strikes, and unemployment have produced far more riots than have racial or ethnic factors.

When intergroup relations have entered the picture as an added factor in rioting, the geographical distribution has been widespread. Examples can be cited from practically every area. Modern Africa has been the scene of violent conflicts between Bahutu and Batutsi (Watusi), Ibo and Hausa. In Asia bloody outbreaks have occurred between Chinese and Vietnamese, Chinese and Burmese, Japanese and Koreans. The examples could be multiplied with many similar occurrences from Europe and the Americas.

Explanations

Collective behavior. Rioting, as a type of crowd behavior, has certain features in common with lynchings, panics, hysterias, and even tearing down goal posts at a football game. In such a crowd the sense of self-awareness diminishes and, along with it, personal responsibility (Turner and Killian, 1957). Ordinary attitudes of self-criticism and restraint are relaxed. Even when individuals are able to preserve a measure of personal responsibility they may fear reprisal from the crowd should they try to alter its course. Instances are known in which mobs have turned their fury on members who have urged restraint. During a buildup of emotion, individuals perceive that their own feelings are acceptable to their fellows, and they are thus stimulated and encouraged. Their feelings are mirrored in the less restrained behavior of those around them. A feedback situation is thus created; individual expressions of intense feeling become both response and stimulus.

The character of the group itself, as it is perceived by its individual members, is an important factor in collective behavior. "Disciplined, organized groups with high morale, i.e., with the confidence of each individual in the orderliness and mutual loyalty of his fellows, do not readily experience panic or other hysterical mass dissociations, even under extreme provocation" (Wallace, 1961, p. 188).

Some scholars believe that collective behavior tends to follow a definite pattern. Research on a number of riots, panics, lynchings, and student revolts has revealed the following key factors (see Smelser, 1962):

1. *Structural conduciveness*—structural characteristics that permit or encourage episodes of collective behavior (for example, religious, economic, class, and ethnic cleavages)
2. *The intensification of structural strains* (like economic depression or collapse, a population shift, the redistribution of political power, or the invasion of territory previously occupied by another group)
3. *The spread of hostile belief*
4. *Environmental factors* (for example, hot, humid weather)
5. *A precipitating event* (like the slaying of a minority member by a policeman, an attack on a majority member by a minority member, a rape, assassination of a group leader)
6. *Mobilization for action.*

Neil Smelser's helpful analysis indicates that social controls determine how fast, how far, and in what direction each episode will develop. "In certain respects," Smelser has written, "this final determinant arches over all the others" (1969,

p. 17). Social controls minimize conduciveness and strain and, in a broad sense, prevent the occurrence (p. 327). If an episode does develop, controls are mobilized through appropriate agencies—the police, the courts, the press, religious authorities, and community leaders.

Urbanization. It is possible to construct a theoretical explanation for violent collective behavior in which the focus is the setting of the event. Such collective outbreaks involve concerted action and necessarily occur in places where population is concentrated. Though riots are not limited to the big city—some riots have occurred in small towns and rural areas—the urban situation does provide a favorable social environment, because the urban situation is more than geographical space. It is social space as well. Two factors seem to be significant: one, the prominence of the impersonal, segmental, social relationships that mark much of contemporary society and, two, the use of secondary, rather than primary, mechanisms of social control. Primary groups, like the family, are no longer sufficient to maintain order.

A heavy in-migration of rural people to urban areas creates a situation in which public facilities are overtaxed and occupational opportunities are limited. Frustration follows. Governments, governmental agencies, or political leaders are then blamed for the misery that grows out of the inequities. Frustrated individuals may also turn to more accessible targets and vent their hostility on scapegoats.

Long-term urban residents may begin to share in the discontent. Many of them may lose jobs or be forced into underemployment as a result of the influx of new workers. These demographic and structural factors have an impact upon one another, to the extent that a single catalytic event can set off an explosion.

Social change and human interaction. Robert E. Park attributed the intergroup conflict of his day to the fact that major social changes were taking place. "There is more conflict," Park said, "because there is more change, more progress" (1964, p. 233). The alteration in social relations that followed in the wake of World War I had not escaped him. He certainly was aware of the tensions that reached a peak during the Red Summer of 1919. Between May 10 and September 30 of that year major explosions had come to Charleston, South Carolina; Longview, Texas; Washington, D.C.; Chicago; Knoxville; Omaha; and Phillips County, Arkansas.

Park explained intergroup tension by linking individual thoughts and attitudes with changes in social structure. Human thought proceeds, Park argued, by the method of classification. According to the rules of Aristotelian logic, we may be said to know a thing when we are able to classify it. We are dependent, more often than we are consciously aware, upon our tendency to categorize people. Everyone we meet inevitably finds a place in our minds in some previously defined category. We thus classify individuals as friends or foes, as neighbors or strangers. The category to which we assign an individual determines, with little conscious reflection on our part, the attitude that we assume toward him.

These mental categories also tend to determine our responses to individuals of other groups. But we must modify mental categories whenever social relations among groups are undergoing change. These categories, however, in order to be functional must be somewhat resistant to change. Individual responses to changed social relationships may therefore range from mild dissonance to militant hostility.

Park saw the same processes occurring at the societal level. He noted that in stable societies there is substantial agreement about categories. Whenever there is a change in status, a change in social organization is involved. "Prejudice—that is caste, class and race prejudice—in its more naïve and innocent manifestations, is merely the resistance of the social order to change" (1964, p. 233).

How does social conflict originate? At the individual level its origin is implicit in the development of self-consciousness. It is in the various responses called forth by social contacts that the personality of the individual is developed and his status defined. "In an effort to maintain this status or improve it, to defend the personality, enlarge its possessions, extend its privileges, and maintain its prestige, conflicts arise." The personality of the individual can become "so bound up with the interests of his group or clan that in a struggle he makes the group cause his own" (Park and Burgess, 1928, p. 576).

Status consistency.   Some social scientists have interpreted minority unrest within the context of status-consistency theory. Status consistency (or rank equilibrium) is the extent to which an individual's rank positions on several status hierarchies are at a comparable level. An example of status consistency would be a White with high education earning a high income at a white-collar job. An example of status inconsistency or rank disequilibrium would be a person from a dominant group (a White in the United States, a Spanish person in Peru) with high education earning low wages at a blue-collar job.

A number of studies indicate that status inconsistency can lead to stressful individual and group situations. Christopher Bagley, for example, thinks that this basic idea is implied in the key concepts of several classic research studies (1970, pp. 267–288):

1. *Relative deprivation—The American Soldier.* During World War II military police who had little chance for promotion showed higher morale than air corpsmen who had good chances for rapid promotion. The researchers on *The American Soldier* (a large-scale research undertaking conducted during World War II) attributed the lower morale of the air corpsmen to the discrepancy between their actual positions and their role expectations. Military police, on the other hand, expected little in the way of advancement and tended to be well satisfied with their positions.

2. *Anomie.* Robert K. Merton (1957) and others, following up an idea advanced by Durkheim, have suggested that *anomie* results from a gap between the goals that society motivates an individual to strive for and the goals that it allows him to reach. Deviance is a typical outcome.

3. *Integration of status.* J. Gibbs and W. Martin (1964), in predicting variations in suicide rates, found that the individuals most prone to suicide are those who occupy "unpopular" (statistically speaking) combinations of statuses.

Using status consistency as an explanatory factor, Bagley argues that minority conflict in America is a result of the *betterment* of economic and educational opportunities for minorities. As occupational and educational barriers have fallen and many minority members have improved their statuses in the hierarchies, they have become more and more critical of the low valuation still placed on them. Bagley argues that this result is precisely what should be expected if we can rely upon the long line of sociological and psychological studies showing that status inconsistency leads to deviance, innovation, and unrest.

Bagley's explanation is deficient in that it fails to account for the *worsening* of the relative economic position of many minority members in the United States. Even though legal barriers have fallen, large numbers of low-income individuals have not benefited from the changes. If anything, the gap has widened for them. Bagley's ideas are useful in that they take into account the gains that some minority members—notably those of the middle and upper classes—have been able to achieve and the ways in which those gains have been perceived.

Militancy. "Patience got us nowhere. We built America, and we deserve—we are going to get—a fair share of the wealth." This statement summarizes the case for violence—a case supported by the massive participation of minority members in the labor force of America. Such feelings are understandable if we know the long history of systematic discrimination and repression minorities have experienced. It seems effective if we take into account the new facilities, funds, and assistance programs that have flowed into the places where earlier disturbances have occurred. Indeed, as long as subordinate groups remain docile and quiet, dominant peoples tend to assume that they are happy and contented. Militant ideology, however, usually ignores or discounts changes that have occurred in intergroup relations as the result of legislative, educational, and judicial activities.

Some writers see current intergroup disturbances in the United States as a preliminary bout before the main event, a full-scale war of global proportions in which Whites will be pitted against non-Whites. In these terms, Whites are overwhelmingly outnumbered. Such a prediction is based on the somewhat questionable assumption that all people of color feel a common bond with one another or at least that they can be made to feel this bond. The facts are, however, that many non-White groups recognize gradations of skin color among themselves and that their intragroup cleavages are influenced by these perceptions.

Revolution. Considerable historical evidence supports the view that oppressed people who perceive of their fate as hopeless do not revolt. Fatalism generally takes forms other than revolution. Revolution—according to Alexis de Tocqueville—is associated with "improvement" and rising expectations:

Nations that have endured patiently and almost unconsciously the most over-whelming oppression often burst into rebellion against the yoke the moment it begins to grow lighter. The regime which is destroyed by a revolution is almost always an improvement on its immediate predecessor . . . Evils which are patiently endured when they seem inevitable become intolerable when once the idea of escape from them is suggested (1856:214).

This view, however, appears to contradict the Marxian proposition that revolution occurs after progressive degradation of the working class has produced despair and anger.

A theoretical *rapprochement* between Marx and Tocqueville has been attempted by James C. Davies in his analysis of revolutions (1962: 5–19). Davies studied the French Revolution (1789), Dorr's Rebellion (1842), the Russian Revolution (1917), and the Egyptian Revolution (1952) and found that revolutions are not likely among those who are well off and hopeful of the future.

Davies found further support from the American Revolution, the draft riots of New York (1863), and the riots of Nyasaland (1959), all of which appear to fit a J-curve pattern. He observed: "It is when the chains have been loosened somewhat, so that they can be cast off without a high probability of losing life, that people are put in a condition of proto-rebelliousness" (1962: 7).

In terms of his theory Davies found only one negative case of revolution that did not occur—the depression of the 1930s in the United States—and concluded:

> The notion that revolutions need both a period of rising expectations and a succeeding period in which they are frustrated qualifies substantially the main Marxian notion that revolutions occur after progressive degradation and the de Tocqueville notion that they occur when conditions are improving. By putting de Tocqueville before Marx but without abandoning either theory, we are better able to plot the antecedents of at least the disturbances here described. (1962, p. 17)

Caution must be exercised in generalizing from these uniformities to present conditions in the United States. In the disturbances that Davies considered, inter-group relations were by no means analogous to their role in contemporary American society. The presence of these factors in the current situation could actually serve as a constraining force to limit the scope of any disturbance to racial or ethnic aggregates alone. That is, aggregates of people of the same socioeconomic status but different groups might not act in concert because of group antipathies.

Social control.   Violent collective episodes are likely when a widespread sense of deprivation and hostility *plus* a reduced fear of retribution are present. Relative deprivation, status inconsistencies, and frustration over grievances can all be considered causes of collective responses, but they are not necessary and sufficient causes (in the sense that they alone produce the responses). Perhaps that is why some investigators who have tested the hypothesis of relative deprivation have found it to be a poor predictor of collective violence during certain historical periods (see Snyder and Tilly, 1972, pp. 520–532, for a study of collective violence in France between 1830 and 1960). The point is that feelings of deprivation and anger provide motivation, but the likelihood of a collective response seems to depend upon a lessened fear of retribution. Fear of retribution tends to be minimized under at least three sets of circumstances.

First, an activity that involves large numbers of people can provide the individual with a sense of impunity. Mob participants, for example, know it is scarcely possible to apprehend and punish everyone involved and, thus encouraged, take their greatly reduced chances. At some rock festivals, individuals who have engaged in behavior defined as illegal by the surrounding society seem to have felt a heightened sense of impunity because of the large crowd present and to have openly engaged in actions that otherwise might have led to arrest. At the rock festivals minority relations were not centrally involved, but the events illustrate how participants in a crowd feel safety in sheer numbers and figuratively thumb their noses at the larger society.

Second, fear of negative sanctions is lowered when members of the frustrated group feel that the establishment is unwilling or unable to enforce its laws. Participants in a strike, riot, or mob may know that the enforcers are weak or ill prepared. Or they may know that the establishment is loath to use force. Whatever the reason, it makes collective violence likely. "It is when the chains have been loosened somewhat," Davies comments, "so that they can be cast off; *without a high probability of losing life,* that people are put in a condition of proto-rebelliousness" (1962, p. 7).

Third, the deterrent effect of reprisal and punishment obviously is less when collective violence comes to be defined as a "good." Then individuals are freed from two types of constraints, the restraint of conscience (internalized norms) and the restraint of possible disapprobation from their reference others. Such a redefinition of the situation actually may enable participants to become highly esteemed by their reference others: Participants in a pogrom against Jews may see themselves as doing the will of God upon an accursed people; participants in the lynching of a Black as upholding White supremacy and, ironically, law and order; and participants in a riot as fighting a rebellion or a revolution against "the Man." If the situation is thus defined, potential participants may welcome the chance to suffer or die for their actions. They may even invite punishment, thus seeking martyrdom. Such an attitude can be fostered through a religious faith or through revolutionary ideology, both of which may call for total commitment to some ultimate value. For example, medieval crusaders against the infidels were told that death in such an undertaking was a duty, yea, an opportunity. Similarly, Julius Lester has written in *Revolutionary Notes* that revolutionaries should care so much that they are willing to die doing their revolutionary duty (1969, p. 24). Whenever such attitudes become deeply felt and widely shared, the effectiveness of coercive and retaliatory techniques is severely diminished.

Patterns in Recent American Riots

Two dimensions of collective behavior are sometimes overlooked: the excitement of the event and the normative character of the event. A riot may provide diversion from the boredom of everyday life.

A reporter has recorded the following interview:

> Reporter: "What were you doing during the riot?"
> Juanita (a cheerful rather charming 16-year-old Negro girl): "That wasn't no riot. That was a rebellion."
> Reporter: "OK, what were you doing during the rebellion?"
> Juanita (grinning with delight): "I was lootin'."
> Reporter: "Do you think there's going to be another rebellion?"
> Juanita (with obvious sincerity): "Oh I hope so." (Alsop, 1967, p. 16)

Similar observations have been made about lynchings. In fact, lynchings have sometimes been called "lynching bees." Some researchers have concluded that a lynching can be viewed as a release of tension for individuals who "crave some excitement, some interest, some passionate outburst" (F. Tannenbaum, quoted in Smelser, 1969, p. 75).

Friedrich Nietzsche observed decades ago that human beings want two things, danger and play. W. I. Thomas, in a similar vein, stated that one of the "four wishes" is the desire for new experiences that lead away from the monotony of life (Park and Burgess, 1928, pp. 599, 442).

Riots are not entirely lawless. Certain rules of the game tend to regulate individual behavior even in the midst of what would superficially seem to be chaotic conditions. For example, some stores and dwellings are regarded as off limits. Observers have also noted that gangs of looters often develop clearly defined divisions of labor. One individual will stand guard while others loot; at the next shop the same individual will take his turn inside while another person stands guard. The term "breakdown of law and order" is thus not very accurate. Instead, collective behavior involves the substitution of one set of norms or relationships[1] for another set. An organized group, with a clearly defined division of labor and

---

[1] A norm is conceptually distinct from a relation. For example, the father-son relationship can be defined and regulated by a variety of norms, even though the relationship itself remains essentially the same. On the basis of this distinction, Jack M. Weller and E. L. Quarantelli have classified collective behavior into four types, two of which are of particular interest here. In the first type, old relationships continue, but new norms emerge. An example would be a police force which, in a riot, begins to riot itself. In the second type, the norms remain the same but the relationships change. An example would be lynchings, of which it has been observed that the same normative patterns were followed "time after time" (1973, p. 678).

governed by explicit norms, may thus emerge from what previously appeared to be a random grouping of people.

Most of those who died during the riots of the 1960s were minority members. Why? Because the disturbances took the form of clashes between minority groups and law-enforcement personnel, rather than clashes between civilian populations. Of the thirty-six people killed in the Los Angeles riot, thirty-three were Blacks. Kenneth B. Clark has declared, "The fact of their deaths, the senseless death of human beings, has been obscured by our respectable middle-class preoccupation with the wanton destruction of property, vandalism and the looting" (1967, pp. 249–267).

Clark has further observed that residents of the slums have no realistic stake in respecting property because in a basic sense they do not possess it. They are possessed by it. When slum dwellers are able to obtain the symbols of the United States' high standard of living—color television sets, radios, washing machines, refrigerators, automobiles—they often must pay the highest prices for the cheapest brands, financed by usurious carrying charges. It is not as widely known as it should be that it is rare indeed for slum dwellers to own their own homes.

Simply providing low-cost *rental* property does not seem a satisfactory solution to the problem. Perhaps what is needed is an opportunity for individuals with low incomes to be able to purchase dwellings.[2] In many instances these individuals already pay rent equal to or in excess of the amount required for monthly mortgage payments.

Who is most likely to take part in a riot? A full answer to that question has not yet been obtained. Perhaps the best partial answer available is based on a profile of the individuals arrested during the 1967 Detroit riot (U.S. Department of Labor, 1968):

He was a single man just over thirty years of age, a Protestant, but not a regular church-goer.

He had dropped out of school by the eleventh grade. His birth place was the South and he had lived in Detroit for fifteen years or more.

[2] Actually, several programs that subsidized the purchase of homes were initiated by the Federal government ("235" homes, Farmers Home Administration programs, and so on) in the aftermath of the disturbances of the 1960s. In certain geographical areas these programs were quite successful. Some areas, however, experienced rather high rates of repossession and various such abuses as overpricing and shoddy construction by builders, fraudulent appraisals, and subterfuge on applications by prospective owners and realtors. These difficulties highlight administrative deficiencies of the programs and do not necessarily invalidate the concept of subsidizing the purchase of residences by low-income families. Nationwide, the repossession rate between 1968 and 1972 for "235" subsidized dwellings was 6.34 percent, a figure that compares favorably with unsubsidized mortgage experience. The administrator of Alabama's program, Jon Will Pitts, has written, "Our record with this program, in my opinion, lays to rest for all time the fear that many banking institutions had that long term mortgage financing for minority families in Alabama was a high risk venture" (unpublished circular letter No. 73-6, HUD, July 3, 1973). The program was terminated during the second term of the Nixon administration.

He was a blue-collar worker in a manufacturing plant, where he earned $120 a week. He was currently employed, but he had experienced more than five weeks of unemployment during the previous year. He had not participated in a government training or poverty program.

He believed that conditions, both for himself and for Detroit Blacks generally, had improved during the previous five years. He was also hopeful that Blacks would someday have everything the White man had.

Prospects for the Future

The violent episodes of the 1960s may have been preambles to intense and continuing warfare. Tom Hayden has predicted, "The conditions slowly are being created for an American form of guerrilla warfare based in the slums" (1967, p. 69). Marxist revolutionaries feel that the class composition of Blacks and Chicanos—which is largely proletarian—puts them in a position to detonate the entire working class.

Further intensification of racism and the polarization of the United States into White and Black may be an accurate prediction. "The key danger," Kenneth B. Clark has written, "is the possibility that America has permitted the cancer of racism to spread so far that present available remedies can be only palliative" (1967, p. 254).

Some observers, however, are not utterly pessimistic about the future. They emphasize the positive consequences of social conflict, correctly maintaining that, once relations have been established through conflict, other types of relations are likely to follow. Indeed, even the bloodiest wars have cross-fertilized previously unrelated cultures and brought about relations where none existed before.

At the level of interpersonal relations, child psychologists report that conflict is often one way in which people engage in relationships (Coser 1956, p. 8). After first quarreling over a toy, children who once were strangers may then begin to cooperate with each other. A child, having been tested in a conflict situation, can now become a playmate. Adult behavior offers many similar illustrations. Hostile interaction may lead to subsequent friendly interaction, conflict being a means of "testing" and "knowing" the previously unknown. "The stranger may become familiar through one's struggle with him" (Coser, 1956, p. 8), because struggle enables combatants to know more about each other (if they do not destroy each other first). Attitudes are not likely to change when one individual is in a situation in which he cannot add to or correct information about others. William Blake has expressed the idea:

> I was angry with my friend;
> I told my wrath, my wrath did end.
> I was angry with my foe;
> I told it not; my wrath did grow.

In sum, it is true that tranquillity breeds boredom and a corresponding desire for excitement, but it is also true that people grow tired of conflict. An ebb and flow of conflict and tranquillity underlies the many accommodations that can be cited in history. Accommodations tend to be unstable, however, and any development that shifts the balance of power usually results in renewed conflict.

Overview

The urban riots of the 1960s have been inaccurately interpreted as a symptom of modern times, uniquely American and racial in origin. An examination of the evidence makes it clear, however, that riots, hysterias, and revolts have occurred throughout the world both in modern and in ancient times. Most riots have resulted from causes other than racial or ethnic factors.

Why do riots and rebellions occur? How do intergroup relations figure in them? Seven theoretical perspectives offer a partial answer:

First, riots and rebellions are forms of collective behavior. They have certain features in common with lynchings, panics, and hysterias. Some scholars believe that collective behavior in a riot or a lynching follows a definite pattern. Certain key determinants affect the development: structural conduciveness, the intensification of structural strains, the spread of a hostile belief, environmental factors, a precipitating event, and mobilization of action. Social controls, however, overarch the entire sequence.

Second, the urbanization process that has changed much of the world has also created a social climate conducive to rioting. Social relations increasingly tend to be impersonal and segmental. As facilities in the crowded cities become overtaxed, frustrated residents and migrants began to blame the government or scapegoats.

Third, collective behavior has a social-psychological dimension. When there is a great deal of change, dissonance is widespread, for the old categories that guide interaction are no longer appropriate. There is more conflict because there is more change.

Fourth, the concept of status consistency (and status inconsistency) helps to explain still another dimension of the dissonance that can lead to hostile outbursts. A number of important studies indicate that status inconsistency can lead to stressful individual and group situations.

Fifth, militancy, as in the riots of the 1960s, may have been the beginning of an all-out global war based upon color. Or these riots may have been desperate flurries before a relatively peaceful period of accommodation.

Sixth is revolution; an analysis of several examples indicates that a revolution is most likely to occur after a long period of improvement, a sharp rise in expectations, and subsequent frustration. In the United States the presence of intergroup tensions may actually have prevented revolution from occurring. Frustrated individuals of the same socioeconomic status often have been unable to unite because of group antipathies.

Seventh is social control. The adequacy of social control must be considered along with relative deprivation, status inconsistency, and resulting frustrations in formulating a satisfactory explanation of collective behavior. Lessened fear of retribution increases the likelihood of violent collective response.

Two aspects of collective behavior are sometimes overlooked: the excitement associated with the event and the normative character of the event. What of the costs? The economic costs of the riots of the 1960s were staggering. Generally, they were not borne by the rioters, primarily because they tended not to be owners of property. As for the loss of life, most who died were minority members. The clashes occurred between law-enforcement personnel and minority members, not between civilian populations.

Some observers are not utterly pessimistic about the future. They base their expectations on the known fact that conflict can open up relations where none existed before. People do grow tired of conflict and seek accommodations with the adversary; that is, if the two do not destroy each other first.

For Further Reading

Many of the items among the references cited may be considered as recommended reading as well.

Carmichael, Stokley, and Charles V. Hamilton. *Black Power: The Politics of Liberation in America.* New York: Random House, 1967.

Coser, Lewis. *The Functions of Social Conflict.* New York: Free Press, 1956.

Davies, James Chowning (ed.). *When Men Revolt and Why: A Reader in Political Violence and Revolution.* New York: Free Press, 1971.

Grier, William H., and Price M. Cobbs. *Black Rage.* New York: Basic Books, 1968.

Hoffer, Eric. *The True Believer.* New York: Harper & Row, 1951.

Lomax, Louis. *The Negro Revolt.* New York: Harper & Row, 1962.

Skolnick, Jerome H. *The Politics of Protest: A Task Force Report Submitted to the National Commission on the Causes and Preventions of Violence.* New York: Simon & Schuster, 1969.

Smelser, Neil J. *Theory of Collective Behavior.* New York: Free Press, 1962.

Thompson, Edgar T., and Everett C. Hughes (eds.). *Race: Individual and Collective Behavior.* New York: Free Press, 1958.

Waskow, Arthur I. *From Race Riot to Sit In: 1919 and the 1960s.* Garden City, N.Y.: Doubleday Anchor, 1967.

Weller, Jack M., and E. L. Quarantelli. "Neglected Characteristics of Collective Behavior," *American Journal of Sociology,* 79 (November 1973). Pp. 665–685.

WAR BEHIND WALLS

EDWARD BUNKER

Edward Bunker is a White convict in San Quentin penitentiary. He has written a frightening piece—frightening because it describes a place where individuals are beaten or even killed on the basis of skin color alone. Here a White man may die because one too many Black men has died in prior fights. Such a killing will even the score, at least for the moment. If the other side of the tally sheet is unequal, a Black man or a Chicano will be killed. The personal characteristics of an individual count for little in choosing a target. What is important is skin color, which, like family name, identifies a person as a member of a tribe. Indeed, what is described here is akin to tribal warfare between ancient peoples or feuds between families in folk cultures.

Perhaps that is what is frightening about the article. Bunker has written a commentary on prisons in the United States, but he also has written a commentary on **Homo sapiens**. It is a description of one of the futures open to the species.

I'm white and I'm a convict, and this story is written from that view. Though I've tried to be dispassionate, I see that bias creeps in, for I'm involved and threatened by the violence, and yet I believe that every word tries to be true and honest. Some things have been written in less than complete detail to avoid murder charges being filed against anyone.

In San Quentin there is so much racial paranoia that provocation is unnecessary to incite the violence. Almost any excuse is enough to start the killing. So it was that the prison's last epidemic (as opposed to the routine stabbings) began with events just slightly related to race.

The 700 inmates of the East cellblock straggled back from the messhall after the evening meal. The five tiers were crowded. Some men waited near their cells for lockup. Others roamed, wagered cigarettes on the NCAA basketball finals, which would be broadcast over the cell earphones, or tried to hustle a bindle of heroin, a tab of acid, a quart of homebrew, or anything that would soften the edges of reality during the long night. A humming roar of noise hung over everything, a sound so common and pervasive in the cellhouse that it went unnoticed by those accustomed to it, the kind of sound that attracts attention when it stops or the rhythm changes.

Tonight the rhythm changed. From the fourth tier came the thud and grunt of struggling bodies. Convicts nearby froze and turned, wary as animals at a sharp sound. Others, on tiers above and below, craned their necks to see what was going on. Tension spread like electricity through connected wires. Men forty yards away knew within seconds that something had happened.

The gunrail guard, his khaki uniform (rather than the usual green worsted) indicating a rookie, was drawn to the sudden jumble of motion. He saw something. His whistle bleated, repeated itself, amputated the last vestige of doubt that someone was being stabbed, for San Quentin convicts long ago gave up fist-fighting to settle disputes. If it's not worth killing about, forget it, for if you punch someone in the mouth they're liable to come back later with a knife. Now silence fell, except for the scrape of running feet. More than one man was breaking through the crowd to get away. The guard leveled his rifle, but was unable to shoot into the press of bodies. He tried to follow along the gunrail, whistle still screaming accusation, but his quarry disappeared down the stairs. Guards on the cellblock floor failed to arrive before the assailants got away.

Someone had been stabbed. The question was: white or black? And then: was the stabbing across racial lines? If a white had stabbed another white, or a black another black, the incident would end with the participants and their cohorts. But if a black had stabbed a white, or vice versa, there was no telling what might happen. Mexicans make up 13 per cent of the convict population, and many are quick with knives, but usually it's on another Mexican; and even if it does cross racial lines it hasn't, as yet, resulted in a general war.

The first rumor had black against black.

Four blacks appeared on the floor, pushing a flatbed handcart used to move laundry hampers and metal trash barrels. Now it carried a "brother" being rushed toward the hospital. He was on his back, legs drawn up, denim jacket open; a red stain spread across his white T-shirt. The blacks who pushed the cart would have let a white man die, and a white convict who gave aid to a black (unless the white was assigned to the hospital) was ostracized by other whites, if not attacked. On the gallery of tiers above, hundreds of convicts watched the exiting group. Rumor now was that he'd been stabbed and thrown from the tier, but that was hard to believe. His head was raised. He was alert. Nothing seemed broken. The human body breaks when it drops thirty feet to concrete.

Extra guards rushed into the building. The public address speaker blared: "Mandatory lockup! All inmates lock up!"

The Watch Lieutenant began questioning inmates with cells near where the incident had occurred. While the officials tried to find out what had happened, the convicts already knew. The tier workers carried the word while making their rounds selling grilled cheese sandwiches (two for a pack of cigarettes) or delivering outfits and narcotics. Two Chicanos had kept lookout while a third Chicano stabbed the black. The anger had commenced in the education building where there had been an exchange of stares, then sneers, and finally hot words. Both assailant and victim came from worlds where it was impossible to conceive, much less articulate, the senselessness of murder arising from locked stares and nothing more.

When word got around that it was Chicano and black, most whites relaxed, uninvolved and glad about it. Some especially militant blacks conspired to retaliate: a brother had been hit and revenge was required. Chicanos recognized the possibility of trouble and readied themselves. Black tier tenders delivered knives from mattresses, ventilators, and drainpipes. Chicano cellblock workers did the same. (Despite repeated searches of the sprawling prison by an elite squad of half a dozen guards with special equipment, any convict wanting a knife can have one in minutes.) No more than ten on each side actually armed themselves, taping large and crudely honed (but deadly) knives to forearm, easy to jerk from a sleeve, or poked a hole in the bottom of pants pocket so the blade rested on a bare thigh and the handle was hidden. It could be drawn in an instant. As in the Wild West, a quick draw sometimes decides who lives.

The prison slept without anticipating that the match was set to the tinder of black hate for Whitey, and that the ensuing flame would continue week after week: stabbings and murders, attack and retaliation, ending only through attrition. Indeed, it isn't over now, not really.

The Yard's Territorial Imperative

Two giant messhalls feed the prisoners. One has sections with murals of California history on the walls, as if it were a high-school cafeteria rather than the feeding place of robbers, rapists and murderers, drug addicts and child molesters. Both messhalls together are unequal to the task of feeding everyone at the same time, so the feeding is in running shifts. The North and West cellblocks, which are honor units, begin breakfast at 6:40 in the morning, and when the prisoners are finished they can go back to the cellblocks or into the yard.

The yard is half again the size of a football field. The immense faded-green cellblocks wall the yard on three sides, holding out the sun until it rises high. The asphalt paving is pitted by decades of being hosed clean with water from the Bay. A high, corrugated weather shed without walls covers half the yard, sheltering prisoners from the frequent rain and the shit of circling seagulls. The shed's roof is marked from bullet holes of warning shots fired upward.

By 7:30 the East and South cellblocks finish breakfast. The yard fills with denimed convicts streaming from the messhalls. The gate from the yard to the rest of the prison's walled areas—shops, factories, and education department— remains closed until 7:50. Just before the gate opens, two thousand convicts fill the yard.

In recent years the races have segregated themselves. Along the North cellblock wall is the ghetto, where the blacks congregate. Thirty yards from the wall is a vague territorial line, unmarked and shifting. When there is no high racial tension (some always exists) the blacks leave their area to go to the canteen or take care of other business. Mexicans and whites have the rest of the yard, but cliques and gangs are commonly found in certain areas, where an individual can seek out his friends when the yard is crowded. In the messhall, Anglo and Mexican eat together, but blacks have again segregated themselves. The mingling of white and Mexican doesn't mean that all Mexicans are friendly to all Anglos, or vice versa, but they are generally closer to each other than either is to blacks.

The morning following the East cellblock stabbing, the yard was silent. The usual flux of movement was also missing. Three hundred blacks stood balefully near the North cellblock staring at the Mexicans, about one hundred of whom were gathered under the shed to the right of the blacks. Another hundred Mexicans stood facing the blacks across thirty yards of empty asphalt. Almost all whites stayed back. Among these were two dozen young Nazis and half that many Hells Angels and sycophants of the motorcycle gang. Twenty or more whites were sprinkled among the Chicanos, ready to back "homeboys" or close friends. One clique of about a dozen whites stood conspicuously against the East cellblock wall. In the last black-versus-white war they had carried the brunt of the killing, and had notched numerous other prison stabbings and murders. It was the strongest white clique, but its numbers in the general population had been depleted by officials locking them up in segregation. Though violent, the clique was not especially racist; that is, it would not *start* a race war. But it had many Chicano friends, and when it had almost had trouble with a larger Mexican clique, other Mexicans had sided with the white clique. Now these Mexicans were in the forefront, facing the blacks.

Guards, too, were aware of the volatile situation. Half a dozen with rifles and a sergeant with an antiquated but effective Thompson submachine gun poised on the gunrail twenty feet above the ground. Most were lined up on the blacks (blacks had killed three guards and stabbed another dozen in other California prisons during the preceding year), but one black guard was conspicuously lined up on the Mexicans. Such was the situation in San Quentin.

The staredown went on for ten minutes while the messhalls continued to disgorge prisoners into the yard, swelling the ranks. The riflemen precluded an open riot. Then, from the sidelines, a black and Chicano appeared. They were friends. The black was a prizefighter so outclassing everyone in the prison that nobody would dare to fight him. He was also a dope fiend and disregarded racial lines to satisfy his vice. He was not known as a militant, though some suspected him of undercover agitation. The Chicano was leader of a clique of fifteen, whose members stood among the Mexicans under the shed. When the pair reached the center of the empty asphalt, the black prizefighter motioned toward the blacks ganged near the wall. Two came forward. One's head was shaved and oiled so that it glistened in the wan morning light. He was high among the Black Muslims. The other wore tiny Ben Franklin glasses and a bushy Afro. Both were tall and slender.

The quartet stood in a tight circle. The blacks spoke, gestured, tense with ire and accusation. The Chicano took over, held the floor, and the conversation went on while the yard gate was opened and the steam whistle blew the morning work call. Half the convicts in the yard streamed out, glad to avoid possible trouble. The warriors on each side remained. So did the riflemen, allowing the conference to go on because it might settle the incident without further bloodshed.

The conference broke up. The Mexican stalked back to his followers, said something and gestured toward the gate. His clique left the yard. The black spokesmen went to the throng along the North cellblock. A dozen blacks crowded tight around them, listening to what was said.

The public address system blared an order to clear the yard.

The confrontation broke apart, became clots of walking men. In minutes the yard was empty except for a few convicts with long-handled dustpans and small brooms sweeping up orange peels from the breakfast ration. Rumor had it that the trouble had been avoided. No whites knew what was said. Days later the truth was revealed. The Mexican clique leader had disowned the assailant, claiming he was a Nazi, not a Chicano; hence no trouble between brown and black. . . .

While the trouble was brewing between Chicano and black at the school building, another fuse was being lighted elsewhere. Two burly whites with reputations as brawlers had swindled a black for twenty papers of heroin, giving him a phony $100 bill. An hour after the confrontation in the yard, the swindled black and his friends trapped the two whites on a stairway in the South cellblock and began swinging knives. The whites, both young and strong, managed to fight off being killed, but they were badly carved up and hospitalized.

The leading white clique knew about the burn, knew what lay behind the stabbing, and judged that it was justice. The knifing was over narcotics, not race. But to the prison's hate-filled young blacks, all events involve race. Nothing occurs unrefracted through racialist lenses, often delusional.

A Religious Doctrine of Hate

The phenomenon of enraged blacks existed in prison long before anyone dreamed of Detroit, Watts, or the hot summers of the late Sixties. Indeed, both Malcolm X and Eldridge Cleaver first experienced racial militance in prison. But what is relatively new and what increases racial polarization in prison beyond conciliation is the mutative leap in black militant rhetoric. This rhetoric is heard within the prison walls by unsophisticated minds and gives those blacks who already hate all whites a rationale for murder. Such a black takes "off the pig" and "ten for one" as a license. He can find murder to be the means of assuming dignity in his own eyes, in having identity. Blacks have taken to killing prison guards, without any hope of getting away, almost as if seeking martyrdom—as a form of suicide.

Everyone understands that blacks have been brutalized by generations of institutionalized racism, and recently by inertia and indifference. What the sympathetic fail to grasp is that sometimes the psychological truncation is so great that it cannot be repaired. Nothing is left but hate. They have no desire—no motivation—for anything except revenge and license for whatever they desire. Additionally, they've decided that they are political prisoners. The black realizes that he has committed a crime, or has acted against the statutes. However, the claim of "political prisoner" comes from the argument that he was formed by a corrupt system, that his acts are a result thereof, and therefore he cannot be held responsible. Secondarily, he feels that he has never been a part of this system, but is still in slavery, and consequently the white laws do not apply to him. Such personalities are often found in prison, where the flower of black racism is blossoming, virulent and paranoid. Many white convicts are equally dangerous and intractable, but they at least intellectually accept that their acts are wrong. And even white racists recognize that their attitudes are no longer approved, to be shouted, whereas blacks are open in their racism. The catechism of Elijah Muhammad's Black Muslims that all whites are "beasts" that Moses raised on their hind legs and led from the caves has wide following in prison. Such doctrines seem absurd, but blacks with third-grade educations and Baptist parents who inculcated them with an inability to function without some religion believe this doctrine as zealously as devout Catholics believe in the Immaculate Conception. Elijah allows them to have God and hate Whitey too. Black Muslims, however, incite no violence. Separatist and racist, the cult eschews violence except in self-defense. Muslims follow a moral code John Calvin would have approved.

Other blacks, particularly the Panthers, have attained a political consciousness transcending racism. They realize it isn't white convicts who oppress them. They will war for their kind, but they do so with misgivings, just as many white warriors do, knowing their enemy is elsewhere. But race relations in California prisons have reached such an impasse that politically aware blacks make no attempt to reach white convicts, a potentially rich vein of revolutionaries; and white convicts, all too aware that guards often seize writings proclaiming white genocide and the joys of bayoneting a pregnant white woman, see all blacks as animals, a direct threat.

The Space between Races

Such was the general situation when the Mexican stabbed the black in the East cellblock (he wasn't hurt bad and immediately informed on his assailant) and the two whites were stabbed over the heroin swindle.

Noon came, and again the yard was filled with convicts. Again there was the open space between races. This time whites faced blacks and a few Mexicans stood with the whites. The stabbing of the whites was well known, but the underlying cause was less well known. All blacks and most whites were unaware that the warrior whites had decided to let the matter drop.

Movement was turgid, sound subdued. The lunch hour was passing. Suddenly a dozen guards rushed through the yard toward the North cellblock. Something had happened there, or on Death Row, which is over the North cellblock. At the appearance of the guards, even the slow movement ceased. All that moved were the seagulls overhead. The silence became complete. Moments later four white convicts rushed from the cellblock, carrying a man on a litter. A guard ran along beside them. As the retinue crossed through the white crowd, convicts walked alongside and asked what had happened. The wounded man had been napping in his cell (doors in the North cellblock are left unlocked) and one or two blacks had crept in and stabbed him while he slept. He didn't know who they were. He'd been selected because he was white and asleep.

On the yard both sides pulled back into tighter ranks. The guards overhead tightened their grips on rifles. A voice cried out in rage: "Goddamn fuckin' niggers." A voice yelled back: "Fuck you, honky!"

Some blacks thought of rushing the whites. The whites were ready. So were the riflemen overhead. Nothing came of it. The white fury was as yet uncommitted to act. Though numerically superior (50 per cent of the population to 35 per cent for blacks) whites are less united along racial lines. Unlike blacks, they cannot believe all whites are their brothers. There'd be nobody against whom they could compete if they believed that way. Indignation swirled, but it hadn't decided to lash outward. The white who'd been stabbed in the North cellblock was just an average convict, not someone special. Trouble might have subsided if that had been it.

But an hour later a fifty-year-old white convict went up the stairs into an old building housing two classrooms. He was being transferred and wanted to say goodbye to a teacher. Three blacks were waiting at the top of the stairs. They knocked the man down and began stabbing him. They'd never seen him before. They'd been waiting for any white. The teacher, hearing the sounds of struggle, opened the door, saw what was happening, and began blowing his whistle. Guards nearby rushed toward the scene, caught the blacks running out the stairway door. As they were led away, they yelled: "Power to the people!" The elderly white convict was slightly wounded.

The order came to lock the prison down. Each department was released separately, the convicts filtered back to the cellhouses in groups that could be supervised. Paranoia ran high, for on the narrow tiers it was impossible to keep the races apart. Who could know when, or if, the long shivs would be pulled. Men without friends, those trying to quietly serve a term and get out, were in the worst predicament. They had no allies. Warriors stayed together, knew many of their opposition, suspected others from hairstyle, mannerism, and association. Whites were indignant and afraid. Blacks were jubilant and afraid, though they waited to yell their joy until they were locked in their cells where their quips and laughter were anonymous.

Guards and freemen began a search of the prison that would continue for days and reveal hundreds of knives. Cellblocks were first. Personnel filed along the fifth tier without warning until two were before each cell. Riflemen behind them gave cover. Security bars were raised and convicts were ordered to come naked onto the tier. As soon as convicts on lower tiers knew what was happening, knives were thrown between the bars, sailing down to clatter on the floor of the bottom tier. Actually, it was unnecessary to discard the weapons, for the searchers were sadly out of physical shape, used to sitting on their asses. Before they'd finished two cells they were panting, unable to do more than perfunctorily raise a mattress. Many just walked into cells and sat down.

On each tier behind the cells is a narrow service passage with plumbing and electrical conduits. Convict electricians and plumbers have access to the passages. Guards found two dozen knives and three roofing hatchets in the East cellblock passageways. The arsenal belonged to whites because the plumber and electrician were white.

The huge cellhouses were silent and motionless as tombs during the evening. Beneath the silence the furies were gathering. It had gone too far to end. Whites had to make a showing. If there was no reprisal the blacks would stab and rip off whenever they had the whim. The decision was made by many individuals rather than collectively, just as the decision to stab was made individually among blacks.

The lockup continued the next day except for essential workers. The few members of the white clique and other white militants out of their cells managed to pass a few words on a grapevine. The idea came to wait to strike until the prison was back on normal routine.

No stabbings occurred on Wednesday. The lockup was too tight. Every convict out of his cell was searched several times during the course of the day. On Thursday the West cellblock returned to normal schedule. A few other workers and clerks were pulled from the breakfast lines and told to report to their assignments.

The associate warden called many inmates. He wanted to know the mood of the prison, the depth and intensity of the anger. But the particular associate warden is too hated, too out of communication, and those to whom he talked lacked prestige or influence in the yard. He appointed a committee to "cool" the situation, but those on the committee were without respect among their peers, especially the blacks on it: the very fact that they'd talk to the "chief pig" closed them away from their brethren.

When the associate warden was holding interviews, the blacks struck again. A fifty-five-year-old semi-nut was coming up the back stairs in the South cellblock.

A prison character, he'd served twenty years and was a compulsive writ writer. He bothered nobody but the authorities. He gave coffee and tobacco to anyone who came to his cell and asked. He was particularly generous to blacks, mainly because they had less and did more asking. Four of these waited on the stairs. They jumped him, stabbed him in the face and neck with a fork bent so that two prongs jutted out. The wounds were superficial. Two attackers were caught immediately. Two got away, but thereafter refused to come out of their cells at mealtime through fear of retaliation. One hid under the bed. When he was locked in segregation he bellowed about the "honky we downed."

A black prison administrator meanwhile summoned three militant white leaders. He wanted them to assure him nothing more would happen. Two stood silent, heads down, preferring to say nothing. The third flushed, stuttered: "Five whites have been downed, old men and strays who didn't do nothin' to nobody. Next they'll want us to pluck our eyebrows and get a black jocker. Me, I'm not promising anything."

The whites' plan of waiting for normal routine was gaining acceptance as it was discussed. Nazis and Hells Angels backed away, claiming that none of their brothers had been hit and they would stay on the sidelines until that happened.

The blacks were still on the offensive, not waiting for Whitey to strike back. A few workers were out of their cells in the East cellblock, sweeping and mopping. Three blacks, also unlocked for chores, were instead roaming the tiers, looking for a victim. Two had been involved in the murder of a white tier tender in 1969.

On the fifth tier a white was standing outside a cell. The tier was empty. The white was an old-line convict and knew the score. When the blacks started toward him, the white knew what was happening. Luckily, the men in the cell before which he stood had a twenty-inch shiv with them. They handed it out. The blacks saw what happened and turned away. It was not exactly cowardice. Even if they killed him, he would certainly wound one of them, and wounds would get them caught.

On the fourth tier, another white, a motor-cycle rider, was in front of a cell, trying to buy a tab of acid. He worked in the messhall scullery and had just gotten off duty. The cell he stood before was in the center of the tier. Two blacks came toward him from the rear. The third black walked along the tier below and climbed up from the front. The white was caught between them. He saw them and sensed danger, for he backed up against the rail, refusing to turn his back. He spread his arms, resting his hands on the rail and leaning back, as if he was looking toward the tier above. He was probably trying to hide any evidence of fear. A smart convict or a warrior, black or white, would have climbed up or down without hesitation. This man was insufficiently afraid to save his life. The black from the front arrived first. He pulled a knife and rushed the last ten feet. The white threw up his hands. The knife went between them and plunged into his chest. The blacks from the rear arrived an instant later. One knifed the man in the back. The biggest of the trio grabbed him from behind, pinned his arms. The first black stabbed at his throat. The blade entered just above the collarbone, drove down through his lungs and punctured his heart. He continued struggling, but he was already dead. The second black with a knife kept stabbing him. There were no screams, just agonized grunts and gasps—and the horrifying sound of tearing flesh. Mirrors jutted from cells along the tier, periscopes of men trying to see what was going on. Whites began yelling and rattling the bars to drive off the killers. They were watching a murder and unable to do anything. Questions were yelled from other tiers: "Dennis! What's happening?" Answer: "Them fuckin' niggers downed a white dude." A black voice: "Gonna get all you honky mother-fuckers!"

The blacks ran to the rear, down the stairs. A score of guards arrived on the run. Only six blacks were out of their cells. All were taken into custody for investigation. A bloody knife was found beneath a pile of dirty clothes at the back of the cellblock.

In an hour, the associate warden ordered the blacks released, saying there was no evidence they'd done it nor even that any blacks had done it. He instead ordered nine whites locked up, friends of the victim who also worked in the kitchen. The logic was that they might try to retaliate. Meanwhile, guards had found blood on the shoes of three blacks, and they'd told conflicting stories when questioned. The associate warden allowed them to be kept locked up.

Inmates in cells near the murder were questioned. Whether any talked in the privacy of an office is known only to officials, but none will testify in a courtroom, a fact evidenced by the months that have passed without an indictment.

During the afternoon the word got out that white guards would look the other way when whites struck back. Bias was long established, but outright license was something new. The unholy alliance of white guards and convicts was not mutual love but shared hatred. Until recent years, most guards have been evenhanded in dealing with convicts. Events in Soledad are what changed things. Three guards were killed within a year, all by blacks; a dozen others were stabbed.

A Paranoiac Tension

The senseless murder in the East cellblock changed the minds of whites about waiting for revenge until the prison was opened. During the afternoon, blacks yelled: "Kill them honkies! The pigs got Brother Leroy and J. T., jive-ass mother-fuckers!"

Whites were quiet, saying nothing. When the slow unlock for supper began, one tier at a time, faces showed how things were going. Groups of blacks were laughing and joking. Whites were glum, brooding.

Whistles suddenly bleated as the fifth tier was unlocked. When the guards arrived, they found two blacks in their cell, lying in their blood. One walked out, seriously wounded. The other was half under the bed, spuming blood from his mouth with each breath, indicating a punctured lung. A gunrail guard had four whites covered, and blacks on the tier were pointing them out. Most guards were uninterested in investigating what had happened. The victims lived. They claimed that two whites had started stabbing them the moment the doors were opened; and that two other whites had held the other blacks at bay. The whites claimed that they were attacked and had taken the knives from the blacks.

Forty-eight hours passed without a stabbing. The lockup separated the antagonists. The weekend approached. Officials discussed return to normal. Kitchen workers were already on fairly regular routine. The kitchen has a locker room and shower area isolated from the rest of the kitchen. To get to it, one must go up a very narrow, concrete-walled stairway. More than one unsolved murder has occurred in this locker room area, the last one a stool pigeon whose jugular was literally torn from his throat. A guard supervises the shower room, but duties sometimes take him elsewhere.

On Saturday morning, half a dozen whites filed up the stairs, each with a knife in his belt. Five blacks were in the room, shaving, showering, rinsing their hands, taking a piss. One saw the attack and ran through a door into a wire enclosure, bracing himself and holding the door closed. The other four blacks had nowhere to go. In seconds, blood was splattering the walls. Blacks were running in circles, bumping into each other, followed by the knives. One black lowered his head and charged at the narrow entrance to the stairs. Two Hells Angels were waiting. He got past them, but when he stumbled out he was wounded several times and a shiv was hanging from his buttocks. He rushed into the kitchen proper where a sergeant was eating a pilfered sandwich. "I'm hit," he said, T-shirt bloody. The sergeant answered: "You ain't hurt that bad, boy. Stand off there until I get finished."

The wounded black who got away saved the lives of the others. The whites, believing the alarm was given, fled before finishing off the other three blacks. One died, his spinal column severed. He went into a coma and never came out of it.

The kitchen sergeant's attitude mirrored the investigation. The victims were never shown photos to identify. Higher officials were crippled by the indifference, if not recalcitrance, of their subordinates, who were not even making an attempt to apprehend anyone.

"Snitch" letters bypassed the guard level to the warden. He ordered several whites locked up. Three were innocent. One of them had been locked in his own cell during the attack. The warden apparently didn't care; he wanted something to show Sacramento.

Blacks stopped laughing. Usually they jump lines, crowd in, bump into someone, and refuse the simple amenity of excusing themselves. Now, suddenly, everyone was respectful of each other—but blacks and whites who'd been friends, some since childhood, passed without speaking, or merely nodded recognition, eyes hard. No more friendships existed across racial lines.

A fistfight broke out between three whites and four blacks on the morning following the kitchen attack. Whistles shrilled; a rifle went off. Nobody was hurt, but more men were locked in segregation. Tension remained near general paranoia. In a world absolutely integrated, each cell identical with each other, each man eating the same food and wearing the same clothes, the race hatred was malevolent and intractable. Nor was there a sanctuary where any man could relax. Even the cells were dangerous. A ten-ounce coffee jar filled with gasoline could be hurled against the bars and a match thrown on it. This had happened before. Going to eat, the prisoners were in crowds. A group of whites or blacks might be gathered in a doorway or on a stair landing. A man of the opposite color had to pass between them to reach his cell. Nobody could know if it was an ambush. A white was attacked in precisely such a setting; he ducked the knife blow and ran. Ten minutes later, in another cellblock, a white lunged at a black, but exposed his knife before he was in range. The black saw it and bolted down the tier.

Convicts in the North cellblock reached a truce. No attacks would be made in the building. Outside the building it was open season. Neither side entirely believed the other (no white can speak for *every* white, nor any black for *every* black).

The associate warden's committee of inmates was allowed to roam the cellblocks at night, hopefully to talk to militants and end the war. One white used the unlock to take a shower. Three blacks trapped him in the showers; he was stabbed in the neck. Miraculously, he survived. (San Quentin's surgeons are probably the world's foremost experts on stab wounds. Many prisoners are saved who would certainly die from similar wounds outside.) Three black guards worked the cellblock that night. They protected the black attackers just as white guards protected whites.

The next day a friend of the latest victim surged into a crowd of blacks with a knife. They scattered. The rifleman fired a shot. He was caught with the knife.

Another Saturday arrived. No stabbings for three days. The prison was on regular schedule, including the weekend movie. One of the blacks involved in the shower stabbing was at the movie. When the lights went on and the crowd surged toward the exits, whites tried to stab him in the back. A black yelled a warning. The intended victim darted through the throng, slightly wounded, so slightly that he didn't go to the hospital.

Minutes later, a hundred blacks bunched under the weather shed, facing an equal number of whites lined up against the East cellblock wall. Chicanos and nonmilitants left the yard. Extra riflemen hurried into position.

And music blared very loud over the public address system.

Only two of the white clique were still on the mainline. The rest were in segregation. Tired of the confrontations leading to nothing, the two whites walked toward the blacks, as if going for a drink of water at a fountain amid them. They reached the fountain and turned, as if drinking. One small black eased forward through the crowd. Half a dozen others moved with him. The whites suddenly turned, one with a roofing hatchet, the other with a shiv, challenging the blacks. The blacks froze. The one who'd been creeping up darted back through the crowd, throwing a knife away, frightened both by the challenge and the staccato clacking of rifle bullets being levered into firing chambers above. Ground guards closed in. The whites, now exposed, turned back to their comrades, many of whom had come off the wall when it looked as if a brawl was starting. A black guard kept one of the two whites in sight, picked him from the crowd, and got the knife. The other white got rid of the hatchet.

A huge, 350-pound black walked beside the guards, pointing out which whites should be searched. He was later locked up for his own protection.

Once more the convicts were locked in their cells. Again the administration returned to normal schedule. Two months passed without a racial stabbing, a hundred men still segregated; others have been transferred. Nobody has been indicted for any of the stabbings or murders. Marin County wants no San Quentin convicts in its courtroom, especially when convictions are hard to obtain. For every convict who'll testify for the prosecution, fifty will testify for the defense.

Nothing has been resolved. The races are more estranged than ever. Weapons are stockpiled. Anyone who talks moderation is in danger of being killed as a "Tom" or a "nigger lover." Men who were moderate are now filled with loathing and hate. Blacks are more certain that all whites are racists bent on genocide, and whites see all blacks as uncivilized brutes. Something will ignite another race war in a week, a month, or six months—and nobody can explain what either side will gain. In California prisons it's too late for rapprochement between races. Could it be a precursor for society as a whole?

11

Altering Intergroup Relations

The problem of the twentieth century is the problem of the color line.

—W. E. B. DuBois, Pan-African Conference, London, 1900

Practically every recent textbook on social problems has included a major section devoted to intergroup relations. There are several reasons.[1] First, there is a widespread conviction that discrimination against minorities abridges human rights and is therefore morally wrong. In social-science literature this conviction is called the *humanitarian* (or ethical) criterion for identifying social problems. Second, discrimination is now recognized as having high social and economic costs: the *utilitarian* criterion. Third, it is also recognized that intergroup tensions can cause society to malfunction seriously: the *functional* criterion. Finally, prejudice and discrimination are not consonant with other important values in American society: the *social-deviance* criterion. Each of these considerations, in varying degrees of importance, underlies the widespread concern about this issue.

[1] See Bernard (1957) and R. R. Bell (1971).

Learning How To Alter Intergroup Relations

Research can be frustratingly slow—so slow that it sometimes requires years to collect full and accurate information on a topic. Many intergroup problems, however, demand immediate attention. Then, one way that social scientists can make useful contributions is through evaluative research. Sometimes they actually participate in the programs that they are evaluating. As a project develops, they assess each stage. They may suggest modifications to administrators, in the light of new inputs, and then evaluate the effect of each change. Such continuous assessment can contribute to the success of the program itself, as well as increasing general understanding of intergroup relations.

This approach to evaluation is somewhat akin to constructing a theory. We begin by formulating the best theory possible with existing evidence. The theory is then formalized, in order to ascertain its implications, which are checked against new data (Blalock, 1969). In contrast to the classical notion of theory construction, however, evaluative research may involve the evaluator in the action. He checks out the implications of his theory on the job and consciously risks contaminating the data in order to obtain continuous feedback. To keep the evaluation honest, a careful researcher attempts also to assess the impact of "contamination." Evaluative research, following a model developed by Daniel Stuffelbeam (1967), involves four generalized stages—*context, input, process,* and *product.*

Context evaluation involves description of the setting in which changes are to occur, determination of unmet needs in that setting, and analysis of the problems that underlie those needs. It also involves establishing "benchmarks" that will later be used to measure how much change has occurred. Context evaluation of a program designed to increase the number of minority members in the construction trades of a particular city, for example, would include careful documentation of the number of minority members presently employed, a breakdown of employment by specific occupational categories, a projection of employment statistics based upon representative minority participation in each category, and an analysis of mechanisms that hinder equal participation.

Input evaluation involves listing the relevant capabilities of the program, as well as strategies that might be employed. The procedure implies analysis of the components that might be manipulated in an action program. As an example, input evaluation of a program designed to upgrade minority housing in a particular city would involve describing possible resources: schools, banks, labor unions, religious organizations, civic clubs, political organizations, and so on.

Process evaluation is focused on the *procedures* that are actually employed in a particular program. Even if the program's objectives are attained, its later usefulness and its adoption elsewhere may depend less on proof of effectiveness than on knowledge of what was done to develop and to secure acceptance of the program. Process evaluation answers the question *How* were changes brought about?

Product evaluation answers the questions *What* changes took place? and *How much* change took place? It involves, first, giving operational definitions of a program's objectives, which permit measurement (quantitative) of any changes that may occur. Second, it deals with the extent to which the program's objectives have been attained; if unanticipated change occurs, this change too is evaluated.

This approach to evaluation is appropriate for many projects that focus on intergroup problems. Much would be accomplished if only a fraction of the programs now underway were properly evaluated and the results made widely available. For several reasons—including a shortage of trained evaluators, smugness on the part of program administrators, and fear of careful evaluation, not to mention inadequate funding—such evaluation has not often occurred.

Similar Problems and Strategies in Other Substantive Areas

Knowledge about altering intergroup relations can be increased through the appropriate use of findings from research on related topics. A basic premise of this book is that relations among ethnic groups are not different in kind from relations among other kinds of groups. Three substantive areas of social science are particularly appropriate to intergroup relations: reference-group theory and research, organizational analysis, and diffusion research. Obviously, these three areas of inquiry do not exhaust the possibilities. Their inclusion here is primarily illustrative.

Each of the areas chosen has a well-developed literature that draws upon literally scores of studies. In the brief discussions that follow, a few important principles from these fields are presented and then applied to intergroup situations. The books and articles cited have been chosen to stimulate further specific studies in these areas.

Reference-Group Theory and Research

Even though the idea of reference groups is an old one, careful formulation of the idea and specific research on the topic dates only to the 1940s. Reference-group theory and research have great potential for understanding behavior change. We pointed out earlier (Chapter 2) that individual attitudes are connected with membership groups (and sometimes with nonmembership groups). This connection suggests that one way to change an individual's attitudes is to change the referents of those attitudes.

It is difficult if not impossible to *talk* people out of their prejudices. "A person convinced against his will," an old adage warns, "is of the same opinion still." That same prejudiced individual, however, just may begin to act in non-discriminating ways if he or she can identify with groups that do not discriminate against minorities. If the objective is to modify intergroup relations toward tolerant norms, situations can thus be structured so that prejudiced individuals will begin to identify positively with new reference groups (or referents). In restructured situations individuals tend to behave in a manner congruent with their perceptions of what a member of the significant group is like. They feel the need to be good church members, gentlemen, ladies, scholars, union members, law-abiding citizens. The rationale for such behavior is that an individual tends to accept new values in the process of strongly identifying with a new group.

Research has shown that the influence of *peers* and other referents can be an important determinant in such matters as vocational aspirations. Only a start has been made, however, in gathering systematic knowledge of the process that is involved when an individual substitutes one reference group for another or of how such behavior can be induced. The following strategies are drawn from reference-group theory (on an a priori basis): limiting a subject's contacts with members of the previous reference group, limiting or restricting communications with the previous reference group, discrediting the old reference group, enhancing the prestige of a new reference group, immersing the subject in the "culture" of a new reference group, application of sanctions consistent with the norms and values of the new reference group. Such techniques might be used to modify the behavior of individuals who are associated with hate organizations and the like.

Actually, reference-group theory is often used implicitly in everyday life. For example, parents seeking to minimize the influence of undesirable companions of their children may apply some of these strategies. But the strategies, as many parents learn, are not uniformly effective. Their application may, in fact, produce effects quite different from those intended; for example, a parent who tries to discredit a youngster's friends may actually make the friends seem more desirable than before.

Students who wish to read a detailed assessment of reference-group theory and research will find the work of Herbert Hyman and Eleanor Singer (1968) especially useful. J. A. C. Brown's *Techniques of Persuasion* (1967) is also quite good.

Organizational Analysis

Systematic study of organizations by sociologists dates from the work of Max Weber. Many additional studies have been conducted under the aegis of industrial engineering, management, industrial relations, political science, and educational administration. Two topics of concern in these studies are relevant to our interests in intergroup relations: organizational responses to change and human relations in organizations.

It is known that programs for implementing changes in social structures are more likely to endure than are those that focus only upon individual attitudes. Individual attitudes tend, over time, to become consonant with behavior that is required within a particular social system. Weber once noted that the mere regularity of certain events confers upon them a kind of "oughtness."

A strategy that focuses upon enlisting individuals who hold key positions in industry, unions, religious organizations, government, and the community will often be successful. Success is further ensured if the program culminates in revised policies, administrative procedures, or laws. For example, if the top management of a corporation and union officials can be induced to establish open hiring and promotion policies, then behavioral changes at lower levels often follow. Lower-level changes do not always occur, to be sure, for it is known that decisions at top levels of management can be ambushed at lower levels. A further commitment to a training program for middle- and lower-level supervisors might help to ensure the success of such a policy.

The desegregation of military organizations during the administration of President Harry S. Truman is a well-known example of a structural change that has profoundly affected intergroup relations. Truman's biographer, Merle Miller, has reported that he ordered the desegregation of the armed forces in 1945 against the advice and protests of almost every admiral and general, as well as of most of his civilian advisers. Today American military units maintain continuing programs of education in intergroup relations for their personnel. Education is thus used to supplement structural changes.

Readers who wish to explore the voluminous literature for findings and general principles on organizations that can be applied to intergroup relations will find the following references helpful:

Amitai Etzioni (ed.). *A Sociological Reader on Complex Organizations* (New York: Holt, Rinehart and Winston, 1969).

James G. March (ed.). *Handbook of Organizations* (Chicago: Rand McNally, 1965).

Herbert A. Shepherd. "Changing Interpersonal and Intergroup Relationships in Organizations." In James G. March (ed.). *Handbook of Organizations* (Chicago: Rand McNally, 1965). Pp. 1115–1143.

Additional materials can be obtained by consulting the articles listed under "Organizations" in the *International Encyclopedia of the Social Sciences* (1968) and by checking in various bibliographies under the following topics: human relations, union-management relations, management, administration (problem solving), and arbitration.

How can information on arbitration or union-management relations be useful in altering intergroup relations? Chiefly by providing tested strategies and methods. For example, a conflict between members of a minority community and a city's public-school board is probably similar in many respects to a labor dispute between a union and management. In order to achieve a fair and efficient solution, arbitrators often are brought into labor negotiations. Social scientists are sometimes brought into intergroup conflicts as problem solvers or as resource persons. (The social scientist is invited less frequently and usually has much less authority than does the labor negotiator, however.)

If social scientists can learn how effective arbitrators avert strikes and solve problems, presumably they themselves can act effectively in intergroup conflict situations. The following problem-solving strategy suggests one way to proceed:

> Union-management relations are often characterized by ingrained hostile stereotypes. In such cases both parties are likely to believe that conflict is unresolvable, not only because of their past experience with each other, but as an ideological conviction. Under these circumstances there is no motivation to move toward collaboration, and it may be impossible to bring the groups together with the third party to attempt restructuring. If there is to be any movement toward a problem-solving relationship, the effort must be initiated unilaterally and carried forward unilaterally for some time. The initiating party needs to understand win-lose dynamics[2] very well, to invent procedures which will prevent the sides from freezing into fixed positions. . . . (Shepherd, 1965, p. 1141)

In order to resolve conflicts that arise between labor and management, some industries maintain full-time arbitrators whose salaries are paid by both sides. In addition, the American Arbitration Association helps to arrange arbitration service for industry-labor clashes on an ad hoc basis. In order to break a deadlock, a third party is brought in to hear both sides of the dispute. Usually, the disputants agree in advance to abide by the decision of the arbitrator. Intergroup conflicts seldom have been resolved through formal third-party mediation, but this approach could well be a future development. (Scholars in business relations say that third-party arbitration is characteristic of "mature" phases of union-management relations.)

Diffusion Research

There are similarities between the ways in which people accept or reject innovations and the ways in which they respond to programs for altering intergroup relations. Social scientists working in our own society and abroad have learned a great deal about the ways in which innovations like the "new math" or improved farming techniques are diffused. They have isolated the factors that agents of change should take into account (Arensberg and Niehoff, 1965):

---

[2] The disputants may perceive an arbitration board's decision to be a victory, a loss, or a compromise (see Davey, 1972).

1. *Awareness of needs.* A target population's perceptions of its problems may not be the same as those of the agent of change. Unless the agent is able to convince members of the target population that there is a real need for change, apathy or even hostility is likely to be encountered.

2. *Interrelatedness of society.* Anthropologists and sociologists have repeatedly demonstrated that a change in one part of a social system will have consequences elsewhere in the system. Discrimination against minorities often seems ingrained because of functional connections with other parts of society—with the economy, status hierarchy, religion, and political structure. One effective way to deal with an intergroup problem, however, is to change another part of the social system (the economy, politics, or demography, and so on).

3. *Behavior and beliefs.* Successful agents of change usually try to avoid open conflict between innovations and traditional values or customs. "Ultimately they may replace the traditional beliefs," Conrad Arensberg and Arthur Niehoff counsel, "but, for the sake of acceptance, it is best that they do not contradict them openly at the outset" (1965, p. 84). Sometimes an agent of change can graft on to some acknowledged belief that, though it contradicts other beliefs, still exists with them in the society. The agent of change behaves somewhat as does a tribesman in a nonliterate society who, when accused of wrongdoing, cites some old proverb to justify what he has done. He pits one tradition against the other.

4. *Visibility.* An agent of change needs a highly visible "success" early in the game, especially if the target population is conservative or skeptical. He or she may view such success as an easy accomplishment, yet it may cause the audience's earlier skepticism to vanish. It may also have a multiplier effect, as the target population spreads news of the event.

5. *Participation of the people.* Some programs fail because the wrong individuals support them or because the right people are not brought in. Others fail because too few people learn how to carry on the necessary activities; when the agent of change leaves the community, the project soon falls apart. Only accurate information about the target population and a careful training program will prevent this result.

6. *Religion.* In some communities, especially rural ones, practically the only viable suprafamilial groups are religious organizations. Accordingly, successful agents of change often try to work with religious organizations when they introduce innovations.

Other characteristics of the diffusion process are relevant to the present topic. For example, diffusion studies have indicated what type of individual is most likely to adopt an innovation first and how he can best be reached with information about the idea. Other studies indicate the approximate length of time required for adoption to occur. The best available summary of these studies is Everett M. Rogers and F. Floyd Shoemaker, *Communication of Innovations: A Cross-Cultural Aprproach* (1971), which summarizes the research findings and provides supporting evidence for 103 generalizations about diffusion.

Specific Programs and Strategies

In the preceding section we have indicated that knowledge about changing intergroup relations can be extrapolated from related fields of inquiry. Clearly, the possibilities are great, but they have only begun to be explored. The major hazard in such an approach is the difficulty in determining whether or not situations are really similar. How similar, for example, are labor disputes and intergroup conflicts? Is it true that the new math and toleration can be diffused in an identical manner? No ready-made guideline is available to answer such questions.

We now turn to the programs and strategies that deal directly with intergroup problems. Some of the programs, like school desegregation, are widely known. Others have attracted far less attention. In fact, some methods seem to work best when they are unobtrusive.

School Desegregation

The use of public schools as a specific strategy for altering intergroup relations in the United States is one of the major developments of this century. Several considerations have been involved: The public-school population is a captive audience representing a cross section of the community. It includes children of labor, management, various religions, political parties, and so on. Activities in school are known to have an enormous impact on individual and group behavior. In the language of social science, students and teachers tend to become important referents. Segregationists have never been blind to this eventuality. That is why they have fought school desegregation so bitterly. When children from segregated communities participate in desegregated schools every day, basic behavioral changes are virtually inevitable.

Resistance to school desegregation has been most pronounced, according to the research of sociologist Beth E. Vanfossen, where the non-White population is highly concentrated and where the economic gap between the Whites and Blacks is great (Vanfossen, 1968, pp. 39–44). The fifteen socioeconomic variables that Vanfossen considered in her research and their correlations are presented in Table 8.

A massive literature has been devoted to the impact of desegregation upon scholastic achievement, personality development, and job attainment. Most investigations have reported favorable results. According to one report sponsored by the U.S. Commission on Civil Rights:

> Disadvantaged Negro children generally perform at higher levels if they have been in school with whites for some time, regardless of the present social class level of their classmates. They perform at even higher levels if, instead of simply being in schools with whites whose family background is the same as theirs, they are in schools where the students are from families of higher educational background.

TABLE 8 VARIABLES RELATED TO RESISTANCE TO DESEGREGATION IN THE SOUTH

Correlation Coefficients, Fifteen Socioeconomic Variables, Southern States, 1960

Variable Number	2	3	4	5	6	7	8	9	10	11	12	13	14	15
1	-.78	.44	.72	.75	-.10	.68	-.18	.45	.15	-.10	-.14	-.29	.15	-.30
2		-.27	-.66	-.84	.29	-.65	.20	-.58	.16	.17	.17	.37	-.33	.40
3			.82	.35	.50	.22	.61	.81	.10	.71	.73	-.81	.73	-.83
4				.81	.07	.39	.27	.84	.03	.39	.43	-.74	.68	-.76
5					-.42	.43	-.19	.57	-.07	-.08	-.04	-.43	.39	-.45
6						.24	.70	.26	.15	.55	.52	-.12	.29	-.15
7							-.21	.24	.23	-.34	-.35	.04	.00	-.0
8								.56	-.15	.88	.87	-.48	.62	-.42
9									-.32	.67	.68	-.82	.87	-.82
10										-.28	-.23	.16	-.36	.01
11											.98	-.62	.74	-.56
12												-.66	.78	-.62
13													-.74	.95
14														-.73

Variables

1. Percent Negro students in school with whites, 1965–66.
2. Percent of population which is nonwhite.
3. Median income of white males, 1959.
4. Median income of nonwhite males, 1959.
5. Nonwhite income as the percentage of white income, 1959.
6. Median school years completed, whites aged 25 and over.
7. Median school years completed, nonwhites aged 25 and over.
8. Percent completed 1–4 or more years of college, whites.
9. Percent of the labor force in white-collar occupations.
10. Percent of the labor force in manufacturing industries.
11. Percent of white males in professional and managerial occupations.
12. Percent of white males in white-collar occupations.
13. Percent of population residing in rural-farm areas.
14. Percent of population residing in urban areas.
15. Percent of labor force employed in farming.

Variable Number 1 is the dependent variable.

SOURCE: Beth E. Vanfossen, *Social Forces*, Vol. 47 (September 1968), p. 40. Used by permission.

The cumulative effect on attitudes is similar. Negro students, who have had contact with whites since the early elementary grades are more likely to feel able to affect their own destiny than those who have not had that experience.

Both the academic performance and attitudes of Negro students, then, are affected by the duration of their school contact with whites. Students whose first contact with whites was late in elementary or early in secondary schools are at a distinct disadvantage when compared with Negroes who have had school contact with whites since the early grades. (1967, pp. 107, 108)

In one national survey of Black adults, individuals who were products of predominantly Black schools revealed lower self-esteem than did those who had attended desegregated schools. This characteristic persisted even when other types of intergroup association, like interaction with White friends and residence in desegregated neighborhoods, were accounted for. The difference also was observed for both sexes and for different social classes and age groups (U.S. Commission on Civil Rights, 1967, p. 112).

Desegregated settings have been detrimental to the performance of minority students, according to some researchers, when the student has felt a sense of isolation or estrangement from other students and when he has had an extreme fear of competition with members of the majority group. A detailed summary of findings is available in a special report of Phi Delta Kappa by Meyer Weinberg, *Desegregation Research: An Appraisal* (1970).

The implementation of certain types of desegregation plans, like mandatory busing, has had a corollary development in many neighborhoods: the flight of White families to outlying suburbs. "Resegregated" inner-city schools have resulted in many places. (In Atlanta, for example, the public-school population in 1973 was approximately 20 percent White and 80 percent Black; a decade before it had been 60 percent White and 40 percent Black.) Mandatory busing has triggered outbreaks of violence in places such as Boston during the fall of 1974. Open enrollment plans—sometimes called "freedom of choice" plans—have had little effect in producing numerical changes; and, perhaps for this reason, they have not aroused much political opposition. Ideally, voluntary busing plans minimize the effects of residential segregation by allowing Black parents to send their children to White schools. In practice, estimates indicate that only 5 to 15 percent of the Black parents exercise this option, even when transportation is free and places are available (Jencks, 1972, p. 41). In the late 1950s and early 1960s freedom-of-choice plans were widely tried, but most were eventually judged unacceptable by Federal courts that ruled on them.

When busing occurs what happens to minority students? As far as academic achievement (as measured by test scores) is concerned, preliminary findings are congruent with earlier studies of desegregation when busing was not an issue: "Since some studies report gains and virtually none report losses, it seems likely that the average effect is a gain" (Jencks, 1972, p. 120). Blacks, on the average, receive somewhat lower grades in desegregated schools than they receive in segre-gated schools, which *may* lead to lower self-estimates of academic ability. As for the impact upon White students, little is presently known. "The most reasonable conclusion at present," Christopher Jencks has written, "is that neither busing nor 'natural' desegregation (that which results from residential desegregation) has much effect either way on whites' test scores" (1972, p. 120).

In 1972 the U.S. Commission on Civil Rights conducted a study on the impact of busing in five cities—Pasadena, California; Tampa-Hillsborough, Florida; Charlotte-Mecklenburg and Winston-Salem/Forsyth, North Carolina; and Pontiac, Michigan. It concluded:

1. Some opposition came from Blacks, but most came from the White community.
2. Parents expressed much more hostility to the plan than did students or teachers.
3. Reports of intergroup violence had been exaggerated. Such incidents occurred usually at the inception of desegregation plans and tapered off sharply after a few weeks.
4. Busing plans did entail additional costs for school systems.
5. No rigorous evaluation of the quality of education was available. Some teachers felt that minority pupils were receiving a better education than before; others believed that the stiff competition in desegregation schools dis-couraged some minority students who felt they were unable to compete success-fully because of their inadequate preparation. "No change in the motivation or performance of White pupils was noted in any school."

The report expressed no real surprise at the difficulties that had been en-countered. "After generations of separateness," the report concluded, "it would be unrealistic to expect integration to be an instant or uniform success" (1972, p. 2).

The Economics of Change

Creation of jobs.   It is an oversimplification to attribute all intergroup problems to any one cause, but it does seem safe to say that economic measures hold great promise for altering intergroup relations. Minority leaders have been quick to point out that it is not worth much to have the right to eat at expensive restaurants if one does not have the money to pay the bill. Economic strategies include such macro-level approaches as maintaining an expanding national economy and such micro-level approaches as projects administered by single businesses or unions. Economists like James Tobin (1965) have maintained that the most effective way to improve the economic status of minorities is to keep employment levels high. This result can be achieved by means of heavy governmental spending at appropri-ate times in order to stimulate the economy.

It must be remembered that high employment levels create inflationary pressures. Economists who favor full employment concede that some inflation is inevitable in expanding economies. They argue, however, that the negative effects of inflation can be countered by protecting individuals on retirement and other fixed incomes through adjusted social-security benefits and the like.

Jobs and money were singled out for special attention by the National Advisory Commission on Civil Disorders (1968). The commission called for a national policy of economic growth that would provide jobs for newly trained workers without displacing older employees. It recommended six basic objectives:

1. Existing programs aimed at recruiting, training and job development should be consolidated . . . to avoid fragmentation and duplication.
2. High priority should be placed on creation of new jobs in both the public and private sectors.
3. Creation of jobs for the hard-core unemployed will require substantial payments to both public and private employers to offset the extra costs of supportive services and training.
4. Special emphasis must be given to motivating the hard-core unemployed.
5. Artificial barriers to employment must be removed by both public agencies and private employers.
6. Special training is needed for supervisory personnel.

(National Advisory Commission, 1968, pp. 415–417)

A number of large corporations now include training in intergroup relations as part of their management-instruction program. United Parcel Service (U.P.S.). for example, distributes *Impartial Employment and Promotion Guide* to each of its 25,000 employees. The following statement appears in the guide:

We have a single set of standards for all applicants for each job. We employ without regard to race, religion, color, or national origin.

We promote from within and fill managerial positions from our ranks. In doing so we take care not to overlook people whose present jobs may keep them out of sight. We will fill a vacancy from the outside only when we cannot find a candidate qualified for promotion from within our organization.

Advancement is based on individual merit and performance. Anyone who performs his tasks capably and has the capacity to assume greater responsibility is eligible. We select the person who seems best fitted for the job, without regard to race, religion, color, or national origin.

Job training versus liberal education.   Even though it is widely recognized that job availability and intergroup relations are closely related, a consensus has not been reached on the kinds of jobs that offer the greatest opportunities for minorities. In fact, two of the most influential Blacks in American history—Booker T. Washington and W. E. B. DuBois—split over this issue. Washington and his associates at Tuskegee Institute wished to avoid direct competition with Whites for jobs during the troubled days that followed Reconstruction. Insisting that industrial training was a sure and practical way to success, Washington wrote:

Many seem to think that industrial education is meant to make the Negro work as he worked in the days of slavery. This is far from my conception of industrial education. If this training is worth anything to the Negro, it consists in teaching him how not to work, but how to make the forces of Nature—air, steam, water, horse-power and electricity—work for him. . . . The Negro in the South works and works hard; but too often his ignorance and lack of skill causes him to do his work in the most costly and shiftless manner, and this keeps him near the bottom of the ladder in the economic world. (1903, pp. 10–29)

DuBois, a sociologist and early civil-rights advocate, emphasized broadly educating those whom he called the "talented tenth" and urged support of the newly established Black colleges:

I would not deny, or for a moment seem to deny, the paramount necessity of teaching the Negro to work, and to work steadily and skillfully, or seem to depreciate in the slightest degree the important part industrial schools must play in the accomplishment of these ends, but I *do* say, and insist upon it, that it is industrialism drunk with its vision of success, to imagine that its own work can be accomplished without providing for the training of broadly cultured men and women to teach its own teachers, and to teach the teachers of the public schools.

The talented tenth of the Negro race must be made leaders of thought and missionaries of culture among their people. No others can do this work and Negro colleges must train people for it. The Negro race, like all other races, is going to be saved by its exceptional men. (1903, pp. 56–75)

DuBois's strategy was criticized on grounds that it would produce an élite group lacking marketable skills. DuBois replied, however, that his approach was compatible with an emphasis on occupational training. Washington's critics thought that his proposal would eliminate Blacks from competition with Whites for high-status jobs and would thus perpetuate White supremacy.

Motivation.   In competitive situations, individuals who have experienced failure may simply quit trying. Even when they are told that conditions have changed, they may not believe it. One Black educator explained:

The hardest job we have is convincing youngsters in grade school—especially boys—that it is really worthwhile to stay in school. For too many years, a filling station job was all that awaited a Black man, even if he had a high-school diploma. Youngsters know that they don't need to finish school to get a filling station job. College is out of the question for many of them because it is too expensive.

Projects like the Pittsburg Youth Motivation Task Force attempt to motivate young people to continue their educations and eventually to embark on careers in business and industry. The task force brings successful industry and business representatives to schools and community centers, in order to provide the youngsters with a variety of role models. It also arranges field trips to offices and plants with the goal of providing in-plant experience. In this way an effort is made to break the low-motivation cycle, a frequent component of minority situations. Interested Negroes—IN—is a project with similar objectives that was begun in Philadelphia in 1968. More than 1,600 boys had participated in the IN program by 1970.

Such programs are dismissed by some minority spokesman as superficial attempts to repair the damage done by an exploitative economic system. They call for basic changes in the economic structure rather than individually focused programs that tend to be primarily ameliorative. Alternative proposals range from such reformist plans as the negative income tax to such revolutionary plans as abolishing inheritance and other mainstays of capitalist systems.

Job information. Lack of information about job openings can be a serious handicap to minority members who wish to enter certain occupations. The creation of job banks at state employment offices during the 1970s may help to remedy this situation. In the past a local employment office could provide information about local jobs and a few out-of-state jobs. Not many blue-chip vacancies were listed, however. Under the job-bank program, employment needs from local offices are forwarded to a district office, then to the state office, and eventually to all state offices. An applicant in a local office has access to all this information. Under an executive order (no. 11598) any company or institution that contracts or subcontracts with the Federal government (for $10,000 or more) is required to list all job vacancies with local employment offices, which means that many universities and most large businesses must cooperate. Even though the job-bank program was not designed just to assist minorities, the fact that it widely disseminates information about jobs should have a marked impact on the economics of intergroup relations.

Federal and state agencies have begun to hire people from minority groups in substantial numbers. In November 1969, according to a survey by the Civil Service Commission, 11,552 minority workers held high-paying jobs with the Federal government—governmental scale (G.S.) 12 or above. That number had increased to 17,013 by November 1972. Minorities also accounted for 28.4 percent of the lowest-paid jobs (G.S. 1 to G.S. 4). Minority workers constituted 22 percent of the postal employees in 1972. Overall, minorities accounted for 20 percent of all Federal employees in 1972—Blacks 15.3 percent, Spanish-surnamed Americans 3.1 percent, Indians and Orientals 1.6 percent.

Because the Federal government is a major employer, the implementation of its nondiscriminatory policy is in itself a major development. Opening whole categories of jobs to minorities offers incentives for achievement, as well as the economic means to achieve personal goals.

What effect does economic prosperity or depression have upon intergroup relations? It oversimplifies matters to say that relations improve during periods of prosperity or that they deteriorate during recessions. During a period when unemployment is increasing, minority members are often the first to be fired: *the principle of disproportionate loss*. And, when the economy is expanding, minority members are usually the last to be hired: *the principle of less than proportionate gain*.

The evidence presented in Chapter 10 suggests that an economic condition that enables considerable numbers of a poor minority group to move upward rapidly through several class strata is also likely to produce a social climate in which its members will be restless and sensitive. Violence initiated by the minority tends to increase. On the other hand, an economic recession tends to produce a sullen and vindictive dominant group. Hostile acts initiated by the dominant group then tend to increase.

Organized labor.   Labor unions—Black leader Bayard Rustin believes—constitute the largest organized segment of American society that is officially committed to improving the welfare of minorities (1971, p. 76). He may be right. The only serious challenger for this distinction would be the religious organizations. Organized labor has long supported "fair employment" and civil-rights legislation. During recent years the civil-rights department of the A.F.L.–C.I.O. has been particularly active. (In 1970, Blacks accounted for an estimated 13 percent of total union membership in the United States.)

Labor leaders at the national and state levels endeavor to keep members politically active by means of local meetings, conventions, the mass media, and, particularly, union newspapers. A typical union newspaper carries reports on pending legislation and issues of concern to labor. It usually has a tally sheet with the voting records of legislators on important bills. Unions lobby for key legislation in Congress and in state legislatures. They conduct voter campaigns and support candidates who are likely to favor their interests. With this kind of leverage, it would indeed appear that minorities have a powerful ally.

Support for minorities, however, is not uniform throughout the labor movement. When Hubert M. Blalock, Jr., reviewed the situation in 1967, he concluded that, despite a slight overall trend in favor of upgrading minority labor, relationships had changed but little since Herbert Northrup's analysis (1944) of intergroup relations in the 1930s and early 1940s. These general patterns can be summarized as follows (Blalock 1967, p. 85):

1. Discrimination against Blacks is more pronounced in craft unions than in industrial unions. (At the time of Northrop's study of the AFL and the CIO had not yet merged, and the distinction coincided "remarkably well" with the distinction between the two confederations.)
2. The structure of the industry itself affects union policy. The steel, mining, and auto industries show the lowest degrees of discrimination. A study by Scott Greer (1959) has corroborated this finding. Blacks and Mexicans were found

to be especially handicapped in unions with "hiring hall" systems. (Hiring halls exist when employers typically ask for given numbers of workers, who are then hired on a day-to-day basis.)

3. Unions that stress the social and fraternal aspects of work organization and those with heavy concentrations of southern workers have been found to be most restrictive.

4. Minorities sometimes benefit when rival unions are competing for members, but not always. "Liberal" unions have been known to tighten their membership policies in order to capture support from Whites.

5. Minorities tend to benefit from unions when national control is strong. Because the AFL–CIO is a federation of affiliates, each with a high degree of autonomy, lower-level units do not always implement national policy. The parent body can urge action, but the affiliates decide whether or not to comply.

Labor unions are, in some ways, victims of their own success. Many union members have used their increased wages and other benefits to move to the suburbs, where they have become less and less responsive to union policies and recommendations. Predictably, they have been less than enthusiastic about busing their children back to inner-city schools. Apparently resisting school busing is more important to them than higher wages, fringe benefits, or a closed shop. In addition, some of these workers feel that their jobs are threatened by minorities. Their resistance to change at the lower levels of union membership seems tied to two emotional issues, schools and jobs. Labor economist Ray Marshall has summed up the impact of organized labor on intergroup relations in the United States:

> I agree with Bayard Rustin that labor has done more for Blacks than any other organized segment of American society. Often the unions were not doing what they did just to help minorities, but because of an interest in assisting whole categories of jobs. To my knowledge, there has been no major civil-rights legislation passed which did not have the backing of organized labor. But labor also has been a major source of trouble. At the grass-roots level, unions have strenuously resisted minority quotas, they have maintained segregated seniority systems, etc. My basic view is that unions are not basic *causes* of Black employment patterns, but they may be used to formalize and perpetuate patterns. (personal conversation, 1973; see also Marshall, 1965, 1967; Marshall, Levitan, and Mangum, 1972)

Legal and Administrative Strategies

The social traditions of some nations are such that the law can be a minority's foe or its friend. Mohandas Gandhi based his strategy for change in India on the legal tradition of the British. He had observed that the British generally would abide by their laws, even when those laws worked to their disadvantage. This trait proved to be the Achilles' heel of their rule in India. One of Gandhi's tactics was to request formally a permit before some planned demonstration. If it was denied, he would go ahead with the demonstration anyway, knowing that he could go to the courts and prove that he had been denied the permit illegally. He thus used the legal structure to bring about change and set in motion a series of events that eventually produced an independent India.

History probably would not show Americans to be quite as scrupulous as the British on this point, but there is certainly a viable tradition of abiding by the law in this country as well. Laws and court decisions in the United States, considered as a whole, profoundly influence our lives. For example, the resistance and the delaying tactics that occurred before the civil-rights act was finally passed attest to the importance and the symbolic significance of the law. "Law cannot order men to abandon their prejudices," R. M. MacIver has written, "but it can strengthen or weaken the conditions under which prejudice develops" (1948, p. 171).

Using the courts either to enforce a law, to clarify an issue, or to decide between contradictory legal ideas customarily calls for long, patient struggle. Ensuring that laws are enacted requires research, little-publicized "understandings," and plodding detail work. A restive minority may turn to speedier and more dramatic measures than legal and legislative maneuvers. To them, understandings reached with an adversary may smack of immoral compromises. Spending time and effort on legal battles to secure basic rights seems wasteful and foolish. Predictably, organizations like the National Association for the Advancement of Colored People have had difficulty maintaining rank-and-file support, despite their victories in important legal and legislative battles.

Which is most effective—legislation, education, or confrontation? Probably it is more essential to ask what conditions favor these different strategies. "Legal action by itself may run into massive resistance or reluctant compliance that returns at once to old patterns when surveillance is removed," George Simpson and J. Milton Yinger have observed, "but in a situation where quiet educational and conciliatory processes have also been at work, gains won by legal coercion may gradually get the support of personal conviction and institutional practice" (1965, p. 525).

Among law-abiding people, a legal code that restrains one group from oppressing another can be a major step toward an ultimate solution. A policy that simply takes wealth or power from one group and gives it to another is not. Why? Because tolerance, as far as human beings are concerned, is not determined by genetics. All human groups—Indian, White, Black, and Oriental—can be ruthless, discriminatory, and cruel if they have sufficient provocation and opportunity. "Power tends to corrupt," John E. E. Acton has written, "and absolute power corrupts absolutely." Groups with power, regardless of their skin color, behave in predictable ways unless their power is limited.

The limitations on power are many, but they may be classified in two categories: those activities that groups and individuals *cannot* perform and those that they *will not* perform. Some groups do not oppress neighboring groups because they *cannot*; they lack the population, the technology, or the organizational efficiency to overpower their neighbors. Other groups—perhaps far fewer in number —do not oppress neighboring groups because they *will* not. The values that they have internalized, or their laws, act as deterrents.

It is conceivable that systems of "checks and balances" can be developed in intergroup relations. Let us suppose that three groups—Purples, Greens, and Oranges—live side by side. The Purples dominate the other two groups because of their larger numbers and superior power. The result is an uneasy peace. While still in power, however, the Purples negotiate with the Oranges and the Greens an arrangement that abolishes all benefits based on color. Under this arrangement, power and privilege will be based upon individual merit. If all three groups can agree on the new arrangement and build in safeguards for its enforcement, each can guarantee its own future. By eliminating discrimination against every color, they eliminate discrimination against their own colors.

Actually, such an arrangement is not as utopian as at first it may seem. The literature on the sociology of religion suggests that religious pluralism is achievable when it has strong legal safeguards. For two centuries the United States has been able to avoid the religious wars and sectarian strife that have marred the history of practically all modern nations. This probably unique experience may be attributed to the fact that the United States has no official state church. By means of the First Amendment, an official alliance between government and a particular religious denomination has been prevented. In effect, the First Amendment has said to religious Purples, Greens, and Oranges that they all stand equal before the law. None can legally use the power or wealth of the government to take advantage of the other.

One further illustration: Abolition of slavery in the United States meant that no group—Black or White—would ever again be held in slavery. In the 1860s Blacks, for the most part, were the slaves. At some future time, it is conceivable that Whites might have become the slaves. Abolishing slavery itself ensured the future freedom of both Blacks and Whites. That point appears to have been in Abraham Lincoln's thoughts. In a message to Congress delivered in December 1862, Lincoln[3] ended with the words, "In giving freedom to the slave, we assure freedom to the free...."

In addition to enacting laws to safeguard the rights of minorities, some gov-

---

[3] Actually, Lincoln was not the first to free the slaves of an enemy group. The British issued an emancipation proclamation in November 1775: "I do hereby further declare all indentured Servants, Negroes or others (appertaining to Rebels) free that are able and willing to bear Arms, they joining his Majesty's Troops as soon as may be, for the more speedily reducing this Colony to a proper Sense of their Duty, to His Majesty's Crown and Dignity" (D. Porter, 1973: p. 52).

ernments establish special administrative units to deal with minority problems. The U.S. Commission on Civil Rights is one such organization. Its primary purpose is to investigate and document instances of discrimination. The impact of the commission has been twofold: First, it has provided Congress with evidence for legislation, and, second, the publicity surrounding its hearings and reports has sometimes been a deterrent to flagrant abuses.

Government regulations that affect government employees sometimes alter intergroup relations. The nation of India, in an effort to undo the disabilities experienced by "scheduled castes and tribes," now assigns a quota of individuals from these lower strata to government jobs. This attitude toward disadvantaged groups is reflected in the Indian constitution (section 330), which provides that seats in legislative bodies be reserved for members of these castes and tribes.

In the United States government employment practices affect not only government employees themselves but also employees of firms and institutions that receive government funds. In recent years corporations and universities holding Federal contracts have been called upon to present evidence that they do not discriminate against minorities. In addition, some organizations have been required to implement "affirmative action plans" by which they make *special* efforts to hire minority members. With this kind of economic leverage, the government's intervention in intergroup relations has been widely felt.

Obviously, such policies force "prejudiced discriminators" (P.D.) to conform to certain norms, but they affect "unprejudiced discriminators" (U.D.) as well. The distinction between *prejudiced* discriminators and *unprejudiced* discriminators is based on the fact that prejudice does not always lead to overt action (discrimination). We expect people who are prejudiced to discriminate, but we are not as often aware that unprejudiced people discriminate too. The unprejudiced discriminator discriminates against minorities, not because of personal ill will, but because of a need to conform to group norms. Thomas F. Pettigrew calls this personality type, the "latent liberal." This person is neither authoritarian nor anti-Semitic but rather has habits and needs of conformity that lead to discrimination (1971, p. 139).

A no-nonsense government policy provides the unprejudiced discriminator (U.D.) with a way out of his dilemma. He can drop discriminatory practices, with the excuse that there is no other choice. He may even join prejudiced discriminators in complaining about governmental policies but from motives different from theirs. This kind of behavior is somewhat like that of a husband who, lacking courage to say "no" to a persistent salesman, instead declines on the grounds that his wife may object to the purchase. In reality his wife could not care less about the particular purchase. Blaming her is simply a gambit—the "coercion gambit," to coin a phrase. In the same way the U.D. who resorts to the stratagem of blaming the government for what he or she may be willing to do anyway is able to stop discriminating without risking personal censure.

Open Housing

Whenever housing is segregated, it is likely that schools, churches, hospitals, and recreational facilities will also be segregated, usually on a *de facto* basis. For this reason, many people believe that open-housing programs hold great promise for altering intergroup relations. They see busing as a short-range strategy and open housing as a long-range one.

The first organized efforts to promote open housing were those of citizens' groups that attempted to stabilize residential patterns in mixed neighborhoods in Chicago and Philadelphia in the 1940s. Many of these early attempts were not very successful, primarily because the areas involved were virtual islands surrounded by neighborhoods which restricted sales to Whites only.

From this shaky beginning, the movement has broadened to include activities that are sponsored by approximately 2,000 local fair-housing groups and related community organizations in the 1970s. Approximately forty professionally staffed metropolitan open-housing centers are now operating. Their activities are coordinated at the national level by the National Committee Against Discrimination In Housing (N.C.D.H.). The N.C.D.H. was formed in 1950 and is composed of fifty major religious, civil-rights, labor, and civic organizations. Its stated goal is to achieve an integrated housing market in which "a decent home and suitable living environment" is available to every American family.

Several important developments have contributed to the growth of the movement:

1. The Supreme Court has upheld an 1866 fair-housing law that forbids racial discrimination in the sale or rental of all housing and land.
2. The 1968 Civil Rights Act bars discrimination in sales and rentals of approximately 80 percent of the nation's housing.
3. Fair-housing laws have been enacted in twenty-seven states (by 1970) and in numerous cities.
4. Federal housing programs that are designed to help low- and moderate-income families purchase homes have been implemented. (see Chapter 10, p. 285)

A useful manual, prepared jointly by the American Friends Service Committee and the N.C.D.H.[4] includes step-by-step instructions for a local program. The heart of the N.C.D.H. concept is the organization of a local fair-housing group. Once organized, a fair-housing group is expected to maintain a speakers' bureau, sponsor "good neighbor" pledge-signing campaigns, conduct periodic surveys, assist minority families in moving, counter rumors, initiate direct action against discriminatory activities, and generally coordinate the work of interested groups and individuals.

---

[4] American Friends Service Committee and the National Committee Against Discrimination in Housing, *Fair Housing Handbook*. Philadelphia: 1968.

An open-housing program is generally most effective in a community that already has provided equitable job opportunities for minority members. Unless minority families are able to obtain the money necessary to purchase acceptable dwellings, a fair-housing policy will obviously have little effect.

The fact that many formerly legal and quasi-legal discriminatory housing practices have now been struck down by law means that minority families have a better chance to buy what they want. But this chance does not prevent White residents from fleeing to new neighborhoods. This kind of panic response is frequently encouraged by unscrupulous realtors who hope to profit from "blockbusting." Blockbusting involves the use of scare tactics to rush residents of a neighborhood into panic sales. The realtor then arranges to buy up their homes and later resell them to minority families at a profit.

Blockbusting is most likely to occur where it is generally believed that property values will decline precipitously. Actually, a number of studies show that prices are far more likely to rise or to remain stable than to decline when minority families enter all-White areas. One of these investigations is based on 10,000 transactions in seven cities over a five-year period. In 85 percent of the instances, prices in mixed neighborhoods were equal to or exceeded those in comparable all-White neighborhoods. In 15 percent of the instances, declines ranged from 5 to 9 percent, were usually short-run declines, and were followed by rises to or above previous prices (American Friends Service Committee, 1968).

Programs for Immigrants

A number of nations provide services to help immigrants adjust to their new homes. Several programs are conducted under the aegis of groups like the Intergovernmental Committee for European Migration. A typical program includes orientation courses, language classes, and technical training. Construction workers migrating to Brazil, for instance, are taught the usual methods of building walls or installing plumbing in that country. Some countries like Australia and Argentina have provided instructors who escort immigrants from their homes and use the sea voyage to conduct information and language courses.

In the United States, the relocation strategy for World War II refugees is a good example of a program that apparently helped to minimize culture shock. First, the refugees did not come to the United States with the hope that they would one day be able to return home. They attempted to acquire the social legacy of their adopted land as quickly as possible. Second, because the refugees were stateless people, they eagerly sought citizenship. Third, a system of sponsorship dispersed these families over a wide geographical area. Finally, the sponsorship system brought the immigrants into primary relationships with members of civic clubs and local churches (Berry, 1965, pp. 93, 94). By contrast, immigrants to this country in earlier years were frequently deprived of face-to-face interaction with local residents. Their contacts were with policemen, immigration authorities, and employers and thus tended to be restricted and impersonal.

Mass Media and Propaganda

The word "propaganda" has a sinister ring to it, probably because of its association with the policies of totalitarian governments. Actually the word has no inherent relation to either truth or falsehood. It refers only to the deliberate use of communications to influence behavior for some predetermined purpose.

After much research, it seems clear that behavior can be manipulated to some extent by propaganda. Researchers know the broad limitations of the media, the kinds of individuals who are most likely to be affected, and the conditions that heighten media impact.

In the days before opinion polls, television ratings, and market surveys, there seemed to be a rather general belief in the unlimited power of advertising and promotion. Coca-Cola's investment in advertising was obviously paying off handsomely. It also seemed obvious that anything could be sold if the seller were only willing to spend enough to put his message across. Ideas like fair play and tolerance could also be sold to the public as Coke had been, or so it seemed.

Gradually, disquieting evidence began to appear in seemingly unrelated places. On farms, in factories and hospitals, during political campaigns, and in university laboratories, researchers found that individuals often did not expose themselves to certain messages and, furthermore, that they distorted some ideas and forgot others. Such behavior also seemed selective, rather than random. As the phenomena were studied further, they came to be known as the "selective processes": *selective exposure, selective perception,* and *selective retention.*

Selective exposure is the tendency of individuals to expose themselves to communications that are consistent with their existing opinions and interests. In a study of voters in a presidential election it was found that Republican partisans tended not to listen to Democratic candidates and the reverse. Rural sociologists found that radio was ineffective in changing farmers' opinions because rural people generally would not listen to views with which they seriously disagreed. An evaluation of a radio program intended to promote friendship among immigrant groups showed that a program about Italians was heard mainly by Italians, a program about Puerto Ricans by Puerto Ricans, and so on. The pattern in each of these studies was clear: Exposure to mass communications was selective.

Additional research showed that individuals who are exposed to a message incompatible with their opinions tend to distort the message or remember only parts of it. The distortion process is called "selective perception," the recall process "selective retention." The line of demarcation between selective perception and selective retention is a fine one. A person who has been exposed to a message may report a distorted or incomplete version of its content. It is thus difficult to ascertain whether it was correctly perceived and not retained or whether the two processes were complementary.

Mass communications are especially vulnerable to selective perception and retention. A study of cigarette smokers showed that smokers are not as likely to perceive the relationship between smoking and cancer as are nonsmokers who read identical newspaper and magazine reports. When subjects in the experiment were tested on the contents of the articles which they all had read, the non-smokers made significantly higher scores than the smokers. In an older study of prejudice, subjects tended to interpret the motives of film characters in a movie (*Home of the Brave*) favoring tolerance in ways that were predictable on the basis of their scores on a previously administered tolerance test.

Communications-research findings have consistently shown that some people are more likely to be influenced by other individuals than by the media. Some "influentials," or "opinion leaders," have impacts upon several groups; others are influential in only one group and in a specific area like politics, fashion, or athletics.

The mass media provide "followers" with what is in effect raw material that can be molded by the opinion leader. Joseph T. Klapper writes:

> After the follower has been influenced by the opinion leader, mass communication may provide material which the follower selectively attends or perceives to buttress his newly adopted opinion. For the opinion leader himself, wide exposure to mass communication provides information and points of view which he may or may not pass on to his less widely exposed followers. (1965, p. 33)

One way in which the media can alter intergroup behavior is to redefine group stereotypes. In earlier decades American Blacks were commonly stereotyped as indolent, shuffling, and amiable, but a campaign to change that image has met with some success. The new image has been based upon concepts like "aggressive," "militant," "Black is beautiful," and "Black power."

Certain kinds of propaganda, especially those that redefine minorities as threatening, run the risk of boomeranging (this boomeranging is sometimes called the Law of Reversed Effect). Films that depict the persecution of minority victims may actually reinforce sadistic impulses of prejudiced individuals, rather than creating sympathy. Evidence also suggests that propaganda that increases anxiety is ineffective, apparently because the anxiety may persist even though the message that induced it is forgotten.

Despite these limitations, propaganda can be used to reinforce the attitudes of the tolerant and to make them less vulnerable to prejudiced propaganda. Tolerant individuals may also be induced to support intergroup action programs and to combat racist activities. In addition, propaganda may be used to indicate to intolerant individuals that public sentiment is running against them.

Religious Activities

A number of important values in American society have their origins in religious beliefs, even though they may seldom be recognized as intrinsically religious. The work ethic (sometimes called the "Protestant ethic") is an example. Certain attitudes toward work persist, even though they have lost their older religious content. The same is true of the origins of certain universities, hospitals, children's homes, and philanthropic enterprises. They are now known as "nonsectarian," but their origins are religious. Many such organizations support a variety of intergroup programs.

The role that organized religion has played in intergroup relations is hotly disputed. Some argue that institutionalized religion, which tends to be conservative, sanctions the economic interests of the ruling class. Detractors observe that religion both justifies the ways of the rich and tranquillizes the poor by promising them "riches" in the hereafter. Others, in defense, cite long and impressive lists of religious benevolences and programs. Is religion, then, villain or hero?

To begin with, it needlessly oversimplifies matters to speak of religion as if it were an *undifferentiated* phenomenon. A number of writers have discussed its complexities. Marked differences occur even within the same denomination. For example, during the 1960s, when Baton Rouge was ordered to desegregate its schools, a local Baptist pastor wrote a prosegregation pamphlet that was widely distributed by the Klan and the White citizens' councils. By contrast, a pastor of another Baptist church in the same city bought space in the newspaper for a proclamation urging compliance with the desegregation plan. Both churches were affiliated with the same denomination, both were located in the same part of the city, and both drew members from approximately the same social class. Attitudinal differences of the respective pastors apparently accounted for this particular development.

It is a matter of historical record that religious groups have been heavily involved in intergroup activities—sustaining the underground railroad, participating in the abolitionist movement, and contributing to hundreds of philanthropies. During this century the civil-rights movement has been heavily supported by religious organizations.

The religious organizations of minority groups have often been a training ground for leaders and a rallying point for political thrusts. During the 1950s and 1960s the Black Church was the usual place where members of the Black community mobilized for action. Traditionally, churches in the Black community have provided sanctuaries where frustrations, hopes, and dreams could be expressed freely. Oliver Cox has written:

> Probably no one who has seen the Negro preacher in his cabin church of the Deep South, marching triumphantly over the King's English amid great surges of "Amen! Amen!" and "Yes, Lord!" leading his congregation in repeated

FIGURE 12   One of the Auca killers of two decades ago, who, with the aid of several tribesmen, was responsible for killing the first missionaries who tried to enter their jungle territory. Now a Christian convert, he tells the world about his new life. (Courtesy of **Decision** magazine.)

affirmations of faith and hope, could fail to realize that these people are far from being resigned in spirit. (1948, p. 442)

During recent years, most large religious denominations have rallied behind the Federal government's moves against discrimination. And the government—prompted partly by economic and political considerations, international relations, and other matters of national interest—has found in religion a moral base for its actions. Religious leaders actually have had a twofold impact: They have legitimated, and they have prodded to further action. Martin Luther King, Jr., it should be remembered, was a Baptist minister, and many of his associates had close ties with church groups.

Religious groups often affect intergroup relations through their proselytizing efforts. Several major religions have attempted to incorporate previously diverse peoples into a single household of faith. As for Christianity, the letters of the Apostle Paul record that the ultimate emergence of the church as a missionary force was accompanied by bitter internal struggles over admitting outsiders. The original commission of the Christian church, however, was universal in its scope: "Go ye into the world and preach the gospel to every creature." A similar tradition is present in the Muslim faith. Muhammad, in his farewell sermon, admonished his followers, "Know ye that every Muslim is a brother unto every other Muslim, and ye are now one brotherhood."

Religious movements when they first begin usually encounter resistance from adherents of older faiths, and they often turn to out-groups like minority peoples for converts. The religious philosophy of the Bahai, a religion founded in the nineteenth century by Baha' U'llah, has such a strategy: "If it be possible, gather together these two races, Black and white, into one assembly, and put such love into their hearts that they shall not only unite but even intermarry" (Bahai Public Trust, 1969, p. 359). This philosophy also has been characteristic of Jehovah's Witnesses, which has a large constituency of minority members. Actually, Jehovah's Witnesses attempt to win converts from all social strata, from both majority and minority. But they have had especially considerable success in recruiting from minorities.

Outside the United States Christian missionaries—Protestant and Roman Catholic—have sought to win native populations to their respective faiths. Their impact as agents of change upon traditional societies has often been considerable and is amply documented in anthropological literature. But missionaries have also affected sponsoring groups at home by prodding them to adopt open admission practices. Awareness of the discrepancy between the practices of the missionary church and the church at home has had a disquieting effect upon the American religious community during the past few decades.

Virtually all the major denominations in the United States have now officially renounced segregation. The idea expressed in a 1946 pronouncement by the Federal Council of Churches (now known as the National Council of Churches) has been repeated in many statements by individual denominations: "The Federal Council of Churches in America hereby renounces the pattern of segregation in race relations as unnecessary and undesirable and a violation of the Gospel of love and human brotherhood . . ." (Loescher, 1972, pp. 41, 42).

Action at the grass-roots level is another matter. Churches that are organized in hierarchical forms of government, like the Roman Catholic church, generally have had more success implementing official policies in local churches than have those with congregational forms of government.

Billy Graham has been quite influential in intergroup relations. He conducted his first desegregated crusade in Chattanooga in 1953, a year before the U.S. Supreme Court's school decision. He did so despite protests, forecasts of trouble, and sparse attendance by Blacks. What is remarkable is that Graham risked losing his base of support in the Bible Belt of the South, which at the time was still rigidly segregated. Predictably, his practice aroused hostility. In 1958 South Carolina Governor George B. Timmerman announced that permission to use the state-house grounds would not be granted to the "well-known integrationist." The general in command of nearby Fort Jackson invited Graham to hold the rally there. Sixty thousand people then attended the "first nonsegregated mass meeting in South Carolina's history."

Graham has consistently adhered to the policy of preaching before integrated audiences. When he visited the Union of South Africa in 1973, the usual segregation regulations were lifted for his meetings. In one such rally, a multigroup audience of 50,000 people overflowed the Durban cricket stadium.

A comment on the general impact of religion is in order. The circuit riders, priests, pastors, and evangelists who for decades have dwelt much on the themes of self-denial and love for our neighbors could not fail to have affected the American national character. One result, considered as an ideal type,[5] is the "person of good will." Such an individual tends to be inner-directed, to have firm beliefs about human rights and the intrinsic worth of personality, and to be somewhat conservative. This individual feels squeamish about the possible disruptions that often accompany sweeping changes, and prefers nonviolent means to secure objectives. Persons of good will are reactionary in the sense that they wait for problems to arise before reacting. Even then they may hesitate if action is likely to lead to personal unpleasantness. They tend not to constitute a strong political force unless they become aroused over some particular issue.

A certain amount of "good will" must be sustained within a society if that society is to continue as an operating concern. If every person and group were to push its respective demands to the limit, the result could be bitter and interminable conflict. Religion, with its preaching of kindness and generosity, mutes some individual and group demands and thus helps to keep abrasive conflicts within limits.[6] Kindness and generosity can, however, be stressed to the extent that a people will not make justifiable demands or defend its legitimate interests. Then religion is indeed an opiate.

---

[5] An ideal type is a hypothetical construct developed from the relevant characteristics of real individuals, groups, and so on is not designed to correspond to any one person or group. The use of ideal types was developed as a technique by Max Weber. Examples of ideal types are the "marginal man," "economic man," "sect," and "church."

[6] The ameliorative impact of religion does not seem to be evenly distributed, for loyalty to a religious in-group can lead to hostility and intolerance toward religious out-groups. "As we have opportunity," one biblical passage states, "let us do good to all men, and especially to the household of faith" (*Galatians*, 6:10). Available evidence suggests that some religious denominations may emphasize the "especially" of that principle more than other denominations. An important study by Charles Y. Glock and Rodney Stark (1966) indicates that certain Christian religious beliefs are causally related to anti-Semitism. A reexamination of the data used by Glock and Stark by Russell Middleton (1973) concluded, however: "Do Christian beliefs cause anti-Semitism in the U.S. today? To this question I must give the response, 'not proved'" (1973, p. 50).

Direct-Action Programs

In a group approach like community action or community development, an agent of change attempts to organize a community behind various projects. He or she may also attempt to promote community development by showing individuals how to conduct meetings, pass resolutions, and present petitions to politicians. In a variation called "community mobilization," he or she tries to break down the apathy of residents by arousing their anger against the local power structure. The agent of change may give community residents instructions for mass action—demonstrations, sit-ins, strikes—to help them obtain power.

Voter-registration campaigns can be effective if the group is numerically significant. This approach is particularly appropriate where coalition politics are feasible. The Lumbees of Robeson County, North Carolina, have gained political power in recent elections by bloc voting with Blacks. If the minority group is not numerically strong, however, it must resort to other activities like demonstrations or litigation.

Many of the strategies of direct action were developed during the civil-rights campaigns of the 1960s. The strategic concept of those years was nonviolence. King and other leaders urged the use of tactics that would dramatize injustice. Their presumption was that there is a social conscience and that citizens will act affirmatively when injustice is dramatized.

Dramatization of a social issue by a poor, numerically weak minority is effective only if it draws support from a larger audience. In a case study of a Harlem rent strike, Michael Lipsky makes precisely that observation:

> The problem of the powerless is that they have little to bargain with, and must acquire resources. Fifteen people sitting in the mayor's office cannot, of themselves, hope to move city hall. But through the publicity they get, or the reaction they evoke, they may politically activate a wider public to which the city administration is sensitive. (Lipsky, 1969, p. 11)

In the 1970s the dominant strategy has shifted in many quarters to one of organizing for power. Proponents of this approach recognize that in an urban society broad power is exercised through mass control. They believe that only organized action is capable of applying the leverage necessary to bring about important changes. "If we cannot remove racism," James Farmer has stated, "we can checkmate racism. This means that people who do not necessarily love one another can live with one another, each respecting the other for his power. We must learn to live and survive in a power equation."

Two manuals discuss the steps that can be taken to organize for action: *A Manual For Direct Action: Strategy and Tactics for Civil Rights and All Other Nonviolent Protest Movements* by M. Oppenheimer and George Lakey (1965) and *How People Get Power: Organizing Oppressed Communities For Action* by Si Kahn (1970). The subtitles of these two manuals indicate the ideological shift away from nonviolence that has occurred since 1965. But, the two manuals do agree on a number of basic points:

Entering the community. Kahn believes that an organizer's decision on how and when to enter a community is the most important one that will be made. Everything that he or she does after arriving in the community will be influenced by the initial impression that is made. Especially in rural communities where all the residents know each other, the organizer represents an element that is new and unknown. Sometimes the very arrival of the organizer can have a catalytic effect upon the community.

An organizer obviously must gain the confidence of poor people. But it is also advantageous to maintain contact with members of the power structure, if for no other reason than to estimate its strengths and weaknesses. Kahn suggests, "An organizer who regularly drops in to visit with members of the power structure, who is friendly, who occasionally helps them out in small ways, may still be hated for what he stands for; but he is less likely to be hated personally" (1970, p. 8).

Bringing people together. The mass meetings that were so important during the early civil-rights campaigns had two disadvantages. They offered little opportunity for individual participation, and the power structure could measure the support that the organization had. Kahn recommends "block organizing" instead. Even though block organizing is usually an urban technique, it can be used in rural areas. In practice, each block or neighborhood organization sends representatives to a central organization, but smaller units may take action on their own or in combination with others. This method is flexible, in that it combines the interdependence of a small group and the power of a large organization. Then, too, opponents are less likely to estimate correctly the strength that is developing.

Choosing leaders. A "negative reputational technique" for choosing leaders is proposed by Kahn. As a first step, he advises the organizer to ask key members of the power structure to identify "responsible" leaders in the poor community. The organizer should be wary of the individuals that are recommended. Instead, the individuals who are labeled "trouble makers," "agitators," and "a discredit to their race" are likely to be key prospects for leadership positions. Those who have incomes protected from pressures of the power structure are especially useful. They should be sought by the organizer and trained. Kahn's advice has obvious limitations. To be out of favor with the power structure may indicate strong leadership potential, but it may also indicate that the individual in question is a poor risk for other than ideological reasons.

Adopting goals and priorities. When a campaign is first launched, the organizer should avoid attacking entrenched problems that are likely to cause defeat. The reason is that early failure may discourage other people from coming into the organization.

Dealing with the power structure. Both manuals emphasize that power structures are seldom as unified as they sometimes appear. There may be intense personal antagonisms, differences in beliefs, and serious conflicts of interest within the structure. These cleavages can be crucial in the development of a direct-action campaign.

Direct action usually passes through several stages, which can be labeled by the reactions of the opponents: indifference, antagonism, negotiation, and accommodation. Once the initial indifference of the power structure has been dispelled, active antagonism is likely. Then every action will be magnified. Experiences that confirm the prejudices of the opponent will be blown up. Those that run counter to old prejudices also will have more impact than usual. This stage is critical because some members of the action group may begin to waver in their purpose. They may complain that the situation is now worse than when they began. Their opinion is probably correct, in the sense that, if the campaign were ended at this point, the two communities would be farther apart than before. The opposing group, however, may also be experiencing disunity within its own ranks.

When the negotiation stage is reached, spokesmen should be firm but friendly. Oppenheimer and Lakey counsel, "Experience shows that a negotiator is not usually effective if he is hostile and uses the sanctions as a threat to the opponent— 'You give what we want or you'll get what's coming to you!' " (1964, p. 25).

Neither manual devotes much space to the problems of implementing and institutionalizing demands, once they have been accepted. Actually, these activities may prove to be more important than the initial victory. Accommodation may take the form of drifting back to traditional patterns after the initial excitement has faded. Then, too, people who have succeeded in throwing out the old power structure may abuse their recently acquired authority by oppressing little people in the same way that their predecessors did before them. Kahn does urge organizers, once their mission is accomplished, to train local leaders carefully to carry on the work that has begun. Before departing, the organizer is advised to visit with members of the power structure to inform them that he will be coming back to the community from time to time just in case he is needed!

Intergroup Contact

Programs that attempt to establish personal relationships between members of different groups are numerous and varied. The Boy Scouts and Girl Scouts, the Y.W.C.A., the Y.M.C.A., colleges and universities, foundations, and church groups are typical organizations that sponsor group-contact programs. An underlying assumption of this approach is that prejudice thrives upon ignorance and that first-hand experience counters it. Forums, intergroup committees, councils, integrated churches and camps, international houses, and housing projects for mixed constituencies have thus been undertaken. Evaluations of these activities have revealed mixed results. Some have produced more favorable attitudes, others have failed to produce changes, and some appear to have reinforced previously held negative stereotypes.

Intergroup contacts generally are more likely to produce favorable attitudes toward other groups under the following conditions: The contacts are between individuals of comparable socioeconomic status (SES), the individuals seek common goals, their tasks make them mutually dependent, and they interact in a setting in which there are such positive sanctions as support from authorities or customers.

In an exploratory[7] study conducted by the author in the Raleigh, N.C., police department in 1968, a sample of twelve policemen expressed more prejudice (on a modified Bogardus social-distance scale) toward Germans and Japanese than toward Blacks. Surprisingly, the majority of respondents indicated that they would not object if a Black were to "move onto their street" or "join their club." Such tolerant views were not commonly held among Whites in Raleigh at the time of the study. In-depth interviews showed the negative attitudes toward Japanese and Germans to be carryovers from World War II experiences. The low scores for Blacks were partly explained by the comparatively high SES of Black officers in the unit. This particular police department had been able to recruit selectively among Blacks, with the result that all Blacks who had been hired had completed high school and several had completed college. The salaries of Blacks and Whites were equal for each rank. All policemen and their families were eligible to join the police club (a recreational facility). Furthermore, the danger of police work tended to make Blacks and Whites dependent upon each other. "If I have to go out on a dangerous assignment with a rookie, I will pick a Black over a White any day," a White veteran told me. "Nine times out of ten, a Black knows how to take care of himself. With a White rookie I might have to take care of him and myself too." Finally, the police chief had issued and implemented clear guidelines on intergroup hiring and promotion practices. On the whole, the responses of the policemen interviewed were consistent with the conditions and expectations of the contact hypothesis.

In a study of residents in an integrated public-housing project in a border city, results generally supported the hypothesis that there is a postive relationship between equal-status intergroup contact and tolerance. The evidence for White residents was rather clear-cut in support of the hypothesis, but for Black residents it was only partially and inconclusively confirmed (Ford, 1973, pp. 1426–1447).

An experimental study of small boys showed contact as reducing group conflict. Twenty previously unacquainted boys from homogeneous backgrounds were brought together in a summer camp. After they had been divided into two groups, each group was encouraged to develop high *esprit de corps*. Rivalry was stimulated

[7] The subjects of the study were enrolled in a college extension course. All students in the class participated in the study. No suggestion is made here that their responses are typical of other policemen in that city or typical of all policemen.

by competitive tasks. Intergroup animosity took the form of derogatory slogans, raids on the other camp, unflattering stereotypes, and desire for complete segregation.

The investigators then brought the boys together to repair a damaged water tank that supplied the whole camp and to raise funds to see a favorite movie. Participating in these cooperative and functionally dependent tasks led to the reduction of group tensions (Sherif and Sherif, 1953).

Social contact and accessibility to a particular group do sometimes heighten prejudice. A report prepared for Israel's Ministry of Education and Culture (Amir, 1969, pp. 338, 339) outlined the following conditions associated with contact situations that lead to negative responses: contact that produces competition between the groups; contact that is unpleasant, involuntary, or tense; contact in which the prestige of one group is lowered; contact that occurs when members of the groups are frustrated or depressed (after a recent defeat or failure, during an economic depression, and so on); contacts between groups whose customs may be mutually objectionable; and contacts in which one group has considerably lower status than the other (Amir, 1969, pp. 338, 339).

Even when contact does reduce prejudice, attitudes and behavior may be focused on very specific situations. According to one description of a mining community in West Virginia, White and Black miners worked amicably together in mixed teams. Sometimes Blacks supervised Whites. At the close of the work day, however, the workers separated at the top of the mine shaft to lead their above-ground lives in segregated neighborhoods. The only above-ground unsegregated territory was the union hall.[8]

Overview

Intergroup relations are considered a social problem on the basis of four criteria—humanitarian, utilitarian, functional, and social-deviance. A general knowledge of evaluative research can be useful in learning how to alter intergroup relations. Unfortunately, many action programs have not been subjected to careful evaluation. Adequate evaluation of an action program usually has four components: context evaluation, input evaluation, process evaluation, and product evaluation.

Knowledge about altering intergroup relations can be gained from studies that deal directly with intergroup problems, as well as from research on similar

[8] This study and others are cited in Amir's review of literature on the contact hypothesis (1969, pp 319–342). Amir expresses concern at the fact that much of the literature describes contrived situations that lead only to casual acquaintances. Furthermore, the reported studies may reflect interviewer bias: Respondents who are lead by a prestigious figure (teacher, researcher) through a series of experiences with other groups may simply cooperate with the leader by providing the changes that they know the leader is seeking.

problems in other fields. Three substantive areas provide especially useful insights into possible strategies: reference-group theory and research, organizational analysis, and diffusion research. The major hazard in extrapolating information from these substantive areas, however, is the difficulty in determining whether or not situations are really similar.

For this reason much of our present knowledge about altering intergroup relations comes from studies of programs that deal directly with such problems. Desegregation of public schools is the best-known program. In fact, it is one of the major developments of American history. Desegregation seems to have little effect on the scholastic performances of majority-group children (as measured by test scores), but academic performance of minority students generally improves. These findings notwithstanding, "White flight" to the suburbs has been a widespread phenomenon of the 1970s.

Occupational programs, especially those that provide jobs and job training for minorities, have been emphasized by many strategists. They correctly argue that entry rights to colleges, restaurants, motels, and theaters are of little value if the minority person does not have the money to use these facilities. Here agreement ends. What kinds of jobs are needed? Who should provide them? What kind of training or education is most appropriate for minority people? These points arouse the major disagreement over job strategy.

Minority members, as participants in the labor force, have potential leverage through organized labor. In fact, some minority leaders believe that labor unions constitute the most important organizational resource for minorities. Present evidence partly supports this claim, but it also shows that unions do not uniformly help minorities. At the local level, especially, some union practices have worked to the disadvantage of minorities. Union policies toward minorities vary according to the type of union and the level of control (local or national).

Programs aimed at changing the law have been particularly important in the United States. In fact, the N.A.A.C.P. has devoted a major part of its resources to achieving this goal. Governmental guidelines and regulations also have had great impact. Some governments have established special agencies to deal with minority problems. The Commission on Civil Rights is one such agency. It provides Congress with information on needed legislation and publicizes abuses of citizen rights.

It has long been known that segregated housing patterns tend to produce segregated schools, politics, religion, and recreation. The fair-housing movement attempts to deal with these interrelations by creating stable integrated neighborhoods. The National Committee Against Discrimination In Housing is the major organization that promotes this effort.

Because problems of newcomers can lead to tension and internal divisions, many nations have programs to help immigrants adjust to their new environments. Some of these programs are operated under the aegis of United Nations agencies.

The mass media and propaganda are frequently used in efforts to reduce prejudice and combat discrimination. Mass communications are not uniformly effective, however, because of phenomena known as the "selective processes." Individuals are known to avoid messages that are not consonant with their existing opinions and interests (selective exposure). If they do see or hear such messages, they either distort them (selective perception) or forget them (selective retention). Mass communications and propaganda seem most effective in reinforcing the attitudes of the tolerant and in encouraging them to act in specific ways (to support action programs, to oppose racist activities, and so on).

The general impact of institutionalized religion upon intergroup relations is hotly disputed. Detractors see religion as legitimating the status quo and as an opiate of the people. Religion's supporters, however, can enumerate long lists of activities for oppressed peoples—the abolitionist movement, various philanthropies, schools and colleges, and so on. Indeed, the civil-rights movement has had some of its most important inputs from various religious groups.

Direct action, as a strategy, uses an agent of change, who attempts to organize a community behind various projects. In a variant approach called "community mobilization," the agent tries to break up the apathy of the residents by arousing their anger against the local power structure. He or she may give instructions for mass action—demonstrations, sit-ins, strikes—to help a minority obtain power. A deficiency of many direct-action programs is too little attention to making changes permanent (institutionalizing the changes). Another shortcoming is the usual disregard of methods for safeguarding "little people" from oppression by groups that succeed in obtaining power.

Intergroup contact is one of the most popular approaches to altering intergroup relations. The underlying rationale is that prejudice thrives on ignorance and that first-hand experience counters it. Unfortunately, intergroup contact may actually increase prejudice and discrimination. It is under the following conditions that intergroup contact is most likely to reduce prejudice and discrimination: Contacts between people of comparable S.E.S., common goals (not requiring competition for scarce resources), mutually dependent tasks, and interaction within the context of clear, positive guidelines from persons with authority or prestige.

ON IMPROVING THE ECONOMIC STATUS
OF THE NEGRO

JAMES TOBIN

In this important article, the distinguished economist James Tobin argues that the government's general economic policies have a critical impact upon the lives of minority people. The author demonstrates that the fluctuations of the economy tend to be more keenly felt by a minority than by a dominant group. "Last to be hired," an old saying states, "first to be fired." Although the article is somewhat dated—its statistics are now over a decade old—many of the economic principles that Tobin articulates have general applicability.

I start from the presumption that the integration of Negroes into the American society and economy can be accomplished within existing political and economic institutions. I understand the impatience of those who think otherwise, but I see nothing incompatible between our peculiar mixture of private enterprise and government, on the one hand, and the liberation and integration of the Negro, on the other. Indeed the present position of the Negro is an aberration from the principles of our society, rather than a requirement of its functioning. Therefore, my suggestions are directed to the aim of mobilizing existing powers of government to bring Negroes into full participation in the main stream of American economic life.

The economic plight of individuals, Negroes and whites alike, can always be attributed to specific handicaps and circumstances: discrimination, immobility, lack of education and experience, ill health, weak motivation, poor neighborhood, large family size, burdensome family responsibilities. Such diagnoses suggest a host of specific remedies, some in the domain of civil rights, others in the war on poverty. Important as these remedies are, there is a danger that the diagnoses are myopic. They explain why certain individuals rather than others suffer from the economic maladies of the time. They do not explain why the over-all incidence of the maladies varies dramatically from time to time—for example, why personal attributes which seemed to doom a man to unemployment in 1932 or even in 1954 or 1961 did not so handicap him in 1944 or 1951 or 1956.

Public health measures to improve the environment are often more productive in conquering disease than a succession of individual treatments. Malaria was conquered by oiling and draining swamps, not by quinine. The analogy holds for economic maladies. Unless the global incidence of these misfortunes can be diminished, every individual problem successfully solved will be replaced by a similar problem somewhere else. That is why an economist is led to emphasize the importance of the over-all economic climate.

Over the decades, general economic progress has been the major factor in the gradual conquest of poverty. Recently some observers, J. K. Galbraith and Michael Harrington most eloquently, have contended that this process no longer operates. The economy may prosper and labor may become steadily more productive as in the past, but "the other America" will be stranded. Prosperity and progress have already eliminted almost all the easy cases of poverty, leaving a hard core beyond the reach of national economic trends. There may be something to the "backwash" thesis as far as whites are concerned.[1] But it definitely does not apply to Negroes. Too many of them are poor. It cannot be true that half of a race of twenty million human beings are victims of specific disabilities which insulate them from the national economic climate. It cannot be true, and it is not. Locke Anderson has shown that the pace of Negro economic progress is peculiarly sensitive to general economic growth. He estimates that if nationwide per capita personal income is stationary, nonwhite median family income falls by .5 percent per year, while if national per capita income grows 5 percent, nonwhite income grows nearly 7.5 percent.[2]

National prosperity and economic growth are still powerful engines for improving the economic status of Negroes. They are not doing enough and they are not doing it fast enough. There is ample room for a focused attack on the specific sources of Negro poverty. But a favorable over-all economic climate is a necessary condition for the global success—as distinguished from success in individual cases—of specific efforts to remedy the handicaps associated with Negro poverty. . . .

The most important dimension of the overall economic climate is the tightness of the labor market. In a tight labor market unemployment is low and short in duration, and job vacancies are plentiful. People who stand at the end of the hiring line and the top of the layoff list have the most to gain from a tight labor market. It is not surprising that the position of Negroes relative to that of whites improves in a tight labor market and declines in a slack market. Unemployment itself is only one way in which a slack labor market hurts Negroes and other disadvantaged groups, and the gains from reduction in unemployment

---

[1] As Locke Anderson shows, one would expect advances in median income to run into diminishing returns in reducing the number of people below some fixed poverty-level income. W. H. Locke Anderson, "Trickling Down: The Relationship between Economic Growth and the Extent of Poverty Among American Families," *Quarterly Journal of Economics*, Vol. 78 (November 1964), pp. 511–524. However, for the economy as a whole, estimates by Lowell Galloway suggest that advances in median income still result in a substantial reduction in the fraction of the population below poverty-level incomes. "The Foundation of the War on Poverty," *American Economic Review*, Vol. 55 (March 1965), pp. 122–131.

[2] Anderson, *op. cit.*, Table IV, p. 522.

are by no means confined to the employment of persons counted as unemployed.[3] A tight labor market means not just jobs, but better jobs, longer hours, higher wages. Because of the heavy demands for labor during the second world war and its economic aftermath, Negroes made dramatic relative gains between 1940 and 1950. Unfortunately this momentum has not been maintained, and the blame falls largely on the weakness of labor markets since 1957. . . .[4]

Unemployment. It is well known that Negro unemployment rates are multiples

[3] Galloway, *op. cit.*, shows that postwar experience suggests that, other things equal, every point by which unemployment is diminished lowers the national incidence of poverty by .5 per cent of itself. And this does not include the effects of the accompanying increase in median family income, which would be of the order of 3 per cent and reduce the poverty fraction another 1.8 per cent.

[4] For lack of comparable nationwide income data, the only way to gauge the progress of Negroes relative to whites over long periods of time is to compare their distributions among occupations. A measure of the occupational position of a group can be constructed from decennial Census data by weighting the proportions of the group in each occupation by the average income of the occupation. The ratio of this measure for Negroes to the same measure for whites is an index of the relative occupational position of Negroes. Such calculations were originally made by Gary Becker, *The Economics of Discrimination* (Chicago, 1957). They have recently been refined and brought up to date by Dale Hiestand, *Economic Growth and Employment Opportunities for Minorities,* (New York, 1964), p. 53. Hiestand's results are as follows:

Occupational position of Negroes relative to whites:

	1910	1920	1930	1940	1950	1960
Male	78.0	78.1	78.2	77.5	81.4	82.1
Female	78.0	71.3	74.8	76.8	81.6	84.3

The figures show that Negro men lost ground in the Great Depression, that they gained sharply in the nineteen forties, and that their progress almost ceased in the nineteen fifties. Negro women show a rising secular trend since the nineteen twenties, but their gains too were greater in the tight labor markets of the nineteen forties than in the nineteen thirties or nineteen fifties.

Several cautions should be borne in mind in interpreting these figures: (1) Much of the relative occupational progress of Negroes is due to massive migration from agriculture to occupations of much higher average income. When the over-all relative index nevertheless does not move, as in the nineteen fifties, the position of Negroes in non-agricultural occupations has declined. (2) Since the figures include unemployed as well as employed persons and Negroes are more sensitive to unemployment, the occupational index understates their progress when unemployment declined (1940–50) and overstates it when unemployment rose (1930–40 and 1950–60). (3) Within any Census occupational category, Negroes earn less than whites. So the absolute level of the index overstates the Negro's relative position. Moreover, this overstatement is probably greater in Census years of relatively slack labor markets, like 1940 and 1960, than in other years.

The finding that labor market conditions arrested the progress of Negro men is confirmed by income and unemployment data analyzed by Alan B. Batchelder, "Decline in the Relative Income of Negro Men," *Quarterly Journal of Economics,* Vol. 78 (November 1964), pp. 525–548.

of the general unemployment rate. This fact reflects both the lesser skills, seniority, and experience of Negroes and employers' discrimination against Negroes. These conditions are a deplorable reflection on American society, but as long as they exist Negroes suffer much more than others from a general increase in unemployment and gain much more from a general reduction. A rule of thumb is that changes in the nonwhite unemployment rate are twice those in the white rate. The rule works both ways. Nonwhite unemployment went from 4.1 percent in 1953, a tight labor market year, to 12.5 percent in 1961, while the white rate rose from 2.3 percent to 6 percent. Since then, the Negro rate has declined by 2.4 percent, the white rate by 1.2.

Even the Negro teenage unemployment rate shows some sensitivity to general economic conditions. Recession increased it from 15 percent in 1955–56 to 25 percent in 1958. It decreased to 22 percent in 1960 but rose to 28 percent in 1963; since then it has declined somewhat. Teenage unemployment is abnormally high now, relative to that of other age groups, because the wave of postwar babies is coming into the labor market. Most of them, especially the Negroes, are crowding the end of the hiring line. But their prospects for getting jobs are no less dependent on general labor market conditions.

Part-time work. Persons who are involuntarily forced to work part time instead of full time are not counted as unemployed, but their number goes up and down with the unemployment rate. Just as Negroes bear a disproportionate share of unemployment, they bear more than their share of involuntary part-time unemployment. A tight labor market will not only employ more Negroes; it will also give more of those who are employed full-time jobs. In both respects, it will reduce disparities between whites and Negroes.

Labor-force participation. In a tight market, of which a low unemployment rate is a barometer, the labor force itself is larger. Job opportunities draw into the labor force individuals who, simply because the prospects were dim, did not previously regard themselves as seeking work and were therefore not enumerated as unemployed. For the economy as a whole, it appears that an expansion of job opportunities enough to reduce unemployment by one worker will bring another worker into the labor force.

This phenomenon is important for many Negro families. Statistically, their poverty now appears to be due more often to the lack of a breadwinner in the labor force than to unemployment.[5] But in a tight labor market many members of these families, including families now on public assistance, would be drawn into employment. Labor-force participation rates are roughly 2 percent lower for non-white men than for white men, and the disparity increases in years of slack labor

[5] In 34 per cent of poor Negro families, the head is not in the labor force; in 6 per cent, the head is unemployed. These figures relate to the Social Security Administration's "economy-level" poverty index. Mollie Orshansky, *op. cit.*

markets.[6] The story is different for women. Negro women have always been in the labor force to a much greater extent than white women. A real improvement in the economic status of Negro men and in the stability of Negro families would probably lead to a reduction in labor-force participation by Negro women. But for teenagers, participation rates for Negroes are not so high as for whites; and for women twenty to twenty-four they are about the same. These relatively low rates are undoubtedly due less to voluntary choice than to the same lack of job opportunities that produces phenomenally high unemployment rates for young Negro women.

Duration of unemployment. In a tight labor market, such unemployment as does exist is likely to be of short duration. Short-term unemployment is less damaging to the economic welfare of the unemployed. More will have earned and fewer will have exhausted private and public unemployment benefits. In 1953 when the over-all unemployment rate was 2.9 percent, only 4 percent of the unemployed were out of work for longer than twenty-six weeks and only 11 percent for longer than fifteen weeks. In contrast, the unemployment rate in 1961 was 6.7 percent; and of the unemployed in that year, 17 percent were out of work for longer than twenty-six weeks and 32 percent for longer than fifteen weeks. Between the first quarter of 1964 and the first quarter of 1965, over-all unemployment fell 11 percent, while unemployment extending beyond half a year was lowered by 22 percent.

As Rashi Fein points out . . . one more dimension of society's inequity to the Negro is that an unemployed Negro is more likely to stay unemployed than an unemployed white. But his figures also show that Negroes share in the reduction of long-term unemployment accompanying economic expansion.

Migration from agriculture. A tight labor market draws the surplus rural population to higher paying non-agricultural jobs. Southern Negroes are a large part of this surplus rural population. Migration is the only hope for improving their lot, or their children's. In spite of the vast migration of past decades, there are still about 775,000 Negroes, 11 percent of the Negro labor force of the country, who depend on the land for their living and that of their families.[7] Almost a half million live in the South, and almost all of them are poor.

Migration from agriculture and from the South is the Negroes' historic path toward economic improvement and equality. It is a smooth path for Negroes and for the urban communities to which they move only if there is a strong demand for labor in towns and cities North and South. In the 1940's the number of Negro farmers and farm laborers in the nation fell by 450,000 and one and a half million Negroes (net) left the South. This was the great decade of Negro economic advance. In the 1950's the same occupational and geographical migration continued

---

[6] See *Manpower Report of the President,* March 1964, Table A-3, p. 197.

[7] Hiestand, *op. cit.,* Table I, pp. 7–9.

undiminished. The movement to higher-income occupations and locations should have raised the relative economic status of Negroes. But in the 1950's Negroes were moving into increasingly weak job markets. Too often, disguised unemployment in the countryside was simply transformed into enumerated unemployment, and rural poverty into urban poverty.[8]

Quality of jobs. In a slack labor market, employers can pick and choose, both in recruiting and in promoting. They exaggerate the skill, education, and experience requirements of their jobs. They use diplomas, or color, or personal histories as convenient screening devices. In a tight market, they are forced to be realistic, to tailor job specifications to the available supply, and to give on-the-job training. They recruit and train applicants whom they would otherwise screen out, and they upgrade employees whom they would in slack times consign to low-wage, low-skill, and part-time jobs.

Wartime and other experience shows that job requirements are adjustable and that men and women are trainable. It is only in slack times that people worry about a mismatch between supposedly rigid occupational requirements and supposedly unchangeable qualifications of the labor force. As already noted, the relative status of Negroes improves in a tight labor market not only in respect to unemployment, but also in respect to wages and occupations.

Cyclical fluctuation. *Sustaining* a high demand for labor is important. The in-and-out status of the Negro in the business cycle damages his long-term position because periodic unemployment robs him of experience and seniority.

Restrictive practices. A slack labor market probably accentuates the discriminatory and protectionist proclivities of certain crafts and unions. When jobs are scarce, opening the door to Negroes is a real threat. Of course prosperity will not automatically dissolve the barriers, but it will make it more difficult to oppose efforts to do so.

I conclude that the single most important step the nation could take to improve the economic position of the Negro is to operate the economy steadily at a low rate of unemployment. We cannot expect to restore the labor market conditions of the second world war, and we do not need to. In the years 1951–1953, unemployment was roughly 3 percent, teenage unemployment around 7 percent, Negro unemployment about 4.5 percent, long term unemployment negligible. In the years 1955–1957, general unemployment was roughly 4 percent, and the other measures correspondingly higher. Four percent is the official target of the Kennedy-Johnson administration. It has not been achieved since 1957. Reading and maintaining 4 percent would be a tremendous improvement over the performance of

[8] Batchelder, *op. cit.,* shows that the incomes of Negro men declined relative to those of white men in every region of the country. For the country as a whole, nevertheless, the median income of Negro men stayed close to half that of white men. The reason is that migration from the South, where the Negro–white income ratio is particularly low, just offset the declines in the regional ratios.

the last eight years. But we should not stop there; the society and the Negro can benefit immensely from tightening the labor market still further, to 3.5 or 3 percent unemployment. The administration itself has never defined 4 percent as anything other than an "interim" target.

Why Don't We Have a Tight Labor Market?

We know how to operate the economy so that there is a tight labor market. By fiscal and monetary measures the federal government can control aggregate spending in the economy. The government could choose to control it so that unemployment averaged 3.5 or 3 percent instead of remaining over 4.5 percent except at occasional business cycle peaks. Moreover, recent experience here and abroad shows that we can probably narrow the amplitude of fluctuations around whatever average we select as a target.

Some observers have cynically concluded that a society like ours can achieve full employment only in wartime. But aside from conscription into the armed services, government action creates jobs in wartime by exactly the same mechansim as in peacetime—the government spends more money and stimulates private firms and citizens to spend more too. It is the *amount* of spending, not its purpose, that does the trick. Public or private spending to go to the moon, build schools, or conquer poverty can be just as effective in reducing unemployment as spending to build airplanes and submarines—if there is enough of it. There may be more political constraints and ideological inhibitions in peacetime, but the same techniques of economic policy are available if we want badly enough to use them. The two main reasons we do not take this relatively simple way out are two obsessive fears, inflation and balance of payments deficits.

Running the economy with a tight labor market would mean a somewhat faster upward creep in the price level. The disadvantages of this are, in my view, exaggerated and are scarcely commensurable with the real economic and social gains of higher output and employment. Moreover, there are ways of protecting "widows and orphans" against erosion in the purchasing power of their savings. But fear of inflation is strong both in the U.S. financial establishment and in the public at large. The vast comfortable white middle class who are never touched by unemployment prefer to safeguard the purchasing power of their life insurance and pension rights than to expand opportunities for the disadvantaged and unemployed. . . .

Increasing the Earning Capacity of Negroes

Given the proper over-all economic climate, in particular a steadily tight labor market, the Negro's economic condition can be expected to improve, indeed to improve dramatically. But not fast enough. Not as fast as his aspirations or as the aspirations he has taught the rest of us to have for him. What else can be done? I shall confine myself to a few comments and suggestions that occur to a general economist.

Even in a tight labor market, the Negro's relative status will suffer both from current discrimination and from his lower earning capacity, the result of inferior acquired skill. In a real sense both factors reflect discrimination, since the Negro's handicaps in earning capacity are the residue of decades of discrimination in education and employment. Nevertheless for both analysis and policy it is useful to distinguish the two.

Discrimination means that the Negro is denied access to certain markets where he might sell his labor, and to certain markets where he might purchase goods and services. Elementary application of "supply and demand" makes it clear that these restrictions are bound to result in his selling his labor for less and buying his livelihood for more than if these barriers did not exist. If Negro women can be clerks only in certain stores, those storekeepers will not need to pay them so much as they pay whites. If Negroes can live only in certain houses, the prices and rents they have to pay will be high for the quality of accommodation provided.

Successful elimination of discrimination is not only important in itself but will also have substantial economic benefits. Since residential segregation is the key to so much else and so difficult to eliminate by legal fiat alone, the power of the purse should be unstintingly used. I see no reason that the expenditure of funds for this purpose should be confined to new construction. Why not establish private or semi-public revolving funds to purchase, for resale or rental on a desegregated basis, strategically located existing structures as they become available?

The effects of past discrimination will take much longer to eradicate. The sins against the fathers are visited on the children. They are deprived of the intellectual and social capital which in our society is supposed to be transmitted in the family and the home. We have only begun to realize how difficult it is to make up for this deprivation by formal schooling, even when we try. And we have only begun to try, after accepting all too long the notion that schools should acquiesce in, even re-enforce, inequalities in home backgrounds rather than overcome them.

Upgrading the earning capacity of Negroes will be difficult, but the economic effects are easy to analyze. Economists have long held that the way to reduce disparities in earned incomes is to eliminate disparities in earning capacities. If college-trained people earn more money than those who left school after eight years, the remedy is to send a larger proportion of young people to college. If machine operators earn more than ditchdiggers, the remedy is to give more people the capacity and opportunity to be machine operators. These changes in relative supplies reduce the disparity both by competing down the pay in the favored line of work and by raising the pay in the less remunerative line. When there are only a few people left in the population whose capacities are confined to garbage-collecting, it will be a high-paid calling. The same is true of domestic service and all kinds of menial work.

This classical economic strategy will be hampered if discrimination, union barriers, and the like stand in the way. It will not help to increase the supply of Negro plumbers if the local unions and contractors will not let them join. But experience also shows that barriers give way more easily when the pressures of unsatisfied demand and supply pile up.

It should therefore be the task of educational and manpower policy to engineer over the next two decades a massive change in the relative supplies of people of different educational and professional attainments and degrees of skill and training. It must be a more rapid change than has occurred in the past two decades, because that has not been fast enough to alter income differentials. We should try particularly to increase supplies in those fields where salaries and wages are already high and rising. In this process we should be very skeptical of self-serving arguments and calculations—that an increase in supply in this or that profession would be bound to reduce quality, or that there are some mechanical relations of "need" to population or to Gross National Product that cannot be exceeded.

Such a policy would be appropriate to the "war on poverty" even if there were no racial problem. Indeed, our objective is to raise the earning capacities of low-income whites as well as of Negroes. But Negroes have the most to gain, and even those who because of age or irreversible environmental handicaps must inevitably be left behind will benefit by reduction in the number of whites and other Negroes who are competing with them.

THE BONUS THAT SAVED THE REPUBLIC
CHARLES F. EYRE

This tongue-in-cheek recommendation skillfully expresses an idea that social scientists have stressed for years: A change in one part of a social system usually results in changes elsewhere in the system. In this instance, a modification in economics (a tax incentive) results in changed demographic and ecological patterns.

I suppose it seems strange to some people, in 1995, that our young people are not able to comprehend the atmosphere of racial bias that existed prior to the end of segregation in the 1970s and the almost miraculous fading of that bias over such a short period. But it has ever been thus, the events of hundreds of years ago are better understood by young people than happenings during their own babyhood. I have no doubt that today's very small fry, when they grow up, will have little knowledge and less understanding of the trials their parents are now suffering with the great waves of "pollution flu" that now and then sweep the world.

However, I am digressing. I want to recall for young readers the end of racial segregation, which finally made this country the true melting pot of the world. Unsuccessful attempts to integrate the races had been continuous since the legal end of slavery, but it only took an idea and the right political climate for the growth of that idea to nurture a pell-mell change in our culture.

The idea came from an obscure college teacher who proposed that an income-tax exemption be given to any person who lived next door to a person of another race. Saying in effect that the government should depend on incentives to achieve integration rather than force, he argued that the tax exemption would promote harmony in the society, especially in housing, and yet would retain a certain measure of freedom for the individual.

Under the peculiar political circumstances of that time, the idea of a racial tax exemption became irresistibly potent. The segregationists saw it as another way to delay forced integration, and the proponents of integration felt that here was at least a token advance for their cause. At any rate, a bill was pushed through Congress. An unexpected feature of the law was the relatively large amount of the exemption, which was set at $4,000 despite the arguments of those who feared the losses in federal revenue would be too great. There was a great deal of inflation and unemployment and a growing fear that tight money policies, which had been followed up to that time, were going to bring on a depression, so the politicians felt compelled to make some gesture that would at least mitigate the unrelenting pressures that had built up around the issue of integration. President Nixon was induced to sign the measure on the understanding that a 5 percent surtax would offset the drain on federal income.

In practical terms the measure as finally enacted meant that any individual residing in an incorporated city of any size who could manage to secure a next-door neighbor who was a Negro, a Mexican, an American Indian, a Puerto Rican or a Filipino would not have to pay any income tax at all until his income reached approximately $5,500 (or higher for a family). And, of course, the exemption applied equally to the members of the minority races named in the law.

The impact was tremendous. Housing that had been tightly closed to them only weeks before was opened up immediately to those families of the prescribed races who had the financial ability to pay the rents and down payments needed. It soon became apparent that there were not enough minority people to go around. Advertisements began to appear in the news media appealing to members of the selected groups to come and live next door. Such advertisements promised a hearty welcome and friendship and extolled the virtues of the local school. Later on bonuses were paid to induce members of the chosen races to move in. Rumors persisted that some families were bribed away from areas after they had already moved in and taken a bonus.

There was a severe shortage of housing for a while as the vast slums lost a majority of their inhabitants. Intensive building activity, aided by heroic financing measures passed by Congress, encouraged other industries, such as automobile manufacturing, and the boom started that has continued unbroken to this time.

Not that there weren't any problems. The Internal Revenue Service found it very difficult to handle the new headaches presented by the legislation. The simplest of these, and the most common, was that many people decided that Mr. and Mrs. So-and-So next door were Indians, Puerto Ricans or whatever and took the exemption, thinking that they could get by with the deception. Word soon circulated that this ploy was unconvincing to the IRS, and those who tried it found themselves in hock to Uncle Sam at the new 10 percent penalty interest rate.

More difficult for the IRS were the cases in which people tried to "pass" so that they could receive bonuses as well as the exemption. Some people managed to get more than one bonus. But these cases were not frequent and those actively seeking "exemption neighbors," as they were called, soon learned to investigate before they paid off. The bonus rage died quickly because it was too difficult to make sure that the expenditure was going to provide the exemption for a sufficient length of time to make the payment of a bonus worthwhile.

Perhaps the most interesting result of the law was the claims by a few families, especially in the southern and midwestern United States, that they were really Negro, even though they had been accepted as white for generations without question. Their claims were aided by some of the old state laws from post-Civil War days, which defined a person as a Negro if as much as one drop of Negro blood coursed in his veins. The services of persons experienced in genealogy and heraldry were much sought after.

Congress was besieged with requests by other groups to qualify them for the tax exemption, but only after a delay until 1975 were Chinese and Japanese accepted. Religious groups set up a great outcry to be included, but nothing came of it, since nearly all of them had the attitude that only they, and no other group, should be included. It was also proposed that the law be scaled so that a larger exemption would be allowed if one were next door to a Negro and a somewhat smaller amount for living next door to a Mexican (of a lighter hue) and so on, but it was generally felt that such changes would have been discriminatory.

The effect on welfare was most unexpected—a sort of serendipity bonus to society. Once welfare recipients coming from the slums were accepted in their new neighborhoods, some force seemed to be set in motion that made them want to "catch up with the Joneses."

The word "neighbor" found a rebirth of meaning in its old sense. There was a great extension of help to those next door, and not all of it for the minority families. Once the barriers were breached in housing, they absolutely disappeared in employment and in nearly every part of American life. Even the unions lowered the subtle barriers that had stayed the invasion of dark-skinned workers into the crafts for so long. No longer were couples of mixed colors and sexes regarded with distrust or even surprise. The whole American society increasingly took on the characteristics of the population of Hawaii in that respect. In 1980 the United States Supreme Court ruled that the granting of an exemption based on race was unconstitutional. But by then the nation was bathed in an absolute plethora of tolerance.

CAIRO, ILLINOIS: A TOWN IN TROUBLED WATERS
JAMES M. HANSON

Cairo, Illinois, has received its share of publicity about intergroup tensions and conflict. Some observers have predicted a continuation of the trend toward polarization, with an inevitable outbreak of passions at some future time. Others are not that pessimistic. James M. Hanson, in providing us with a history of the situation, delineates some of the major factors that have contributed to the strife. His article reads as if the author were following a checklist similar to the one presented in Chapter Two: politics (election results), demography (population ratios), economics (median family income, welfare data), attitudes, and so on. He specifies some alternatives to violence: litigation, boycott, voter-registration plans, social structures for communications between Blacks and Whites. Hanson then describes the limitations of these strategies in Cairo.

Welcome to Cairo, deep in the Southland where Magnolia vies with the Mimosa.

Here on an inland island, surrounded by the Ohio, the Mississippi and the Cache Rivers spanned by five fine bridges, guarded by a multi-million dollar levee system excelled by none in the world, is Cairo, the cross-roads of the nation . . .—
Cairo Chamber of Commerce

*Cairo, Illinois, is on the verge of a total blood bath resulting from polarization and open war between Whites and Blacks.—*Cairo United Front

Cairo, Illinois, at the southern tip of Illinois between the Ohio and Mississippi

Rivers, is a town used to troubled waters. Its massive levee system, capable of withstanding a 60-foot flood crest, has saved the city from the violence of floods for one century, since 1871.

Cairo, at the crossroads of the world, in the Land of Lincoln with a Black population total approaching that of the White population, is a town distinguished by racial conflict, and there are no systems, physical or social, which appear capable of stopping the violence.

About 200 incidents of gunfire have occurred in the past three years, many of them involving the police. The United Front boycott of white retail establishments is now more than two years old, one of the longest in the history of American race relations.

Distrustful of the City's governmental institutions, which have remained in the control of whites, blacks have created a neighborhood council, their own version of local government. They have achieved some economic autonomy with the establishment of two cooperatives, one for food and another for clothing. Their separatist movement has also extended to housing, with the creation of the United Cairo Housing Board.

"Mediation Impossible"

The conflict centers on two opposing groups, the predominantly black United Front and the exclusively white United Citizens for Community Action. Both groups sponsored candidates in the April elections for City Council. The two UF candidates lost, while all three UCCA candidates won. The mayor, who favored the election of independent candidates, spoke once about the possibility of resigning but decided to continue. As in the recent defeat of the police community relations program, 3–2 council votes are not infrequent, with the three UCCA-affiliated Commissioners comprising the majority and the mayor and an elderly Commissioner of Finance the minority.

The UF sponsored boycott has also brought the Cairo Merchants Association into the conflict. Both sides have presented proposals for ending the boycott, but no negotiation has occurred. Disillusioned over whatever hope for reconciliation the election had offered, the United Front anticipates a continuation of the boycott, the violence, and the struggle against the white sector of Cairo.

"At this point, mediation appears impossible," says Ripley Young, a CDS consultant working with the United Front at the latter's request. "The local whites who might be predisposed to cooperate with United Front proposals or programs are fearful of doing so."

An integrated recreation program was started in the Summer of 1969 by the Cairo Committee for Recreation, with help from Frank Kowal, another CDS consultant. Directed by a bi-racial 16-member board, the Committee still meets regularly and sponsors indoor and outdoor activities primarily for youth. The indoor activities were curtailed when the Cairo school system, apparently under pressure from many whites in the community, denied the Committee access to its school buildings and facilities. Both the UF and UCCA have refused to support the Committee, and though the Committee has succeeded in gaining bi-racial cooperation in recreation activities, its example has not stimulated cooperation in other realms of community living.

The United Front offered two proposals to end the boycott, one in June 1969 and another in December 1970. The December resolution, entitled "Cease Fire Resolution," included eight points. The mayor, Albert "Pete" Thomas, interpreted the resolution title as an admission that the United Front was involved "in the shooting, the sniping, and such."

The Mayor and the Merchants Association had offered a proposal in September 1970 for ending the boycott but the United Front rejected the proposal. The merchants tried again in February 1971, offering 10 full-time jobs and 4 part-time jobs, this time with the support of a newly formed black organization named the People for Improvements of Cairo. A United Front leader angrily denounced the proposal: "Whites are still playing games. The people they're meeting with didn't start the boycott. How are they going to end it?" The boycott continued, and the new organization collapsed.

Objective Conditions

Oddly enough, all the parties involved agree about the importance of economic and general living conditions. The 1960 Census reported a median family income in Cairo of $3,385, the lowest for all Illinois communities over 2,500 population. Because of the economic effects of the boycott, the dwindling population and the general mistrust and violence in the community in the later 1960's, little has changed.

Welfare recipients constituted almost 40 percent of Cairo's population during the 1970–71 Winter; of those about 80 percent were black. Unemployment varies from about 8 to 11 percent, with over 20 percent for blacks. Poor whites and blacks compete for the same jobs. Wages are depressed, and blacks have become especially antagonized with the employment of whites living outside Cairo.

An investigating committee of the Illinois General Assembly concluded in 1969 that "low employment generally and among black males in particular has intensified the racial problem. Job competition among poor blacks and poor whites, including recent immigrants from surrounding depressed areas, has provoked harsh feelings. The high welfare rate has antagonized the white community and the tax base is seriously overburdened."

POPULATION FROM 1850–1970

Year	Population	Per Cent Negro
1850	2,242	3.3
1860	2,188	2.1
1870	6,267	29.5
1880	9,011	37.2
1890	10,324	35.9
1900	12,566	30.8
1910	14,548	37.4
1920	15,203	32.0
1930	13,532	33.8
1940	14,407	38.1
1950	12,123	36.1
1960	9,348	37.5
1970	6,177	40 + (est.)

Business and industrial activity have been decreasing. At least five stores in the downtown district have closed because of the boycott. Arson has brought about the destruction of a wood products plant and has resulted in damage to a lumber company and three warehouses. As a result, the Chamber of Commerce has attracted little industry.

The lack of adequate housing has persisted as a problem. Housing surveys for the last 15 years have consistently found about half of Cairo's housing to be substandard and in need of major repair. The mayor and City Council had established an authority, without consulting the United Front. The United Front established its own authority, with a bi-racial board, and eventually obtained a $40,000 planning grant from the state and federal agencies. The UF sponsored authority has attempted to purchase land from the City, but the City Council, disgruntled with the make-up of the authority, has refused to sell.

If writers such as Robert Ardrey are correct, Cairo could be predicted as a tension-prone community solely because of spatial limitations. The usual white middle class escape from poverty-ridden and black-controlled neighborhoods has been the movement to the outer edges of the city. But Cairo is surrounded by dikes and water; there is no ecological escape valve.

"Although more extreme, Cairo's problems are not much different than those of other communities," Young says. "But in Cairo, there is no moving away, there is no escaping the tensions of poverty and racism. We're all here on this small plot of ground surrounded by the levees and the rivers. There is no room to hide from the issues or the people."

Racial attitudes are also important, which Young describes as "a southern racist mentality." At 37 degrees north latitude, Cairo is as close to Jackson, Mississippi as to Chicago, Illinois. About one-third of its population is from out-of-state, with all of the larger contributing states being south of Illinois—Kentucky, Tennessee, Missouri, Mississippi, Arkansas, Alabama, Louisiana and Texas.

White racism forestalled until 1963 the integration of all public places. School integration was not completed until 1967. Separate public housing projects, one for low income whites and one for low income blacks, remain intact. The Protestant Churches remain virtually segregated, as do civic and fraternal organizations. When in cafes and other white controlled establishments, blacks habitually take the seat or booth nearest the doorway.

Racial antagonism is intensified by a generation gap. The white leadership is old; the black leadership is young. The typical white merchant or town leader is in his early sixties; the typical United Front member is in his early twenties.

The poverty, high unemployment, declining economy, poor housing, inadequate education, the dwindling population and tax base, the spatial crowding, the southern racist attitudes, and the traditional struggle of the young black turks against the old white guard—all these conditions have worked to intensify differences, the result being violence approaching civil warfare and polarization with little trust or willingness to compromise by either side.

Alternatives to Violence

Racially inspired violence occurred in Cairo in 1962, when a civil rights campaign was waged to desegregate public places. Many white residents responded by organizing the White Citizens Committee in order "to see that the rights of white persons in Cairo are protected," according to its first president, Fred Sullivan, a local poolroom proprietor.

Civil rights issues continued to promote racial tension in the mid-1960's. Whites reorganized in 1967, as the Cairo Chapter of the Committee of Ten Million. Recognized as an "auxiliary" police force by the City Council, the Chapter's members became known as the "White Hats," an appellation referring to the headgear they wore while conducting armed patrols through Cairo's streets. Shootouts became frequent, as blacks attempted to keep the White Hats out of their neighborhoods, especially the all-black Pyramid Courts housing project area.

The White Hats were disbanded in 1969, in accordance with a ruling by Illinois Attorney General William J. Scott. Whites reorganized again, forming the present United Citizens for Community Action. Later in the same year, a second white activist group was formed, the Cairo chapter of the White Citizen's Council with headquarters in Jackson, Mississippi.

FIGURE 13   State patrolmen move into position during a raid at residences of all-Black Pyramid Courts. (Courtesy of Community Development Newsletter.)

Blacks organized the United Front in 1969, after continued shooting into Pyramid Courts. It immediately retaliated with the boycott of downtown businesses. Since the time of its organization, the United Front has claimed the occurrence of over 150 "attacks on the black community."

Proper law enforcement, the obvious solution to the shooting and violence, has never been achieved. Cairo Police have usually failed to stop the shooting incidents or investigate them. Even with the presence of State Police in town, the firing of automatic weapons can be heard for two or three hour periods, most frequently on Saturday nights. State Police can be seen routinely re-routing traffic around the area of shooting.

In a study done in early 1970, the International Association of Chiefs of Police concluded that the Cairo Police Department was "ill-trained and lack the necessary leadership to accomplish its mission." It added, "there has been an indifference and lack of understanding by various governmental officials with regard to the current social and political issues."

With the help of the Lawyers Committee, a national organization of lawyers created in 1962 to help implement civil rights legislation in the South, the United Front has pursued legal means to protect the rights of blacks. Five different cases are currently being litigated, including one on law enforcement practices.

Unlike other black organizations in both the North and South, the United Front has not exploited the alternative of voting power. Its candidates have lost elections, and one sympathetic observer has attributed the failures to the United Front's neglect to wage a door-to-door voter registration campaign.

As a matter of tactics, the United Front has placed its emphasis on the boycott. Strategies are usually discussed in global terms, in reference to the traditional abuses of blacks and of the need for black awareness and unity. Charles Koen, a young, vociferous minister in the style of Jesse Jackson and director of the United Front, regards the Cairo struggle as an example of what is wrong with white America and what can be achieved in black America.

"Nehemiah rebuilt a city. But in doing so he had to protect himself and his workers. He carried his tools in one hand and his weapon in the other," says Koen. "The white man's response to our liberation has been typical—violence. He has shot at us. He has injured and killed our people. He has burned our businesses. He had had us arrested."

The way to liberation is black solidarity, Koen stresses. Blacks can no longer remain dependent on whites; blacks must create their own institutions and organizations. Help from whites must be initiated and defined by blacks, to the end of helping blacks help one another and of obtaining power in the community and nation.

The United Front has succeeded in unifying blacks, but liberation is still remote. Participating blacks no doubt feel a sense of inner liberation, but overt repression from the white community and local officials has increased. Nehemiah would not likely regard Cairo as a city being rebuilt.

The alternatives to the violence and continued polarization are almost inconceivable, once one becomes acquainted first-hand with Cairo, with its near total absence of trust or good will. As one resident put it, "there are no liberals in Cairo, and even if you don't want to be a radical on one side the other side doesn't leave you much choice."

Because of the polarization, there is no real communication in Cairo. There is only force, or the threat of force; there is the biological force of killing, the economic force of buying or selling, the political force of gaining an office and the legal force of winning a suit and obtaining injunctions.

The community of Cairo is battered and tossed by these forces. Like the river waters which engulfed the town earlier in its history, the conditions and forces of disintegration have swept through every street, into every home. Now 100 years after its last physical flooding, the protection of Cairo demands a new kind of levee-builder, to better channel the onrushing passions of its people and institutions.

THE IMPROBABLE CHANGE AGENT AND THE PH.B.

MARK HANSON

Chapter 11 discusses how an individual can sometimes alter intergroup relations by working as an evaluator. In the following selection, Mark Hanson tells what is involved in evaluating an action program. His account is candid and good-humored. The program he evaluated—Concerted Services—was designed to improve the living conditions of Pueblo Indians, Spanish Americans, as well as Anglos who resided in a poor county in New Mexico.

I had the good fortune to meet Rupert Cordova, the improbable change agent, during the period of time that is described here. Mark Hanson has done social scientists a good turn by providing this account of evaluation, and by putting Rupert Cordova into the literature.

I was an Ab.D. before I got the magical Ph.D. The Ab.D. is normally an unenviable condition, but even the grayest clouds can yield a silver lining. So it was for me. I want to share my learning. . . .

Everything began one day for the Ab.D. as he was sitting in the corner of the grad lounge sipping coffee and rebounding possible thesis topics. The chairman of his doctoral committee entered and performed a replay of the act so well depicted by Michaelangelo's "The Creation of Adam." As the story unfolded it appeared that the members of a high level, government task force were trying out a new change agent strategy to dissolve a pocket of poverty in the wilds of the southwest and they wanted to know if it was working. The young candidate was asked to do the study because of his fluency in Spanish (cultivated in Colombia) and his training in field research methodology. With no way to gracefully dodge "the king," and being on the verge of bankruptcy, he accepted with relief.

The study was to be located in a rural, economically depressed county in the southwest. It wasn't just a run-of-the-mill poor county; it was 1 of the 100 poorest in the nation. President Johnson's War on Poverty was in full swing at the time and his advisors were concerned because most of the millions were being sloshed up by the large urban cities and only a trickle was reaching the rural poor. Local people submitting grant proposals through locally-based organizations were the key to receiving development money. Many of the organizations entitled to receive Federal grants and sponsor new programs were found in both urban and rural centers, such as the Office of Economic Opportunity, Office of Public Health, Bureau of Indian Affairs, Welfare Department, Public Schools, City Government, and so forth. The President's men responded to the puzzling situation by placing a change agent in Pobre County to see if this approach would breathe some local initiative into the rural-based organizations.

In boning up on the subject, the young researcher found that the change agent concept suggests some form of intervention in the normal operations of an organization resulting in a restructuring of events. Interestingly enough, in the classical approach, the change agent is usually an outsider to the organization and does not have the authority to make decisions for any part of the system. He is an outsider because an insider frequently cannot see the forest for the trees, or he has his own vested interests, or he is somehow a part of the problem himself. The change agent cannot make decisions for the organization because the ultimate responsibility for the system is not his.

The change agent must work gingerly enough that the people in the organization accept his presence and deal openly with his initiatives. A threatening presence or a misplaced step on a sore toe can destroy the working effectiveness of the agent through a psychological or physical rejection from the system. His working tools are a product of his training, such as industrial psychology, managerial systems analysis, operations research, organizational theory, and so forth.

In examining the research literature on the change agent strategy, the researcher found that the personal characteristics of the agent are also quite important to his effectiveness. Charismatic leadership, psychological security, and affability in social relationships comprise a fine combination in the personal makeup of an agent. The prospects of the study had fired the imagination of the researcher and he dug into the literature with a zeal.

Going into the field to begin a study is always an exhilarating moment. The arrival, however, is often a deflating realization that the imagination had done its work and things weren't as they were going to be. Driving into the county seat of Pobre County the researcher was depressed. Grinding poverty was everywhere evident. Stopping in front of a worn and beaten 1 story stucco on a street spaced with worn and beaten 1 story stuccos, the researcher entered to meet his subject.

The inside of the building was slightly more agreeable than the outside. A reception room came first, with 2 secretaries and a mass of filing cabinets. Ushered through to the back office, the researcher finally met Rupert Cordova—change agent in residence. As Mr. Cordova extended his greeting and his hand, the researcher thought that the whole configuration of his body suggested he was made to sit in a chair. Charismatic leader was definitely not the appropriate word. In fact, this fellow could probably get lost in a crowd of 3 people. Education—none visibly evident. With a sudden sinking feeling the researcher sensed that the year ahead would indeed be a long one. Here he stood, literally dripping with all the latest sociological theories on the woes of the world and his prospects of using them seemed quickly approaching zero.

The next morning, with little vim but a lot of vigor, the researcher settled down to work. The research problem was easy enough to visualize. The people of

Pobre County wanted desperately to improve their socioeconomic state and the government wanted equally as much to eliminate the pockets of poverty that Pobre County typified. In a sense, 2 systems desired to converge for a mutual undertaking. Unfortunately, in the business of getting together something was not working in the rural-centered organizations that was working in the big city-centered organizations.

Seeking the roots of this problem would entail a probing look at the history, geography, cultural norms, economy, and life style of the identifiable groups in Pobre County. This effort would be no mean task because the cast of characters resembled an old, John Wayne movie—Apache, Navajo, and Pueblo Indians resided in the area along with a slim majority of Spanish-Americans and a few pale faces called Anglos. In other words, Pobre County represented several cultures, several histories, and several futures.

The next step of the study would be to determine what was lacking with respect to the government's response in reaching out to assist the people of Pobre County. Finally, it would be necessary to determine what the change agent was doing, or not doing, to create missing linkages between the government's organizations of delivery and the organizations in the County which were seeking that delivery.

To the researcher, those first few weeks on the job resembled the day of the long night; no corners were turned, no light at the end of the tunnel, no meaningful patterns fitting nicely into the puzzle. He poured over yards of file material taking copious notes on endless pads of yellow paper. He sat inconspicuously in the background at dozens of meetings trying to detect the sum and substance of the energy flow as well as the role played by the change agent—who always seemed to be present when 3 or more people assembled for whatever purpose.

The change agent would travel with his shadow in tow around the County from organization to organization talking and drinking coffee with agency directors, talking and drinking coffee with agency employees, talking and drinking coffee with anyone who happened to be in the area. "You can't push too hard with these people," Mr. Cordova would say. "If you move too fast they will never talk to you again."

After the first 2 or 3 months, the community began to accept the researcher as harmless, but only after a low-key selling job by Mr. Cordova. "This fellow here is a friend of mine," he often would say, "he's here to learn the business." Other times he would say, "My friend here came down from the university to see if I was doing a good job for you people. Better watch what you tell him cause he's smart; he's studying for his Ph.B." The researcher never quite understood what was meant by the Ph.B. comment.

In the early days of the study the researcher was always ready to rip off a few paragraphs of fluent Spanish to impress the locals, but they rarely seemed impressed. In fact, they didn't seem to follow it well. It wasn't long before the young outsider began to realize that the indigenous language of the Spanish-American was neither Spanish nor English. It seemed to be an insiders code grafted with English and Spanish constructions, saturated with idiomatic expressions and punched up with innumerable nonverbal cues. English rather than "Spanglish" proved to be the most precise language of communication for the doctoral candidate.

Much valuable information was picked up as the change agent and the researcher drove across the rock and sand basin of that beautiful but impoverished land. The researcher would dangle a tape recorder from the rearview mirror and ask endless questions which Mr. Cordova seemed to enjoy answering. A knowledge base was beginning to build and some patterns began to fall into place.

The receipt of Federal development money was dependent on local organizations acting on their own initiative sending up to Washington, or a regional office, a precise and comprehensive project proposal. The granting process depended on the local organizations knowing which Federal agency had available funds, what type of projects the agency was funding, and the specific proposal specifications which had to be met. In the grantsmanship effort, the large urban cities proved to have every advantage over the rural communities. For example, the Federal government's communication net went in a direct line from Washington to the regional offices to the large urban centers and terminated. Any organization located in a large urban center could simply call around the city looking for information on grant money.

Also, large professional organizations such as the city planning office, the chamber of commerce, or institutions of higher learning had expert writers who could generate proposals at the first smell of money. These organizations also had a power structure that could command the ears, and often the throat, of the decision-making process in Washington. Of no small import was that the directors of organizations in the big cities were upwardly mobile and every proposal they could get funded would reflect favorably on their careers as well as provide a beneficial service for the poor.

In Pobre County there was no extension of the Federal communication net, therefore little or no proposal information was available. It wouldn't occur to anyone to call the big city and ask about project money—the fast moving world of high finance can be very intimidating to someone who has not had a high school education. Besides, a phone call to the city would be a long distance call, and who has that kind of money? Going to the big city and trying to make a point at a public meeting can also be hazardous. The researcher attended a number of meetings in which small clusters of poor people held their tongues because they did not understand parliamentary procedure and did not want to appear foolish in public by talking at the wrong time.

There were virtually no professionals living in Pobre County. A high school diploma was the sign of an educated man. There was no tradition of forming tough, task-oriented groups in this rural area. Absolutely no one could read and comprehend the bureaucratic verbiage and unintelligible expressions that made up the project proposal guidelines. One local group tried 4 times to get a proposal through and each time it was returned because of insufficient data. It finally quit trying.

Before the arrival of the change agent, there was no one in the county who could write a proposal and there was no money to pay an expert, professional writer. There was no planning commission, no chamber of commerce, or no university to lend expertise or political muscle. In fact, there was no political muscle anywhere in the county. Also, many of the local organization directors were found to be rather unenthusiastic about bringing on additional responsibilities and all the unstable dynamite that came with War on Poverty funds. They were hanging onto their jobs waiting for retirement and had no vision of personal, upward mobility.

In essence, success in local grantsmanship was dependent on a well-organized effort which could draw on various types of professional expertise as well as politically exploit the decision-making process in Washington. Before the arrival of the change agent, Pobre County didn't have a chance. An impoverished rural area such as Pobre County had few, if any, of the ingredients that it took to obtain development money intended for the poor. In fact, the poorer a county happened to be the less chance it had to obtain the funds necessary for local development.

As the months passed, the researcher became increasingly aware that he was watching a master chess player who had 2 games going simultaneously. The first involved a subtle operation to organize segments of the county into a sophisticated operation intended to obtain Federal funds. The change agent was not pushy in this task and to the casual observer it must have looked as though he was following the community rather than leading. His office became a clearinghouse for proposal information which was fed into his own communication net that spread into every corner of the county.

When the agent's 2 very capable secretaries were volunteered to become the official recorders of most of the development organizations in the county, the meetings quickly began to take on a professional tone and communication into the outside world became sophisticated and well-reasoned. Mr. Cordova, in the meantime, was busy searching out uninvolved people with leadership skills and ushering them into key roles. The change agent would never accept an official position in a development organization, but always chose to reside in the background and act in the role of consultant when called upon. Even when he was successful in stage-managing a masterful bit of grantsmanship, he quietly stood back and let the plaudits of the community fall on the leadership of the organization that stood as sponsor of the project.

Jostling the county level agencies out of their comfortable levels of satisfaction was a significant problem that Mr. Cordova had to face. Much of the War on Poverty had to be conducted through these types of local government agencies and their aggressive participation in seeking poverty program grants and sponsoring projects was crucial to the overall strategy. The change agent's approach to the local agency was a patient program of educating them to the need and possible payoff to Pobre County. All those conversations over cups of coffee that the researcher had wondered about entered into this effort. Unfortunately, many local agency directors assumed that the potential cost to them and their well-regulated agencies outweighed the possible benefits, thus their resolve to keep the status quo quickened.

The change agent's response to stiffening defenses was a rather unique form of escalation. He very subtly and skillfully injected into and around a target agency an ever increasing level of tension that could only be relieved by the director making the decision that Mr. Cordova advocated. Also, he was able to do this without attracting attention to himself or getting himself cut off from the friendly, working relationships he had established. The change agent accomplished this by convincing subordinates of a target agency that the benefits to the local people far outweighed the costs to the agency. The subordinates, of course, did not have the same set of vested interests that their director held dear. After this initial fissure between the director and some of his staff had been silently engineered, the entire situation would mysteriously go public. This new development would mean that the stubborn agency director was not only faced with a division in his own organization, but he was also faced with an irate public demanding that immediate and forceful steps be taken to obtain the Federal money intended to help the poor. About this time Mr. Cordova would come around for a chat and a cup of coffee and have an answer—surprise, surprise—to get the agency director off the hook. In no time at all a proposal would emerge from the change agent's office, but always over the signature of the newly converted director.

The second chess game that the change agent had going was with the maze of little and big men that made up the decision-making machinery in the Federal bureaucracy. After a clean and comprehensive proposal surfaced from a potential sponsoring organization in Pobre County, Mr. Cordova would begin to orchestrate a set of inspired moves that frequently left the researcher spellbound. The change agent knew that the bureaucracy in Washington could intentionally or unintentionally suffocate the most creative efforts arising from the hands of the very people it was supposed to serve. The change agent also knew that the bureaucracy, like any creation of man, had its share of Achilles heels and with a few surgically placed strokes, the insulation surrounding the system could be breached.

When encountering a formidable opponent in Washington, the change agent would often play upon the same variable that he used so effectively at the county level—the creation of tension around the decision maker. His use of tension could be deceptively simple or extremely complex depending on the nature of the problem faced. An example of the former might be a letter sent to a Washington office which plays a critical role in project funding. The body of the letter would request positive action on funding a specific proposal, and at the bottom the reader would find: "Copy sent to: Secretary of HEW; U.S. Senator Sam Jones; U.S. Representative Sam Smith." A letter with this type of audience cannot be taken lightly by its intended recipient.

The change agent's more complex strategies were often worthy of an Academy Award. Mr. Cordova knew that the men with the heavy titles in Washington liked to visit the field so they could occasionally rub elbows with genuine poor people. The residents of Pobre County had seen these VIP's before and the important people always seemed to bring along a 2-part message. The first part was an expression of how much Washington loved the rural poor and would do anything in its power to help and the second part was a statement of how the government's limited resources couldn't cover everything; therefore, the people of Pobre County shouldn't expect much help for the present. When Mr. Cordova began orchestrating the VIP visits, he created a situation in which the visitor would receive a 2-part message. After a scenario including a tour of an Indian reservation, an economically depressed Spanish-American hamlet, and a number of run-down houses in the county seat, the VIP would suddenly find himself in a room with 30 mad-as-hell Navajo Indians. Just as General Custer must have been impressed, for a short time at least, with the needs of the Sioux Nation, so was the VIP visibly impressed with the needs of the Navajo. This inspired group of Indians would tell the visitor in no uncertain terms that they were not happy with the way things were going and that they held him personally responsible. A number of proposals were funded after this type of unforgettable visit to Pobre County.

For the young researcher, the final weeks of the study came and went all too quickly. During the course of his study, he had seen a major vocational school complex constructed, a vocational training program initiated, adult education classes begun, recreation facilities developed, irrigation ditches cemented, health programs expanded, several hundred hard-core unemployed residents trained for productive jobs, and many other worthy projects completed which made a significant impact on the lives of hundreds of people in the county. As the researcher packed his yellow pads of paper for the last time, he couldn't help but think that one man really can make a difference in the face of a seemingly hopeless situation—especially if the man understands how the bureaucratic system works and is skilled enough to use the system against itself rather than be used by it.

The young researcher finally received his doctoral degree and his study was published and soon forgotten. But the young man never forgot the education he received in Pobre County and he always felt that Mr. Cordova should have received the Ph.D. and the researcher should have received that Ph.B.

For Further Reading

Many of the items among the references cited may be considered as recommended reading as well.

Arensberg, Conrad M., and Arthur H. Niehoff. *Introducing Social Change: A Manual For Americans Overseas.* Chicago: Aldine, 1964.

Brown, J. A. C. *Techniques of Persuasion: From Propaganda to Brainwashing.* Baltimore: Penguin, 1967 (originally published in 1963).

Elkouri, Frank. *How Arbitration Works.* Washington, D.C.: Bureau of National Affairs, 1973.

Klapper, Joseph T. *The Effects of Mass Communication.* New York: Free Press, 1960.

Lewin, Kurt. *Resolving Social Conflicts: Selected Papers on Group Dynamics.* New York: Harper & Row, 1948.

Pettigrew, Thomas F. *Racially Separate or Together?* New York: McGraw-Hill, 1971.

Rein, Irving J. *Rudy's Red Wagon: Communication Strategies in Contemporary Society.* Glenview, Ill.: Scott, Foresman, 1972.

Rogers, Everett M., and F. Floyd Shoemaker. *Communication of Innovations: A Cross-Cultural Approach.* New York: Free Press, 1971.

Silberman, Charles E. *Crisis in Black and White.* New York: Random House, 1964.

Suchman, Edward A. *Evaluative Research.* New York: Russell Sage, 1967.

U.S. Commission on Civil Rights. *School Desegregation in Ten Communities.* Washington, D.C.: Clearinghouse Publication No. 43, June 1973.

Weinberg, Meyer. *Desegregation Research: An Appraisal.* Bloomington, Ind.: Phi Delta Kappa, 1970.

Williams, Robin M., Jr. *The Reduction of Intergroup Tensions: A Survey of Research on Problems of Ethnic, Racial, and Religious Group Relations.* New York: Social Science Research Council, 1947.

Young, Whitney M., Jr. *Beyond Racism: Building an Open Society.* New York: McGraw-Hill, 1971.

Epilogue

Two sets of forces are always present in society. One furthers incorporation of individuals into larger aggregations; the other promotes specialization, isolation, and separateness. Attaining a humane *rapprochement* between these counterforces, which have been compared to centrifugal and centripetal forces, is perhaps the basic problem of intergroup relations.

Such a *rapprochement* requires a perspective—a world view—that can tolerate differences. One of the most perceptive statements on this subject is that of the astronaut Frank Borman:

> The view of the earth from the moon fascinated me—a small disk, 240,000 miles away. It was hard to think that that little thing held so many problems, so many frustrations. Raging nationalistic interests, famines, wars, pestilence don't show from that distance. I'm convinced that some wayward stranger in a spacecraft, coming from some other part of the heavens, could look at earth and never know that it was inhabited at all. But the same wayward stranger would

FIGURE 14 View of earth, as seen from the moon. (Courtesy of the National Aeronautics and Space Administration.)

certainly know instinctively that if the earth were inhabited, then the destiny of all who lived on it must inevitably be interwoven and joined. We are one hunk of ground, water, air, clouds, floating around in space. From out there it really is "one world." Borman et al., 1969, p. 28)

It may be that Borman's ideas are too detached and too rational to sway everyday affairs in modern society for long. The differences are probably felt too deeply. Ways must thus be sought to let the differences exist but to keep their expression within bounds. "And if we cannot end now our differences," John Fitzgerald Kennedy once said, "at least we can help make the world safe for diversity."

Relations among groups can be visualized as a continuum, with separation at one end and complete assimilation at the other. Pluralism is located between these poles. Pluralism implies pride of group, but it probably is true of groups, as of individuals, that respect for others is impossible without self-esteem.[1] Admittedly, group pride can lead to tribalism; but it need not if it can be coupled with tolerance.

Whether or not this goal can be attained is not clear. The ability to cope with the problems that emerge from diversity probably will continue to be uneven. In some places and at some times racism will prevail to such an extent that only two choices will be open: protest without hope of change or acquiescence. Indeed, Isaac Deutscher once wrote that such a choice often confronts the intellectual, not just in intergroup relations, but on many social issues as well. Some societies will fare better than others, probably because they will be able to develop greater capacities than others for accepting diversity.

[1] Howard J. Ehrlich refers to an analogous phenomenon at the individual level as the *principle of self-congruity*: "The more favorable are a person's self-attitudes, the greater the number of acceptable targets and the more positive their attitudes toward them; the more negative the self-attitudes the greater the number of unacceptable targets and the more negative are attitudes toward them" (1973, p. 130).

References

Aberle, D. K., A. K. Cohen, A. K. David, M. J. Levy, Jr., and F. X. Sutton. "The Functional Prerequisites of a Society." *Ethics, 60* (1950), pp. 100–111.

Adorno, T. W., Else Frenkel-Brunswik, D. J. Levison, and R. L. Sanford. *The Authoritarian Personality.* New York: Harper & Row, 1950.

Allport, Gordon W. "Attitudes." In C. Murchison (ed.), *Handbook of Social Psychology.* Worcester, Mass.: Clark University Press, 1935.

———. *The Nature of Prejudice.* Garden City, N.Y.: Doubleday, 1958 (originally published, Addison-Wesley, 1954).

Alsop, Stewart. "Affairs of State." *Saturday Evening Post, 240,* No. 19 (1967), p. 16.

American Anthropological Associations, *Newsletter,* 13 (1972).

American Friends Service Committee and the National Committee Against Discrimination in Housing. *Fair Housing Handbook.* Philadelphia: 1968.

Amir, Y. "Contact Hypothesis in Ethnic Relations." *Psychological Bulletin, 71* (1969), 319–342.

Aptheker, Herbert. *A Documentary History of the Negro People in the United States*

From the Colonial Era to the Founding of the NAACP. Vol. 1. Secaucus, N.J.: Citadel, 1951.

————. *A Documentary History of the Negro People in the United States From the Emergence of the NAACP to the Beginning of the New Deal (1910–1932).* Secaucus, N.J.: Citadel, 1973.

Arensberg, Conrad M., and Arthur H. Niehoff. *Introducing Social Change: A Manual For Americans Overseas.* Chicago: Aldine, 1965 (originally published, 1964).

Babel, Isaac. "You Must Know Everything." In Nathalie Babel (ed.), *Stones, 1915–1937*, trans. by Max Hayward. New York: Farrar Straus and Giroux, 1969.

Bagley, Christopher. "Race Relations and Theories of Status Consistency," *Race*, 1970, *11*, No. 3, pp. 267–288.

Baldwin, James. Quoted in Charles E. Silberman, *Crisis in Black and White*. New York: Random House, 1964.

Bane, Mary Jo., and Christopher Jencks, "Five Myths About Your I.Q." *Harper's, 246* (1973), pp. 28–40.

Banton, Michael. *Race Relations.* New York: Basic Books, 1967.

————. "Africa South of the Sahara." In Melvin M. Turnin (ed.), *Comparative Perspective on Race Relations.* Boston: Little, Brown, 1969.

Barth, Frederick. *Ethnic Groups and Boundaries.* Boston: Little, Brown, 1969.

Beadle, George W. "Genes, Culture, and Man." In Morton H. Fried (ed.), *Readings in Anthropology.* Vol. 1. New York: Crowell, 1968.

Beals, Ralph E., and Harry Hoijer. *An Introduction to Anthropology.* New York: Macmillan, 1965.

Bell, Daniel. "National Character Revisited: A Proposal for Renegotiating the Concept." In Edward Norbeck, Douglas Price-Williams, and William M. McCord, *The Study of Personality: An Interdisciplinary Appraisal.* New York: Holt, Rinehart and Winston, 1968.

Bell, Robert R. *Social Deviance.* Homewood, Ill.: Dorsey, 1971.

Bendix, Reinhard, and Seymour Martin Lipset. "Karl Marx's Theory of Social Classes." In Reinhard Bendix and Seymour Martin Lipset (eds.), *Class, Status, and Power.* New York: Free Press, 1966.

Benedict, Ruth. *Patterns of Culture.* Boston: Houghton Mifflin, 1959 (originally published, 1934).

Bennett, Lerone, Jr. *The Negro Mood.* New York: Ballantine, 1964.

Berger, Morroe. *Equality by Statute.* Garden City, N.Y.: Doubleday, 1968.

Bernard, Jessie. *Social Problems at Mid-Century.* New York: Dryden, 1957.

Berne, Eric. *Games People Play.* New York: Grove, 1967 (originally published, 1967).

Berreman, Gerald D. "Caste in India and the U.S." *American Journal of Sociology, 64* (1960), 120–127.

Berry, Brewton. *Almost White.* New York: Macmillan, 1963.

————. *Race and Ethnic Relations.* Boston: Houghton Mifflin, 1965.

————. *The Education of the American Indians: A Survey of the Literature.* Columbus: Research Foundation, Ohio State University, 1968.

Beveridge, Albert J. *The Life of John Marshall.* Vol. 4. Boston: Houghton Mifflin, 1919.

Billingsley, Andrew. *Black Families in White America.* Englewood Cliffs, N.J.: Prentice Hall, 1968.

Black Panther: Black Community News Service. Vol. 14, no. 12. San Francisco: Ministry of Information, Black Panther Party, 1970.

Blalock, Hubert M., Jr. *Toward a Theory of Minority Group Relations.* New York: Wiley, 1967.

————. *Theory Construction: From Verbal to Mathematical Formulations.* Englewood Cliffs, N.J.: Prentice-Hall, 1969.

Blauner, Robert. "Internal Colonialism and Ghetto Revolt." *Social Problems, 16* (Spring 1969), 393–408.

Blumer, Herbert. "Race Prejudice as a Sense of Group Position." *Pacific Sociological Review, 1* (Spring 1958), 3–7.

Blumer, Herbert, and Andrew W. Lind. *Race Relations in World Perspective.* Honolulu: University of Hawaii Press, 1955.

Boas, Franz. *The Mind of Primitive Man.* New York: Free Press, 1965 (originally published, 1911).

Bogardus, E. S. "Measuring Social Distances." *Journal of Applied Sociology, 9* (1925), pp. 299–308.

————. "Comparing Racial Distance in Ethiopia, South Africa, and the United States." *Sociology and Social Research, 52* (1968), pp. 149–156.

Bolton, E. B. "Effect of Knowledge Upon Attitudes Toward the Negro." *Journal of Social Psychology, 6* (1935), 68–90.

Borman, Frank, Jim Lovell, and Bill Anders. "Our Moon Journey." *Life,* Vol. 66 (1969), No. 2, pp. 26–31.

Brown, Claude. *Manchild in the Promised Land.* New York: New American Library, 1965.

Brown, J. A. C. *Techniques of Persuasion.* Baltimore: Penguin, 1967.

Caplow, Theodore. *Two against One: Coalitions in Triads.* Englewood Cliffs, N.J.: Prentice-Hall, 1968.

Carmichael, Stokely, and Charles V. Hamilton. *Black Power: The Politics of Liberation in America.* New York: Random House, 1967.

Cheng, C. K., and Douglas S. Yamamura. "Interracial Marriage and Divorce in Hawaii," *Social Forces, 36* (1957), 77.

Clark, Kenneth B. *Prejudice and Your Child.* Boston: Beacon Press, 1955.

————. "The Wonder Is There Have Been So Few Riots." In Milton B. Barron (ed.), *Minorities in a Changing World.* New York: Knopf, 1967.

Clark, Kenneth B., and M. P. Clark. *Racial Identification and Preference in Negro Children.* New York: Holt, Rinehart and Winston, 1947.

Clébert, Jean-Paul. *The Gypsies.* Baltimore: Penguin, 1969 (originally published, 1961).

Coleman, James S., *et al. Equality of Educational Opportunity.* Washington, D.C.: Government Printing Office, 1966.

Coolidge, Mary. *Chinese Immigration.* New York: Henry Holt and Company, 1907.

Comas, Juan. *Racial Myths.* Paris: UNESCO, 1951.

Coon, Carleton, S., S. M. Garn, and J. B. Birdsell. *Races: A Study of Race Formation in Man*. Springfield, Ill.: Charles C Thomas, 1950.

Cooper, Thomas, and David J. McCord (eds.). *Statutes at Large of South Carolina*. 10 vols. Columbia, S.C.: 1836–1841.

Cornford, Francis Macdonald (trans.). *The Republic of Plato*. New York: Oxford University Press, 1945.

Coser, Lewis A. *The Functions of Social Conflict*. New York: Free Press, 1956.

Coser, Lewis A. "Conflict." In David L. Sills (Editor), *International Encyclopedia of the Social Sciences*, Vol. 3. New York: The Macmillan Company, pp. 232–236, 1968.

Cox, Oliver C. *Caste, Class, and Race: A Study in Social Dynamics*. New York: Doubleday, 1948.

Crain, Robert L. "School Integration and Occupational Achievement of Negroes," *American Journal of Sociology, 75* (1970), 593–606.

Dabaghian, Jane W. (ed.). *Mirror of Man*. Boston: Little, Brown, 1970.

Dahrendorf, Ralf. *Class and Class Conflict in Industrial Society*. Stanford: Stanford University Press, 1959.

Dane, J. K., and B. Eugene Griessman. "The Collective Identity of Marginal Peoples: The North Carolina Experience." *The American Anthropologist, 74* (June 1972), 694–704.

Darrett, Mary Ellen, and Achsah J. Davey. "Racial Awareness in Young Mexican–American and Anglo Children." *Young Children, 26* (1970), *No. 1*, 19–20.

Davey, Achsah J. *Contemporary Collective Bargaining*. Englewood Cliffs, N.J.: Prentice-Hall, 1972.

Davies, James C. "Toward a Theory of Revolution." *American Sociological Review, 27* (1962). Pp. 5–19.

Davis, Kingsley. *Human Society*. New York: Macmillan, 1949.

DeFleur, M. L., and F. R. Westie. "Verbal Attitudes and Overt Acts: An Experiment on the Salience of Attitudes." *American Sociological Review, 23* (1958), 667–673.

Dill, S. *Society in the Last Century of the Western Empire*. London: Macmillan, 1925.

Dobzhansky, Theodosius. *Mankind Evolving: The Evolution of the Human Species*. New Haven: Yale University Press, 1962.

Dollard, John. *Caste and Class in a Southern Town*. Garden City, N.Y.: Doubleday, 1957 (originally published 1937).

Dollard, J., L. Doob, N. Miller, O. Mowrer, and R. Sears. *Frustration and Aggression*. New Haven: Yale University Press, 1939.

Doob, Leonard W. *Becoming More Civilized: A Psychological Exploration*. New Haven: Yale University Press, 1960.

Doyle, Bertram. *The Etiquette of Race Relations in the South*. New York: Schocken, 1971 (originally published 1937).

Drake, St. Clair, and Horace R. Cayton. *Black Metropolis: A Study of Negro Life in a Northern City*. New York: Harper & Row, First Torchback Edition, 1962 (originally published, 1945).

DuBois, W. E. Burghardt. "The Talented Tenth." In *the Negro Problem: A Series of Articles by Representative American Negroes of Today.* New York: Pott, 1903. Pp. 560–575.
———. *Dusk of Dawn.* New York: Harcourt, 1940.
Durkheim, Émile. *Division of Labor in Society.* New York: Free Press, 1947.
———. *Suicide: A Study of Sociology,* trans. by J. A. Spaulding and G. Simpson. New York: Free Press, 1951.
———. *The Rules of Sociological Method.* New York: Free Press, 1966 (originally published, 1938).

Ehrlich, Howard J., *The Social Psychology of Prejudice: A Systematic Theoretical Review and Propositional Inventory of the American Social Psychological Study of Prejudice.* New York: Wiley, 1973.
Eisenstadt, S. N. *The Absorption of Immigrants: A Comparative Study Based Mainly on the Jewish Community in Palestine and the State of Israel.* London: Routledge, 1954.
Eisenstadt, S. N. *Social Differentiation and Stratification.* Glenview, Illinois: Scott, Foresman and Company, 1971.
Elkins, Stanley M. *Slavery: A Problem in American Institutional and Intellectual Life.* Chicago: University of Chicago Press, 1959.
Elkouri, Frank. *How Arbitration Works.* Washington, D.C.: Bureau of National Affairs, 1973.
Essien-Udom, E. U. *Black Nationalism.* New York: Dell, 1962.
Eysenck, H. J. *The I.Q. Argument: Race Intelligence and Education.* New York: Library Press, 1971.

Fallers, L. A. (ed.). *Immigrants and Associations.* Paris: Mouton, 1967.
Fanon, Frantz. *Black Skin, White Masks.* New York: Grove, 1967.
———. *Wretched of the Earth.* New York: Grove, First Evergreen Black Cat Edition, 1968.
Finley, John H., Jr. (trans.). *The Complete Writings of Thucydides: The Peloponnesian War.* New York: Modern Library, 1951.
Fisk, Margaret (ed.). *Encyclopedia of Associations.* Detroit: Gale Research Co., 1973.
Foote, Nelson N. "Identification as the Basis for a Theory of Motivation." *American Sociological Review, 16* (February 1951), 17.
Ford, W. Scott. "Interracial Public Housing in a Border City: Another Look at the Contact Hypothesis." *American Journal of Sociology, 78* (May 1973), 1426–1447.
Franklin, John Hope. *The Future of Negro American History.* New York: Social Science Research Council, 1969.
Frazier, Franklin E. *Black Bourgeoisie: The Rise of a New Middle Class.* New York: Free Press, 1957.
Frazier, Franklin E. *The Negro Family in the United States.* Chicago: The University of Chicago Press, 1939.
———. *The Negro in the United States.* New York: Macmillan Company, 1949.

Freeman, Howard E., J. Michael Ross, and Thomas F. Pettigrew. "Color Gradations and Attitudes Among Middle-Income Negroes." *American Sociological Review, 31* (1966), 365–374.

Freud, Sigmund. *Civilization and Its Discontents*, trans. by James Strachey. New York: Norton, 1962.

"The Gangs of Chinatown." *Newsweek,* July 2, 1973, p. 22.

Garnett, Bernard E. "Black Banking in the Black Community." *Race Relations Reporter,* Vol. 3, No. 1 (January, 1973).

Gayarre, Charles. Quoted in David Lowenthal, "Race and Color in the West Indies." In J. H. Franklin, *Color and Race.* Boston: Houghton Mifflin, 1968. p. 332.

Gibbs, J. and W. Martin. *Status Integration and Suicide.* Eugene, Oregon: The University of Oregon Press, 1964.

Gharye, G. S. *Caste and Class in India.* Bombay: Popular Book Depot, 1957.

Glock, Charles Y., and Rodney Stark. *Christian Beliefs and Anti-Semitism.* New York: Harper & Row, 1966.

Gobineau, Arthur de. *Essay on the Inequality of Human Races.* New York: Fertig, 1915 (originally published, 1854).

Goldsby, Richard A. *Race and Races.* New York: Macmillan, 1971.

Goldschmidt, Walter. *Man's Way: A Preface to the Understanding of Human Society.* New York: Holt, Rinehart and Winston, 1959.

Gordon, Chad. *Looking Ahead: Self-Conceptions, Race and Family as Determinants of Adolescent Orientation to Achievement.* Washington, D.C.: American Sociological Association, 1972.

Gordon, Milton M. *Assimilation in American Life: The Role of Race, Religion and Natural Origins.* New York: Oxford University Press, 1964.

Gossett, Thomas F. *Race, The History of an Idea in America.* Dallas: SMU Press, 1963.

Gouldner, Alvin W. "The Sociologist as Partisan: Sociology and the Welfare State," *The American Sociologist, 3* (1968), 103.

Greer, Scott. *Last Man In.* New York: Free Press, 1959.

Grier, William H., and Price M. Cobbs. *Black Rage.* New York: Bantam, 1968.

Griessman, B. Eugene. "Toward an Understanding of Urban Unrest and Rioting." *Journal of Human Relations, 16* (1968), 315–332.

————. "An Approach to Evaluating Comprehensive Social Projects." *Educational Technology*, Vol. 9, No. 2 (1969), pp. 16–19.

————. "The American Isolates." *The American Anthropologist, 74* (1972), pp. 693, 694.

Haley, Alex. *The Autobiography of Malcolm X.* New York: Grove, 1966.

Hall, Edward T. *The Hidden Dimension.* New York: Doubleday, 1966.

Hamilton, Charles V. "The Black Revolution: A Primer for White Liberals," *The Progressive,* (1969), 29–31.

Harding, John, Harold Proshansky, Bernard Kutner, and Isidor Chein. "Prejudice and Ethnic Relations." In Gardner Lindzey and Elliot Aronson (eds.), *The Handbook of Social Psychology.* Vol. 5. Reading, Mass.: Addison-Wesley, 1969, pp. 1–76.

Harvey, Herbert R. "The Florentine Codex." *Natural History,* 79 (1970), 42.

Hayden, Tom. *Rebellion in Newark: Official Violence and Ghetto Response.* New York: Vintage, 1967.

Henry, Jules. "American Schoolrooms: Learning the Nightmare." In Frank Lindefeld (ed.), *Radical Perspectives on Social Problems.* New York: Macmillan, 1968. Pp. 56–66.

Herodotus. *History of the Greek and Persian Wars,* trans. by George Rawlinson. New York: Washington Square Press, 1963.

Herrnstein, Richard. "I.Q.," *Atlantic Monthly,* 228 (1971), 44–64.

Hertzberg, Hazel W. *The Search for An American Indian Identity: Modern Pan-Indian Movements.* Syracuse: Syracuse University Press, 1971.

Hertzler, J. O. *American Social Institutions.* Boston: Allyn & Bacon, 1961.

Himes, Joseph S. "A Theory of Racial Conflict." Paper presented at Annual Meeting of the Southern Sociological Society, Atlanta, May 1970.

Hitler, Adolf. *Mein Kampf.* Munich: S. Eher, 1943.

Hoffer, Eric. "Real Originality." *News and Observer* (Raleigh, N.C.), March 21, 1969, p. 12.

Holmes, O. W., Jr. "Law and Science and Science and Law." In O. W. Holmes, Jr., *Collected Legal Papers.* New York: Peter Smith, 1952.

Hörmann, Bernhard L. "Racial Complexion of Hawaii's Future Population," *Social Forces, 25* (1948), pp. 68–72.

House, Floyd N. "Viewpoints and Methods in the Study of Race Relations," *American Journal of Sociology, 40* (1934), pp. 440–452.

Howard, John R. "The Making of a Black Muslim," *Transaction, 4* (1966), 19.

Hraba, Joseph. "The Doll Technique: A Measure of Racial Ethnocentrism?" *Social Forces, 50* (June 1972), 522–527.

Hraba, Joseph, and G. Grant. "Black is Beautiful: A Reexamination of Racial Preference and Identification." *Journal of Personality and Social Psychology, 16* (November 1970), 398–402.

Hunt, Chester L., and Lewis Walker. *Ethnic Dynamics: Patterns of Intergroup Relations in Various Societies.* Ontario: Irwin-Dorsey, 1974.

Hunter, Guy. *South-East Asia: Race, Culture, and Nation.* New York: Oxford University Press, 1966.

Hutton, J. H. *Caste in India.* New York: Oxford University Press, 1963.

Hyman, Herbert H., and Eleanor Singer (eds.). *Readings in Reference Group Theory and Research.* New York: Free Press, 1968.

Irwin, M., T. Tripodi, and J. Bieri. "Affective Stimulus Value and Cognitive Complexity." *Journal of Personality and Social Psychology,* Vol. 5 (1967), pp. 444–449.

Jencks, Christopher. "Busing—The Supreme Court Goes North." *The New York Times Magazine,* November 19, 1972, p. 41.

Jencks, Christopher, *et al. Inequality: A Reassessment of the Effect of Family and Schooling in America.* New York: Basic Books, 1972.

Jenkins, Herbert. *Keeping the Peace.* New York: Harper & Row, 1970.

Jensen, Arthur R. "How Much Can We Boost IQ and Scholastic Achievement?" In *Environment, Heredity, and Intelligence.* Cambridge, Mass.: Harvard Educational Review Reprint Series No. 2, 1969, pp. 1–123.

———. *Genetics and Education.* New York: Harper & Row, 1972.

Johnson, D. W. "Racial Attitudes of Negro Freedom School Participants and Negro and White Civil Rights Participants." *Social Forces, 45* (1966), 266–272.

Jordan, Winthrop D. *White Over Black: American Attitudes Toward the Negro, 1550–1812.* Baltimore: Penguin, 1969.

Kahn, Si. *How People Get Power: Organizing Oppressed Communities for Action.* New York: McGraw-Hill, 1970.

Katz, Erwin, and Patricia Gurin. *Race and the Social Sciences.* New York: Basic Books, 1969.

Kennedy, Gerald Bishop. *Fresh Every Morning.* New York: Harper & Row, 1966.

Kennedy, Ruby Jo Reeves. "Single or Triple Melting Pot? Intermarriage Trends in New Haven, 1870–1940." *American Journal of Sociology, 49* (1940), 331–339.

———. "Single or Triple Melting Pot? Intermarriage Trends in New Haven, 1870–1950." *American Journal of Sociology, 58* (1952), 56–59.

Killian, Lewis M. *The Impossible Revolution.* New York: Random House, 1968.

Kimura, Yukiko. "Locality Clubs as Basic Units of the Social Organization of the Okinawans in Hawaii," *Phylon, 29* (1968), 331–338.

Klapper, Joseph T. *The Effects of Mass Communication.* New York: The Free Press, 1960.

Klineberg, Otto (ed.). *Characteristics of the American Negro.* New York: Harper & Row, 1944.

———. "Negro-White Differences in Intelligence Test Performance: A New Look at an Old Problem." *American Psychologist, 18* (1963), 198–203.

Kluckhohn, Clyde. *Mirror for Man.* New York: Fawcett, 1965 (originally published, 1944).

———. *Culture and Behavior.* New York: Free Press, 1962.

Knowles, Louis L., and Kenneth Prewitt. *Institutional Racism in America.* Englewood Cliffs, N.J.: Prentice-Hall, 1969.

Kuhn, Thomas S. *The Structure of Scientific Revolutions.* Chicago: University of Chicago Press, 1962.

Kutner, B. "Patterns of Mental Functioning Associated With Prejudice in Children," *Psychological Monographs, 72* (Whole No. 460) (1958)

Kutner, B., and N. B. Gordon. "Cognitive Functioning and Prejudice: A Nine-Year Follow Up Study." *Sociometry, 27* (1964), 66–74.

LaBarre, Weston. "Personality From a Psychoanalytic Viewpoint." In Edward Norbeck *et al.* (eds.), *The Study of Personality: An Interdisciplinary Appraisal.* New York: Holt, Rinehart and Winston, 1968. Pp. 65–87.

Lambert, W. E., and O. Klineberg. *Childrens' Views of Foreign Peoples.* New York: Appleton, 1967.

Lasswell, Harold. *Politics: Who Gets What, When, How.* New York: Meridian, 1958.

LeBon, Gustave. *The Crowd.* London: Unwin, 1896.

Lenski, Gerhard E. *Power and Privilege: A Theory of Social Stratification.* New York: McGraw-Hill, 1966.

Lester, Julius. *Revolutionary Notes.* New York: Grove, 1969.

Lestschinsky, Jakob. "Ghetto." In Edwin R. A. Seligman (Editor), *Encyclopedia of the Social Sciences.* New York: The Macmillan Company, Vol. 6, pp. 646–650, 1931.

Lewin, Kurt (ed.). *Resolving Social Conflicts: Selected Papers on Group Dynamics.* New York: Harper & Row, 1948.

Lieberson, Stanley. "A Social Theory of Race and Ethnic Relations." *America Sociological Review, 26* (December 1961), 902–910.

Liebow, Elliot. *Tally's Corner. A Study of Negro Streetcorner Men.* Boston: Little, Brown, and Company, 1967.

Lienhardt, Godfrey. *Social Anthropology.* London: Oxford University Press, 1966.

Lincoln, Eric E. *The Black Muslims in America.* Boston: Beacon Press, 1961.

Lind, Andrew William. *Hawaii's People.* Honolulu: University of Hawaii Press, 1967.

Linnaeus, Carolus von. *A General System of Nature, Through the Three Grand Kingdoms of Animals, Vegetables, and Minerals.* Vol. 1. London: Lackington, 1802–1806.

Linton, Ralph. *The Study of Man.* New York: Appleton, 1964 (originally published, 1936).

Lippmann, Walter. *Public Opinion.* New York: Macmillan, 1922.

Lipsky, Michael. "Rent Strikes: Poor Man's Weapon." *Transaction,* Vol. 6, No. 4, (February 1969), pp. 10–15.

Litt, Edgar. *Ethnic Politics in America.* Glenview, Ill.: Scott, Foresman, 1970.

Loescher, Frank S. *The Protestant Church and the Negro.* New York: Associated Press, 1972 (first published, 1948).

Loewen, James W. *The Mississippi Chinese: Between Black and White.* Cambridge, Mass.: Harvard University Press, 1971.

Lomax, Louis E. *The Negro Revolt.* New York: New American Library, 1963.

Long, Margaret. "The Imperial Wizard Explains the Klan," *The New York Times Magazine,* July 5, 1964, p. 8.

Loomis, Charles P. *Social Systems: Essays on Their Persistence and Change.* Princeton, N.J.: Van Nostrand, 1964.

Lowenthal, David. "Race and Color in the West Indies." In J. H. Franklin (ed.), *Color and Race.* Boston: Houghton Mifflin, 1968. Pp. 325–335.

Lyman, Stanford M. "Marriage and the Family Among Chinese Immigrants to America," *Phylon, 29* (1968), pp. 321–330.

Lyman, Stanford M., and Marvin B. Scott. "Territoriality: A Neglected Sociological Dimension," *Social Problems, 15* (1967), 236–249.

McGuire, William J ."The Nature of Attitudes and Attitude Change." In Gardner Lindzey and Elliot Aronson (eds.), *The Handbook of Social Psychology.* Vol. 3. Reading, Mass. Addison Wesley, 1969. Pp. 136–314.

MacIver, R. M. *The More Perfect Union.* New York: Macmillan, 1948.

Malinowski, Bronislaw. *Sexual Life of Savages.* New York: Harcourt, 1962.

Mann, J. H. "The Relationship between Cognitive, Behavioral, and Affective Aspects of Racial Prejudice." *Journal of Social Psychology, 49* (1959), 223–228.

March, James G. (ed.). *Handbook of Organizations.* Chicago: Rand McNally, 1965.

Marcus, Jacob R. *The Jew in the Medieval World: A Source Book.* New York: Meridian, 1960 (originally published, 1938).

Marden, Charles F., and Gladys Meyer. *Minorities in American Society.* New York: Van Nostrand, 1972.

Marshall, Ray. *The Negro and Organized Labor.* New York: Wiley, 1965.

———. *The Negro Worker.* New York: Random House, 1967.

Marshall, Ray, Sar Levitan, and Garth Mangum. *Human Resources and Labor Markets.* New York: Harper & Row, 1972.

Marx, Gary T. "Religion: Opiate or Inspiration of Civil Rights Militancy Among Negroes?" *American Sociological Review, 32* (1967), pp. 64–72.

———. *Racial Conflict, Tension and Change in American Society.* Boston: Little, Brown, 1971.

Merton, Robert K. *Social Theory and Social Structure.* rev. ed. New York: Free Press, 1964 (first published 1949).

Messick, David M. *Mathematical Thinking in Behavioral Sciences.* San Francisco: Freeman, 1968.

Middleton, Russell. "Do Christian Beliefs Cause Anti-Semitism?" *American Sociological Review, 38* (February 1973), pp. 33–52, 59–61.

Mill, J. S. "The Cours de Philosophie Positive." In J. M. Robinson (ed.), *Essays on Ethics, Religion, and Society.* Toronto: University of Toronto Press, 1969, pp. 308, 309.

Mills, C. Wright. *The Sociological Imagination.* New York: Grove Press, Evergreen Edition, 1961.

Montagu, Ashley (ed.). *The Concept of Race.* New York: Free Press, 1964.

———. *On Being Human.* New York: Hawthorn, 1967.

Moore, Wilbert E. "Theories of Social Change." *American Sociological Review, 25* (1960), pp. 810–818.

Morland, J. K. "Racial Acceptance in Preference of Nursery School Children in A Southern City." *Merrill Palmer Quarterly, 8* (1962), 271–280.

Moynihan, Daniel P. *Employment, Income and the Ordeal of the Negro Family.* Washington, D.C.: Government Printing Office, 1965a.

———. *Negro Family: The Case for National Action.* Washington, D.C.: Government Printing Office, 1965b.

Mundy, Mike, and Ted Williams. Untitled Research Report, Lee County (Ala.) Head Start, 1970.

Murch, Arvin W. "Political Integration as an Alternative to Independence in the French Antilles," *American Sociological Review, 33* (1968), 559.

Myrdal, Gunnar. *An American Dilemma.* New York: Harper & Row, First Torchback Edition, 1962.

Nabokov, Peter. "La Raza, the Land and the Hippies." *The Nation, 210* (1972), 464–466.

National Advisory Commission on Civil Disorders. *Report.* New York: Bantam Books, Inc., 1968.

National Urban League, *Fortieth Anniversary Year Book.* New York: 1951.

Niagara Movement, Constitution and By-Laws, 1905. In Monroe Nathan Work Papers, Box 2, Tuskegee Institute Archives, Tuskegee Institute, AL.

Noel, Donald L. "A Theory of the Origin of Ethnic Stratification," *Social Problems, 16* (Fall 1968), 157–172.

Norman, Barbara and Kazuko Tatsumura. "The Soaring Popularity of Japanese restaurants." *Holiday,* Vol. 45, No. 3 (July, 1969), p. 59.

Northrop, F. S. C. *The Meeting of East and West.* New York: Macmillan, 1946.

Northrop, Herbert R. *Organized Labor and the Negro.* New York: Harper & Row, 1944.

Olcott, Mason. "The Caste System of India." *American Sociological Review, 9* (1944), 648–657.

Olsen, Marvin E. "Social and Political Participation of Blacks." *American Sociological Review, 35* (August 1970), 682–697.

Oppenheimer, Martin, and George Lakey. *A Manual for Direct Action.* Chicago: Quadrangle, 1965.

Orum, Anthony M. "A Reappraisal of the Social and Political Participation of Negroes." *American Journal of Sociology, 72* (July 1966) 32–46.

————. *Black Students in Protest: A Study of the Origins of the Black Student Movement.* Washington, D.C.: American Sociological Association, 1972.

Paine, Nathaniel. "Early American Broadsides 1680–1800." *Proceedings,* American Antiquarian Society, 1897, p. 465.

Park, Robert E. "Human Migration and the Marginal Man," *American Journal of Sociology, 33* (1928), 892.

————. *Race and Culture.* New York: Free Press, 1950.

————. "Our Racial Frontier on the Pacific." In Everett C. Hughes (ed.), *Race and Culture: Essays in the Sociology of Contemporary Man.* New York: Free Press, 1964 (originally published, *Survey Graphic,* 1926), pp. 138–151.

Park, Robert E., and Ernest W. Burgess. *Introduction to the Science of Sociology.* Chicago: University of Chicago Press, Fifth Impression, 1928.

Parsons, Talcott. *The Social System.* New York: Free Press, 1951.

————. "The Problem of Polarization on the Axis of Color." In John Hope Franklin (ed.), *Color and Race.* Boston: Houghton Mifflin, 1968. P. 353.

Patai, Raphael. *Society, Culture, and Change in the Middle East.* Philadelphia: University of Pennsylvania Press, 1971.

Pettigrew, Thomas F. *Racially Separate or Together?* New York: McGraw-Hill, 1971.

Phillips, Ulrich B. *American Negro Slavery: A Survey of the Supply, Employment and Control of Negro Labor as Determined by the Plantation Regime.* New York: Appleton, 1918.

Pirenne, Henri. *Medieval Cities.* Garden City, N.Y.: Doubleday, 1956.

Pitts, Jesse R. "Social Control." In David L. Sills (ed.), *International Encyclopedia of the Social Sciences,* Vol. 14. New York: Macmillan, 1968, pp. 381–396.

Pollitzer, William S. "The Physical Anthropology and Genetics of Marginal Peoples of the Southeastern United States." *American Anthropologist,* Vol. 74, No. 3 (June, 1972), pp. 719–734.

Pollock, John. *Billy Graham: The Authorized Biography.* Grand Rapids, Mich.: Zondervan, 1966.

Popper, Karl R. *Conjectures and Refutations: The Growth of Scientific Knowledge.* New York: Basic Books, 1962.

Porter, Dorothy B. "The Black Role During the Era of the Revolution." *The Smithsonian,* Vol. 4, No. 5 (August, 1973), p. 52.

Porter, Judith D. R. *Black Child, White Child: The Development of Racial Attitudes.* Cambridge, Mass.: Harvard University Press, 1971.

Prichard, James Cowles. Quoted in Godfrey Lienhardt (ed.), *Social Anthropology.* London: Oxford University Press, 1966.

Race Relations Information Center. "States Have 250 Black Troopers" Associated Press Release. Nashville, Tennessee, December 10, Issue No. 21, 1970, p. 4.

Radke, M., H. Trager, and H. Davis. "Social Perceptions and Attitudes of Children." *Genetic Psychology Monographs,* 40 (1949), 327–447.

Rainwater, Lee, and William L. Yancey. *The Moynihan Report and the Politics of Controversy.* Cambridge, Mass.: MIT Press, 1967.

Reed, John Sheldon. "Percent Black and Lynching: A Test of Blalock's Theory." *Social Forces,* 50 (1972), 356–360.

Reuter, Edward B. "Fifty Years of Racial Theory." *American Journal of Sociology,* Vol. 50, No. 6 (May, 1945), pp. 452–461.

Rogers, Everett M., and F. Floyd Shoemaker. *Communication of Innovations: A Cross-Cultural Approach.* New York: Free Press, 1971.

Rogers, Michael. "Some Quiet Hours With Huey Newton." *Esquire,* 79 (May 1973), 158.

Rogow, Arnold A. "Anti-Semitism." In *International Encyclopedia of the Social Sciences.* Vol. 1. New York: Free Press, 1968.

Rohrer, John R., and Monro Edmonson. *The Eigth Generation Grows Up: Cultures and Personalities of New Orleans Negroes.* New York: Harper & Row, First Harper Torchback Edition 1964.

Rokeach, Milton. "Prejudice, Concreteness of Thinking, and Reification of Thinking." *Journal of Abnormal and Social Psychology,* 46 (1951), 83–91.

———. "Political and Religious Dogmatism: An Alternative to the Authoritarian Personality." *Psychological Monographs,* 70 (1956), 1–43.

———. *The Open and Closed Mind.* New York: Basic Books, 1960.

Rokeach, Milton, and B. Fruchter. "A Factorial Study of Dogmatism and Related Concepts." *Journal of Abnormal and Social Psychology,* 53 (1956), 356–360.

Rose, Peter I. *The Subject is Race: Traditional Ideologies and the Teaching of Race Relations.* New York: Oxford University Press, 1968.

Rosenberg, Morris, and Roberta G. Simmons. *Black and White Self-Esteem: The Urban School Child.* Washington, D.C.: American Sociological Association, 1972.

Rothman, Jack. *Promoting Social Justice in the Multigroup Society: A Casebook for Group Relations Practitioners.* New York: Association Press, 1971.

Roucek, Joseph S. *Social Control.* Princeton, N.J.: Van Nostrand, 1956.

Rousseau, Jean Jacques. *The Social Contract.* Baltimore, Md.: Penguin Books, 1972.

Rowan, Carl. *Atlanta Constitution,* September 11, 1970, p. 19.

Rubin, Morton. "Land and Cultural Change in a Plantation Area," *Journal of Social Issues, 10* (1954), 28–35.

Rustin, Bayard. "The Blacks and the Unions." *Harper's, 242* (1971), 76.

Salvemini, Gaetano. *Prelude to World War II.* Garden City, N.Y.: Doubleday, 1954.

Schary, Dore. In *Not the Work of a Day.* New York: Anti Defamation League of B'nai B'rith, 1965.

Schermerhorn, R. A. *Comparative Ethnic Relations: A Framework for Theory and Research.* New York: Random House, 1970.

Scott, Austin. "The Black Panther Party Today." The Columbus (Ga.) *Enquirer,* November 29, 1970, p. 5.

"Shame City." *Newsweek.* January 4, 1971, pp. 25, 28.

Shapiro, Manheim. "The Sociology of Jewish Life." In Belden Menkus, *Meet the American Jew.* Nashville: Broadman, 1963. Pp. 97–98.

Shelton, Robert. Interview. *Playboy, 12* (1965), 45–55, 85–90.

Shepard, Herbert A. "Changing Interpersonal and Integroup Relationships in Organizations." In James G. March (ed.), *Handbook of Organizations.* Chicago: Rand McNally, 1965. Pp. 1115–1143.

Shepherd, Herbert A. "Changing Interpersonal and Intergroup Relationships in Organizations." In James G. March (Editor), *Handbook of Organizations,* (Chicago: Rand McNally, 1965), pp. 1115–1143.

Sherif, Muzafer, and C. W. Sherif. *Groups in Harmony and Tension: An Integration of Studies of Intergroup Relations.* New York: Harper & Row, 1953.

Shibutani, Tamotsu, and Kian M. Kwan. *Ethnic Stratification: A Comparative Approach.* New York: Macmillan, 1967.

Shockley, William. "Dysgenics, Geneticity, Raceology: A Challenge to the Intellectual Responsibility of Editors." *Phi Delta Kappan,* Vol. 53, No. 5 (January, 1972), pp. 297–307.

Silberman, Charles E. *Crisis in Black and White.* New York: Random House, 1964.

Sills, David. "Voluntary Associations: Sociological Aspects." In David Sills (Editor), *International Encyclopedia of the Social Sciences,* Vol. 16. New York: Macmillan, 1968, pp. 362–379.

Simpson, George E. "Assimilation." In *International Encyclopedia of the Social Sciences.* Vol. 1. New York: Free Press, 1968, pp. 438–444.

Simpson, G. E., and J. M. Yinger. *Racial and Cultural Minorities: An Analysis of Prejudice and Discrimination.* New York: Harper & Row, 1965.

Skolnick, Jerome H. *The Politics of Protest.* New York: Simon & Schuster, 1969.

Slater, Marian K. "My Son the Doctor: Aspects of Mobility Among American Jews." *American Sociological Review, 34* (1969), pp. 359–373.

Smelser, Neil J. *Theory of Collective Behavior.* New York: Free Press, 1969 (originally published, 1962).

Smith, Arthur L. *The Rhetoric of Black Revolution.* Boston: Allyn & Bacon, 1966.

Smith, Constance, and Anne Freedman. *Voluntary Associations: Perspectives on the Literature.* Cambridge, Mass.: Harvard University Press, 1972.

Snyder, David, and Charles Tilly. "Hardship and Collective Violence in France, 1830 to 1960." *American Sociological Review, 37* (October 1972), 520–532.

Snyder, Louis L. *The Idea of Racialism.* New York: Van Nostrand, 1962.

Society of Friends. *A Statistical Inquiry into the Condition of the People of Colour of Philadelphia.* Philadelphia: 1849.

Southern Episcopalian. Charleston, South Carolina, April 1854. Cited in Leslie H. Fishel, Jr. and Benjamin Quarles, *The Negro American:* A Documentary. *History.* Glenview, Ill.: Scott, Foresman and William Morrow, 1967, p. 114.

Spykman, Nicholas J. *The Social Theory of George Simmel: Adaptation from Works of George Simmel.* New York: Atherton, 1966.

Stampp, Kenneth. *The Peculiar Institution.* New York: Knopf, 1956.

Stephenson, H. W., and N. G. Stephenson. "A Development Study of Race Awareness in Young Children." *Child Development, 29* (1958), 399–410.

Stouffer, Samuel A. "An Analysis of Conflicting Social Norms." *American Sociological Review, 14* (1949), pp. 707–717.

Stufflebeam, Daniel L. "The Use and Abuse of Evaluation in Title III." *Theory into Practice, 6* (1967), 126–133.

Suchman, Edward A. *Evaluative Research: Principles and Practice in Public Service and Social Action Programs.* New York: Russell Sage, 1967.

Swain, Joseph Ward. *The Ancient World.* Vol. 2. New York: Harper & Row, 1950.

Texas Commission on Law Enforcement Procedures. *Handbook for Texas Law Enforcement Officers.* Austin: 1967.

Theodorson, George A., and Achilles G. Theodorson. *Modern Dictionary of Sociology.* New York: Crowell, 1969.

Thomas, W. I., and Dorothy S. Thomas. *The Child in America.* New York: Knopf, 1928.

Tobin, James. "On Improving the Economic Status of the Negro." *Daedalus, 94* (1965), pp. 878–898.

Tocqueville, Alexis de. *Democracy in America.* New York: Vintage, 1945.

———. *The Old Regime and the French Revolution,* trans. by John Bonner. New York, Harper, 1856.

"The Touchables." *Newsweek.* April 2, 1973, p. 88.

Toynbee, Arnold J. *A Study of History.* abridged ed. New York: Oxford University Press, 1947.

Triandis, H. C., and L. M. Triandis. "Race, Social Class, Religion, and Nationality as Determinants of Social Distance." *Journal of Abnormal and Social Psychology, 61* (1960), 110–118.

Turnbull, Collin M. "The Lesson of the Pygmies." *The Scientific American, 208* (1963), 6.

Turner, F. J. *The Frontier in American History.* New York: Henry Holt and Company, 1920.

Turner, Ralph H., and Lewis M. Killian. *Collective Behavior.* Englewood Cliffs, N.J.: Prentice-Hall, 1957.

United Nations Educational, Scientific and Cultural Organization. *The Race Concept: Results of an Inquiry.* Paris: 1958.

United Nations Educational, Scientific and Cultural Organization. *Research on Racial Relations.* Paris: 1966.

United States Bureau of the Census. *Statistical Abstract of the United States.* Washington, D.C.: Government Printing Office, 1970.

————. *Current Population Reports.* Washington, D.C.: Government Printing Office, Series P-23, No. 33, 1970.

————. *Current Population Reports.* Washington, D.C.: Government Printing Office, Series P-60, No. 75, 1970.

United States Commission on Civil Rights. *Racial Isolation in the Public Schools.* Vol. 1. Washington, D.C.: Government Printing Office, 1967.

————. *Political Participation.* Washington, D.C.: Government Printing Office, 1968.

————. *Mexican Americans and the Administration of Justice in the Southwest.* Washington, D.C.: Government Printing Office, 1970.

————. *Five Communities: Their Search For Equal Education.* Washington, D.C.: Government Printing Office, 1972.

————. *School Desegregation in Ten Communities.* Washington, D.C.: Government Printing Office, Clearinghouse Publication No. 43, June 1973.

United States Department of Agriculture. *Farm Population by Race, Tenure and Economic Scale of Farming, 1966 and 1970.* Washington, D.C.: Economic Research Service, Agriculture Economic Report No. 228, June, 1972.

U.S. Department of Health, Education and Welfare, Public Health Service. *Statistical Notes,* 26–50, 1971.

United States Department of Housing and Urban Development (HUD). Unpublished circular letter No. 73–6, July 3, 1973; in possession of the author.

United States Department of Labor. *The Detroit Riot: A Profile of 500 Prisoners.* Washington, D.C.: Government Printing Office, 1968.

Van den Berghe, Pierre L. *Race and Racism: A Comparative Perspective.* New York: Wiley, 1967.

Vanfossen, Beth E. "Variables Related to Desegregation in the South." *Social Forces,* 47 (1968), 39–44.

Vidulich, R. N., and F. W. Krevanick. "Racial Attitudes and Emotional Response to Visual Representations of the Negro." *Journal of Social Psychology,* 68 (1966), 85–93.

Wagatsuma, Hiroshi. "The Social Perception of Skin Color in Japan." In John Hope Franklin, *Color and Race.* Boston: Houghton Mifflin, 1968, pp. 129–165.

Wagner, Nathaniel N., and Marsha J. Nang. *Chicanos: Social and Psychological Perspectives.* St. Louis: Mosby, 1971.

————. *Culture and Personality.* New York: Random House, 1961.

Warner, W. Lloyd, and Leo Srole. *The Social Systems of American Ethnic Groups.* New Haven: Yale University Press, 1945.

Washburn, S. L. "The Study of Race." *American Anthropologist,* 65 (1963), 521–531.

Washington, Booker T. "Industrial Education for Negroes." In *The Negro Problem: A Series of Articles by Representative American Negroes of Today.* New York: Pott, 1903. Pp. 10–29.

————. *Up From Slavery: An Autobiography.* Garden City, N.Y.: Sun Dial Press, 1937 (originally published, 1900, 1901).

Waskow, Arthur I. *From Race Riot To Sit-in, 1919 and the 1960's.* Garden City, N.Y.: Doubleday, 1967.

Wax, Murray L. *Indian Americans: Unity and Diversity.* Englewood Cliffs, N.J.: Prentice-Hall, 1971.

Weber, Max. *On Law and Economy and Society,* trans. by Edward Shils and Max Rheinstein. New York: Simon & Schuster, 1967.

Weinberg, Meyer. *Desegregation Research: An Appraisal.* Bloomington, Indiana: Phi Delta Kappa Report, 1970.

Weisz, P. B. *The Science of Biology.* New York: McGraw-Hill, 1963.

Weller, Jack M., and E. L. Quarantelli. "Neglected Characteristics of Collective Behavior." *American Journal of Sociology,* 79 (November 1973), pp. 665–685.

West, Ralph L. *The Adjustment of the American Indian in Detroit: A Descriptive Study.* Detroit: Wayne State University Press, 1950.

Williams, Robin M., Jr. *The Reduction of Intergroup Tensions: A Survey of Research on Problems of Ethnic, Racial, and Religious Group Relations.* New York: Social Science Research Council, 1947.

————. *Strangers Next Door: Ethnic Relations in American Communities.* Englewood Cliffs, N.J.: Prentice-Hall, 1964.

Wilson, Robert A. "Anomie in the Ghetto: A Study of Neighborhood Type, Race and Anomie." *American Journal of Sociology,* 77 (1971), 66–88.

Wirth, Louis. "The Ghetto." *American Journal of Sociology,* Vol. 33 (1927), pp. 57–71.

Wirth, Louis. "The Problem of Minority Groups." In Ralph Linton (ed.), *The Science of Man in the World Crisis.* New York: Columbia University Press, 1945. P. 365.

Wolff, Kurt H. *The Sociology of Georg Simmel.* New York: Macmillan, 1950.

Woodword, C. Vann. *The Strange Career of Jim Crow.* New York: Oxford University Press, 1966.

Wrong, Dennis H. "Social Inequality Without Social Stratification." *Canadian Review of Sociology and Anthropology, i* (1964), 1.

Yancey, William L., Leo Rigsby, and John D. McCarthy. "Social Position and Self-Evaluation: The Relative Importance of Race." *American Journal of Sociology,* 78 (September 1972), 338–357.

Young Socialist Alliance. *Introduction to the Young Socialist Alliance.* New York: 1970.

Zanden, James W. Vander. "The Klan Revival." *American Journal of Sociology,* 65 (1960), 456–462.

NAME INDEX

SUBJECT INDEX

W. deC. Hachler, Ph.D.